Ford/Southampton Studies in North/South Security Relations

Managing editor: Dr JOHN SIMPSON

Executive editor: Dr PHIL WILLIAMS

The Soviet Union and the strategy of non-alignment in the Third World

T0370716

*Ford Foundation Research Project 'North/South Security Relations',
University of Southampton*

Principal Researchers:
    Professor P. A. R. CALVERT
    Dr J. SIMPSON
    Dr C. A. THOMAS
    Dr P. WILLIAMS
    Dr R. ALLISON

*While the Ford Foundation has supported this study financially, it does not
necessarily endorse the findings. Opinions expressed are the responsibility of the
author.*

The Soviet Union and the strategy of non-alignment in the Third World

ROY ALLISON

Lecturer, Centre for Russian and East European Studies
University of Birmingham

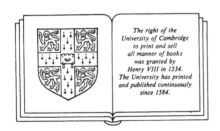

The right of the
University of Cambridge
to print and sell
all manner of books
was granted by
Henry VIII in 1534.
The University has printed
and published continuously
since 1584.

CAMBRIDGE UNIVERSITY PRESS

CAMBRIDGE

NEW YORK   NEW ROCHELLE   MELBOURNE   SYDNEY

CAMBRIDGE UNIVERSITY PRESS
Cambridge, New York, Melbourne, Madrid, Cape Town, Singapore, São Paulo, Delhi

Cambridge University Press
The Edinburgh Building, Cambridge CB2 8RU, UK

Published in the United States of America by Cambridge University Press, New York

www.cambridge.org
Information on this title: www.cambridge.org/9780521102506

First published 1988
This digitally printed version 2009

A catalogue record for this publication is available from the British Library

Library of Congress Cataloguing in Publication data
Allison, Roy
The Soviet Union and the strategy of non-alignment in the Third World/Roy Allison.
   p.   cm.
Bibliography.
Includes index.
ISBN 0–521–35511–7
1. Soviet Union – Foreign relations – Developing countries.
2. Developing countries – Foreign relations – Soviet Union.
3. Nonalignment. I. Title.
JX1555.Z7D443 1988
327.47 01724– –dc 19   88–10230 CIP

ISBN 978-0-521-35511-7 hardback
ISBN 978-0-521-10250-6 paperback

Contents

Acknowledgements

This book was researched and written at St Antony's College, Oxford and the Department of Politics, the University of Southampton. I am particularly grateful for the support received from both these institutions. St Antony's College provided a most congenial intellectual environment for broad research on Soviet foreign policy. I remain endebted to the Centre of Russian Studies for the use of its facilities during my attachment to the College as a post-doctoral research fellow. Many fellows and students helped motivate my research in different ways; Mr A. Brown and Professor E. A. Roberts are to be thanked in particular. The Department of Politics at Southampton University also provided me with excellent facilities for the completion of the manuscript and generously offered me a senior research fellowship for 1986–87, which was attached to the Ford Foundation project on North/South Security Relations. I am very grateful to all the project members for their consistent encouragement and assistance, Dr J. Simpson, the project coordinator, deserves special thanks.

I am also beholden to the Law Faculty of Moscow State University for making me welcome during a productive six week visit under an exchange scheme arranged by the British Council. Various Soviet academic institutes were helpful during this visit, including IMEMO and the Institute of State and Law. I am thankful in addition to the academics I met in the Jawaharlal Nehru University and to numerous Indian diplomats and officials who were interviewed during a research visit to New Delhi. Mrs S. Morphet offered very useful comments on the early chapters of the manuscript. Caroline Kennedy assisted greatly in checking the script.

I thankfully acknowledge the financial support I received from the ESRC, which provided for my fellowship at Oxford, and from the Ford Foundation for my period of research in Southampton.

Introduction

Western analysts are in general agreement that since the mid 1950s the Soviet Union has made strenuous attempts to capture the middle ground between the Eastern and Western alliance systems. Soviet leaders have had little interest in sustaining the intermediate position of states between the primary military structures for its own sake, but they have accepted the tactical necessity of supporting and promoting such independence as part of a broader competition with the West. Soviet officials made it abundantly clear in the 1950s and 1960s, however, that their view of international affairs is premised on an underlying struggle between two opposing and irreconcilable socio-economic systems. The emergence of a considerable number of new states which ideologically and politically were committed to neither East nor West did not shake this Soviet postulate.

The non-bloc states became an established and numerically significant component of the international order, which Soviet leaders were among the first to acknowledge. But Soviet officials have remained circumspect about their broader strategic designs for such militarily 'uncommitted' states. This warrants a systematic examination of how successive Soviet leaders have sought to coordinate their policies with the 'Non-Aligned World' and how Soviet policy-makers have employed the idea of military non-alignment as a specific strategic device in the Third World.

The focus of Western studies of Soviet political and military involvement in the Third World has tended to reflect the primary concern of Western statesmen – the assertive Soviet use of direct military and political instruments in pursuit of unilateral gains in Third World regions. Particular attention has been paid to Soviet conduct in regional crises or conflict, Soviet power projection capabilities and Soviet arms transfers.

Soviet force projection and the provision of military supplies undeniably are significant instruments enabling the Soviet Union to enhance and sustain political influence for periods in specific countries or regions. But such military links as the Soviet Union has cultivated have arisen generally on an *ad hoc* basis and have been of uncertain duration. For most of the post-war period they have been rather negligible as countermeasures to Western-sponsored or Western-oriented alliance structures and bilateral military agreements in the Third World. Throughout the 1950s and 1960s Soviet doctrine predisposed Soviet leaders to expect that their military position in the Third World would eventually improve in the wake of revolutionary structural socio-economic changes which, they believed, would orient the policies of the majority of developing countries firmly against the West. It was apparent by the 1970s that such economic determinism could not be relied on to develop Soviet political influence or military capabilities in the Third World. To be sure, Soviet support for a number of new revolutionary regimes developed into close bilateral military relationships, but these by no means offset Western military and political preponderance in Asia, Africa and Latin America. The underlying Soviet strategy, in this situation of comparative disadvantage, has been one of military *denial* to the Western powers, of impeding Western access to military assets in Third World regions.

The Soviet strategy of military denial in the Third World was originally intended to hamper the creation of new alliance systems by the West in the 1950s and to retard military links between the newly independent states and the Western powers. This design, to deny the territories of Third World states for Western military purposes, to anticipate and decry ensuing forms of political and economic dependency, was congruent in many respects with the anti-bloc impulse which governed the emergent policies of neutralism and non-alignment among an increasing number of developing states in the 1950s and 1960s. Soviet leaders sought both to dissuade countries from entering Western-dominated alliances and pacts and to encourage those already within them to resist integrative influences. Third World tendencies towards military abstention in the Cold War contest could be realised in the creation of 'zones of peace' free of Western military ties. The states in such regions were expected, however, to be sympathetic to Soviet initiatives on international security issues. These military objectives did not appear over-ambitious in view of the strong anti-colonial and by extension anti-Western sentiments of many newly independent states. From the Soviet perspective a strategy of non-alignment could combine military denial of 'third areas' to the West with the propagation

2

among them of broad Soviet initiatives on regional security and disarmament.

Moscow regarded neutralism and non-alignment, therefore, as an integral component of the competitive struggle between East and West, rather than a disengaged influence on this struggle. This assessment was reinforced by the Soviet doctrinal outlook which assumed that the policy of non-alignment actually pursued by states is linked to their socio-economic formation. Consequently, both neutralism and non-alignment were conceived as transitional and developmental drawing their character from changes in the domestic and international environments. Soviet spokesmen believed that the global 'correlation of forces' would shift in favour of the 'socialist system of states'. They characterised the policy of non-alignment, therefore, as a process which over the passage of time should orient the states led by its principles towards ever closer political and military association with the Soviet led group of states. Non-alignment in their view could not be conceived as a static condition of political equidistance. In this sense Soviet officials, at least until the late 1970s, considered non-alignment ideally as a policy of short-term military and political denial to the West which prefigured a longer-term tendency common to the Third World as a whole of increasing political and possibly military integration with the Eastern system of states.

At this point it should be emphasised that such a conception of non-alignment diverges substantially from the notion which Third World and Yugoslav statesmen originally elaborated more than a quarter of a century ago. Non-alignment and its precursor neutralism were conceived as an independent approach to foreign policy, as a means for the new African and Asian states to avoid becoming drawn into the Cold War competition of the superpowers. The key requirement was non-participation in entangling Great Power alliances. Neutralism in essence constituted a rejection of the East–West rivalry represented by the Cold War and a wholesale renunciation of the value system engendered by this contest. Since the late 1940s numerous decolonised states professed this outlook which, contrary to the Eurocentric and international legal status of neutrality, had no legal substance and embraced a wide range of diplomatic behaviour.

In the 1960s influential leaders of the non-bloc states who wished to assume a more active role in mediating East–West conflict and to project their own demands on the North–South agenda cultivated the notion of non-alignment. This displaced the more passive and isolationist policy of neutralism. Neutralism anyway had a confusing character since the term had been employed in the 1950s in the context of debate over the military aspects of East–West relations within Europe. It has surfaced periodically also as a term to convey resistance to the military integration of the Western alliance from within that structure itself.

Non-alignment has never been a concept which applies exclusively to the conduct of Third World states. Yugoslavia had a formative influence on the character of non-alignment and played an influential role in its gradual institutionalisation into the Non-Aligned Movement of states. Tito of Yugoslavia, Nasser of Egypt and Nehru of India were the primary figures behind the convention of the first summit of non-aligned states in Belgrade in 1961. Nevertheless, the political programme which became associated with non-alignment contains a Third World rather than European ethos. Non-alignment has become somewhat of a misnomer therefore when used to refer to the non-bloc aspects of European neutral countries such as Sweden. The term is still used occasionally in the context of neutrality in Europe but this should be distinguished from the foreign policy approach promoted by the Non-Aligned Movement.

As far back as 1947 Prime Minister Nehru of India explained the difference between neutrality and the Indian policy of non-alignment. He noted that India would not attach itself to any particular group in the Cold War contest but regarded this as unrelated to neutrality or passivity. While it would be rather difficult to remain neutral in world war, Nehru stated that 'we are not going to join a war if we can help it; and we are going to join the side which is to our interest when the choice comes to it'.[1] This understanding was developed at a conference of the Uncommitted Countries held in Cairo in June 1961 in preparation for the Belgrade Conference held later that year.

The Cairo participants formulated certain criteria of non-alignment which did not preclude membership in all multilateral/bilateral alliances and regional defence arrangements, but only those conceived in the context of the Cold War, of 'Great Power conflicts'. The concession of military bases by non-aligned states was prohibited also only within this context. These provisions were directed against military alignment in the Cold War, conceived as full membership in non-regional multilateral pacts, and as such expressed a neutralist impulse. Their qualified character reflected the fact, however, that nine of the Belgrade participants had strong military ties, outside of the main Cold War alliances, with the United States or Great Britain.[2] It should be emphasised that such military ties and the receipt of large quantities of military aid and supplies (even by belligerent states backed by rival superpower patrons) have continued to characterise the foreign policy of states remaining in the Non-Aligned Movement.

If one adopts a far stricter interpretation of non-alignment to preclude all involvement by the small powers in military arrangements with a Great Power it would be necessary to conclude that a large minority of the 'Non-Aligned' have appeared aligned to the West (and to the East since the late 1970s). This would ensue from membership of the Organisation of American States, multilateral links with France or bilateral links with the United States, Great Britain or France.[3] The Third World states concerned have not considered such links to detract from non-alignment. But these secondary military relationships certainly have encouraged Soviet officials to regard a number of states participating in the Non-Aligned Movement as constituents of the East–West balance rather than as independent actors.

The 1961 Cairo preparatory conference ruled additionally that non-aligned states should consistently support movements for national liberation and follow an independent policy based on peaceful coexistence and non-alignment or show a trend in favour of such a policy. Neutralism may have formed a strong undercurrent in the commitment of many new states to the policy of non-alignment, but the emphasis on anti-colonialism expressed at Cairo has meant that non-alignment has always constituted more than a revamped neutralism. Since the European neutral states in the United Nations tended to side with the colonial powers, this provision confirmed that non-alignment was not synonymous with non-bloc status. This distinction was underlined in the 1960s by the relatively low priority given to the issues of Great Power military alliances and bases in the communiqués of the summit conferences of the non-aligned states.[4] Soviet leaders understood that the phenomenon of non-alignment expressed positive political aspirations in addition to negative military commitments. They anticipated correctly that on colonial questions such goals in general would conflict with Western policies. The majority of non-aligned states have interpreted their independence in foreign policy to mean acting according to their own best judgement. In principle this has not precluded support for Soviet-sponsored initiatives on an *ad hoc* basis. Soviet officials have sought, therefore, to steer the non-aligned states behind various Soviet proposals on disarmament and military security. Moscow gave collective statements by these states greater attention as the Non-Aligned Movement became more institutionalised in the 1970s.

The phenomenon of neutrality should be distinguished from that of non-alignment. Although the distinction between war and peace has become more difficult to draw since the Second World War, the classical notion of neutrality has a strict legal basis premised on non-involvement in the wars of third parties. Certain European neutral states have in addition drawn up specific guidelines to help regulate the practice of their policy of neutrality in peacetime, but these guidelines remain subject to the interpretation of the neutral states themselves. In the 1950s and 1960s Soviet spokesmen tended to confuse this peacetime policy of the European neutrals with the neutralism professed by many Third World states. This confusion in categories has led to the assumption by some Western analysts that Moscow sought to impose the broad principles of the Third World neutralist or non-aligned states on the European neutrals or to place the conduct of the former under the legal constraints of the latter.[5] The concept of non-alignment is not historically rooted in the institution or status of neutrality. But the Soviet view of neutrality is pertinent to this study since European neutrality became a component of Moscow's broad strategy of military denial to the West which was expressed in an altered form in the Soviet approach to non-alignment in the Third World.

The legally determined Eurocentric concept of neutrality is closely linked to the process of neutralisation, which involves guarantees from the Great Powers for the neutralised status of a state or territory and undertakings from that state to abstain from relationships which may prejudice its neutrality. There have been some attempts to apply a watered-down form of neutralisation to Third World states or regions involving both the United States and the USSR as guarantors. Soviet policy towards such proposals, which is the subject of Chapter 3 of this study, is particularly revealing. It illustrates the very limited conditions under which Soviet leaders are prepared to establish the formal neutrality or even non-alignment of specific Third World areas to deny both themselves and the Western powers military access to or influence over the states involved.

In contrast the first two chapters of this study analyse the manner in which Moscow has sought unilateral benefits from non-alignment and the Non-Aligned Movement of states. Chapter 1 addresses the evolution of Soviet perceptions of non-alignment and the composition of the Non-Aligned Movement. The attempts of Soviet officials and specialists to reconcile these phenomena with their ideological preconceptions of the international system are considered in some detail. The sensitive subject of non-alignment as an option for smaller socialist states requires a separate assessment. This provides the background for Chapter 2 which analyses the Soviet stand in relation to the practical measures sponsored or supported by the Non-Aligned for enhancing international security. It becomes clear that the Soviet attempt to coordinate and converge policy with the Non-Aligned has met only partial success.

The Soviet Union has sought to use the Non-Aligned Movement as an instrument in its broader strategy of political and military denial to the West outlined above. This strategy is further illustrated in the examination contained in Chapter 4 of Soviet policy and attitudes towards various forms of military alignment in the Third World. Since the USSR has felt militarily dispossessed in the Third World for most of the post-war period it has sought to exert various levers, including the encouragement of indigenous neutralist sentiment, to exclude the military presence of the Western powers. Simultaneously Moscow has tried to direct attention away from the military relationships which it has gradually cultivated with Third World states. This raises the question of whether the extension of Soviet military commitments in the Third World and the Western response to this Soviet military presence has tended to undermine indigenous collective Third World efforts to avoid alignment with the Great Powers. The 'strategy of non-alignment' developed by Third World states may have lost some of its former military significance in these circumstances and Soviet efforts to exploit non-alignment to deny Western states military and political assets in Third World regions may be less productive than in earlier decades.

THE SOVIET VIEW OF NEUTRALITY

Soviet interest in the peacetime condition and status of neutral policy developed only in the 1950s. Soviet diplomats had accepted neutrality previously simply as a tactical measure, directed at the possible outbreak of war. Such tactical considerations underlay the commitments on neutrality assumed by the young Soviet state in a series of bilateral non-aggression pacts signed in the 1920s. Soviet diplomats recognised the phenomenon of permanent neutrality but they displayed little enthusiasm for the idea of Western states declaring themselves neutral in peacetime since this did not suit their definition of international relations as the class relations of antagonistic social systems. In contrast, Soviet theorists developed the idea in the 1920s that the position of the Soviet socialist state, outside the conflicts of interest which were believed to divide capitalist states, placed Moscow in the best position to practice real neutrality.[6] The Soviet position at the beginning of the Second World War could be considered as the last attempt to realise such 'socialist neutrality'. However, Hitler's attack on the USSR in 1941 threw the concept into doubt. Soviet writers subsequently claimed that in 'just' wars – those with a revolutionary content – neutrality was unjustifiable. The USSR, like the Western powers, denounced the wartime neutrality of states such as Sweden and Switzerland for aiding and abetting the fascist attacker.

In the immediate post-war years neutrality both as a legal concept and as a political category remained suspect in the Soviet Union. For Soviet international lawyers neutrality was incompatible with the newly inaugurated system of collective security. Their criticism primarily concerned the *ad hoc* status of neutrality during war. But the prevailing Manichaean light in which international relations were regarded in both East and West, also ruled out Soviet endorsement of the permanent neutrality of distinct states. Eastern and Western statesmen regarded neutrality as a means of circumventing a clearcut stand on the crucial ideological divide out of a sense of defeatism. Soviet leaders made no concessions to neutral tendencies in Eastern Europe, although they came to recognise the positive content of Swedish neutrality in as much as it provided an alternative to military integration in NATO. In Western Europe, states which had traditionally pursued neutrality, like Belgium, the Netherlands and Luxemburg, still impressed by the German violation of their neutrality, accepted membership in the Atlantic Alliance.

As early as 1950 there were some signs that a far-reaching re-evaluation of the conduct of Soviet foreign affairs was underway. By early 1951, in apparant anticipation of a change in Soviet policy, the West European communist press openly proclaimed the positive value of the principle of neutrality.[7] Soviet leaders foresaw the political and strategic benefits which a neutralisation of Central Europe could offer, and in March 1952, already before the death of Stalin, they proposed the reunification of Germany in return for its non-participation in any coalition or military alliance directed against any of Hitler's wartime opponents. But a full reappraisal of the status of neutrality only occurred in Moscow after the death of Stalin, especially once Bulganin and Khrushchev had taken charge of foreign policy. Molotov suggested provisions for neutralising Germany at the Berlin conference of foreign ministers in January–February 1954. In April 1955 an Austrian delegation conducted successful negotiations in Moscow leading to the signing of the Austrian State Treaty in May and the Austrian declaration of permanent neutrality in October of that year. These acts resulted in international recognition of Austria's status as a permanently neutral state.

The Geneva Conference of Heads of Government in July 1955 finally expressed an authoritative Soviet endorsement of neutrality. Bulganin declared the Soviet government's opinion that 'should any nation desiring to pursue a policy of neutrality and non-participation in military groupings, while those groupings exist, raise the question of having their security and territorial integrity guaranteed, the Great Powers should accede to these wishes'. He avowed that 'as far as the Soviet Union is concerned, it is prepared to take part in such guarantees'.[8] The Warsaw Pact states issued a joint statement after a meeting in January 1956 which defined neutrality as the common goal of those European, Asian and African countries which had decided on an independent foreign policy free of ties to either of the power blocs. When the Twentieth Party Congress met in February 1956 Khrushchev confirmed that one of the most urgent tasks of Soviet foreign policy was to support countries which refused to join military blocs quite irrespective of their social order and economic system. At the same time he emphasised in his report the Soviet intention to 'develop and strengthen friendly relations with Finland, Austria and other neutral countries'.[9] The previous month the Soviet Union had evacuated the military and naval base it had occupied on Finnish soil at Porkkala, and in the following year the first references to Finland's 'neutral foreign policy' appeared in joint Soviet–Finnish communiqués.

At this stage Soviet statesmen regarded neutrality as a phenomenon confined primarily to Europe. At the time the Austrian State Treaty was signed there existed a widespread Western view that the main reason the USSR had accepted the neutralisation of Austria was to create a model for the subsequent solution of the problem of German reunification. However, Soviet leaders did not consider neutrality as a goal in itself. It was perceived as a means to forestall close political and economic association between the Federal Republic and Austria, to prevent the strengthening of West Germany. Moscow would have considered the military and economic potential of even a neutral reunified Germany as constituting a danger for the future. From the Soviet perspective a neutral Austria could perhaps serve instead as a model for a divided Germany, for the neutralisation of the Federal Republic and perhaps of Italy. A few days after the signing of the Austrian State Treaty Bulganin told the Warsaw Conference, then in the process of constructing the Warsaw Pact, that it would be wrong to assume that the Austrian government alone regarded neutrality as a course with great potentialities for promoting cooperation between East and West since 'there are quite a number of states, both in Europe and in Asia, which are averse to joining aggressive military blocs'.[10] The Soviet press at this time urged the Italians and West Germans to consider the Austrian example.

Apart from the significance of neutrality in Europe, the 'third position' adopted by many former European colonies by the mid 1950s had impressed itself on Soviet statesmen. Khrushchev set into motion a broad theoretical reappraisal of the Soviet international outlook, which would encourage and justify a diplomatic drive among those Third World states which remained or became militarily disengaged from the West. At the Twentieth Party Congress Khrushchev discarded Stalin's cherished and simple model of a two-camp world by identifying a further category, a 'zone of peace'. embracing neutral countries and the uncommitted Asian and African states. His identification of this zone was a response *inter alia* to the emergence of an Afro-Asian political identity symbolised by the Bandung Conference held the previous year.

Soviet spokesmen explained the position of such intermediate states, in a world which in their view was still divided at the most fundamental level into two contradictory ideological systems, by adjusting the time scale of necessary historical development. Soviet theorists created a category of 'transitional states', which were deemed to be neither fully capitalist nor socialist in social structure and neutral in their foreign policy and affiliations. This corresponded to the general Marxist supposition of a correlation between the foreign-policy conduct of a state and its domestic socio-economic structure. Such states were not conceived to be in static equilibrium between capitalism and socialism. Instead, struggling 'progressive forces' within these historically transitional states were expected to encourage them over time to cooperate ever more closely with the socialist camp, since such cooperation in the long run was conceived as the 'objective guarantee' of their security. In the Soviet view 'it naturally would be sensible to join the camp of peace-loving states' but on account of 'causes of an internal and international character' certain states could not do this. In such conditions a policy of non-participation in military blocs and coalitions was accepted as 'practical'.[11]

This distinction between short-term and long-term historical prospects gave Soviet theorists and diplomats considerable flexibility in their approach to the 'intermediate' states. But in practice it was left to Soviet legal specialists to formulate definitions of neutrality and its obligations. These definitions were not only legal pronouncements. They had a political function in indicating the parameters within which the Soviet Union has expected neutral states should form and conduct their foreign policy.

Soviet international lawyers had little disagreement with their Western counterparts over the wartime obligations of permanently neutral states since these were laid down in the Hague Conventions of 1907. On 7 March

1955 the Soviet Government declared its respect for the Hague Conventions and declarations which Imperial Russia had ratified earlier to the extent that they do not conflict with the United Nations Charter and have not been modified or replaced by subsequent international treaties signed by the USSR.[12] Soviet legal specialists admitted that so long as the phenomenon of war exists there remains a basis for wartime neutrality, and the greater the number of neutral states during war the broader the 'zone of peace'. But the optimistic prognosis of the 1961 Communist Party Programme shaped their view that 'wartime neutrality as an institution of international law will not exist for ever'. Indeed, with the victory of communism throughout the world 'all social and national causes giving rise to all kinds of war will finally be eliminated' and in these conditions there will be 'no place for the laws of wartime neutrality'.[13] Soviet specialists in the 1960s called for the conclusion of a multilateral convention to determine anew the rights and obligations of neutral states in peace and war. The USSR wished this convention to modify and update the Hague Conventions, for example by prohibiting violations of neutrality by acts from space. In the Soviet view this new convention should also 'reflect the existence and interests of states of the socialist type'.[14]

Since the mid 1950s Soviet spokesmen have been reserved about the notion of wartime neutrality. Their contention has been that the characteristic features of the post-war international system make evident the inherent indivisibility of war and peace and consequently of their respective legal codes. Soviet lawyers have described the policy conducted by a permanently neutral state itself as 'one of the forms of peaceful coexistence and the peaceful cooperation of states'.[15] Soviet leaders came to conceive of neutrality as an institution in which the principles of the new doctrine of peaceful coexistence could be expressed. This was part of a broader attempt to invest international law with a new content appropriate to these principles.

The specific Soviet emphasis on neutrality as a peacetime code or course was expressed during a congress of the Soviet-inspired International Association of Democratic Jurists in October 1960. This body formed a commission to work out a definition of neutrality. It determined that neutral status obliges non-participation in military groupings and prohibits the presence of foreign military bases or foreign troops on the territory of the neutral. The Soviet-sponsored commission stated also that neutrality prohibits the use of the neutral's air space for the aims of espionage or the possession of atomic arms by the neutral, and it obliges neutral states to maintain good relations with all states without exception. Neutral states, furthermore, should not render any assistance on their territory or give any direct or indirect support to aggressors and should withdraw from all pacts which create obligations incompatible with their status.[16] These requirements extend far beyond the Western understanding of permanent neutrality. But more than a decade later the Soviet Diplomatic Dictionary of 1971 still referred to the resolutions of the 1960 Congress as its primary source defining the distinct rights and obligations of neutral states.[17] Soviet legal specialists accompanied this Eastern definition of neutrality with an appeal for a multilateral convention (as in the case of wartime neutrality) to define permanent neutrality. Such a convention could establish, for example, the principle that permanent neutrals cannot take part in political and economic preparations for war nor locate on their territory or test weapons of mass destruction.[18]

Soviet specialists have accepted that permanent neutrality in a legal sense is the highest form of neutral policy. Such neutrality is based on an international treaty or is written into constitutional law. Austria and Switzerland represent the best examples.[19] The peacetime rights and duties of these states should form a guideline for all other forms of neutrality. However, Soviet definitions of Austrian and Swiss neutral policy have been permeated by the underlying concerns of the USSR towards the foreign policies of these states. This could be expected since Soviet leaders made it evident that Austria is responsible for its policy of neutrality to the guarantors of that neutrality, which include the USSR. As one of the principal signatory powers of the Austrian State Treaty the Soviet Union gained a position of control over the interpretation of Austria's neutrality, which gave it formal legal grounds to influence the formation of Austria's conception of neutrality.

A Soviet scholar maintained that in the military sphere the permanent neutral was permitted 'moderate' armed forces serving the aims of self-defence, but the 'significant strike force' maintained by Switzerland was considered to contradict the wish to observe permanent neutrality. The permanent neutrals were denied the right to possess nuclear arms, to permit the armed forces of foreign states on their territory or to allow the passage of such forces through their territory. This directly reflected Soviet strategic concerns. In the economic field Moscow ruled out the participation of permanent neutrals in economic boycotts and blockades directed at foreign states (except against 'reactionary regimes', such as South Africa), or their entry into economic alliances or groupings which directly or indirectly may draw them into military conflicts or organisations. This was interpreted to mean that permanent neutrality barred

Austria and Switzerland from entering the European Economic Community. In the ideological realm a Soviet specialist denied such neutral states the right 'to permit propaganda' on their territory 'which is aimed at provoking hatred and hostility towards other states'. Finally, the permanent neutrals were considered 'obliged to carry out a struggle for peace and the peaceful coexistence of states'.[20]

Soviet commentators devised a separate category for Sweden and Finland. The neutrality of these states derived from unilateral proclamations rather than international treaties. Moscow accepted that such states have greater independence in forming their foreign policy than the permanent neutrals and are under no direct obligation to other states to follow a neutral course, but do so of their own free will. The unfortunate vagueness of this category resulted in confusion among Soviet specialists in the 1950s and 1960s between the policies considered desirable for the European 'unilateral neutrals' and those advocated for the newly emergent Third World 'neutralists', since both groups of states were generally described in these years as pursuing a 'policy of neutrality' or 'positive neutrality'. However, an emphasis on the 'traditional' character of Swedish neutrality developed. This reflected Sweden's voluntary and consistent commitment to neutrality over an extended period of time. Soviet writers accepted that Sweden, like the Third World neutralists, could at any moment break off the custom of pursuing neutrality. Austria and Switzerland in contrast were unable to do this.

Soviet legal specialists did not regard the concept of neutralism as closely related to that of formal neutrality in war. However, they asserted that certain international legal principles of 'positive neutrality', drawn from the case of Indo-Chinese neutrality in the 1960s, were suitable more broadly for Third World neutralist states. The Soviet contention was that the states which participated at the Geneva Conference in July 1962 were led by an understanding of contemporary neutrality in general when they worked out the principles and norms relating to the neutrality of Laos. Although Laos could not alter its new status unilaterally, Soviet spokesmen tended to describe it as observing a legally based policy of neutrality rather than permanent neutrality. Moscow sought to use the ambivalent status of Laos to influence the character and requirements of Third World neutralism. Soviet leaders also sought a neutralisation of Cambodia comparable to that of Laos in the 1960s (see Chapter 3).

A more recent example of the merging of categories in Soviet thinking on neutrality is the case of Malta. In 1981 Malta declared itself: 'a neutral state which is adhering to a policy of non-alignment and abstaining from participation in any military alliance, actively striving for international peace and social progress'. In a joint Soviet–Maltese communiqué the Soviet Union welcomed Malta's declaration of its novel status and pledged its support for Maltese efforts to win the recognition and respect of other states for it.[21] For Soviet writers this demonstrated 'the possibility of combining the status of neutrality and non-alignment in the international legal position of one or other state', which for Malta had become a 'generally recognised fact'.[22] In the 1970s a group identity emerged which drew the neutral and non-aligned states within Europe together on certain issues. However, Soviet leaders have preferred to conduct their relations with the European neutral states on a separate basis to their relations with Third World non-aligned states. This has been particularly evident with respect to issues of military security.

Soviet spokesmen have criticised the traditional orientation of neutral states towards wartime conditions and urged them to concentrate on peacetime activities. The intensity of the military polarisation between East and West ensured that the forms of neutrality adopted by European states in peacetime could influence the continental military equation. The intermediate position of neutral states also gave them opportunities to work for a reduction of military tensions around them. Soviet officials encouraged the European neutrals to concentrate on this objective.

Soviet leaders paid close attention to the interpretation the European neutrals gave to the relationship between neutrality and their military forces. Foreign military bases were obviously, and in Austria's case crucially, impermissible on neutral territory. But international law has not traditionally defined the volume and type of weaponry the neutral country should stock. The assumption has existed that the military potential of the neutral states should be sufficient to ensure its ability to defend itself against possible infringements of its neutral status. Soviet specialists accepted that the desire of a neutral state to re-equip its armed forces to strengthen its defence capability should be regarded favourably by other states. They argued, however, that such a course should not lead to 'overstepping reasonable limits', the armaments 'should not be excessive, should be limited to the actual requirements of defence'.[23] As previously observed, the Swiss armed forces have been subject to Soviet criticism for exceeding such limits.

Austrian statesmen have defined one aspect of Austrian neutrality since its inception as a policy of preparatory armament. Soviet leaders did not favour such 'military neutrality'; they pressed their Austrian counterparts to focus instead on specific 'peace-promoting' policies designed to reduce the danger of war.[24] In practice, the Austrian policy of permanent military neutrality has constantly been restrained by limitations imposed on Austrian armaments by the Austrian State Treaty. Soviet leaders have repeatedly rejected Austrian interpretations of the Treaty which favour Austria's understanding of armed neutrality. The restrictions on Finland's armed forces laid down in its Peace Treaty of 1947 have also served to hamper the development of notions of armed neutrality in Finland. In this case, however, the USSR has permitted the Finns to circumvent some of the legal constraints imposed on Finland's military development.

The Soviet Union has been firmly opposed to neutral states acquiring nuclear weapons. The Soviet contention has been that the possession of such weapons would exceed the requirements of defending neutrality, and render neutral states totally dependent on foreign suppliers and impair their independence of action. Austria and Finland were already denied such weapons in their peace treaties. At the end of the 1950s Switzerland and Sweden were strongly criticised for considering the acquisition of tactical nuclear weapons. The Soviet Government argued that the acquisition of these weapons would intensify the atomic arms race and sharpen the international situation, which 'contradicts the very spirit of neutrality as a form of peaceful coexistence'.[25] In a novel initiative in 1958 the Soviet government declared its readiness 'jointly with other powers to secure reliable international guarantees of the "atomic neutrality" of the participant states of zones free of atomic arms in order to exclude the likelihood of the use of such arms in this zone'.[26] This initiative was directed not only towards the neutral states but also at West Germany and Italy. In March 1958 Nikita Khrushchev claimed that alongside the development in Italy of 'neutral tendencies in the broad sense of the term', 'voices have been raised ever more loudly in Italy, demanding that it be included in a nuclear-free zone, demanding Italy's atomic neutrality'.[27] The Soviet declaration in favour of 'atomic neutrality' was the precursor of numerous Soviet appeals to establish nuclear-free zones.

The Soviet concept of 'atomic neutrality' was advanced as an adaptation of classical neutrality, which sought to avoid involvement in a conventional war, to the realities of an age of potential nuclear war. On a practical level it was directed against non-nuclear states becoming involved directly or indirectly in the nuclear strategy of NATO and the nuclear arms race. States committed to atomic neutrality would be obliged not to produce, maintain, or obtain nuclear arms for their own purposes. The location of nuclear arms of every kind on their territory would be prohibited. Such states would not permit the construction of 'nuclear arms facilities' on their territories and 'the use of atomic arms against the territories of such states...would be banned'.[28] Atomic neutrality, Soviet writers argued, should enter into the content of permanent neutrality, since in a sense it was permanent neutrality, although only in relation to atomic arms.[29] Soviet writers claimed that the entry of neutral states into broad 'zones of peace', zones free of atomic arms, would best respond to their national security interests, while acquiring atomic arms would contradict their role in the struggle for disarmament and the prohibition of atomic arms.

Soviet statesmen developed hopes that the European neutral states could contribute materially to the creation of a 'collective security system' on their continent. By this they meant broad agreements on defence policy between the European states preferably on Soviet terms. By the mid 1950s Soviet international lawyers had reversed their earlier claim that neutrality and collective security are incompatible and the neutral Scandinavian countries were urged to join an all-European collective security agreement. Soviet specialists now discerned a complementary element in the relations between neutrality and collective security, although, at least in principle, they considered the latter 'as a barrier to aggression' to form 'a higher form of struggle for peace than the policy of neutrality'. This meant that 'a retreat from collective security in favour of neutrality would be a step backwards not forwards in international relations'.[30]

Although neutrality was regarded by Soviet spokesmen in the 1950s and 1960s as a factor contributing towards a collective security system, it was not endorsed at the expense of the latter objective. The phenomenon of peacetime neutrality, a Soviet writer observed in 1958, developed in the specific conditions formed by the existence of two powerful military groupings of states. He maintained, however, that the 'recognition of the significance of neutrality in these conditions does not mean that we stand for the preservation of the division of the world into military blocs'. In his view, 'the elimination of these blocs and the creation of a united system of collective security in Europe', as proposed by the USSR, would instead be the most reliable means to establish peace in Europe.[31] At the conference of European Communist and Workers' parties in Karlovy Vary in 1967, Brezhnev declared that 'for a series of countries, including ones of North Europe, the alternative to their participation in military–political groupings of powers may be to take to neutrality'. He called simultaneously for recognition of the 'principle of neutrality and of unconditional respect for the inviolability of neutral countries' within a European security system.[32]

Soviet encouragement for the spread of neutrality in Western Europe was designed to meet the military and strategic interests of the USSR. Soviet acceptance of the neutralisation of Austria in the heart of Europe had similarly been motivated primarily by strategic considerations,[33] although Soviet leaders have tended to describe their military interests in relation to Austria in rather general terms. When Kosygin visited Austria in 1973 he noted that 'Austria accepted the obligation not to permit the creation of military bases of other states on its territory'. This position, he asserted, 'is directed at the relief of military dangers in Europe'. Kosygin maintained that the Soviet Government saw 'the positive significance of Austrian neutrality' in the pursuit of this task.[34] Soviet spokesmen suggested on occasions in the 1950s and 1960s that a comparable neutralisation of Germany might be possible; this meant an 'independent Germany, neutral in military relations' with its international status guaranteed by the Great Powers in a peace treaty.[35] Soviet leaders may not have realistically expected the Western powers to accept the idea of a reunified, neutralised Germany. Nor is there any clear evidence that they themselves identified strategic benefits in such an arrangement which would outweigh those derived from a permanently weakened and divided Germany. The incorporation of East Germany into the Warsaw Pact and Khrushchev's attempts during the Berlin Crisis in 1961 to gain Western recognition of the GDR were hardly calculated to facilitate a future reunification of Germany. In contrast the Soviet leadership naturally welcomed the unlikely prospect of a neutral West Germany (with the status of East Germany unaffected). The USSR also gave encouragement to neutralist tendencies in the smaller NATO states. In relation to Brezhnev's Karlovy Vary appeal, a Soviet writer explained that 'to a certain extent the neutral policy of Finland and Sweden holds down the northern plans of NATO'. He speculated that 'if Denmark, Norway, Sweden and Finland were to form a common neutral region, free from NATO influences, then the peaceful future of Scandinavia would be secured'.[36] However, such proposals were double-edged since Eastern Europe could not altogether be insulated from Soviet encouragement of a geographical extension of neutrality in Western Europe.

Soviet views on the application of neutrality to states within the Eastern military and political bloc have been in marked contrast to their advocacy of neutrality in Western Europe. The Soviet leadership, aware of the dangers of political example and strategic loss, rules out the possibility of individual states withdrawing from the Warsaw Pact. On 1 November 1956 Imre Nagy renounced the Warsaw Pact, declared Hungary's neutrality, and called upon the USA, Great Britain and France to guarantee this neutrality. This act, by forces the Soviet Union had already branded as 'counter-revolutionary', precipitated a large-scale intervention of Soviet troops in Hungary that autumn and the reintegration of Hungary into the Pact. Soviet propagandists claimed that 'world democratic opinion unanimously saw this maneuver of the reactionary clique as a step towards the enslavement of Hungary and her conversion into a springboard for imperialist warmongers'. In this context, a Soviet legal specialist quoted the view of the leader of the Dutch Communist Party that 'for those countries over which America at present rules neutrality guaranteed by both world camps would be a step towards national independence' but 'for a socialist country neutrality would be a step backwards towards subordination to American imperialism and its sphere of influence'.[37] Soviet theorists developed the notion of the 'transitional state', which had a historical orientation to the East, but they regarded any move by an established Eastern state towards neutrality as historically regressive. This line of reasoning stemmed from Soviet concern for the political as well as military integrity of the Eastern bloc. They feared that military disengagement from the Eastern bloc would inevitably be bound up with political disengagement (whereas the West European neutral states remain integrated within the Western political and economic system).

Soviet strategic and political interests are also reflected in the measures in the field of defence recommended for the West European neutral states towards creating a European system of security. These were outlined by a Soviet writer before the convention of the Conference on Security and Cooperation in Europe (CSCE) in 1973-5. He suggested that the permanently neutral states implement a scheme leading to their full disarmament. The United Nations (or its Security Council) could then recognise such states as having fully disarmed, as an example of the potential of peaceful coexistence, and it could offer guarantees of the territorial integrity of the disarmed states. In addition the neutral states should take an active part in concluding treaties on creating nuclear-free zones in various regions of Europe; they should support schemes to conclude treaties for the withdrawal of all foreign troops from the territory of European states and the elimination of foreign military bases; and they should struggle to eliminate the 'aggressive NATO bloc'. The neutrals were exhorted, furthermore, to recognise the German Democratic Republic and the inviolability of the existing European borders.[38] These appear to have been maximal Soviet expectations of the European neutrals; since

1972 Soviet spokesmen have been unwilling to lay down such specific programmes for the European neutrals in the military field.

During the years of European *détente* Soviet leaders identified a less controversial role for the neutrals in the field of general European cooperation. During a visit by the Austrian Chancellor to the Soviet Union in 1974 Kosygin argued that *détente* had opened up a 'broader field of activities in international affairs' for neutral states. These states, he noted, 'actively assist the organisation of international meetings, their representatives are enlisted for cooperation in zones of conflict, and mediate in questions of peace settlements'. He commented on the 'positive role' played by the neutral states in the preparations for the CSCE and in 'the negotiations on reducing armed forces and arms in Central Europe'.[39] The importance of the neutral countries working to complement political *détente* with military *détente* also found its way into Soviet communiqués with neutral states in the 1970s.[40]

On a broader political level Soviet diplomats expected the European neutral states to work towards the establishment of permanent inter-parliamentary links, the conduct of systematic political consultations on the government level, and economic cooperation on a general European basis. These hopes were not abandoned, despite the acrimonious exchanges during the follow-up meetings to the CSCE conference. When East–West relations deteriorated in the early to mid 1980s Soviet diplomats, if anything, placed greater emphasis on the mediating role which the neutral states together with the European non-aligned countries (the N and N group formed after the European Security Conference) could perform. For example, at the Twenty-Sixth Congress of the CPSU in 1981 Brezhnev paid a particular tribute to Finland's contribution to 'the consolidation of European security'.[41] The first and final sessions of the CSCE had been held in Helsinki. Andropov welcomed the compromise draft for the final document of the Madrid Review Conference submitted by the heads of state and government of Austria, Cyprus, San Marino, Finland, Sweden and Yugoslavia in March 1983 and gave these states credit for their efforts in this field.[42]

The success of the Stockholm conference on confidence-building measures in 1986 has persuaded the Gorbachev leadership that the European neutral and non-aligned states should be encouraged to work more directly towards measures to strengthen confidence and military-strategic stability in Europe. This was apparent from a statement issued by a meeting of the foreign ministers of the Warsaw Pact states in March 1987. This statement addressed the Vienna Conference of representatives of CSCE states which was underway, and it advocated 'the active participation of neutral and non-aligned countries in the examination of the military aspects of European security at all stages'. The Eastern bloc ministers expressed their belief that these states 'in view of their positive role in the all-European process could make a tangible contribution to the cause of disarmament in Europe too'.[43] Soviet leaders sought to involve the 'N and N states' within a new forum for discussing and negotiating conventional arms reductions in Europe.

A Soviet scholar argued in 1984 that greater democratisation in international relations had permitted the European neutral and non-aligned nations to take some useful and positive initiatives 'without undermining the existing alignment of forces in world affairs'. He noted that these states contributed in certain ways to the stabilisation of *détente* and the development of cooperation in Europe. At the same time he stressed the continued symbolic importance of the neutral states as they 'represent a Europe not divided into hostile military blocs' and 'the idea to eliminate military blocs in Europe has its most visible effect in the existence of these states'.[44] However, the new Soviet leadership has placed its emphasis on the need to gradually reduce the military activity of NATO and the Warsaw Pact rather than on the need to abolish these alliances. It appears likely that Moscow will continue to value the presence of the neutral states in Europe more as a stabilising influence, in conformity with current Soviet views on the 'all-European process', than as an example encouraging a radical disruption of West and East European military structures.

I   The Soviet view of non-alignment in the international order

THE CONCEPT OF THIRD WORLD NEUTRALISM

The key to the development of non-alignment is to be found in the course of Soviet relations with Yugoslavia in the 1940s and 1950s.[1] Since Yugoslav non-alignment was formulated at the expense of the USSR it has been ignored or disparaged in Soviet accounts of the early years of non-alignment and the inaccuracies this introduces into Soviet writings and statements on non-alignment should be borne in mind (see Chapter 2). Instead Moscow developed a confused notion of Third World neutralism with a legal and prescriptive basis influenced by the conduct and character of the European neutral states.

The prominence the Soviet leadership gave to neutrality in its policies towards Western Europe from the mid 1950s was strong evidence of the revision underway in the orthodox Stalinist conception of international relations. Under Stalin Soviet spokesmen had drawn a close link between the ideological and military polarisation dividing East and West; this orthodoxy had precluded any real appreciation of a 'third way'. Khrushchev, however, recognised the significance of the decision by a large number of states to reject military–political integration in Western-sponsored military alliances. Following the death of Stalin, Soviet statesmen were particularly impressed by the course pursued by India and Egypt. Initially, Soviet obervers regarded certain European neutrals and the Third World 'extra-bloc' countries as part of a single international phenomenon. Soviet officials believed that these states shared important common attributes and accepted similar restraints on their foreign policies. Moscow termed them 'neutralists' or the 'positive neutrals'. However, this categorisation tended to obscure for Soviet officials the nature, motive force and objectives of the Third World extra-bloc states in the 1950s and 1960s.

In early 1957 Khrushchev expressed his understanding and sympathy for states such as India, Indonesia, Burma, the United Arab Republic and Cambodia 'adhering to a policy of non-participation in military blocs'. He separately praised 'the benefits of the neutrality of countries such as Switzerland and Sweden'.[2] The Soviet Diplomatic Dictionary of 1961 did not accept this pragmatic distinction between Third World and European states. 'Positive neutrality' was defined as a foreign policy implemented by a number of European, Asian, African and Latin American countries which represented a choice to abstain from military alliances with great powers, to deny them their territory for military bases and to strive to establish friendly relations with other countries. This policy was described also by the terms 'neutralism', 'policy of non-participation in blocs' and 'policy of freedom from alliances'.[3] Soviet leaders were sufficiently pragmatic to realise that the *modus operandi* of European and Third World states would remain at variance despite their common opposition to integration in military blocs. But this proliferation of terms reflected Soviet uncertainty about what could reliably be expected from Third World neutralism in the early 1960s.

Khrushchev sought to argue that neutralism could not apply to the ideological divide between East and West. He observed in 1963 that 'many countries which recently liberated themselves from colonial domination wish to take the socialist path', but 'the statesmen of some of these countries say that they intend to manoeuvre between the two military blocs, confusing the concepts of "bloc" and "system"'. Such confusion, he asserted, assisted the colonialists to preserve their position in these countries.[4] The idea that neutralism obliges the new states to adopt an intermediate path between capitalism and socialism in their internal policy was unacceptable to Soviet spokesmen. They maintained that 'positive neutralism applies exclusively to the sphere of international relations and is absolutely not suited for the regulation of relations between classes within a particular country'. Soviet doctrine determined that 'antagonistic classes cannot be "neutral" on account of the irreconcilability of the contradictions between them'. The notion of a third neutral trend between capitalism and socialism was viewed as a pernicious attempt to 'disorientate the masses'.[5]

Soviet leaders were aware that the foreign policy of many neutralist states was exercised by elite groups. Orthodox Marxist thinking required them to accept that the policy of neutralism has a class character, expressing the will of the dominant classes of a given country. But Soviet theorists qualified this admission with the claim that since the struggle for peace, as expressed in neutralism, is an important task for all strata of society 'the broad mass of people consider the policy of positive neutralism as their life blood and exert pressure on the ruling circles consistently to conduct this policy'.[6] While the attitude of the neutralist state towards communism or capitalism was viewed as its internal affair, which should not influence an appraisal of its neutral policy,[7] Soviet writers still anticipated that the neutralist course would contribute 'to the transition of a national state on socialist lines'.[8]

In his report to the Twenty-Second CPSU Congress in 1961 Khrushchev strictly defined the limits of neutralism in the international sphere. 'These countries are often called neutralists', he stated, 'though they may be considered neutral only in the sense that they do not belong to any of the existing military–political alliances.' To the Soviet leader most of these states were 'by no means neutral when the cardinal problem of our day, that of war and peace, is at issue', for 'as a rule, those countries advocate peace and oppose war'.[9] This definition was used to develop the basic Soviet view that in international systemic conflict neutralism represents a form of anti-imperialist struggle. Neutralism was defined as the foreign policy concept of certain states 'which expresses on the one hand their anti-imperialist tendencies, and on the other, an unwillingness for too broad economic and political cooperation with the socialist countries'.[10]

By 1963 Moscow perceived the foreign policy goals of the neutralists 'to correspond largely with the political course of the socialist states'. Evidence for this was taken from the joint condemnation of colonialism by the two groups of states and from their coincident approach towards the issues of full and universal disarmament and the elimination of foreign military bases. The appeal issued by a large group of neutralist states to the United Nations' General Secretary to hasten the settlement of the Cuban missiles crisis and avert war in 1962 was advanced as further evidence of their 'peace-promoting' role.[11]

In December 1963 Khrushchev reported to the USSR Supreme Soviet that for the first time a conflict leading to serious military clashes had arisen between a socialist and a neutralist country. Rather than supporting China in the Sino-Indian conflict Khrushchev explained that 'the policy of non-alignment with blocs, the neutralist policy of India has won great moral and political weight in the world' and he proceeded to weigh up the Chinese and Indian positions on the conflict even-handedly. Soviet neutrality in this conflict was a clear sign of the importance attached by Soviet leaders not only to Indian military disassociation from the West but to neutralism in general. Moscow had no interest in exacerbating the Sino-

Soviet rift for its own sake. The Soviet press accused the West of claiming that neutralism was 'a policy that left a country without friends or help in trying times' and of anticipating India's 'total abandonment of neutralism' which by force of example would, it was believed, lead to 'the death-warrant of non-alignment...in the Afro-Asian world'. Instead, the Soviet media proclaimed, neutralism 'came forward actively to frustrate imperialist intrigue against the Asian states'.[12]

In the 1960s the USSR expected the neutralists to withdraw ever more from the capitalist West in their economic planning just as they were already believed to have done in their political and ideological relations. Soviet officials anticipated the growth of 'progressive' forces in these countries and the realisation of deep social transformations within them. This would draw them, in various degrees and at different paces, ever closer to the socialist countries. Soviet specialists believed that in contemporary conditions the two groups of states would form a sphere of peaceful coexistence, 'and tomorrow a system of states with various levels of social progress, but motivated in a common direction'.[13] This claim that the foreign policy principles of the neutralist and the socialist states were drawing together became an established premise in the Soviet view of the non-bloc states. But it is rare, however, to find such an explicit forecast in Soviet writings that eventually the two groups of states will form a common state system.

The legal implications of neutralism became a subject of some controversy among Soviet international lawyers. Many of them accepted the view that neutralism did not endow a state with any special international legal status. Nor in their view would any special legal obligations or rights arise for other states in relation to the neutralist state. But they argued that the unilateral declaration of a policy of neutrality by a state established a set of obligations which the neutralist assumes. Since, in their view, these voluntary obligations were based on the sovereign will of the state it 'has the right to determine itself the extent of these obligations'. More generally, since the neutralist state defined the principles of its foreign policy it had 'the right unilaterally to change them' provided this did not infringe principles of international law.[14] Although there were a series of general principles of neutralist policy, a Soviet specialist on Africa recognised that there existed no 'single model of neutralism, a once-and-for-all defined form suitable forever and every-where in Africa'.[15]

These views were openly criticised by a second group of Soviet lawyers in the 1960s who asserted that in the contemporary era it was insufficient to examine positive neutrality only as foreign policy course. In their opinion it also represented 'a distinct international legal position', which 'presupposes mutual rights and obligations' in the relations between the states exercising positive neutrality and the powers which recognise their status. The characteristic feature of this novel status was identified only in the ability of the positive neutrals, in contrast to permanently neutral states, freely to determine their position upon the outbreak of a war. These lawyers interpreted Khrushchev's maxim of 1961, according to which the neutralists advocate peace and oppose war, to mean that such states were neutral 'only in relation to the aggressive blocs of imperialist states'. Consequently, the involvement of troops of African neutralists (through the agency of the United Nations) against European colonial powers in the Congo crisis was regarded as quite legitimate.[16] The qualification remained that neutralist states should not take part in 'aggressive wars, the military adventures of imperialist powers, and other activities representing a threat to peace or an infringement of it'.[17] This is reminiscent of the earlier Soviet distinction between the legitimacy of neutrality in just and unjust wars.

This second school of Soviet thought provided opportunities for Soviet officials to try to regulate the peacetime conduct of neutralist states along strict lines through citing international legal principles. Certain Soviet spokesmen adapted planks from the political platform of the European neutrals for use in the Third World context. Soviet lawyers also claimed that the Geneva Conference on Indo-China in 1954 had already contained a multilateral legal recognition of positive neutrality. They developed the argument that the norms and principles regulating the rights and duties of neutral Laos worked out by the fourteen participant states at the Geneva Conference on Laos in July 1962 were particularly relevant for Third World neutralists. They based this on the view that these rights and duties had received broad international recognition and that Laos pursued a legally formulated peacetime policy of neutrality.[18] Such principles acted at least as a background influence on Soviet diplomats in their dealings with Third World neutralist states.

In the military field, apart from the traditional prohibition for neutrals against participation in alliances, the Geneva Agreement forbade Laos to create foreign military bases and strongpoints or any other military installations on her territory. It stipulated that all foreign military troops and personnel should be withdrawn from Laos and that they should not return. From the Soviet legal standpoint this established contractually the principle that the presence of such personnel was incompatible with a neutral status. The Agreement prohibited the import of nuclear arms into

Laos. To Soviet lawyers this represented the formulation of a further principle that 'the arming of a neutral state with nuclear arms' conflicts with neutrality.[19] In the diplomatic field, it was written into the Geneva Agreement that Laos would realise the principles of peaceful coexistence, develop friendly relations and establish diplomatic relations with all countries on the basis of equality. Laos was barred from taking part in any agreements, military or non-military, incompatible with its neutrality. In the Soviet interpretation this obliged Laos not to conclude international agreements hindering 'the establishment of diplomatic relations with states independent of their social structure' (in other words with the socialist states). Soviet analysts stressed that Laos was obliged not to receive any foreign military assistance tied to political or military conditions. In their view the Agreement contained distinct legal guarantees defending Laos from the attempts of 'imperialist' states 'to tie it to unequal economic agreements, which are accompanied by one-sided political conditions'. They stressed the significance of these understandings 'for all neutralist states developing their economies, as a rule, with the assistance of other countries'.

Finally, Soviet spokesmen noted that the Declaration on the Neutrality of Laos adopted by the Geneva Conference on 23 July 1962 includes a provision requiring the parties to the declaration to abstain from all kinds of direct or indirect interference in the internal affairs of Laos and from the use of the territory of any state for such interference. Soviet commentators hoped these regulations could be used by the neutralists in their struggle 'against the intrigues of the imperialists'.[20] Overall, the understandings worked out at Geneva on the position of Laos were interpreted in Moscow as a kind of charter for the neutralists in their opposition to the West. Since in the 1960s the Western states had a more active diplomatic and military presence in the Third World than the USSR, the restrictions on relations with neutralist states outlined above were calculated to work in favour of the Soviet Union. The contemporary Soviet view held that Afro-Asian neutralism 'essentially limits the sphere of operations of the imperialist and colonial powers, narrows the sphere of influence of the imperialist and colonial powers and simultaneously extends the zone of peace'.[21]

Quite apart from the legal 'code of conduct' for neutralist states drawn from the Geneva Conference in Laos, in the 1960s Soviet specialists presented a whole series of political objectives of the Bandung Declaration of Afro-Asian States (April 1955) and the Belgrade Declaration of Non-Aligned States (September 1961) as normative prescriptions for states pursuing a course of 'positive neutrality'. The obligations identified included the need: 'to render effective assistance' in the struggle to eradicate colonialism and neo-colonialism and liberate territories still under foreign domination; to observe the status of Africa as an atomic free zone; to support universal and full disarmament; to support the universal prohibition of racial discrimination; to actively assist the peaceful resolution of international conflicts and disputes; and to develop broad economic, scientific–technical and cultural cooperation with all countries.[22] Moscow also hoped to benefit strategically from Third World neutralism as a policy of specific military denial to the West. This was reflected in the broad range of military obligations identified by certain Soviet specialists to flesh out and add to the principles advanced in relation to the agreement on Laos. Until at least the beginning of the 1970s the military obligations and functions identified by Moscow for the non-aligned group of states remained substantially those specified earlier in the 1960s for the less cohesive neutralist group.[23]

In 1963 a Soviet writer stipulated that the new military requirements for the neutralist states included a prohibition against using their air space for hostile aims against other states, such as espionage, nuclear war and the transport of missiles; an obligation not to permit or assist activities on their territory supporting aggression; an obligation not to take part in 'military measures of the imperialist powers'; a prohibition against the possession and testing of nuclear weapons on their territory.[24] Soviet analysts did not consider the conclusion of alliances of a defensive character by neutralist states, as in the case of the 1966 treaty of defence between Syria and the United Arab Republic, as illegitimate. But 'joint manoeuvres of the armed forces of neutralist states and imperialist powers' in their view would 'contradict the idea of positive neutrality'. Such a 'contradiction' was discerned, for example, in the joint manoeuvres of the Indian air force with the air forces of the United States and Great Britain over Indian territory in the early 1960s. Western military assistance to the neutralists created a similar contradiction in Soviet eyes since such assistance was considered almost by definition to be 'accompanied by binding political conditions'. An example given by the Soviet press in 1963 was the claim that the United States was attempting to link assistance to India with restrictions on Indian anti-aircraft defence.[25] Soviet writers accepted the legitimacy of military assistance from neutralist states to other states striving for independence despite the proclaimed 'illegality' of military cooperation between the neutralists and the Western countries.[26] They were also careful not to deny the neutralists the option of turning to the Soviet bloc for assistance.

Although Soviet analysts accepted that Third World neutralist states like the European neutrals had the right to remain neutral in the event of war, as Khrushchev had implied in his speech to the Soviet Party Congress in 1961, they regarded neutralism as directed essentially against participation in the Cold War. This corresponded to Western views on neutralism in the 1960s. According to one commonly accepted Western definition, 'neutrality means keeping aloof from shooting wars whereas neutralism means disassociation from the Cold War, while perhaps involving efforts to remove, or at least mitigate, some of the harshness of the Cold War struggle'.[27] The neutralists sought to find acceptable channels of communication across Cold War barriers, but it was understood that neutralism does not preclude participation in conflicts lying outside the East–West polarisation, or even participation in actual wars.

At times, however, Soviet writers tried to introduce an ideological component into the neutralist renunciation of the Cold War. One specialist contended, for example, that it would be inadmissible for a neutralist government to locate radio installations on its territory directing 'subversive transmissions against other countries', or even to permit on its soil 'reactionary organisations which direct provocative activities against other governments and stir up anti-communist attacks in the press'. The blurring of the traditional two-camp thesis was reinforced by the claim that Soviet respect for the rights of the positive neutrals and the broad economic assistance they received from the socialist countries on the basis of equality and mutual benefit illustrated the principles of 'proletarian internationalism in action' between the two groups of states. This degraded the assertion by the neutralists that they were playing a 'third role' in world affairs. The neutralist countries argued that classical international law favours the status quo powers and does not necessarily represent the global community of states. But even in this area Soviet writers claimed that the neutralists or the non-aligned, as they began to be termed in the 1960s, were leading 'the struggle to establish new international legal principles such as the principle of universal and full disarmament and the principle of prohibiting war propaganda' not independently but 'together with the socialist camp'.[28] In other words, Soviet diplomats gave a legal dressing to their favoured political principles in an attempt to enshrine them in the foreign policy conduct of the neutralist states.

The Soviet Union and Afro-Asian solidarity

Khrushchev's identification of a vast 'zone of peace' between the two ideological systems was primarily intended to encourage the new sovereign African and Asian states to reject the blandishments and resist the pressures of Western states, to form an anti-Western political coalition motivated by broad universalist principles and opposition to alliances but inclined towards support of Soviet proposals in the international arena. Soviet leaders sought to steer the emerging anti-Western Afro-Asian political identity along lines favourable to the socialist bloc. Alongside formal support for the conferences of Afro-Asian states they tried to achieve this through promoting and sponsoring 'solidarity' meetings of diverse radical groups in the new African and Asian states.

The Afro-Asian Conference at Bandung in April 1955 provided proof to Soviet leaders that the Afro-Asian states were breaking away from Western military bonds. In later years Soviet spokesmen, as many Third World statesmen, tended to trace back the origins of the Non-Aligned Movement to this seminal conference. But such prospects were not predicted by Soviet observers in 1955 who were fully aware of the diversity of political and military links held by the states represented at Bandung. They could anticipate that the presence of communist China at the conference would be more than balanced by the presence of states with military pacts with the United States such as the Philippines, Iraq, Thailand, Turkey and Pakistan. The Soviet media claimed that Washington had allotted the delegations of these countries the role 'of a kind of ideological mine' in order to 'blow up the conference from inside'.[29] The participation of such states at Bandung ensured that Western defence pacts would not be condemned. Rather, the sixth of the Ten Principles adopted at Bandung recognised the right of individual or collective self-defence provided that collective defence does not serve the private ends of any Great Power and that there are no pressures on countries to join defence pacts.

The Soviet leaders responded to Bandung with an attempt to bring the anti-colonial momentum represented by the conference under Soviet or socialist control. They sponsored the first meeting of the Afro-Asian Peoples' Solidarity Organisation (AAPSO) in Cairo in late December 1957. In contrast to the Bandung Conference there were no official state representatives at Cairo. In their place there assembled a diverse group of delegates from the 'social organisations' of forty-five Afro-Asian countries, including the Soviet Union. Although the Cairo Conference reaffirmed the

Ten Principles adopted at Bandung, the major addresses at Cairo implicitly denied Principle Six and criticised Western defence pacts and the Afro-Asian states which had joined them.[30] Non-communist African and Asian circles tended to regard the AAPSO's independent character with scepticism or disbelief, especially after it took a further leftward turn in 1961. Indeed during the AAPSO conferences in Moshi in 1963 and Winneba in 1965 formal references to the Bandung Principles were phased out, and anyway the Organisation showed little inclination to recommend neutralism or non-alignment as a major strategy to realise its goals.[31]

The USSR appeared to have strong organisational influence over the AAPSO, but by the mid 1960s the debate in the Organisation was racked by competition between the Soviet Union and China. Although the conference in Winneba, Ghana was supposed to increase 'peoples' solidarity', the head of the Soviet delegation admitted that the discussion held was 'at times quite stormy' since 'those who met in the conference hall were people of very different political convictions'. He stressed that the Soviet delegation assured the participants that 'the peoples of the USSR will fulfil their internationalist duty to the fullest and will give all-out support and assistance to the peoples waging a just struggle'.[32] This sounded rather like Soviet assurances at international Communist Party meetings. Indeed, the Winneba meeting adopted a decision to the effect that representatives of the 'solidarity committees' of the European socialist states should be invited as observers to all subsequent AAPSO conferences. China managed, nevertheless, to gain a majority in favour of holding the next AAPSO meeting in Peking in 1967. This never happened, since a key session of the AAPSO Council in February 1967 managed to relocate the venue to Algiers and expel the pro-Chinese African representatives.[33] Hereafter the AAPSO became a dutiful proponent of the views of the Soviet-led socialist bloc in the Third World.

The crucial discussions over Soviet involvement in the Afro-Asian movement did not take place in the AAPSO but over the question of Soviet participation in a second Bandung Conference originally planned for 1964. Soviet leaders were clearly equivocal over the benefits to be gained from pressing for Soviet participation. In spring 1964 the Chinese opposed the idea of inviting the Soviet Union to the Afro-Asian conference at a preparatory meeting in Jakarta. In response a statement by the Soviet Government sought to justify the 'desire of a number of member countries' of the Afro-Asian movement to see the USSR in the conference. Moscow argued its case firstly on the grounds that 'the Soviet Union is not only a great European but a great Asian power', and secondly on the basis of Soviet sacrifices 'at the risk of being involved in very grave developments' (meaning, no doubt, a confrontation with the West) to avert encroachments on the independence of the newly free nations.[34] By August the Soviet Government maintained that it had 'by no means considered' that it should 'necessarily' attend the conference, and that it could not allow the question of being invited to become an 'embarrassment' to the Afro-Asian countries or to cause disharmony among them'.[35] This pragmatic approach was reversed the following year when the Soviet media pressed strongly for Soviet representation at the conference in Algiers. Moscow asserted that if 'the international prestige of the USSR, backed by its might, is put on the scales, this will doubtlessly multiply the strength of the conference countries and help them achieve their aims'.[36] Soviet spokesmen also stressed the ideological rationale behind the Soviet position; the conference was regarded as a potential forum for an anti-colonialist and anti-imperialist front to which the USSR was wedded by virtue of its internationalist obligations.[37]

A coup in June 1965 toppled Ben Bella of Algeria, the host country for the Afro-Asian conference. This provided a formal pretext to postpone further the conference.[38] Over the following months the Soviet Union maintained her pressure for admission. However, following the overthrow in October of Sukarno of Indonesia, China's strongest ally in the Third World, China requested a çancellation of the conference, which confirmed its collapse and the 'demise of Afro-Asianism as a Third World organising principle'. It has been observed that China's distinctive ideological posture at an Afro-Asian meeting would have been a polarizing rather than a unifying factor,[39] but this would have been equally true of Soviet participation. Nevertheless, the Soviet contention was that the events of autumn 1965 'reaffirmed the importance of cooperation with the socialist countries, notably the USSR, in strengthening Afro-Asian solidarity'.[40] This only underlined Soviet unwillingness to accept the Afro-Asian group as an independent body of states free of close organisational links with the Soviet bloc.

THE CONCEPT OF NON-ALIGNMENT AND THE NON-ALIGNED MOVEMENT

Non-alignment is a term which has come to cover the interrelated phenomena of a foreign policy doctrine, the practical policy of distinct countries, and the interstate union of Non-Aligned countries and its activities. The Soviet understanding of non-alignment as a doctrine or policy has been tightly bound up with its general characterisation of the Non-Aligned Movement and its expectations of this body. Within the Soviet doctrinal outlook the Non-Aligned Movement has been part of the overall process of social development of the Third World, a manifestation of the national liberation movement directed against colonialism and 'imperialism'. The national liberation movement, alongside the international working class and the world socialist system in turn are regarded as integral parts of the struggle beween the two world social systems. Khrushchev had already used this categorisation in an attempt to explain the phenomenon of neutralism. From this perspective Soviet officials conceived the Non-Aligned Movement, despite its disavowal of military blocs, as part of the conflict between the political–ideological systems of East and West.

Soviet officials had supported neutralism as a foreign policy course since the late 1950s, but initially they were ambivalent in their responses to the Non-Aligned Movement. In the early 1960s the meetings of the Non-Aligned had to compete with the Afro-Asian movement for legitimacy in representing Third World views. Until the summit conference in Lusaka in 1970 the gatherings of non-aligned states were episodic; they lacked the frequency, continuity and momentum characteristic of a movement. Another factor which contributed to Soviet reluctance to encourage multilateral diplomacy based on non-alignment was the association of this concept or policy with Yugoslavia. Tito had used non-alignment as a strategy to stake out an independent foreign policy in Eastern Europe. The first summit of non-aligned nations was held in Belgrade and Tito's efforts were behind the organisational revival of the Non-Aligned group in the late 1960s which resulted in the Lusaka Summit in 1970.

By the time the Lusaka Conference was convened Soviet diplomats recognised that the phenomenon of neutralism or positive neutrality in the Third World had been overtaken and absorbed by the more active, policy-oriented doctrine or strategy of non-alignment. They were also aware that the policies Third World states associated with non-alignment shared common ground with various Soviet objectives. In a tactical shift Soviet spokesmen begun to blame the difficulties 'non-alignment' had experienced in the 1960s on its former association with neutralism. They identified a central contradiction between the passive and active elements in neutralism. These were manifested in its attempt to combine non-interference in global international conflicts at the 'high level' with an attempt to constructively contribute towards the resolution of pressing world problems. The USSR anticipated a more active, prominent role in the 1970s for states pursuing a course of non-alignment. During the Lusaka Summit the Soviet press criticised attempts to turn the non-aligned states into a kind of contemporary 'court of arbitration' in the 'neutral zone' as 'impracticable and untenable'.[41] Throughout the 1970s the neutralist strain in the Non-Aligned Movement and the policy of 'equidistance between East and West' which it has sustained were gradually subjected to more persistent Soviet criticism for their alleged passivity.

The Soviet press acknowledged that the participants at the Lusaka Non-Aligned Summit 'had no clearcut common view as regards the concept of non-alignment, because the different forces within the movement interpret its principles in their own way and invest it with different meanings'.[42] Soviet observers dwelt on the problems in defining the essence of non-alignment which arose at a conference devoted to issues of non-alignment held in Belgrade in January 1969. The Soviet Diplomatic Dictionary of 1971 set down its own definition of a policy of non-alignment: 'the foreign policy course and international legal position of a state in peacetime which is characterised by abstention from joining any military bloc and grouping, aggressive or defensive'. This policy allegedly exhibited 'an anti-imperialist, anti-war, anti-colonial thrust', which resulted in the greater part of the non-aligned states supporting 'the resolution of the problem of universal and full disarmament, banning nuclear arms, the creation of atomic free zones, the elimination of racial discrimination' and 'the proposals of the Soviet Union and the socialist countries on the easing of international tensions'.[43] This indicates that at the beginning of the 1970s the policy of non-alignment was considered by the Soviet authorities to combine a characteristic neutralist opposition to military blocs with a 'progressive' anti-Western policy and support for Soviet-sponsored security proposals. As late as 1973 the definition of non-alignment provided by a Soviet legal specialist remained permeated by the concept of neutralism. He listed the requirements of non-alignment as: 'equal relations with the states of both socio-economic systems, non-participation in military–political blocs, the elimination of military bases, and determining positions freely in a possible war of third countries'.[44]

The concept of non-alignment could not easily be absorbed into the doctrinal outlook on international affairs accepted by Soviet analysts in the 1970s. They could not simply regard non-alignment as a new, more active foreign policy course, since they were predisposed to believe that foreign policies are determined by the class interests they realise, and the participants of the Non-Aligned Movement represented a great variety of socio-economic formations. A Soviet specialist resolved this theoretical dilemma with the argument that non-alignment is invoked 'to secure the foreign policy goals and tasks of a state by means of non-participation in the military blocs of imperialism and the defensive agreements of socialist states, by means of an independent approach to international problems'. In other words, non-alignment was the foreign policy means and method of approach to attain particular goals. Non-alignment was used to work out the tactics and strategy of diplomacy 'in the contemporary conditions of the division of the world into two social systems and the refusal of a given state to participate in their military agreements'. In the broader sense non-alignment was defined as 'a general democratic interstate movement of countries being led in their foreign policies by the stated method'. It was perceived as 'a manifestation of the global process of our epoch – the transition of states from capitalism to socialism'.[45]

Soviet spokesmen rejected the widespread notion that there exists a basic global division between the poor South and the rich North on doctrinal grounds. In their view this outlook displaced class struggle as a distinct phase of social development and set the USSR and other socialist countries in opposition to the Third World. Soviet analysts asserted that the 'poor–rich' division was copied from the social structure of bourgeois society, although they admitted that the weak economic development of the overwhelming number of new states often created a 'favourable propagandist-psychological base' for this notion.[46] As early as the Cairo Non-Aligned Conference in 1964 the Soviet press accused delegates who referred to a North–South division of theoretical confusion or unscrupulousness, of a racist desire 'to bring about a clash between the "coloured" races and the white race'.[47] Soviet officials were concerned about the influence of this concept among the pro-Chinese delegations. Again, before the Lusaka Conference the USSR attacked attempts to counterpose the 'poor South' to the 'rich North'. It disparaged the argument that the Non-Aligned Movement should be used only to solve problems specific to the 'small and poor countries'. This was described as a means 'to squeeze the underlying principles of non-alignment into an artificial framework, to force the young national states onto the road of cooperation and compromise with imperialist powers'.[48]

When discussion arose in the West at the beginning of the 1970s suggesting that the world was moving from a 'bipolar' to a 'multipolar' epoch, the thesis developed among many non-aligned states that in these conditions the 'small and medium states' had a special role to play. The Non-Aligned Movement was characterised as a representative body of the small and militarily weak states. Prominent non-aligned statesmen believed that the Non-Aligned group could benefit by maintaining a 'balance of power' between the Great Powers. Soviet writers contended, however, that the Non-Aligned could not sustain such a role as a 'third force', acting as a balancer between the Great Powers. They argued that this position logically would require the Non-Aligned to interfere on behalf of one side or another if the equilibrium between them were upset, in which case the entire basis of non-alignment would collapse.[49] The Soviet Union was concerned that the attractiveness of the 'two superpowers' notion would increase Chinese influence among nationalist Third World leaders and distance them from the Soviet bloc.

In the 1970s Soviet specialists also began to outline a legal framework governing the rights and obligations associated with non-alignment and the Non-Aligned Movement. This involved shedding much of the legal framework Moscow had sought to attach to Third World neutralism (influenced by the Soviet view of European neutrality) and identifying more pragmatic legal criteria relevant to a more organised group of independently minded states and Soviet interests towards them. Soviet writers argued in the first place that the legal obligation to observe a status of non-alignment had been fixed in a wide range of unilateral declarations, in domestic legislation, in communiqués and bilateral treaties, in joint resolutions at Non-Aligned conferences, and in multilateral treaties. This in turn created an obligation for other states to respect the assumption of this status. From the Soviet perspective the countries in the League of Arab States (through a special resolution against alliances in 1954) and the Organisation of African Unity (through articles in the OAU Charter) had bound themselves especially to observe non-alignment.[50] the OAU Charter was described in Moscow as the first multilateral treaty which juridically confirmed the obligatory nature of non-alignment for its signatories.

Soviet lawyers sought secondly to tie an extensive range of obligations to the status of non-alignment which would direct it firmly against the Western states. For example, while non-aligned states in their view had the right to create regional economic organisations, the activities of these organisations had to comply with the legal basis of non-alignment – peaceful coexistence. Non-aligned states were obliged to observe fully the principles of peaceful coexistence and to help secure them in international relations. The Soviet corollary was that 'in this connection, anti-communism and anti-Sovietism in the foreign policy of non-aligned states would be illegal'. Non-aligned states had the right to dissolve agreements infringing the principles of non-alignment and had the corresponding obligation not to conclude such agreements. They were obliged to strive to eliminate 'imperialist military bases' on their territory.[51] Soviet analysts were more cautious in considering whether the decisions of the Non-Aligned Movement had legal force. They accepted that in practice the resolutions of organs of the Movement are recommendations, representing morally committing agreed views which express the joint political positions of the member states.[52]

As the prominence of the Non-Aligned Movement grew Soviet leaders began to consider its long-term strategic goals. They encouraged the Non-Aligned to adopt a political programme which would conform with Soviet strategic interests in the Third World. A Soviet writer identified certain political objectives for the Non-Aligned at the Lusaka Summit in 1970 in addition to their traditional opposition to military alliances and foreign military bases. These included peaceful coexistence, the strengthening of the role of the Non-Aligned in the United Nations, a struggle against colonialism and racism, a resolution of conflicts by peaceful means and curtailing the arms race.[53] The development of *détente* only extended the range of 'open and urgent' tasks required of non-aligned states. A Soviet scholar listed these in 1977 as follows: the struggle to avert a new world war and assist the process of *détente*; the elimination of conflicts between individual liberated countries; active participation in the process of restructuring international economic relations on the basis of equality and justice; the confirmation of the sovereign rights of nations over their natural resources; the elimination of the military bases of imperialist powers and the destruction of plans for the creation of new aggressive groupings in various regions of the Third World.[54] By the beginning of the 1980s Soviet spokesmen also placed the democratisation of international relations in general on their political agenda for the Non-Aligned Movement.[55]

It could be argued that the pursuit of such a far-reaching programme calls for the maximum organisational cohesion between the non-aligned countries. However, Soviet spokesmen have been adamant that the Non-Aligned Movement should not form a third bloc; this was evident from their rejection of the notion of the Non-Aligned as a 'third force' between the Great Powers. Soviet officials are aware that a current of opinion has favoured the creation of such a bloc to oppose the two superpowers, but they have argued that the decision by the non-aligned states at the 1961 Belgrade Conference against the formation of a bloc remains binding. In Soviet eyes this precludes the Non-Aligned Movement turning into an international intergovernmental organisation in the ordinary sense. It is defined instead as a new institution of international relations and international law. Soviet specialists describe the relationship between the Non-Aligned Movement and the United Nations as one of mutual influence. The former body exerts a technical influence on the course of discussions within the United Nations on issues of world politics and the creation of international law, for example in the Conference on the Law of the Sea.[56]

Soviet officials were suspicious of the tendency towards a further institutionalisation of the Non-Aligned Movement in the 1970s. A Soviet scholar explained in 1981 that this movement 'was and remains a free forum of joint action and coordination of foreign policy activities'. He believed that its participants were not formally committed to particular positions but in practice, especially in international organisations, were more or less bound to 'firm moral discipline' in relation to resolutions previously adopted in Non-Aligned conferences.[57] Soviet specialists have generally argued for the 'political–organisational solidarity' of Third World international organisations. They feared, however, that efforts to tighten the organisational structure of the Non-Aligned Movement could engender its fragmentation through the withdrawal of a whole number of states. They view the existing mechanism of the Movement as flexible enough and accept that the recommendatory character of decisions adopted by the Non-Aligned Movement preserve the unity of action of the participants.[58] However, to ensure the anti-Western consensus of the Movement, Soviet officials have expected it to maintain selective entrance requirements.

Distinct criteria of non-alignment were adopted in June 1961 by representatives at the preparatory conference in Cairo for the Belgrade Non-Aligned Summit. They determined that the states invited to the Belgrade Conference should not be in multilateral military alliances concluded in the context of Great power conflicts, they should not be in any bilateral military arrangements with a Great Power or in regional defence pacts if these are deliberately concluded in the context of Great Power conflicts, nor should they have conceded any military bases to a Great Power in the context of Great Power conflicts. The states invited to Belgrade were expected additionally to have adopted an independent policy based on peaceful coexistence and on non-alignment, or be showing a trend in favour of such a policy, and to have consistently been supporting the national liberation movement.[59] The 1985 Soviet Diplomatic Dictionary provides an exact rendering of the military criteria of non-alignment formulated in Cairo.[60] Until the 1980s, however, Soviet publications hardly ever quoted these criteria in full and tended to misrepresent them by stating that non-alignment prohibited any collective military agreement or bilateral union with a Great Power. Soviet writers chose to interpret these criteria in a manner calculated to exclude states with close military links with the Western powers from the Non-Aligned Movement, and to bring pressure to bear on these states. Soviet spokesmen also appealed to the political criteria of 1961 in their efforts to direct the non-aligned states against the West. In June 1969, before the preparatory meeting for the Lusaka Conference, Soviet specialists asserted that the numerical increase in participants at Non-Aligned conferences 'undoubtedly has its natural limits'. They warned that 'any erosion and especially alteration of the basic principles will undoubtedly undermine the whole concept of non-alignment', and attacked attempts 'to include among the non-aligned states neutral countries and some states which are either members of imperialist military blocs or maintain broad military and political relations with the United States and Britain', such as Australia.[61]

A proposal to introduce South Korea and the Philippines into the Non-Aligned Movement was rejected in August 1975 at the Lima Conference of Non-Aligned Foreign Ministers. Soviet writers commended this decision on the grounds that these states have military agreements with the United States and have accepted foreign military bases and foreign troops on their territories. Soviet observers expressed concern over press rumours at the beginning of the Colombo Non-Aligned Summit Conference in 1976 that some states planned to propose the candidatures of states such as Australia, New Zealand, Portugal, Pakistan, Turkey, South Korea and China for the summit. Those in favour of this proposal argued that the inclusion of such countries in the Non-Aligned Movement would assist the dissolution of the blocs. The Soviet response was that any revision of the criteria of non-alignment in favour of such 'limitless expansion' could lead 'to a breakup of the movement into contradictory groupings, not to a strengthening but on the contrary to a weakening of its influence in international affairs'.[62] Soviet diplomats no doubt welcomed the decision reached by a Non-Aligned conference in Algiers in June 1976 that 'participants in military pacts' could only be represented in meetings of the Non-Aligned holding the status of 'guests' on a renewable basis.

Soviet observers in the mid 1970s still believed that the military–political conditions for entry into the Non-Aligned Movement were 'softening'. They referred to the acceptance of certain states into the Movement which were linked by military agreements to Western powers, such as Singapore,

Malaysia, Trinidad and Tobago and Panama. They noted that a number of countries had entered the Non-Aligned Movement with foreign military bases on their territory, such as Cyprus, Cuba, Malaysia, Panama, Trinidad and Tobago and Jamaica, and some still retained them. Moscow accepted that in those cases where these bases were retained participation in the Movement contributed to the removal of the bases. But certain countries, such as Oman and Saudi Arabia, were attacked for their unwillingness to eliminate military bases on their territory and for their conclusion of one-sided treaties contrary to the Belgrade criteria of non-alignment.[63] Soviet writers also sought to use the criteria of non-alignment against the participation of African non-aligned countries in military agreements and alliances with France, although this state lay outside the formal military structure of NATO.[64]

By the beginning of the 1980s the USSR directly accused the Non-Aligned Movement of ignoring the activities of members 'whose foreign policy course in many respects contradicts the principles of non-alignment'. The American military agreements with Egypt, Morocco and Saudi Arabia, and Western military bases in non-aligned states, were referred to as evidence that easing the criteria of entry into the Movement 'negatively affects the movement's effectiveness'.[65] It was understood that the presence of foreign troops and military bases on the territory of a state was not 'an insuperable obstacle' to the possession of Non-Aligned credentials if such troops and bases were retained against the will of the non-aligned state and if it sought to remove them.[66] But this hardly vindicated the continued membership of Afghanistan in the Non-Aligned Movement after the entry of Soviet troops into this country. Soviet spokesmen also sought to use the political criteria of non-alignment identified at Cairo in 1961 to preclude 'pro-imperialist regimes' from access to Non-Aligned meetings and to brand them as international pariahs. Soviet writers stressed that it was the 'non-correspondence' of the South Korean regime to these criteria which had led to the rejection of its request in 1975 for admission into the ranks of the Non-Aligned. The Soviet Union approved certain cases where the 'social tendency and character of power' of states had been taken into account. An example was the condemnation of the 'reactionary military junta of Chile' by the Lima Conference of Non-Aligned Foreign Ministers in 1975 and its subsequent exclusion from the Non-Aligned Movement.[67]

In the 1980s Soviet writers have questioned the premises behind a trend towards 'universalism' or 'globalism' in the Non-Aligned Movement. They are concerned that not only countries of Latin America but a number of small and medium-sized European states have in some form become attached to the Non-Aligned Movement. They recognise that the 'objective coincidence' of the positions adopted by a significant mass of Afro-Asian countries and those assumed by a number of Latin American states and certain West European countries on a series of international issues is 'undoubtedly a positive fact'. But their concern is that the proponents of the 'globalism' concept are states in the Non-Aligned Movement with relatively developed economic relations, which often claim the role of regional centres of political and economic influence and seek association with the capitalist countries of 'medium' development, such as Spain, Portugal and Greece, rather than with the majority of socially and economically backward Afro-Asian countries.[68] The Soviet Union fears that the growing influence of large semi-developed states, mostly in Latin America, whose natural economic orientation is towards Western Europe will further erode the radical anti-Western thrust of the Non-Aligned body of states.[69]

Soviet commentators have found it difficult to explain such a deradicalisation of the Non-Aligned Movement. They welcomed the growth of the sphere of operations and international activity of this body. Their doctrinal and methodological approach to the Third World predisposed them to assume that the change in the global 'correlation of forces' evident in the 1970s involved an intensifying crisis in the political and economic relations between the developing world and the Western states.[70] Yet the radical thrust of the Non-Aligned Movement evidently abated in the 1980s. In an attempt to explain away this contradiction between theory and reality Soviet writers identified 'deepening socio-political and economic contradictions' within most developing countries. A more pragmatic Soviet assertion has been that an influx of new members into the Non-Aligned Movement coincided with a generational change among its leaders. A Soviet commentator explained in 1981 that former leaders of the Non-Aligned who had greatly influenced the activities of the Movement, like Tito, Nasser, Sukarno and Nkrumah, had undergone a 'severe schooling in the struggle for national liberation' against colonialism and imperialism. In contrast the new generation of Non-Aligned leaders were the spiritual products of the post-colonial era, and as such led primarily 'by the realities of present international relations'. Their priorities were 'the problems of development, the struggle for natural and energy resources, the internal tensions of many developing societies, the nuclear threat' and so on. These were the issues which motivated their foreign policy courses.[71]

Soviet analysts maintain that the objectives of the Non-Aligned

Movement developed in stages reflecting changes in the international environment. According to their schema the 1950s and 1960s were a period of concentrated Non-Aligned struggle against colonialism. A second stage of Non-Aligned activity, tightly linked to *détente* and beginning in the first half of the 1970s, was oriented primarily towards achieving economic independence and restructuring international economic relations. Moscow characterises the Non-Aligned Movement in the third stage since the end of the 1970s as particularly active on issues concerning the preservation of peace and international security. Soviet spokesmen explain that this shift reflected a recognition by many Non-Aligned leaders that the deterioration in international conditions had not only adversely affected the security of their states but also had shattered their hopes of effectively resolving the necessary tasks for economic development. The Non-Aligned Movement was also confronted by an increasing number of conflicts within the developing world itself.[72] This change in priorities suited a central Soviet strategic objective in the 1980s: to coordinate Soviet proposals on broad issues of international security and disarmament with those of the great majority of non-aligned states (see Chapter 2). Soviet leaders seek to steer the diffuse, and for some states more residual, anti-Western radicalism, still expressed in the consensus of the Non-Aligned Movement, towards this goal.

NON-ALIGNMENT AND THE SOCIALIST SYSTEM

The Soviet ideological and doctrinal outlook on international affairs has equipped Soviet leaders poorly to understand and appreciate non-alignment as an independent strategy pursued by states. Traditional Marxist–Leninist thinking in the USSR on the clash between the Eastern and Western systems has been modified since the 1950s, but not sufficiently to accept the degree of autonomy of action the majority of the non-aligned states ascribe to their status of non-alignment. Soviet spokesmen have drawn from their ideological ballast in discussing various aspects of non-alignment and the Non-Aligned Movement. These include the general relationship between the internal policies of states and their pursuit of non-alignment, the relative independence or distance of non-aligned states from the Eastern and Western systems or blocs, the political–ideological composition of the Non-Aligned Movement overall, the relationship between socialist and non-aligned principles, and the correspondence in objectives between non-aligned states and the 'socialist community'. All these issues are examined below.

One premise of Soviet analysts has been the existence of a relationship between the internal regime, politics and social forces of non-aligned states and their policy of non-alignment. In the early and mid 1960s neutralism and non-alignment were linked to the nature of socio-economic change within the neutralist or non-aligned state. Soviet specialists claimed that the more a given country identified itself with the 'non-capitalist path of development' the more vigorous and viable its non-aligned stand became. Khrushchev identified the 'non-capitalist path' in the 1950s as an intermediary and transitional category of socio-economic development. Neutralism and non-alignment became regarded as the foreign policy manifestations of this course. In the Soviet view the 'most active fulfillment of neutralist principles' was found among the Afro-Asian liberated countries which had chosen the non-capitalist path.[73] During the Cairo Non-Aligned Summit in 1964 the Soviet media went one step further in rejecting the view that the principle of non-alignment would be violated by the decision of a Third World country to adopt a 'socialist way of development'. This view was described as a deliberate confusion of 'the question of ways of development with that of orientation towards military blocs'.[74] The domestic underpinnings of a policy of non-alignment were minimally expected to be non-capitalist, but possibly also socialist.

According to the characteristic Soviet view in the 1960s, while positive neutrality or non-alignment carried a class character and expressed the will of the dominant classes of a given country it did not exclusively reflect ruling-class interests. Soviet specialists contended that since non-alignment was directed at the defence of national interests and the maintenance of peace it acquired 'broad support among all layers of the population of these [non-aligned] countries'.[75] In the early 1970s Soviet writers still relied on 'progressive forms of social development' and the non-capitalist path to assist the formation of 'positive principles' in the Non-Aligned Movement. Support for such principles was expected from 'revolutionary democratic communists', workers parties, trade unions and youth organisations. The 'national bourgeoisie' were also perceived as a reservoir of support for non-alignment.[76] However, throughout the 1960s and 1970s Moscow became progressively more disillusioned over the prospects of the non-capitalist path and this cast the class basis of non-alignment into doubt. In the 1980s Soviet spokesmen maintain that the basic goals and 'anti-imperialist' content of a policy of non-alignment still 'objectively' serve working-class and peasant interests in the liberated countries. But they admit that in many cases these social groups have been unable directly to influence the foreign policies of their countries, which have suffered instead from the 'class limitations' of Third World ruling elites.[77] Soviet scholars now argued that the foreign policies of non-aligned Third World states reflected retrogressive tendencies in their societies and their economic relations. In this context they singled out the pernicious influence of the ideology and practice of nationalism. In retrospect Soviet writers characterise the 1970s as a period of internal polarisation of the socio-political forces in non-aligned countries and of greater 'differentation' in their foreign policies. The Soviet contention is that these processes have subsequently been expressed in a polarisation of forces within the Non-Aligned Movement. All this has aggravated the consequences of conflicts between non-aligned countries which have arisen out of the nationalist claims of their ruling classes.[78] 'Inconsistencies and fluctuations' in the foreign policies of the non-aligned countries are blamed on the continued financial dependence of the majority of these on the West.

These arguments serve to camouflage a basic change that has been underway since the late 1970s in the Soviet theoretical appraisal of the foreign policy dynamics of non-aligned and Third World states. This shift is expressed in the Soviet admission that since the 1970s 'the foreign policy and general social-class orientation' of the developing countries have not always coincided. Moscow has been compelled to recognise that states which are relatively homogenous in their social structures and the class nature of their dominant groups conduct quite different courses in international affairs. This is explained by 'the enhanced autonomy of the political decisions of the ruling groups, particularly in the foreign sphere'.[79] As a result Soviet spokesmen and diplomats are no longer expected to strain the credibility of their analyses in proclaiming that there exist strong deterministic links or relations of dependence between the internal socio-economic order or class structure of non-aligned (and other Third World) states and the foreign policies or forms of non-alignment of those states. This admission of reality assists Soviet foreign policy-makers to justify the development of pragmatic relations between the USSR and a whole series of countries, regardless of the socio-economic structure of these states or their standing according to traditional Marxist–Leninist criteria.

In the Soviet doctrinal outlook the Non-Aligned Movement has been viewed as part of the overall process of socio-economic transformation of the Third World. At this level of generality Soviet observers have accepted since the mid 1970s that the forms of non-alignment and foreign policies adopted by Third World non-aligned states are most varied and do not necessarily correlate with their diverse levels of socio-economic development. The Non-Aligned Movement as a whole is characterised as a social process which should be sustained and consolidated to advance the class struggle on the international level. For Soviet officials the process of socio-economic transformation represented by the Non-Aligned Movement could in principle be promoted through a strategy of economic aid and political support for those non-aligned nations already far advanced in this process.[80] In reality Soviet assistance to non-aligned states was determined by more pragmatic factors. By the mid 1980s it became apparent that Soviet leaders did not regard a revolutionary domestic policy in a non-aligned state as sufficient grounds to claim such assistance.

Soviet theorists eventually modified their original conception of the relationship between the domestic socio-economic processes and foreign policies of non-aligned states. However, in another crucial area Soviet ideologists refused adamantly to compromise their perception of non-alignment. From the Soviet perspective it remains inconceivable that the Non-Aligned Movement can act effectively as an autonomous body in world affairs let alone pursue principles and objectives equally opposed to those adhered to by the Eastern and Western political constellations. This was evident already in the early 1960s from Khrushchev's complaints about the tendency of the neutralists to confuse the concepts of bloc and system, and from the belief that neutralism was a transitional phenomenon. In the 1960s the anti-colonial and anti-Western rhetoric of the new Asian and African states and their general commitment to independent economic development were sufficient to convince those schooled in Marxism–Leninism that the non-aligned states were part of a broad historical front directed against the Western order, which could not be divorced from the Soviet-led socialist system. In the Soviet view states could position themselves outside military blocs but they could not exist in a limbo between the two political systems or jockey for an equidistant position from these systems.

In the 1960s Soviet leaders did not consider it very likely that the new non-aligned states would rapidly assume overtly pro-Soviet orientations. They were satisfied with non-alignment meaning primarily non-alignment with respect to military blocs accompanied by diffuse anti-Western criticism. The leading non-aligned states also saw no need to balance their judgements on the policies of the East and West. In opening the Belgrade Conference in 1961 Tito argued that it was unnecessary to speculate whether the course arising from the conference would be pro-Western or pro-Eastern since the conference had been convened not to support blocs 'but to define clearly and coordinate our positions on the most important problems...and then it will become clear where our stands differ and where they coincide with those of one or the other side'.[81] Ben Bella, the Algerian President, expressed the mainstream opinion of the Non-Aligned at the Cairo Conference in 1964 when he argued that to be non-aligned means to be determined to be independent but not to 'seek a position half-way between East and West, or endeavour to practice, vis-à-vis the great powers, a policy involving constant acrobatics'.[82]

During the Cairo Conference a Soviet Third World specialist claimed that the 'socialist world' gave the non-aligned states 'the necessary aid without any strings attached'. He questioned how non-aligned states under these circumstances could be 'equally antagonistic' to both Eastern and Western states.[83] The Soviet press attacked the 'Western' interpretation of non-alignment, 'obliging one not to transcend certain boundaries in relations with the Soviet Union and the other socialist states' as a betrayal of the policy of non-alignment calculated to 'prevent the newly liberated countries from choosing friends of their liking'.[84] Moscow praised the documents of the Cairo Conference for denouncing the 'specific prosecutors of an imperialist policy', and noted that 'efforts to saddle the non-aligned countries with anti-communist slogans failed'.[85]

Soviet leaders were confident that they could steer the anti-colonial radicalism of non-aligned states along channels which would set the Non-Aligned Movement in coordination with the Soviet camp into some kind of structural opposition to the Western powers. But, as the anti-colonial political thrust of the Non-Aligned was progressively displaced in the 1970s by broader issues of global economics and *détente*, the general political orientation of the Non-Aligned Movement became much harder to identify. This was underlined by the expansion of the Movement to embrace a far broader range of states and regimes. A core of ideologically pro-Soviet states became vociferous participants in the Movement from the middle of the decade. The views of states in the Non-Aligned Movement became more polarised as its composition increasingly reflected the political diversity to be found in the Third World as a whole.

By 1973 a Soviet writer divided the non-aligned countries into three broad categories: those of socialist orientation, those forming a right wing and those occupying a centrist position. Algeria, Burma, Guinea, Egypt, Iraq, Yemen, Congo, Mali, Syria, Somalia and Tanzania were placed in the first category. These states, alongside India, Bangladesh and certain other countries formed 'the progressive left wing of the non-aligned countries'. The notion of socialist orientation, a more explicitly political category and one obviously slanted to the East, had replaced the non-capitalist path as the desirable orientation of the most eligible non-aligned states. States characterised by a pro-Western orientation, tight cooperation with Western states and 'excessive nationalism', were grouped on the right wing of the Non-Aligned Movement. These included Liberia, Lesotho, Gabon, Indonesia (after 1965), Saudi Arabia and Tunisia. The third category was composed of states like Zaire, Zambia, Morocco, Senegal and the UAR, which strove to escape clear statements on open political issues, occupied a middle line and often worked out compromise resolutions.[86] However, by 1981 these Soviet categories had been adjusted. Certain states of the left wing of the Non-Aligned Movement had in the Soviet view shifted to the right wing, which was now composed of Pakistan, Egypt, Somalia, Saudi Arabia, Oman, Singapore and certain ASEAN states. Moscow admitted that the majority of non-aligned countries were developing along the capitalist path, although India among these was still praised for strengthening and preserving the 'progressive fundamental principles' of the Non-Aligned Movement. The 'centrist' group of states in the Movement was now expected to strive for or support 'anti-imperialist activities', although certain of them linked to Western powers were still prone to conduct a 'policy of compromise'.[87]

By the mid 1980s Soviet analysts regarded the Non-Aligned Movement as polarised to a still greater extent. The 'progressive wing' of the Movement now embraced 'socialist states [Vietnam, Laos, Kampuchea and Cuba], countries of socialist orientation [Angola, Mozambique, Ethiopia, Afghanistan and South Yemen in particular] and states with progressive regimes affiliated to them, which orient themselves to world socialism'. A more numerous group among the Non-Aligned was identified as states with 'moderate, liberal regimes on the path of capitalist development, but occupying a distinct position in the world capitalist economic system'. These states were criticised for making 'various compromises with imperialist circles concerning individual issues of world politics', but praised for not accepting the 'bloc policy' of the Western powers, opposing war and military dangers and expressing a 'readiness to maintain friendly and equal relations with the countries of the socialist community'. In the third group were placed countries of a 'pro-Western foreign policy orientation' whose position meant 'an indirect and often also direct complicity' with the Western powers against the Soviet bloc. Even these states were alleged to be frequently in 'collision' with the Western powers.[88] Such a breakdown preserved intact the basic Soviet premise that somehow the 'essence' of the Non-Aligned Movement, despite its heterogeneity, remained anti-Western. Soviet writers currently classify about twenty non-aligned states as 'radical', about twenty as 'conservative' and some fifty or sixty as 'centrist'. According to their revised view the 'main watershed' in the Non-Aligned Movement since the mid 1970s has been between the socialist and socialist-oriented countries on the one hand and those proceeding on a capitalist path of development on the other.[89]

As the Non-Aligned Movement became polarised during the period of Cuban chairmanship in 1979–83, Soviet officials directly attacked the view, which had long been advocated by the more conservative non-aligned states, that non-alignment requires the maintenance of a degree of political distance from both superpower blocs. In October 1980 Boris Ponomarev, head of the International Department of the Soviet Central Committee, complained of recent attempts to split the ranks of the Non-Aligned Movement, to 'counterpose them to the socialist community' through the concept of 'equidistance'.[90] Primakov, a prominent Soviet specialist on the Third World, also criticised the advocacy by certain non-aligned states of 'a plague on both houses'. In his view such an approach would lead to a transformation of the Non-Aligned Movement into some kind of 'third force' opposing NATO and the Warsaw Pact in equal measure. He scorned the idea that the Non-Aligned could secure themselves an independent role through distancing themselves equally from 'world socialism and world capitalism'.[91]

A wide spectrum of views was expressed by the non-aligned delegates at the Havana Summit in 1979. However, the Soviet press identified an 'anti-imperialist orientation' (that is anti-Western) 'in literally all of the questions discussed by the conference'.[92] At the Delhi Conference of Non-Aligned Foreign Ministers in 1981, which addressed the issue of Soviet intervention in Afghanistan, the Soviet press still regarded the 'anti-imperialist orientation' as 'distinctly evident'.[93] It was not until the Harare Non-Aligned Summit in 1986 that Soviet political commentary accepted that 'differences between political and ideological interests and disparities between ideological principles' were a serious political failing in the Non-Aligned Movement.[94]

It became clear from Soviet statements in the 1980s that whatever the economic policies adopted by non-aligned states (and former Soviet optimism in this area gradually faded) the greater part of the Non-Aligned Movement is expected to remain anti-Western in its political orientation. Soviet spokesmen currently recognise that the overwhelming majority of the Non-Aligned occupy 'a particular place in the world capitalist system' but they still maintain that 'non-alignment as a foreign policy orientation signified and signifies above all an unwillingness of a given state to associate itself with the [political] policies of this system'. This included a rejection of Western attempts to use Third World states for their military-strategic and political interests. The Non-Aligned aspiration was perceived as one of 'distinctive "dissociation" from imperialism' and its policies;[95] in *political* relations the non-aligned states were not 'a component part of the imperialist system'.[96]

According to the prevailing Soviet view, 'the desire to remain outside the military–political groupings of the two basic political systems will remain for the majority of the non-aligned countries the dominant orientation of their foreign policy courses'. In practice this would invariably lead to the adoption of 'positions coincident with or close to the positions of the USSR and other socialist states on the majority of issues' but 'positions close to the interests of the USA and other Western states' on other issues.[97] One Soviet estimate of the voting pattern of the non-aligned countries in the United Nations in recent years was that in about eighty per cent of cases the stand of the United States did not coincide with the overwhelming majority of non-aligned countries.[98] Soviet spokesmen only had to refer to American reactions to the documents issued by Non-Aligned conferences to reinforce their argument that political 'equi-distance' was not a necessary component of the policy pursued by the Non-Aligned.

In October 1981 Ambassador Jeane Kirkpatrick sent a letter to the representatives of sixty-four non-aligned countries attacking a com-muniqué they had issued the previous month in New York for containing no mention of the USSR but referring negatively to the United States 'nine times by name and dozens of times by implication'. The United States State Department described the political declaration issued by the Delhi Non-Aligned Summit in 1983 as 'in many ways an unbalanced and argumentative document that does not reflect the principles of non-alignment proclaimed by this movement'. Washington observed that this declaration contained numerous criticisms of American international activities but avoided any criticism of the USSR.[99] Soviet spokesmen considered that their conception of non-alignment as political dissociation from Western policies was reaffirmed at the Harare Summit in 1986. They asserted that the political declaration issued at Harare mentioned the United States 'in anything but complimentary terms' more than twenty-five times and again contained no criticism of the Soviet Union'.[100] It may be revealing in this context to consider next how Soviet spokesmen have characterised the relations between socialist or Soviet-bloc states and the Non-Aligned Movement and its principles. This should shed light on Soviet expectations of the likely future development of relations between the non-aligned states and the Soviet bloc, and help reveal Soviet views on the long-term prospects of non-alignment and the Non-Aligned Movement.

In the 1960s Soviet comments on the relationship between non-alignment and socialism were an essential ingredient of the polemics between Soviet and Yugoslav leaders, especially on the nature of peaceful coexistence (see following section). The Bandung Conference had passed a resolution endorsing the 'Ten Principles of Cooperation Among States', and the Belgrade Non-Aligned Summit devoted a passage in its Final Declaration to the policy of peaceful coexistence. The terminology of peaceful coexistence has littered Soviet descriptions of non-alignment. But for the original group of non-aligned states, and Yugoslavia in particular, the principles of peaceful coexistence were not, as Moscow claimed, applicable merely to relations between capitalist and socialist states. The Non-Aligned regarded these principles as the sole basis of international relations in general. Following the 1964 Cairo Conference the Soviet press attacked the 'erroneous story' aimed at 'discrediting socialism in the eyes of the non-aligned countries... that peaceful coexistence in relations between the Soviet Union and the United States allegedly extends to ideology as well'.[101] According to Soviet doctrine the competing ideologies were irreconcilable.

'Socialist' Cuba remained quiescent at Non-Aligned conferences in the 1960s, but became gradually more prominent in the 1970s. In 1972 a Soviet writer acknowledged that in current conditions in Latin America 'the participation of socialist countries of the Western hemisphere in the Non-Aligned Movement in one form or another is evidently inevitable'.[102]

Cuban activism and the continued challenge posed by Yugoslav theorists and diplomats finally induced Soviet writers to specify the implications of non-alignment for the foreign policy of a socialist state. The non-aligned character of such states had appeared compromised by the basic Soviet premise that the relations between socialist states are governed by the principles of socialist internationalism. Tuzmukhamedov, a primary Soviet specialist on non-alignment, determined that:

For socialist states, by social class, politically and ideologically a component part of the world socialist system, there should be no question, in the presence of the opposition of the two systems, of non-alignment towards one or other of them. It is possible not to be a member of the military–political unions of the socialist states, but it is impossible to set oneself outside the bounds of operation of the principles of socialist internationalism regulating the relations between all socialist states.

This was a clearer formulation of the standard Soviet view that non-allignment could apply to blocs but not systems. Tuzmukhamedov claimed additionally that it would be wrong from the international legal standpoint to set the principles of socialist internationalism in opposition to those of non-alignment. For socialist states there was 'no need for choice between one or other alternative'.[103] This was not merely an abstract theoretical point since it could be related to the Soviet failure to support socialist China in her border conflict with non-aligned India. Khrushchev had failed to provide such support in December 1962 and Brezhnev if anything was even less willing to fulfil the principle of socialist internationalism in this way in the 1970s.

In the 1970s Yugoslav spokesmen claimed at times that the principles of non-alignment could take priority over those of socialist internationalism even for a socialist state. This was anathema to Moscow. In his editorial comments to the Russian language collections of Non-Aligned conference documents Tuzmukhamedov asserted that, 'in the event of a conscious or unconscious contradiction of non-alignment to socialist internationalism, which as is known regulates the relations between socialist states independent of whether or not they enter into an alliance agreement, no doubt arises over the priority of socialist internationalism because it fully expresses the class essence of socialist states'. Reference was made to a speech by Fidel Castro at the Algiers Non-Aligned Conference in 1973 (his début at a Non-Aligned summit), which underlined Cuba's primary orientation as a Marxist state linked closely to socialist states (see section below). This endorsed a line set by Cuban delegates at the Lusaka Conference in 1970. From the Soviet perspective the socialist countries within the Non-Aligned Movement simultaneously form part of an independent international force, in both political and class terms, that of the world socialist system.[104] Moscow regards Cuba and other countries classified as socialist as a distinct group among the Non-Aligned with separate ties based on political affinities.

The USSR would greatly benefit from formal recognition by the Non-Aligned Movement of the legitimacy of the principles of socialist and proletarian internationalism. Yugoslavia, concerned by the possible implications of fraternal assistance from the USSR, has managed, however, to block such recognition. Moscow sought to avert criticism by the non-aligned states of the Soviet invasion of Czechoslovakia in 1968 through resorting to various arguments. Before the Lusaka Summit was convened Soviet spokesmen asserted, for example, that those who urged the non-aligned countries to condemn Soviet 'fraternal assistance' to Czechoslovakia also cast doubt on the right of the Afro-Asian states to use armed forces against Western efforts 'to restore or maintain colonial and racialist regimes'. This was clearly a spurious comparison.[105] For the non-aligned states it failed to validate military invasion as the application of 'proletarian internationalism'.

Western observers disparaged the non-alignment of a number of regimes in the late 1970s on the grounds of their self-proclaimed Marxist–Leninist ideology, their support for the views of the Soviet Union and their receipt of Soviet arms. To Soviet spokesmen this was false logic since it implied the need to query also 'whether countries which ... [had] adopted the capitalist economic system and received arms from the Western countries could be regarded as non-aligned'. Ultimately this would mean that 'no single country could be considered non-aligned, and consequently there would be no such thing as a Non-Aligned Movement'.[106] According to the principles of non-alignment, a Soviet writer sought to argue, non-aligned states could enter political and economic relations with any state outside the Non-Aligned Movement provided that the foreign policy of the latter state is based on the principles of peaceful coexistence and aimed at securing the independence of peoples, international peace and security.[107] Such a definition could be used by Soviet officials to denigrate Western relations with non-aligned states wholesale. It also left intact the contentious Soviet 'natural alliance' theory.

The 'natural alliance' thesis originated in the early 1970s. A premise of Soviet thinking was that the growth of non-alignment was one reflection of the shift in the global 'correlation of forces' in favour of the 'socialist community'. Soviet doctrine justified the theoretical and practical need of unity and mutual support, and the creation of organisational links, between socialist and non-aligned states in a struggle with Western states.[108] One reflection of this emphasis on state solidarity was Soviet hostility to the notion of creating a separate youth organisation for the Non-Aligned Movement. Moscow claimed that 'a movement at the level of state and government of the non-aligned countries cannot be shifted over to the youth level'. In the Soviet view this plan (which has not been realised to date) risked 'splitting the solidarity and unity of the democratic youth movement of the world, of ... isolating the youth of the developing countries from the youth of the socialist states'.[109] Even at the state level the USSR regarded the expediency of participation by socialist states in the Non-Aligned Movement as determined by 'the interests of socialism, inseparable from the interests of consolidating the world socialist system'. Such states were obliged to strive for the 'most consistent and full realisation of the anti-imperialist functions of the Movement',[110] in other words to mobilise the anti-Western sentiments of the Non-Aligned in harmony with the Soviet bloc.

Soviet spokesmen were cautious in their public statements on the relations between the Non-Aligned Movement and the Eastern bloc before the 1973 Algiers Non-Aligned Summit. However, at Algiers the Soviet media praised Castro's speech for revealing 'who the genuine ally of the developing countries is'.[111] *Pravda* argued that the foreign policy of the USSR promotes in every way the realisation of the tasks assumed by the Movement, that the success of these tasks 'in many ways depends on the support of the socialist states', and that the non-aligned countries had 'come to the conviction that the socialist states are their most reliable and natural ally'.[112] Soviet commentators expanded on this thesis during the Colombo and Havana Non-Aligned summits. Moscow rejected the possibility of any 'fundamental differences or hostility' between the foreign policy principles of socialist and non-aligned countries, and alleged that the policies of these two groups were based on a 'community of objectives and aims, close or coinciding views on world development'.[113] This encouraged an abortive Cuban attempt to introduce the 'natural alliance' thesis into the official resolutions of the Havana Summit.

To assist the propagation of Soviet views among non-aligned countries Moscow urged 'decolonisation in the sphere of information'. This notion, which was directed at the monopoly held by the Western states in international news circulation, became a familiar subject of UNESCO debates in the early 1980s. When the non-aligned countries held a conference in January/February 1984 on this topic in Jakarta, Moscow gave its backing to the struggle against 'informational imperialism'.[114] The Soviet leader Yuriy Andropov warned that if certain states tried to set themselves against the 'community of states' cooperating in UNESCO 'the peoples will once again see for themselves who is their friend and who is their enemy'.[115] However, Moscow failed to make much political capital in the Non-Aligned community from the American decision to opt out of UNESCO.

It was clear by the mid 1980s that the Non-Aligned Movement was highly unlikely to accept the degree of solidarity with the Soviet bloc sought by Soviet leaders. Soviet publications still perceived the gradual formation of a 'united front' of socialist and non-aligned countries as 'an objective law-determined development of the system of international relations in the contemporary epoch'.[116] They acknowledged, however, that the need for such a 'front' or 'alliance' had not yet been broadly accepted by the non-aligned states. A Soviet specialist admitted that although 'the progressive forces of the developing world consider the socialist commuity as an objective ally', the leaders of other Third World states 'consider that non-alignment towards blocs is incompatible with the recognition of one of them as a natural ally and the other as the natural opponent of the non-aligned countries'.[117] In these circumstances Soviet officials can only hope that the policy objectives of the pro-Soviet radical states within the Non-Aligned Movement will eventually exercise greater influence on the general orientation of this body.

By the early 1980s Cuba had been joined in the Non-Aligned Movement by a number of radical regimes and organisations close to the USSR in their foreign policy outlook. North Korea, Vietnam, Angola and the PLO were all admitted to the Movement at the 1976 Colombo Summit. Revolutionary regimes were installed in Ethiopia and Afghanistan. Other participants in the Movement such as Laos, Libya, Mozambique, South Yemen (PDRY) and Syria also tended in varying degrees to support Soviet foreign policy proposals and identify convergent interests with this power. As previously indicated, Soviet specialists avowed that non-alignment was compatible with a socialist foreign policy, but they preferred not to emphasise non-alignment in relation to the policies of those states in the Non-Aligned Movement classified as socialist: Cuba, Vietnam, North Korea, Laos and Kampuchea. Such caution has not characterised Soviet descriptions of so-called 'socialist-oriented' Third World states. According to a Soviet writer in 1981 'the leaders of countries such as Angola, Mozambique, Ethiopia, PDRY, and Afghanistan resolutely declare the compatibility of non-alignment and alliance with the forces of socialism'.[118] These states were portrayed alongside Vietnam, Laos and Cuba as the 'true "prime movers"' of the Non-Aligned Movement 'which make it dynamic and effective'.[119] Such 'socialist-oriented' members of the Non-Aligned Movement, which pursue revolutionary domestic programmes and cultivate close political links with the Soviet bloc, have typified the form of 'non-alignment' Soviet leaders regard as desirable for Third World states in general. In Soviet analyses these new regimes displace the more traditional and independent Non-Aligned radicals such as Algeria. Soviet analysts observed that all the new 'socialist oriented' Third World regimes had opted to enter the Non-Aligned Movement. The transition of a non-aligned country to a path of socialist orientation should not, in their view, 'be accompanied by abstention from a policy of non-alignment' since non-alignment reflected 'an independent foreign policy course, creating favourable preconditions for the conduct of deep socio-economic transformations'.[120] The category of 'socialist orientation' to some extent displaced the earlier category of the 'non-capitalist path of development' in representing for Moscow the form of internal socio-economic order desirable for a non-aligned state.

Soviet descriptions of the left-leaning non-aligned states have exaggerated the similarity of their policies and displayed considerable wishful thinking. The Soviet specialist Ya. Etinger portrayed the foreign policy of the 'left wing' of the Movement in 1981 as distinguished by:

militant anti-imperialism, active struggle against the remnants of colonialism and racism, the development of tight political, economic and other cooperation with the socialist states, an ever greater role of the principles of socialist internationalism in foreign policy, and an emphasis on the need for a strategic alliance with the USSR and other socialist states.

He noted that this understanding of the goals of the Non-Aligned Movement coincided with the objectives of the socialist states.[121] In an authoritative work in 1985 Etinger used the same definition to describe the foreign policy course of 'socialist-oriented' states. On this occasion he referred additionally to the possibility of 'defence cooperation' between such countries and the socialist states, although he spoke of their 'tight links' rather than their need for a 'strategic alliance' with the Soviet bloc.[122] This indicates the optimal Soviet scenario for the non-socialist radical regimes in the Non-Aligned Movement in the long term: that they adopt and pursue foreign policy objectives almost indistinguishable from 'socialist' Third World states and assume diverse and ever more pronounced political and military ties with the Soviet bloc.

This doctrinaire approach appears to coexist among Soviet specialists with less optimistic, more pragmatic expectations of the evolution of the non-aligned world in the near future. The continued Western dominance in international economic and trade relations with the Third World has sapped Soviet confidence in the future course of the 'socialist-oriented' non-aligned states. As previously indicated, by the mid 1980s Soviet publications admitted that although 'the overwhelming majority of non-aligned countries left or strive to break away from the political system of imperialism...almost all continue to take part in the world capitalist economic system'. This 'intermediate' position of non-aligned states in the contemporary world was blamed for the 'complexity and internal contradictory nature' of their foreign policy courses, for 'inconsistencies, zigzags, and changes in approach' towards international issues.[123] Furthermore, Soviet writers have begun to acknowledge that situations have arisen 'when countries of capitalist orientation (for example, India or Mexico) sometimes occupy on distinct questions a more active anti-imperialist position than certain countries which have developed a socialist orientation'.[124] This admission has led to Soviet recognition that the foreign policy and 'social-class orientation' of states in the Third World may be at variance (see above). Indeed, since about 1982-3 Soviet officials have more openly expressed doubts about the likelihood of the 'socialist oriented' states developing towards the 'higher stage' of socialism. This is reflected, for example, in the classification of these states as 'revolutionary-democratic states' by the authoritative Third World specialist Karen Brutents in an analysis of the Non-Aligned Movement in 1984.[125] These developments cast doubt on the overall utility for the USSR of concentrating politically on ties with 'socialist oriented' states to the exclusion of links with other, more moderate, non-aligned states.

The prevailing view among Soviet specialists on international affairs appears to be the pragmatic one that the Non-Aligned will continue to polarise and become more heterogeneous. Soviet writers refer to the operation of 'a long-term tendency of "erosion" of all groups of developing countries' as certain states join the world socialist system whole others, which are more advanced on the 'capitalist path', draw closer to the group of developed Western countries. The Non-Aligned Movement is recognised as an intergovernmental political union embracing practically all the countries of the Third World. From the Soviet perspective 'this does not, ultimately, change the fundamental characteristics of the political structure of the contemporary world – its division into contradictory social systems'. It 'does not create a third centre equivalent to the two main "poles" in world politics'.[126] The Soviet Union would wish the Non-Aligned Movement as a whole to assume the political objectives of its pro-Soviet 'left wing'. The adoption of these goals evidently could transform the Movement into a vast political reserve for the Soviet bloc. But Moscow does not encourage over-hasty attempts to realise this ambition, which may threaten a paralysing polarisation of the Non-Aligned Movement or its breakup. When the Libyan leader Gaddafi argued at the Harare Summit for dismantling the Non-Aligned Movement, for the unity of small nations 'in a strong alliance against imperialism', the Soviet reaction was unenthusiastic. Gaddafi based his suggestion on the belief that the world was divided simply between the camps of 'liberation' and 'imperialism' and that 'being in the camp of liberation does not mean joining the Warsaw Pact, but to rally with it to confront the imperialist camp'.[127] A Soviet broadcast noted that Gaddafi's criticism of the Non-Aligned Movement for its alleged ineffectiveness 'met with no support at the conference'.[128]

The Soviet Union accepts that the Non-Aligned Movement 'does not pursue socialist goals', although its activity is described as resting 'on a general democratic progressive basis'.[129] This provides scope for a broad range of common contemporary interests, goals and positions between the 'socialist community' and the Non-Aligned. These were defined in the mid 1980s as:

the struggle for *détente*, for disarmament, for the elimination of the hotbeds of military conflict, for strengthening security in various regions of the world, in particular in Asia, for the elimination of the military bases of imperialist powers and the withdrawal of their troops from the territory of the countries of Asia, Africa and Latin America, for the breakup of the aggressive military blocs created by the imperialists, for extending the national liberation movement and the abolition of the remaining strongpoints of colonialism.[130]

These are the medium-term Soviet objectives for the Non-Aligned, around which a consensus on joint interests with the Soviet bloc may be formed. In his message of greetings to the Harare Non-Aligned Summit in 1986 Gorbachev studiously refrained from any terminology of the 'natural alliance' variant. After the conference, however, a Soviet Foreign Ministry spokesman reiterated that the non-Aligned Movement's support for Soviet initiatives was 'indicative of the community of approach to these problems' and of the potential for further cooperation.[131] Soviet leaders will bide their time and nourish their hopes that eventually the states in the Non-Aligned Movement sympathetic to Moscow will impress their priorities and outlook on its agenda. Meanwhile they seek to draw together the objectives of Soviet policy with those expressed by the Movement as a whole across a broad field of international activity. They will seek to pursue a programme towards this end in the United Nations' structure, or through regional and bilateral negotiations.

This Soviet tendency in the 1980s towards greater pragmatism on ideological matters is also illustrated by the Soviet reaction to the development of organisational links between the Non-Aligned Movement and the West European socialist movement.

The Non-Aligned Movement and the Socialist International

The Soviet Union has traditionally been critical of links between Western states/political groups and the Non-Aligned Movement, fearing that such links may dilute the anti-Western, anti-colonial thrust of the Non-Aligned and suggest or support alternative developmental patterns to those of the 'non-capitalist path' or 'socialist orientation'. However, by the 1980s anti-colonialism in the strict sense was no longer at the forefront of the concerns of the majority of non-aligned states and Soviet commentators admitted that most of the non-aligned states remained firmly in the Western economic orbit or system. Towards the end of the 1970s and in the early 1980s a development took place which the USSR regarded with a mixture of interest and apprehension. The West European based Socialist International, which represents West European socialist and social democratic parties, began to establish contacts with the Non-Aligned Movement. A coincidence of the basic political goals of the two organisations was declared after a meeting between the General Secretary of the Socialist International and the Chairman of the Coordinating Bureau of the Non-Aligned Movement in August 1979. They resolved to work out a mutual 'alternative policy to that conducted by the "superpowers"'. Castro, the incumbent chairman of the Non-Aligned Movement, was invited as its representative to take part in the work of the Fifteenth Congress of the Socialist International in Madrid in 1980.[132]

There are mixed benefits for the Soviet Union in this association. Soviet writers note that in the disarmament field both international bodies are interested in working out joint proposals or ones similar in content. While the Socialist International tends to regard the arms race as reflecting the rivalry of the two superpowers, its appeals to end the arms race are believed to coincide basically with corresponding Soviet initiatives. Soviet writers accept that there may be certain common features in the positions found in the programmes and documents of the Socialist International and the Non-Aligned Movement on global problems but they point out that their lines and proposals in relation to actual conflicts in the developing world are frequently wholly different. They refer to the failure of the socialists and social democrats in France and West Germany when in power to fulfil the recommendations of the Socialist International, especially its Programme of Action on Southern Africa. They upbraid the Socialist International for supporting the Camp David deal in the Middle East, which was condemned by the majority of the non-aligned nations. But they admit that the problems of the Latin American states occupy a large place in the activities of the Socialist International, and that the Latin American countries which have chosen non-alignment as their foreign policy course are often just those which have made initiatives for tighter links between the Non-Aligned and the Socialist International.[133] This reflects the more Europeanised nature of these non-aligned states, their traditionally closer ties politically and economically with West Europe.

Soviet writers in the mid 1980s predicted that the Socialist International 'evidently will pay great attention to the Non-Aligned Movement also in the future and search for means to expand its influence in it'. This prognosis is supported by three arguments. In the first place Soviet specialists maintain that while the resolutions of Non-Aligned meetings are not binding they influence the formation of the political and economic concepts and actions of a huge number of states. This fact compels the Socialist International to take account of the positions of the Non-Aligned Movement, 'to work out more effective methods of "exporting" the social democratic model of the "third way" to the developing world' and of expanding their influence to the maximum extent among the new Third World states. Secondly, in the Soviet view the Socialist International is taking advantage of the fact that 'the majority of the non-aligned states remain part of the world capitalist economic system, striving to achieve an improvement in their economic position by means of gradual reform within this system'. It is understood that many of the economic and political objectives of the Non-Aligned, set out in the documents of their conferences, 'attract the leaders of the Socialist International as to a certain extent they coincide with the "recipes" in relation to spreading "democratic socialism" which the Socialist International provides the developing countries'. Moscow has regarded the Brandt Commission Report as an example of such reformist ideology applied to resolving Third World economic problems. Soviet writers admit that the participants of the Socialist International and the Non-Aligned Movement have been prepared mutually to consult on certain aspects of international economic relations since they have coincident views on these matters.

Thirdly, Soviet spokesmen believe that the Socialist International will strengthen contacts with the Non-Aligned Movement since it requires the support of the Third World to realise its foreign policy goals. They detect and foresee attempts to introduce social democratic concepts into the Movement and to influence the positions of the Non-Aligned on the more important international issues. They argue that the Non-Aligned Movement in turn hopes that cooperation with the Socialist International will help achieve Non-Aligned goals in the international arena. This would result from the influence which the social democrats could exert on the governments of the West European countries. The Soviet Union is concerned that the Socialist International and 'certain circles' among the Non-Aligned 'aim at working out a general platform with the intention of creating some "third force" equally opposed to the two basic military–political alliances'. Soviet writers claim that the West European social democrats are trying to assume the role of 'the distinctive ideological guardians of the [Non-Aligned] Movement', which involves pressing on the developing countries the global task of 'opposing communist doctrine' and instilling into them 'different variants of "democratic socialism", pluralism, bourgeois parliamentarism'. It is evident that the Soviet view of the links between the Non-Aligned and the Socialist International will continue to form a mixture of ideological wariness and suspicion, and pragmatic approval. This is expressed in the Soviet assertion that 'progressive forces' in the Third World strive on the one hand 'to neutralise the negative consequences of the activities of the social democrats in the developing world, and on the other to make use of the positive features which cooperation with the Socialist International brings, primarily in the struggle for peace and for a new just order in international economic relations'.[134]

NON-ALIGNMENT AS AN OPTION FOR SMALL SOCIALIST STATES

From the perspective of the Non-Aligned it is natural that Soviet views on the strategy and policy of non-alignment have not necessarily been congruent with the view of non-alignment held by smaller socialist states lying outside the military structure of the Warsaw Pact, such as Yugoslavia, or even Cuba. The primary determinant of these Soviet views, the Non-Aligned would argue, has been the Soviet Union's status as a Great Power rather than its ideological world outlook. If broader political and strategic objectives shape Moscow's doctrinal perception of non-alignment and the Non-Aligned Movement, as described in the previous section, then it is not surprising that certain similarities in professed ideology between the USSR and more independent socialist or communist states are not sufficient to ensure a common evaluation of non-alignment. Indeed, for a European socialist state such as Yugoslavia non-alignment has been a strategy to resist the integrative influences of the Soviet dominated military bloc. The case of Yugoslavia deserves examination in this study despite its location in Europe since the foreign policy principles and outlook of Yugoslavia have so much in common with those of Third World states. A broader study of the Soviet view of non-alignment in the foreign policy of distinct states, which is not undertaken in this study, would need to consider the cases of countries such as Algeria, Egypt, India, Indonesia and Zimbabwe. However, it can be argued that the Third World has not been exclusively extra-European and that since the early 1950s Yugoslavia has had a strong influence on the ideology and autonomous world view of the Third World. The Yugoslav example has even encouraged an Eastern bloc member, Romania, to seek closer attachment to the developing countries.

During the 1960s Yugoslavia was indisputably the most influential self-proclaimed non-aligned state. Yugoslavia's conception of non-alignment and its role in the evolution of the Non-Aligned Movement brought it international renown and prestige. Tito used Yugoslavia's non-alignment to increase the scope and latitude of the country's foreign relations, to resist Soviet pressures to integrate politically into the East European bloc. Yugoslav non-alignment challenged Soviet domination in Eastern Europe. Indeed, since 1954, Yugoslavia has been a signatory to a defence treaty with Greece and Turkey, both of which were full-fledged members of NATO (the Three Power Defence Treaty signed at Bled on 9 August 1954). Yugoslavia has continued to regard the military implications of this treaty as compatible with her non-alignment.

Tito's challenge to Soviet authority aroused vehement Soviet criticism of Yugoslavia's position at times in the 1950s and 1960s. Khrushchev's contention in the late 1950s was that 'neutrality' for the 'true communist' would assist the enemies of the working class; non-alignment was unacceptable for a socialist country. As previously observed, this issue had aroused serious concern within the Soviet leadership in 1956 when Imre Nagy had attempted to proclaim the neutrality of Hungary. The essence of Tito's views had already been expressed in 1955 at the Bandung Conference. He stated that 'the greatest danger threatening us is the division of the world into blocs'; the means to promote peace, in his view, was through 'an active policy of conciliation leading to coexistence'.[135] During the build-up to the Geneva Four Power Conference the Soviet press was prepared to quote Tito's views, but Soviet leaders have never actually accepted Yugoslav views on either blocs or peaceful coexistence.

The Yugoslav commitment to the abolition of blocs and camps irrespective of their 'systemic' character had no basis in Soviet doctrine. For the Yugoslavs the advancement of socialism on a global scale has been a goal which transcends the confines of any particular camp. Tito would not accept the discipline and subordination to the central Soviet authority which the Soviet two-camp thesis implied for Yugoslavia; non-alignment was premised on independence. Micunovic, the Yugoslav ambassador in Moscow, affirmed in 1956 in this vein that 'anyone who doesn't accept Soviet hegemony is immediately declared to be "anti-Soviet", from which it follows that anyone who does accept that hegemony automatically becomes "pro-Soviet"'. In his view the Russians were 'deaf to the idea that anyone in the socialist world can be on terms of equality with them and still remain a friend without being either "pro-" or "anti-" Soviet'.[136] The Yugoslavs have favoured the relaxation of bloc ties within the socialist camp, and for this reason opposed Moscow's convocation of an international communist conference in June 1969 to tighten bloc discipline and isolate the Chinese.

The Yugoslavs have tended to regard the new developing states as national entities seeking an independent existence like themselves, whereas Soviet leaders have perceived them as a potential 'reserve' for the socialist community within the national liberation movement or the 'zone of peace'. In the 1960s the Yugoslavs believed that Soviet leaders in fact hoped for increased fragmentation in the Third World, for the transformation of the Non-Aligned group into a looser more disparate conglomerate, which could more easily be controlled. Yugoslav leaders in contrast have sought to promote cooperation and integration among the Non-Aligned.[137] This difference is evident in the persistent Soviet opposition to a further institutionalisation of the Non-Aligned Movement and in the Soviet stress that the Non-Aligned should ensure in every way that their original decision against forming a 'third bloc' is upheld. For many years Yugoslavia has maintained that no incompatibility exists between being non-aligned and being a socialist state. This dual status only began to be accepted in the USSR in the early 1970s. Yugoslav spokesmen have also long been involved in formulating the theoretical basis of non-alignment and its relationship to international trends. Yugoslav theorists were investigating the relationship between the policy of non-alignment and the evolution of socialism as a social system and process of development many years before their Soviet counterparts began such studies. Indeed, as outlined in the previous section, it was only in the 1980s that Soviet interest in this area began to disseminate outwards from a few specialists.

The Soviet Union welcomed the early commitment of the Non-Aligned group to the principles of peaceful coexistence. These can be traced back to the 'Ten Principles of Cooperation Among States' drawn together by the delegates which assembled at the Bandung Conference. However, since the 1961 Belgrade Conference, the Yugoslav and Soviet conceptions of peaceful coexistence have diverged to a varying extent. Soviet leaders traditionally have claimed that peaceful coexistence implies recognising the existence of the two hostile blocs formed by the two contradictory socio-economic systems. Yugoslav officials in contrast have interpreted peaceful coexistence as the parallel coexistence of states regardless of their socio-economic and political systems. At the Belgrade Conference Tito attacked two conceptions of peaceful coexistence. The first presumed that 'coexistence and war are part of a lasting state of international relations, particularly of the relations between blocs'. Its advocates believed it possible 'both to pursue a policy from positions of strength and to support coexistence'. However, in Tito's view these 'fundamentally different policies' excluded one another. He did not wish peaceful coexistence to be used as the rationalisation for maintaining colonial or Great Power domination over large areas of the world. He pointed out that the supporters of this line considered coexistence to be only one of the bases for cooperation between states, while for the Yugoslavs 'it is not one but the only basis under present conditions'. Secondly, Tito criticised the Soviet theory that peaceful coexistence between blocs is possible. While he admitted that 'even this, as a temporary solution in order to avoid a conflict, is better than war', he likened this to an 'armistice' since it remained temporary and unstable. For Tito, peaceful coexistence had to be examined on a world scale and should be implemented 'not only among states and peoples with different social systems but also among states and people with kindred systems'.[138] For the Yugoslavs genuine coexistence would tend to break down blocs formed on ideological, military and political lines.

The Sino-Soviet divide in the 1960s, and the value attached by Soviet leaders to Yugoslav identification with the Soviet position on this controversy, had the gradual effect of moving the Soviet conception of non-alignment closer to that of Yugoslavia. As Soviet leaders recognised the need to compete effectively with China in the Third World, and the stake of Soviet diplomacy there increased, the USSR began to accommodate itself to the Yugoslav variant of active and peaceful coexistence and to praise the international significance of non-alignment in general. In contrast, Belgrade did not abandon or alter a previously held position out of deference to Soviet wishes on any major issue involving non-alignment.[139] Nevertheless, Soviet spokesmen continued to discourage the emphasis of the Non-Aligned on the pernicious character of blocs. Even when Soviet officials eventually accepted that non-alignment need not be regressive for socialist states, they remained at odds with Yugoslav theorists over the relationship of non-alignment to the principles of socialist inter-nationalism. Nor would Moscow agree with the Yugoslav proposition that socialism can be built in the Non-Aligned world by non-Communist parties.

Although Tito's conception of the principles and purposes of non-alignment clashed with Soviet views in many areas, he remained a socialist. Therefore, he opposed attempts to portray peaceful coexistence as a policy of defence of the *status quo* in internal social relations. At the Belgrade Conference he declared that the assertion of a policy of coexistence 'does not mean that no further progressive processes and changes will take place in contemporary society, since coexistence is an integral part of those changes, which are historically ineluctable'. For Tito the policy of coexistence 'should ensure that these changes be effected without war'. With Yugoslavia's sensitive position in mind he insisted additionally that in each individual country internal social development should be 'a matter to be decided exclusively by the people concerned'.[140] Fifteen years later at the Non-Aligned Summit in Colombo, which introduced a number of new radical regimes into the Non-Aligned Movement, Tito still maintained that 'we do not identify non-alignment with ideological options, nor should we allow a country to be qualified as non-aligned to a lesser or greater degree depending on its political system'. He regarded every country as 'sovereign in searching for the best solutions to its own problems'.[141]

By the 1970s Yugoslavia had earned the respect of other non-aligned states for refraining from attempts to disseminate its form of Marxism–Leninism and for avoiding interference in the domestic affairs of non-aligned countries despite its commitment to international socialism. Tito wished to preserve non-alignment as a foreign policy course and, out of concern for Yugoslavia's independent position in Eastern Europe, was careful not to endorse Soviet views about the necessary interrelation between non-alignment and the domestic path of development of a state, whether 'non-capitalist' (as in the 1960s) or 'socialist-oriented' (as from the late 1970s). Tito also had to resist attacks in the 1970s by radical participants in the Non-Aligned Movement on the 'capitalist' or 'feudal' social order of many, more conservative non-aligned states. Throughout the 1960s and early 1970s the Yugoslav role as a socialist state in the Non-Aligned group remained unique. Cuba was politically inert as a member of this group in this period. Despite its differences with the USSR, it remained in Yugoslavia's interest, therefore, to prevent the Soviet Union or the ideas of communism and socialism in general from being discredited in the Third World, since this would also reduce the unique character and significance of Yugoslav participation in the Non-Aligned Movement.

Yugoslav socialist principles provided the anti-colonial impetus for this state, which the Third World non-aligned states already possessed by virtue of their history. Tito proclaimed this aspect of Yugoslav policy, for example, at the Colombo Non-Aligned Conference. He urged the Non-Aligned to 'devote particular attention to the mobilisation of all democratic and progressive forces so that the anti-colonial and liberation struggle ... may win its ultimate victory as soon as possible'.[142] The independence of post-war Yugoslavia had not, however, been wrested nor come under threat from Western colonial powers, as could be argued in the case of socialist Cuba. This underlay the clash which developed towards the end of the 1970s between Yugoslavia and pro-Soviet radical states in the Non-Aligned Movement. At a meeting of the Non-Aligned in Belgrade in 1978, Tito described the policy of non-alignment as directed against all forms of 'foreign domination and exploitation...power politics, political and economic hegemony, and every kind of external interference and dependence'. These terms clearly covered both Soviet and Western activities. Tito criticised 'attempts to establish in the vitally important regions of the non-aligned world, primarily in Africa, new forms of colonial presence or of bloc dependence, foreign influence and domination'.[143] Cuban troops under Soviet guidance had become prominently involved in Africa since the mid 1970s. Tito's words could be understood, therefore, as an indirect critique of Soviet as well as Western policy.

The prestige of Tito at the 1978 Belgrade meeting of Non-Aligned Foreign Ministers and at the Havana Non-Aligned Summit the following year helped ensure in advance the failure of any attempt by Cuba to present the contentious 'natural alliance' thesis. Castro was astute enough to avoid a direct confrontation on this issue. Soviet leaders also saw no benefit to be derived from encouraging rivalry and antagonism between the two major socialist states in the Non-Aligned Movement. This would have adversely affected the Soviet image among many Third World states, discredited the socialist path of development, and threatened to rupture the Non-Aligned Movement at a time when Soviet spokesmen were further encouraging the solidarity of this body on anti-Western lines.

There remained a basic divergence between Soviet and Yugoslav conceptions of the Non-Aligned Movement. At the 1978 Belgrade Conference Tito reaffirmed his view that this body 'does not visualise the future of the world as resting on the balance of bloc power, or on the supremacy of one bloc over the other'. He characterised the Movement as 'an independent, united and autonomous factor in world politics, and such', he stated, 'it must remain'. By the mid 1980s Soviet writers acknowledged the Yugoslav contribution to working out the concept of non-alignment. But they still rejected the Yugoslav emphasis on the 'autonomy, anti-bloc nature and "anti-hegemonism"' of the Non-Aligned Movement and Yugoslav 'support for a "balance of power"' within it. Soviet writers criticised the tendency of Yugoslav scholars 'to exaggerate the role of non-alignment in world affairs, to globalise the applicability of its doctrine', and to set in place of 'the historically conditioned polarisation of the world into two opposing social systems...the universalisation of an intermediate existence between them'.[144]

Until the early 1970s, Soviet spokesmen were critical of the apparent priority given by Yugoslav officials to the principles of non-alignment over those of socialist internationalism. Later in the decade they detected signs that Yugoslav officials wished to restore some kind of balance between these principles. As Soviet leaders began to acknowledge the broader significance of the Non-Aligned Movement, and the opportunities presented by the infusion of revolutionary regimes into the Movement, they developed expectations that their bilateral relationship with Yugoslavia could be used more effectively as a channel to engage the support of the Non-Aligned for specific Soviet foreign policy proposals. The Yugoslav tendency to side with the USSR over its dispute with China had not compromised the Yugoslav non-aligned image among the majority of the Non-Aligned since Yugoslavia had given the appearance of adopting a principled line on this issue which did not influence her general attitude to non-alignment.

In November 1976, following a visit by Brezhnev to Yugoslavia, Tito and Brezhnev agreed that there existed a 'coincidence or closeness' of their countries on 'key issues of world politics'. They confirmed their view of the Non-Aligned Movement as 'one of the most important factors of world politics'.[145] According to Brezhnev's definition Yugoslavia was a socialist country which actively participated in the Non-Aligned Movement, and which alongside the Soviet bloc supported the defence of peace and 'equal peaceful cooperation against imperialist dictate and tyranny in international affairs'. Brezhnev expressed his conviction that Yugoslavia could contribute greatly to the expansion of cooperation between the socialist countries and the Non-Aligned Movement.[146] In the 1980s Soviet commentators describe Yugoslavia as pursuing a policy of 'peaceful coexistence with all countries, independent of their social system, and non-alignment towards the existing military–political groupings'. The emphasis is on the 'broad possibilities for interaction' in international relations between Yugoslavia and the USSR.

In the post-Tito years the Yugoslavs have concentrated instead on independent activity within the Non-Aligned Movement. In the communiqué issued after Soviet–Yugoslav talks in July 1985 both parties referred to the role of the Movement in promoting measures for international security and cooperation. However, the Yugoslavs separately 'pointed out topical issues concerning the activity of the Non-Aligned Movement as an independent and global factor of international relations'.[147] During discussions between the Soviet and Yugoslav foreign ministers in January 1986 the Yugoslavs confirmed that 'socialist non-aligned Yugoslavia was continuing to proceed along the road as laid out by Tito'.[148] Foreign Minister Dizdarevic declared that the contribution of the Non-Aligned Movement 'to the revival of the so much needed political dialogue, negotiations and agreement-reaching, the consolidation of *détente* as a universal process, is without doubt recognised and sought after'.[149] This mediation function of the Non-Aligned at times of increased hostility and sensitivity in East–West relations has raised the respectability of Yugoslav non-alignment in Soviet eyes. The Yugoslavs have been commended in particular for their work in the neutral and non-aligned group on European security issues in the follow-up meetings of the CSCE Conference. Belgrade has been praised by Moscow for supporting the idea of transforming Europe into a 'continent of peace and equal cooperation'. In this respect Yugoslav non-alignment can acquire positive connotations for the USSR even in Europe, quite irrespective of Yugoslav involvement in the Non-Aligned Movement.

Soviet leaders have been insistent that Yugoslav non-alignment be regarded as *sui generis* rather than an example for other East European states. There are limits beyond which other East European states cannot proceed (excepting Albania) however envious they may be of the autonomy achieved by Yugoslavia. This is illustrated by the case of Romania.

As a signatory of the Warsaw Treaty Organisation there has been no question of Romania being considered a non-aligned state. Since the mid 1960s, however, Romanian foreign policy has deviated sufficiently from its socialist allies, including the USSR, to be described sometimes as 'partially aligned'. Although Romania is located in a military alliance with comparatively developed states its foreign policy orientation strongly emphasises links with the developing and 'small and medium-sized' states. It professes to share common objectives with the Non-Aligned Movement in numerous areas. Romanian spokesmen call for the restructuring of the international political and economic order to improve the situation of the developing countries and they strongly support proposals for a new international economic order. This 'democratisation of international relations' should take place, they believe, at the expense of the Great Powers. Romania now defines itself as a 'socialist developing country' and appeals for an end to the division of Europe into blocs.[150]

In 1975 Romania was invited with guest status to the Non-Aligned Foreign Ministers' Conference in Lima. The Romanian leadership proceeded to lobby for observer status at the forthcoming Non-Aligned Summit in Colombo. For Nicolai Ceausescu and the Romanian Communist Party (RCP), the participation of Romania and other socialist countries at the conference expressed the 'solidarity and collaboration which exists between the socialist and Third World countries'.[151] The RCP argued that what was essential was not so much whether a state belonged to different systems or military alliances but its position with respect to affirming new principles of international relations and the right of each nation to independent development.[152] Romania denied that her interest in participating as an observer in the activities of the Non-Aligned contradicted her membership in the Warsaw Pact or her position as a socialist developing country in 'solidarity with all progressive forces'. Romanian spokesmen referred to their support for the simultaneous dissolution of NATO and the Warsaw Treaty and for the dismantling of military blocs in general.[153]

Romania's request for observer status at the Colombo Summit was turned down. This appeared to be determined largely by opposition from the Indian delegation which feared that Romania's bid could set a precedent for Pakistan. Moscow's opposition to such maverick Romanian behaviour may have acted as a secondary factor. Many non-aligned states regretted the decision even to maintain Romania's status at Colombo as a guest, and Romania failed in its efforts to become more integrated into the Non-Aligned Movement. However, it has retained a distinct interest and view of non-alignment and the Non-Aligned Movement, which a senior Romanian scholar, C. Vlad, clarified in 1984.

In contrast to Soviet views, which stress the ultimate systemic division of the world, Vlad characterised the Non-Aligned as 'a response to the trends of excessive ideological polarisation in international relations' and as 'an alternative to the efforts of certain power centres co-opting other states of the world...into their fold'. He accepted that non-alignment 'is neither equivalent, nor reducible, to a passive or equidistant position with respect to certain powers or groups of states'. In his view it involved a direct commitment to a peaceful, democratic transformation of inter-national relations and the abolition of 'anachronistic policies and institutions', which generate tensions and conflicts. He rejected the 'old outdated equilibrium' based on opposed military blocs. In a speech in this vein in June 1982 President Ceausescu predicted that 'the new equilibrium will be based on a greater diversity of power centres, will take account of the role of the Third World, of the small and medium-sized countries, of the developing and non-aligned nations'. Romanian spokesmen agree with the Non-Aligned consensus that 'the political–military blocs, the foreign military presence – troops and/or bases – on foreign territories, bilateral military arrangements concluded with some of the Great Powers – all represent the game of Great Power politics'. This position clearly reflects the limitations Romania has placed on its military involvement with the Warsaw Pact. The Romanians also agree more specifically with Yugoslavia that the effectiveness of the Non-Aligned Movement involves among other matters its intention 'to preserve its autonomy, and its independent international force outside blocs'.[154]

All this shows that Romania by no means expresses the views of the USSR or even of other members of the Soviet-led 'socialist community' on non-alignment or the Non-Aligned Movement. This distinction is evident in the statements of various East European officials and writers. For example, a statement published in 1979 by the Deputy Foreign Minister of Hungary, Robert Garai, criticised attempts 'to mould the Non-Aligned Movement into some kind of third force'.[155] Polish scholars rejected the interpretation 'forwarded by many non-aligned countries... of the division of the world into the opposed blocs'. Like the Bulgarians they were prone to use the terminology of the 'natural alliance'.[156]

In the 1980s Romanian spokesmen have continued to claim that Romania 'being a developing socialist country, promoter of an independent foreign policy, and member of small and medium-sized nations, attaches special importance to non-alignment as a foreign policy, and also to the Non-Aligned Movement in general'. In his message to the 1983 Non-Aligned Delhi Summit Ceausescu praised the Non-Aligned Movement as a 'significant factor in the struggle against any forms of domination and oppression, for the assertion of a new type of democratic policy based on equality and mutual respect, on the right of each nation to pursue its free development'.[157] Romanian writers have argued that Romania 'as most other states that are pursuing a non-aligned foreign policy today, struggled for a long time against foreign political, economic and military domination, and... for a free and independent development'. They have referred to Romania's 'solidarity' with and support of national liberation movements, and claimed that the interest of the non-aligned nations in the creation of a new international economic order places these nations 'among the new and advanced, democratic forces of the world'. This has resulted in the assertion that:

Romania considers that the develoment of its bilateral and multilateral relations with the non-aligned nations, within the context of the Non-Aligned Movement, suits the long-term needs of the evolution of Romanian foreign policy and that these do not run counter to the regional political, legal or military commitments assumed and implemented by that country.

In other words Romanian foreign policy activity within the framework of relations associated with the Non-Aligned should not contradict her Warsaw Pact commitments. This is further implied in the claim that Romania 'nurtures relations of cooperation and collaboration with the non-aligned nations, without any discrimination or conflict with its close relations with a certain group of states'.[158] In this context Romanian spokesmen have tried to divert attention from Romania's bloc commitments and reaffirmed instead Romanian efforts directed at the simultaneous dissolution of the existing military–political blocs.

It is evident from the foregoing statements that Romania would wish to set its relations with the Non-Aligned group of nations on firmer foundations. Some Western observers have speculated that Ceausescu could attempt to replace Tito as the European non-aligned statesman. To develop this role he would need to demonstrate his concern for Third World issues and persevere in his arguments for the erosion of military blocs and a reduction of tension in Europe. As in the case of Yugoslavia this could provide some protection for Romania when under threat through developing broad international visibility. It could also assist in the creation of national legitimacy and prestige at home.[159] However, Romanian policy, much more than Yugoslav policy, is determined by the breadth of Soviet tolerance, and such a scenario may be frustrated in advance through Soviet pressure on the Romanians to conform on foreign policy issues. Soviet latitude in this area may reflect the future state of Sino-Soviet relations. Romania's deteriorating economy is also likely to act as a constraint. It is unlikely that Soviet leaders will favour closer Romanian association with non-alignment or the Non-Aligned Movement since Romania is not prepared to act at a conduit for Soviet views among the Non-Aligned. Nor is it in the Soviet interest to encourage pressures for a further loosening of Romania's military ties within the Warsaw Pact.

Cuba is the only Marxist state in the developing world which has assumed a prominent position in the Non-Aligned Movement. Since Cuba has retained close bilateral ties with the USSR and the Soviet bloc in general this warrants an investigation of the Cuban role in the Movement. It has been a common Western assumption that for many years Cuba has acted as a Trojan horse for the Soviet Union in this body. Soviet ambitions have been perceived behind Cuban proposals within the Movement. The very notion of 'Cuban non-alignment' has been ridiculed by the majority of Western observers, although they have accepted the non-aligned credentials of Third World states closely affiliated to the West. In contrast, the majority of Third World non-aligned states have chosen not to regard Cuba as an instrument of struggle between East and West. If Yugoslavia symbolised independence for the Non-Aligned in East–West terms, Cuba sought to raise the banner of struggle between North and South. It is indisputable, however, that Cuban radicalism has displayed an ideological colouring which has been reflected in views closely parallel to those of Moscow on many foreign policy issues.

Cuba was among the founding states of the Non-Aligned group and their sole Latin American representative in the 1960s. Cuba's exceptional invitation to attend the 1961 Belgrade Non-Aligned Summit was, to a considerable degree, an expression of Third World hostility to the Bay of Pigs invasion and support for an American withdrawal from the Guantanamo naval base. Had the option been available Cuba may have accepted a formal Soviet commitment to her security, which would have denied her access to Non-Aligned forums. The Cubans were not prominent at Non-Aligned meetings in the 1960s and President Castro attended his first Non-Aligned conference only in 1973 at Algiers. Soviet writers have tended retrospectively to exaggerate the Cuban role in these early conferences.[160] During Soviet–Cuban consultations on the Belgrade Summit soon after its conclusion the Soviet Government claimed only that the Cuban delegation at Belgrade had 'helped to pass decisions aimed at further expanding the national liberation movement'.[161] Cuba was cautious not to isolate herself through adopting an explicitly pro-Soviet line at these early conferences. This was precluded anyway by material differences between Cuban and Soviet foreign policies, especially in the mid 1960s.[162]

The new activism of Cuban foreign policy in the early 1970s was paralleled by greater interest in the Non-Aligned Movement. The consensus in the Movement had shifted leftwards as international economic issues and anti-colonial wars in Africa came to the fore. Despite the rhetoric of Cuban officials Cuba did not itself reflect the consensus or lead the radicalism of the Non-Aligned on international economics or Southern Africa in the 1970s. On the former Algeria was the primary actor and on the latter a number of key African countries.

Cuban–Soviet relations had overcome their difficulties by the time the Algiers Summit was convened in 1973. The support and understanding Cuba had expressed for the Warsaw Pact countries' action in Czechoslovakia in 1968 had drawn it closer to these states and had initiated a period of intimate political relations. By the early 1970s Cuba and the

USSR expressed almost identical views on most foreign policy issues. At Algiers, unlike Cuban spokesmen at previous Non-Aligned conferences, Castro spoke directly of Cuba's socialist character and of its friendship with the Soviet Union. A Cuban–Soviet declaration in February 1974 accepted that the Non-Aligned Movement had 'begun to assume an important role in world politics in the last few years'.[163] This coincided with a Soviet reassessment of the relationship between 'socialist' states and the Non-Aligned.

At the Algiers Non-Aligned Summit Castro decried 'any attempt to pit the non-aligned countries against the socialist camp' as 'profoundly counter-revolutionary'. He described any 'estrangement' from this camp as a 'stupid stragegy' calculated to weaken the Non-Aligned. The implications of this line broadened when Cuban troops entered first Angola in 1975 in support of the Popular Movement for the Liberation of Angola (MPLA), and then Ethiopia in 1978–9 against Somali irredentism. In the former case Moscow provided logistical assistance and in the latter the Cuban military operated under integrated Soviet command. At the Colombo Summit in 1976 the Cuban representative proclaimed that it was the 'determination of the Soviet Government' which gave the Angolan and Cuban fighters the means to crush the South African offensive. For Havana this illustrated 'the solidarity provided by the men and women of several non-aligned countries and the power of socialism joined together'.[164] In the event the Colombo Summit endorsed and even commended Cuban action in Angola, but avoided any 'natural alliance' terminology. Most non-aligned states were convinced of the legitimacy of Cuban action in Angola by Cuba's long support for the MPLA, by evidence that Cuba had acted on its own initiative, and by the South African invasion.

Cuban intervention in Ethiopia was more contentious and Havana's close coordination with the USSR during this crisis threw the independence of its foreign policy decision-making under suspicion at the Belgrade meeting of Non-Aligned Foreign Ministers in 1978. Soviet publications admitted that certain non-aligned states which at the previous conference in Colombo had supported Cuban action in Angola were distinctly critical of Cuban policy in Africa at the Belgrade meeting. They maintained, however, that the majority of non-aligned states shared the perception that Cuba action in Angola and Ethiopia had been directed against violations of the UN and OAU Charters, and had been based on the principles of non-alignments, which require *inter alia* respect for the sovereignty and territorial integrity of states.[165] Cuba persuaded the Non-

Aligned at Belgrade in 1978 that the Somali attack on Ethiopian territory in the summer of 1977 openly infringed the principle of the inviolability of established borders. Cuba thereby avoided even implicit censure of its actions in Africa and ensured the rejection of a resolution condemning foreign military intervention in Non-Aligned member states. This shored up Cuba's position for the Non-Aligned summit in Havana the following year.

In advance of the Havana Summit the Soviet media sought to argue the benefits for the Non-Aligned of 'strengthening African–Cuban cooperation'.[166] Moscow may have been angling for a conversion of the support won by Cuba over the Angolan and Ethiopian issues into a more explicit adoption of the Cuban and Soviet 'natural alliance' thesis at Havana. It remained a Soviet priority, however, to avert a headlong collision between Cuba and Yugoslavia on this issue. Soviet commentaries described the view that Yugoslavia and Cuba were vying for leadership within the Non-Aligned Movement, that one of these two may 'head' the socialist states in the Movement, as 'dangerous'. They underlined instead the agreement reached between Tito and Castro that the member states of the Non-Aligned Movement should join forces to ensure the success of the conference.[167] It could be predicted that Moscow's portrayal of the Havana Conference would aggrandise Castro's role and stature. He was linked by a 'unity of views and actions' with such former influential statesmen in the Non-Aligned Movement as Nehru, Nasser and Boumedienne. Soviet writers admitted differences only in 'accent' between the statements of Castro and Tito. Castro was praised for his 'outstanding political tact' in dealing with those differences which had arisen at Havana on 'less important issues'.[168]

Chinese spokesmen led a spirited attack on the Cuban role at Havana. They asserted that the relations between 'non-aligned' Cuba and Vietnam and the USSR were 'closer than they would be if open alignment were proclaimed'. For Beijing 'Soviet meddling and influence' and 'the continuous splittist activities by Cuba and Vietnam' had seriously harmed the unity of the Non-Aligned Movement. This conduct was contrasted with that of Yugoslavia, which had 'held aloft the banner of the Movement and firmly defended the principles of non-alignment'. Certain non-aligned countries allegedly believed that Cuba 'should be ousted from the Movement because its actions have proved it to be a Soviet agent'.[169] The Chinese media maintained that Cuba took advantage of its host country status at the Havana Summit to manipulate the conference and control speeches, 'trying to cater to the Soviet blueprint for destroying the

Movement and having it augment the Soviet global strategic position'. This plan was aborted, but China predicted that in subsequent years the Cuban authorities would 'abuse their power as the "current chairman" to push the Soviet conspiracy to sabotage the fundamental principles and orientation [of the Non-Aligned Movement]'.[170]

Chinese conspiracy theories of Soviet-inspired Cuban manipulation at the Havana Conference were an extreme variant of the Western media presentation of this summit. The course of events was in fact much less confrontational or dramatic. In his opening speech Castro admitted that the Cubans were 'radical revolutionaries' but reiterated that 'we don't impose our ideology or system on anyone, either inside or outside the [Non-Aligned] Movement'. Bearing in mind Yugoslav susceptibilities, Castro asserted that 'no one has ever tried to tell us what role we should play in the Movement...no one except the Movement itself can determine what it should do and how to do it'.[171] However, Castro did make an effort to introduce clauses favourable to the USSR in the documents of the summit. By virtue of hosting the summit the Cubans were entitled to present the initial draft of its Final Declaration. In fact this availed them little since this declaration had been revised so heavily by the conclusion of the summit that it bore little resemblance to the original Cuban draft. All the general appeals for cooperation with the Soviet Union were deleted. The requests for support which were retained concerned the conflicts in Southern Africa and the Middle East, where the value of Soviet aid was regarded as of particular importance in a specific, current conflict.[172] It is true that the Cubans ought to manipulate the voting over the Non-Aligned credentials of Kampuchea.[173] However, the composition of the Non-Aligned Movement and the results of previous Non-Aligned meetings in 1978 and 1979 made it a foregone conclusion that the summit would fail to endorse the Cuban Marxist outlook or the 'natural allies' thesis.[174]

The Havana Non-Aligned Summit defined the limits of the possible for Castro. The consensus within the Non-Aligned Movement remained opposed to distinctly closer association with the Soviet Union and its socialist allies. The results of the Havana Summit and the contention surrounding Soviet intervention in Afghanistan later that year constrained Castro from abusing the chairmanship of the Non-Aligned to steer the Movement in a more radical direction than that warranted by the resolutions of the Sixth Summit. Cuba's 'revolutionary socialist' support for the Soviet position over Afghanistan damaged Castro's image as chairman of the Non-Aligned Movement. Cuba opposed the crucial resolution in the United Nations in mid January 1980 calling for the withdrawal of foreign troops from Afghanistan which was adopted by 104 nations. In early January the non-aligned states, led by India and Nigeria, arranged for the withdrawal of Cuba's candidature for a UN Security Council seat – a matter which had been deadlocked for some time – and the subsequent election of Mexico.

As chairman of the Non-Aligned Movement between 1979 and 1983 Castro was expected to work towards a solution of the Afghan crisis. But little momentum was achieved in this task, and it seemed that Castro's close relations with the USSR tended to impede rather than contribute to such a solution. Probably Castro avoided any great exertions over Afghanistan in his capacity as Non-Aligned chairman in order to avoid compromising Havana's commitment to the principles of 'socialist internationalism' – which meant support for the Soviet position over Afghanistan. Nevertheless, the political declaration of the 1983 Delhi Non-Aligned Summit vindicated Cuban 'internationalism' in Africa by renouncing the 'linkage' sought by the United States between the independence of Namibia and the withdrawal of Cuban forces from Angola as 'unwarranted interference' in Angola's internal affairs. Moscow found it significant that the conference also appealed to non-aligned and 'other peace-loving countries' to render multilateral assistance to strengthen the defence potential of the frontline Southern African states.[175]

The relationship between Cuban 'internationalism' and her involvement in the Non-Aligned Movement cannot be abstracted from the ideological component in Cuban foreign policy. For Cuba there does exist some link between the ideology of a state and its suitability to take part in the Non-Aligned Movement. Soviet writers in the 1980s maintain that non-alignment is not an ideological concept for Cuba but they accept that in broadening the composition of the Non-Aligned Movement Havana has favoured countries committed to a programme of radical reform.[176] At the Colombo Conference in 1976 the Cuban delegate argued that while he did not demand 'ideological continuity in successive representatives of a country' in the Non-Aligned Movement, membership implied adherence to a programme of change enabling 'the peoples to overthrow colonial or neo-colonial slavery'.[177] Havana aimed specifically at excluding the new Chilean junta from the Movement. This was exceptional, and more recently the Cubans have refrained from calling for the exclusion of states from the Non-Aligned Movement on ideological grounds.

It remains true that Cuban involvement in the Non-Aligned Movement is influenced by principles which ostensibly define Cuban relations with other socialist states outside the Non-Aligned context. Soviet writers have taken the line that Cuban foreign policy activities 'demonstrate that the principles of proletarian internationalism do not contradict and cannot contradict the principles of the Non-Aligned Movement, for they do not have any aims besides rendering disinterested assistance to nations which require it'. But this is qualified by the admission that Cuba as 'a member of the socialist community, defends its interests in the Movement'. The Soviet camp is one constituency among others the Cubans are expected to support. From the Soviet perspective, Cuban conduct at the Havana Summit had shown that 'it defends not only the interests of socialism but also the specific interests of the developing world in the Movement, in particular the countries of Latin America'.[178] It remains unclear which interests have taken precedence for Cuba.

The Havana Summit rejected the explicit link between non-alignment and socialist interests. It can be argued, however, that while the majority of non-aligned countries disagreed with the Soviet line over Afghanistan and the Vietnamese invasion of Kampuchea, Cuban influence prevented Non-Aligned meetings on either subject or critical reference to the USSR in the official declarations of the Non-Aligned. In the opinion of a Western specialist Moscow could use channels to coordinate positions and convey guidance to pro-Soviet radicals in the Non-Aligned Movement well in advance of Non-Aligned conferences. Soviet officials monitoring ministerial or summit meetings are believed to have easy access to 'client' delegations without concern that their presence will be interpreted as interference in Non-Aligned affairs. By the end of Castro's term as chairman of the Non-Aligned Movement in 1983 the existence of an 'aligned minority' within it was much discussed in private among non-aligned states. This was one result of a general polarisation of the Movement and was reflected in increasing cohesion among about twenty 'like-minded' and 'moderate' non-aligned states, which met regularly in the early 1980s as a counterweight to the Cuban group.[179]

In 1982 a Yugoslav ambassador directly accused 'a small group of non-aligned countries' of linking themselves 'ever more closely with the Warsaw Pact'. He noted that these states belong to 'consultative groups of the socialist community' at the United Nations, attend military manoeuvres of the Warsaw Pact, and 'approve *a priori* the foreign political moves of the leading bloc power, including actions involving intervention against the non-aligned countries'.[180] In this context it was significant that as the Delhi Non-Aligned Conference approached Raul Castro held extensive pre-summit consultations in Moscow. The leaders of other Non-

Aligned radicals such as Nicaragua and Mozambique made quiet stops in Moscow *en route* to the summit.

Castro's direct influence over the agenda of the Non-Aligned Movement may have declined after he relinquished the chairmanship to Indira Gandhi but the ideologically radical group maintained a high profile in this body. Their influence, as well as that of the African lobby, was indicated by the decisions to hold the 1985 Foreign Ministers' Conference in Angola and to convene the Eighth Non-Aligned Summit in Zimbabwe. At the Harare Summit in 1986 Castro appeared to shelve the provocative and divisive 'natural alliance' thesis. He referred to an appeal by Tito in 1964 for the Non-Aligned to work jointly 'with the socialist countries and other forces'. But instead of calling specifically for unity with the socialist bloc he suggested that 'the unity of our forces with those which in Europe, Japan and North America itself oppose any decision leading to war will enable us to neutralise those who attempt to unleash it'.[181] This emphasis on a broad intermediate coalition of forces did not fit the image of Cuba as a Soviet proxy among the Non-Aligned.

Despite her partial responsibility for the polarisation of the Non-Aligned Movement Cuba has had independent interests within it since its inception. The Non-Aligned group became a constituency of constant support for Cuba over the Guantanamo naval base and American pressures and sanctions. The value of establishing links with the non-aligned countries increased for Cuban leaders after the missile crisis of 1962 had indicated the limits of Soviet commitment to Cuba. The emphasis of the Non-Aligned group on the assertion of national autonomy through resisting forms of dependence reflected Cuban foreign policy aims. In the 1970s Castro had an independent interest in riding the Non-Aligned tide over international economic issues. He counteracted Cuban reliance on the Soviet Union – which remained a question of political survival – with a rapprochement with Latin American countries and an attempt to lead a campaign against the underdevelopment of this continent. Castro sought to steer Latin American nationalism and extend support to 'national liberation movements' outside Latin America.

Soviet leaders were not necessarily cognisant of Cuban plans as it pursued its ambitions among Third World and non-aligned states. The former Soviet Ambassador to the United Nations, Schevchenko, relates in his memoirs that Castro intended to be 'actively involved' in the Non-Aligned Movement 'often disregarding coordination and guidance from the USSR'. While Moscow 'did not object to Cuba's promoting its ideas among the non-aligned nations,' Schevchenko notes, 'it was not much pleased with Castro's growing influence in the Third World'. More specifically, Schevchenko argues that at the United Nations 'the Cubans tended to ignore unofficial gatherings of the socialist countries'. The Cuban delegate often would not show up at meetings convened by the Soviet Mission, which were intended as briefings of the Soviet position on the particular issue, before major votes in the General Assembly. When the Cuban Ambassador to the UN did show up at these meetings 'he would not share information fully with the Soviet Ambassador about what was going on at meetings of the non-aligned countries', and if asked directly 'he would smile knowingly and remain silent'.[182]

Castro maintained a high profile as a radical Third World spokesman also outside Non-Aligned forums. More recently, for example, he has tried with scant success to mobilise the Latin American debtor states against the United States on the basis of a common Latin American identity. It is difficult to maintain that the Cuban sponsorship of and support for anti-Western resolutions on regional and global issues in the Non-Aligned Movement is simply Soviet inspired when in many respects the extent of the Cuban internationalist commitment to states such as Angola and Nicaragua exceeds Soviet wishes and even embarrasses the USSR.

By the mid 1980s Soviet leaders were urging moderation on Castro over the regional crises in Central America and Southern Africa out of concern for summit diplomacy with the United States. At the Twenty-Seventh Party Congress of the CPSU in Moscow in February 1986 it was Castro rather than Gorbachev who drew the audience's attention to national liberation struggles in the Third World, to the need for solidarity between the socialist community and the Third World. The East–West priorities on the Soviet agenda did not harmonise well with Cuban North–South priorities. Castro had described Cuba as a 'frontline' state in 1985, and in February 1986 he encouraged a rift with the Soviet Union by making a fiery commitment to increase aid to Angola and Nicaragua.[183] In pledging to keep Cuban troops in Angola until apartheid has been dismantled Castro could count on the support of the African Non-Aligned constituency. Castro's independent commitment to Southern African politics had been expressed earlier at an Extraordinary Ministerial Meeting of the Coordinating Bureau of the Non-Aligned Movement on the question of Namibia in April 1981. His affinity with the Palestinian cause similarly ensured a high Cuban profile at extraordinary sessions of the Non-Aligned on Palestine and Lebanon in the early 1980s. In pressing the Non-Aligned to support the candidature of Nicaragua for the UN Security Council in 1983 Cuba likewise needed no prompting from the Eastern bloc.

In the final analysis Cuba's political relationship with and ideological attachment to the Eastern bloc precludes a genuinely autonomous non-aligned course and the Cuban optimal strategy for the Non-Aligned Movement has not been acceptable to this body. But Cuban policy is still committed to authentic if radical Third World objectives on many issues and from the perspective of many non-aligned states this gives Cuba a credible role to play outside the primary military blocs of East and West.

2 The Soviet Union and the search for international security by the non-aligned states

SUPERPOWER CONFLICT PREVENTION

A central objective of the Non-Aligned group of states in the 1960s was to secure a more stable international environment through eliminating the sources of regional and global conflict, dampening down existing conflicts and providing against their resurgence. From its inception the Non-Aligned group was ill-equipped to deal with disputes between states in its midst. The non-aligned states instead directed their energies outwards towards reducing tensions and averting disputes threatening Great Power hostilities. At the Belgrade Non-Aligned Conference in 1961 Jawaharlal Nehru argued that whenever there arises 'a crisis involving the possibility of war the very fact that we are unaligned should stir us to action'.[1] In its initial phase the strategy adopted by the Non-Aligned to deal with the dangers posed by Great Power rivalry had three major components: the encouragement of negotiations between the superpowers and where possible the creation of a non-aligned communication link between them, strengthening collective security arrangements at the global and regional levels, and work for general and complete disarmament. The Soviet attitude to the first two tasks will be examined here; the disarmament question will be treated separately.

In the early 1960s Soviet spokesmen encouraged the non-aligned states to pursue this ambitious agenda and promoted their influence in international affairs. Soviet officials were impressed by the growing weight of the non-aligned countries in the overall global constellation of power. Before the Second Non-Aligned Conference in 1964 a Soviet commentator asserted that 'the policy of non-alignment, with new backing, has become still more effective...it can safely be said that no important problem is solved today without the participation of the neutrals [the neutralists]...their opinions can no longer be disregarded by anyone'.[2] This

79

endorsed and anticipated an active role for these states in the years to come.

The central theatre of competition between the Great Powers in the early 1960s remained in Europe and the conflict which most fully engaged the attention of the Non-Aligned group in these years was the dispute over Berlin and the political configuration of Germany. Although the Final Communiqué of the Bandung Conference in 1955 did not mention the German question Tito had already referred to the issue of German reunification during this conference. In his belief it was necessary 'to give the German people themselves the opportunity to express their own views'. He predicted that they would find 'their own form of democracy, which may be neither purely Western nor purely Eastern'.[3] As chairman of the Belgrade Non-Aligned Summit in 1961 Tito delicately steered clear of this topic. But Soviet statesmen regarded the attitude of the summit to the conflict over Germany as a test case for the Non-Aligned. Before the summit the Soviet press forwarded the view 'that if the Belgrade Conference is really intended to play an important role in strengthening peace it...must express itself concerning the conclusion of a peace treaty with Germany and the settlement on that basis of the situation in West Berlin'.[4] The USSR hoped that the Non-Aligned could be induced to favour and bolster the Soviet position. Chancellor Adenauer on his part sent memoranda to the heads of government of the non-aligned countries in August 1961 presenting the views of the Federal Government on the German question. According to Soviet reports he asked them to treat the German question at the Belgrade Summit on the lines expressed in his memoranda.[5]

At the conclusion of the summit the Soviet media claimed that heads of government of non-aligned countries such as Sukarno, Nkrumah, Tito and Nehru had called for recognition of the existence of two German states and had declared that the 'feverish rearmament' of the German Federal Republic 'was a danger to world peace and the security of nations'.[6] A statement by a representative of the Foreign Ministry of the Federal Republic that the views of those present at Belgrade corresponded to those of the Federal Government was emphatically denied; the non-aligned states had instead 'worked out their own views' on the German question.[7] In fact the declaration finally agreed on at Belgrade was circumspect. It only called upon the parties concerned not to threaten or resort to the use of force to solve the German question or the problem of Berlin. The Soviet media chose to believe, however, that the measures taken by the Soviet Government 'for achieving a peaceful settlement of the German problem' had found 'the full understanding and support of the broad public in the neutral states'.[8] The Non-Aligned states deputed Nehru and Nkrumah to Moscow (and Sukarno and Modibo Keita of Mali to Washington) on a peace mission. This probably had only a marginal effect on the outcome of the crisis but Khrushchev replied to the letter on the global situation he received from the Non-Aligned delegations with a reaffirmation that the USSR would be prepared to negotiate towards a German peace treaty and a normalisation of the situation in West Germany on this basis.[9]

Soviet leaders had failed to rally the Non-Aligned unequivocally behind the Soviet stand on the German question, but they continued to press for support from non-aligned states for a divided Germany. On the eve of the Cairo Non-Aligned Summit three years later the Soviet press claimed that 'a realistic approach to...[the German] problem is beginning to break through' among the non-aligned countries, 'an understanding of the need...to recognise the fact of the existence of two German states is growing'. Support for this 'tendency', Moscow opined, could 'lend significant international authority to the resolutions of the Cairo Conference'.[10] In fact the Programme for Peace and International Cooperation drafted by the summit failed to refer to Germany specifically even in its section on the problems of divided nations. The Soviet Union had to recognise that the Non-Aligned group would refrain from backing the USSR in Great Power conflicts, especially when non-aligned states were not among the parties directly involved.

A more realistic Soviet expectation was that the Non-Aligned could act in a mediatory capacity during crises. After the Cuban missile crisis in 1962 a Soviet correspondent observed in this vein that 'in the days of the Caribbean crisis' the activity of 'neutralism' in 'the cause of world peace and security was conspicuously to be seen'. He noted that 'the steps taken by the non-aligned nations at that anxious juncture, their appeal to U Thant [the UN Secretary General] to do his utmost to resolve the crisis, helped not a little towards warding off disaster'.[11] Despite this praise, the non-aligned states were comparatively helpless during this crisis. India was in fact at war with China. An escalation of the crisis was averted by Soviet restraint and concessions.

Soviet leaders undoubtedly expected that the influx of new developing non-aligned states into the United Nations Organisation in the 1960s could tip the balance against the Western nations and in favour of the Soviet bloc in this body. The Soviet media applauded the decision of the Belgrade Non-Aligned Conference to work for structural changes in the United Nations to give the non-aligned states broader representation in the executive body of the UN Organisation. This decision was regarded as confirmation of the legitimacy of the Soviet suggestion that the UN Secretariat comprise representatives of three groups of countries: the socialist, the Western and the non-aligned countries.[12] But the Soviet 'troika' proposal was never realised and as the non-aligned states became the largest group in the General Assembly of the UN, Soviet diplomats fell back on rallying support for Soviet initiatives in this forum.

Soviet leaders clearly relied much more heavily on their own diplomatic exchanges with the Western states than on the potential mediation of the Non-Aligned in the resolution of East–West conflicts. In 1961 Khrushchev called on the non-aligned states at Belgrade to 'take measures to put out the remaining sources of war and curb the forces of aggression and revenge'.[13] But at the Sixteenth Session of the UN General Assembly he rejected an appeal by the Non-Aligned group for a resumption of his discussions with Kennedy. Almost a decade later Kosygin informed the Lusaka Non-Aligned Summit that it could 'make a contribution toward improving the international situation and to the struggle to remove from international relations whatever harbours a threat to world peace'.[14] But Soviet leaders had done nothing to encourage the convention of this summit out of concern that its participants would criticise the 1968 Soviet invasion of Czechoslovakia.

Outside Europe the 1967 crisis in the Middle East was defused primarily through the moderating influence of the superpowers on the belligerents. The non-aligned states only performed a secondary role and found themselves unable to remain impartial during this crisis. The record of the Non-Aligned as crisis managers in relation to the Middle East crisis in 1973 was no more encouraging. The political stand of the superpowers effectively blocked attempts by non-aligned states to push through a cease-fire resolution in the United Nations. A cease-fire became possible only after the superpowers had reached agreement between themselves and jointly moved a resolution in the Security Council.[15]

The commencement of relations of *détente* reduced the likelihood of direct conflict between the Great Powers in the early 1970s and encouraged direct negotiations and communication between East and West. But contrary to the original expectations of the Non-Aligned group this did not appear to enhance the security of weaker Third World states. The Lusaka Summit noted that the tendencies towards *détente* had 'not yet contributed to the security of the small, medium-sized and developing countries or prevented the danger of local wars', and argued that the arms race acted as a spur to limited wars. Since security was not purely a function of external military relations, the Chinese argument, that the Soviet Union was colluding with the West to freeze the status quo in the Third World in exchange for strategic understandings at the superpower level, also began to gain support among the Non-Aligned.

It was a Soviet priority to undercut the influence of Chinese views on *détente*. Before the Algiers Non-Aligned Summit in 1973 the Soviet Party official and Third World specialist Karen Brutents argued that the changing international situation in favour of *détente* did not '"abrogate" and cannot "abrogate" the national-liberation struggle, which is predicated on objective factors'; *détente* would create more favourable conditions for this struggle. He maintained that cold war and its very atmosphere was a 'nutrient medium for the intensification of anti-democratic trends in international relations and the flouting of the developing states' rights'. The processes of international *détente* would instead facilitate 'the development of crisis phenomena in the military–political blocs and groupings created by the imperialists'.[16] A Tass statement affirmed that the decisions of the conference would be 'all the weightier the more successfully they are able to...solidify the positive shifts in the world arena, so that the favourable changes in East–West relations become irreversible'. Assertions about 'some USSR–USA "collusion", about the redistribution of "spheres of influence" between the two "superpowers" at the expense of the developing countries' were strongly refuted.[17]

In the Soviet message to the summit Kosygin and Podgorny presented the relaxation of international tension as the beginning of 'a fundamental rebuilding of international relations' in the vital interests of the non-aligned states among others.[18] Soviet spokesmen argued that the Soviet and American understanding to refrain from acts which might constitute a danger to the two parties or their allies (the 1972 Basic Principles Agreement) had restricted the 'scope of the forces of neo-colonialism' (understood as Western states) and provided additional safeguards for the peace of mankind including the developing states.[19]

Soviet leaders desired above all an endorsement of their *détente* policy at the Algiers Non-Aligned Conference. But the Non-Aligned remained uncertain about the relationship between *détente* and their ambitions for a new international economic order. While they accepted at Algiers that the rapprochement between East and West and the progress towards solving European problems were 'positive steps in the direction of establishing peace' and that *détente* indicated a 'stronger tendency towards peace in the advanced world', they qualified this by noting that 'in other areas there are still sources of tension which are becoming more acute because of deteriorating economic conditions in the developing countries'.[20] Soviet leaders correspondingly tried to rally support for their policy after the Algiers Summit by rejecting an exclusive notion of the operational sphere of *détente*. The Havana Non-Aligned Summit was praised for calling for 'the broadening and deepening of international *détente* and its extension outside Europe'.[21]

In practice the Soviet Union showed little interest in the 1970s in concluding agreements with the West on more explicit norms of Great Power conduct towards the non-aligned states or the Third World. Soviet leaders tried instead to draw on the interest of the non-aligned states in strengthening collective security arrangements, to steer their support behind Soviet proposals for regional or global security regimes. An example was the Soviet scheme for collective security in Asia, which Brezhnev first advanced in 1969. Soviet writers identified a 'coincidence or proximity of the Soviet principles of ensuring security in Asia with the principles advanced by the developing and non-aligned states in collectively worked-out documents, and reaffirmed in the decisions of the third and fourth conferences of the leaders of the non-aligned nations'.[22] However, none of the Asian non-aligned states besides Marxist Afghanistan were willing to endorse the Soviet collective security plan in their bilateral discussions with the USSR. Nor has this scheme been endorsed by the conferences of the Non-Aligned.

A more promising basis for coordination of policy between Moscow and the Non-Aligned on conflict prevention seemed to be the 'zone of peace' concept. This notion had become a standard component of the Soviet outlook on international security issues already in the late 1950s. At that time Soviet officials had expatiated on the formation of one vast zone of peace encompassing the newly free or neutralist states and the socialist states rather than on the formation of such zones in distinct regions. An emphasis on regional zones of peace developed in the early 1960s. This was paralleled by an independent interest within the Non-Aligned group in this security concept. Since the creation of zones of peace or any extensive demilitarisation in Third World regions implied the dissolution of Western alliance systems the idea was warmly approved by Soviet officials. But in practice it proved most difficult to delineate, establish and maintain 'zones of peace' and the concept remained abstract and idealistic. A more practical Soviet objective involved the extension of Soviet proposals for nuclear-free zones in Europe into Third World regions. Here there arose again a certain coincidence of Soviet views and those of non-aligned states. The Non-Aligned group adopted a declaration on creating a nuclear-free zone in Africa in 1964 and ten years later the Non-Aligned advanced a proposal for a nuclear-free zone in the Middle East. The Soviet Union supported such proposals as a means of strengthening the non-proliferation regime, of supplementing it with new provisions. Moscow perceived an interest in pre-empting the nuclearisation of volatile Third World regions.

The Soviet advocacy of zone of peace initiatives, which in Western strategic parlance could be termed military 'no-go zones' for the Great Powers, or perhaps 'crisis-controlled zones', became more pertinent to Third World conditions in the 1970s. This resulted from growing evidence of the catalytic nature of conflict in the Third World and the extent of the buildup of conventional arms in developing countries. According to Soviet definitions, the creation of zones of peace now presumed the adoption of effective measures to limit and curtain the arms race in large distinct regions of the world, particularly in areas of tension where there existed the greatest likelihood of military conflict. For Soviet leaders this strategic concept remains broader than that of a nuclear-free zone since alongside provisions against the dissemination of nuclear weapons it requires the implementation of measures to limit and reduce the level of military and military–economic activity and the observation of various international legal norms.[23]

The most lengthily debated security initiative on which the non-aligned states and the Soviet Union have in principle been in agreement is the proposed transformation of the Indian Ocean into a zone of peace.[24] This idea was first formulated at the Lusaka Non-Aligned Summit in 1970 and since then it has remained consistently on the agenda of the United Nations and the Non-Aligned Movement. A group of non-aligned states were behind a declaration on blocking military preparations in the Indian Ocean and turning it into a zone of peace, which was adopted at the Twenty-Sixth Session of the UN General Assembly in 1971. This appealed to the Great Powers and the Indian Ocean littoral states to begin joint negotiations to realise the declaration. Resolutions on the issue were adopted at the Colombo and Havana Non-Aligned conferences and in 1979 the UN General Assembly approved a decision to conduct an international conference on the Indian Ocean in 1981. This conference was not convened and Soviet spokesmen accused the Western powers of hindering discussion of the issue. At the same time Moscow loudly proclaimed the coincidence or 'significant proximity' of its position on the Indian Ocean discussions with the majority of non-aligned and Indian Ocean states.

Since the Colombo Summit the documents of the Non-Aligned have identified the source of tensions in the Indian Ocean, however, in the 'rivalry of the Great Powers'. Soviet commentators have rejected this view as 'incorrect factually, unobjective politically, and unfair to the Soviet Union'.[25] In July 1979 the Soviet observer at a conference of Indian Ocean littoral and mainland states, Ambassador L. I. Mendelevich, argued that the USSR had never taken part in and never intends to participate in any military rivalry in the Indian Ocean. He considered the thesis of 'rivalry' as unobjective since it ignored the differing interests of the superpowers: 'For us the military situation in the Indian Ocean is a security factor, a factor of threat to our national territory. For the United States it is not.' In his view this 'gives us a greater right to ensure our security militarily in this region'.[26] Nevertheless, the Non-Aligned still refuse to attribute responsibility for the insecurity in this region solely to the United States as Soviet officials would wish.

Soviet leaders realistically may never expect a comprehensive agreement on an Indian Ocean zone of peace to emerge and it is arguable whether ultimately they would wish themselves to be bound to such an agreement. But they are aware that the proposal focusses the attention of the Non-Aligned on American military strategy which has a higher profile than Soviet strategy in the region and that this provides a suitable lever to prise apart the United States and the Non-Aligned world. Soviet commentators can point out that they have no base equivalent to Diego Garcia in the region. The Soviet Union consequently proclaims its verbal support for concrete proposals towards an Indian Ocean zone of peace, although since the buildup of Soviet naval forces in the region the Soviet emphasis has been more on the denuclearisation of the region rather than on the need to withdraw extra-regional conventional forces from it. Thus the USSR currently supports 'the demands of the littoral states for the elimination of all foreign military bases in the Indian Ocean, for not locating nuclear and other types of arms of mass destruction in this region, and also the demands not to use nuclear arms against littoral and hinterland states, not to locate armed forces and arms which would threaten the...countries of this region, not to draw these states into military groupings in which nuclear powers take part'.[27]

During his state visit to India in November 1986 Gorbachev proposed a number of more detailed, practical measures for the demilitarisation of the Indian Ocean. These included negotiations on 'substantially reducing the size and activities of naval forces there', on 'confidence-building measures in the military field applicable to Asia and the adjacent waters of the Indian and Pacific oceans', and on working out 'guarantees of the safety of sea lanes' throughout the Indian Ocean, including the Persian Gulf and the straits of Hormuz and Malacca.[28] Such specific proposals are intended both to demonstrate to the Non-Aligned the continued sincerity of Soviet purpose and to draw the Indian Ocean onto the agenda of superpower negotiations even if this occurs outside the much discussed prospective conference on transforming the region into a zone of peace.

In the Soviet presentation the non-aligned and socialist states have jointly been urging 'the recommencement of the Soviet–American negotiations, broken off by Washington, on the limitation and subsequent cessation of military activities in the Indian Ocean' and the most rapid conclusion of an international agreement on transforming the Indian Ocean into a zone of peace.[29] The primary forum for this joint activity became the United Nations *Ad Hoc* Committee on the Indian Ocean. This body was mainly composed of states in this region when set up in 1972, but was enlarged in connection with the preparations for the conference on the Indian Ocean to include among others the permanent members of the Security Council, Bulgaria, the GDR, Poland and Romania. Soviet writers point out that the GDR and Bulgaria submitted a working document in 1982 on the possible structure of the conference and its various stages, which was ostensibly impeded by the Western states. They refer similarly to the support of the socialist states for a draft of a General Assembly resolution submitted by the non-aligned states to the *Ad Hoc* Committee in July 1983, which envisaged the opening of the conference in June 1984, but which 'came up against a solid wall of obstruction by the US and its allies, who categorically objected to all the most essential points of the draft resolution'.[30]

In reality Soviet leaders cannot place much faith in the resolution of such complicated multilateral negotiations. Already in 1983 Soviet spokesmen lamented that the American position had induced 'paralysis' in the *Ad Hoc* Committee on the Indian Ocean which 'could become chronic' with the result that 'the chances of an international conference on the Indian Ocean being convened would be reduced to nil and the idea of making the Indian Ocean a zone of peace would not materialize'.[31] They carefully avoid mention of the Western argument that it had been Soviet intervention in Afghanistan which had radically altered security perceptions on the Indian Ocean and had contributed to deadlock on the zone of peace idea.[32] This is in spite of the fact that in the 1980s Moscow has linked the Indian Ocean zone proposal with Brezhnev's initiative for a zone of peace in the Persian Gulf, and in connection with this initiative has admitted that there is a link between security in the Gulf and the situation around Afghanistan (see Chapter 3). Since the Twenty-Seventh Party Congress in 1986, which advanced the concept of a comprehensive system of international security, Soviet officials have underlined that 'the USSR proceeds from the premise that the Persian Gulf is part of the Indian Ocean' and have referred to active Soviet efforts to turn the ocean into a zone of peace.[33] Soviet leaders will continue to use the Indian Ocean scheme to try to create the appearance of and encourage broad-based coordination between the non-aligned states and the Soviet bloc on substantive questions of Third World security, although the prospects for the realisation of this scheme appear slender.

Another more recent initiative by the Non-Aligned welcomed by Soviet leaders is aimed at declaring the Mediterranean Sea region a zone of peace, security and cooperation. Resolutions on transforming the Mediterranean into a zone of peace and cooperation were adopted at the Colombo and Havana summits and the idea was approved as a United Nations' resolution. The 1981 meeting of Foreign Ministers of the Non-Aligned called again on all states to implement these resolutions. The Delhi Non-Aligned forum in 1983 supported a Maltese initiative to create a conference of Mediterranean non-aligned countries and other interested states to discuss the issue. The participants at the Delhi Conference stressed the need to stop the arms race in this region, to reduce confrontation and tensions, and to normalise cooperation in all fields. The first regional conference of Mediterranean countries in the history of the Non-Aligned Movement assembled in the Maltese capital in September 1984. Soviet observers noted that the declaration adopted by the conference contained firm proposals to resolve problems in the Mediterranean which were 'positively appraised' by the Non-Aligned Movement.[34] An appeal was issued at the Luanda Non-Aligned Conference in 1985 for all the non-aligned states to support this initiative and the decision of the Mediterranean states to extend their consultations was welcomed. Other Mediterranean European states and all states were urged 'not to use their armaments, forces, bases and military facilities against Non-Aligned Mediterranean members'.[35] Another conference of the Mediterranean non-aligned countries was convened in Malta in 1986. At the Harare Non-Aligned Summit the decision of the Mediterranean non-aligned states to hold high-level meetings to promote functional cooperation in the region was welcomed.[36]

A concrete proposal for a Mediterranean zone of peace was presented by the Soviet leader Gorbachev when he called for the demilitarisation of the Mediterranean Sea in March 1986 (see Chapter 3). After he had unveiled this proposal Gorbachev explained that 'in the Soviet Union the initiatives of the non-aligned Mediterranean countries...are viewed with understanding'. But he proposed a broader conference similar to the Conference on European Security and Cooperation, which could be attended by the United States and other interested countries as well as the states of the Mediterranean and those adjoining the region.[37] Western officials disparaged these proposals, and it is likely that Soviet leaders will try to use Western indifference to the Mediterranean peace zone idea to exacerbate differences between the Mediterranean non-aligned states and the Western powers.

The USSR regards itself as militarily disadvantaged in the Mediterranean and the proximity of this region to Soviet borders turns it into a particularly sensitive security concern. In this sense it is apparent that there are regions where the formation of so-called zones of peace would meet genuine and mutual interests of the USSR and the Non-Aligned, although at the expense of the prevailing military predominance or presence of the West. In a related fashion Soviet leaders have recently commended the political declaration of the Harare Non-Aligned Summit for assisting the process of building a consensus in favour of an international conference on the 'Near East'.[38] This is evidently an area where little progress can be made without joint efforts by both superpowers. But if the superpowers continue to fail to reach understandings on Third World security it is probable that the USSR will seek to encourage various regional initiatives by the Non-Aligned Movement or by groups of non-aligned states, which would tend to hamper the military presence of Western powers more than that of the Soviet Union. When Soviet leaders find that the brunt of such an initiative is directed instead at the Soviet presence in a particular region they will ignore or stigmatize such endeavours (see Chapter 3).

It was not until the spring of 1981 that the Soviet Union set out a code of conduct for Great Power involvement in the Third World. During an official visit to Libya Brezhnev identified certain 'generally recognised norms of international law' suitable for relations with the new Third World states in contemporary conditions. These included 'respect for the status of non-alignment, chosen by the majority of states of Africa, Asia and Latin America' and 'abstaining from attempts to draw them into military–political blocs of powers'.[39] Western states did not respond to Brezhnev's suggested norms of conduct, although on one level they were a reaction to the accusation by Western statesmen that the breakdown of *détente* resulted from uninhibited Soviet activity in the Third World.

The current Soviet leadership still maintains, however, that Great Power understandings on non-alignment would help to eliminate sources of conflict in the Third World. During a visit to Moscow by the current chairman of the Non-Aligned Movement, Rajiv Gandhi, in May 1985, the Soviet leader Mikhail Gorbachev argued, for example, that 'conflicts in different regions of the world...stem as a rule, from attempts by imperialist powers to interfere, in some form or other, in the affairs of newly independent countries' rather than from a 'rivalry of the superpowers'. He proposed that every permanent member of the United Nations Security Council should assume an obligation not to draw the 'newly independent states' into military blocs, 'which would help remove seats of tension and promote the peaceful settlement of a number of conflicts in Asia, Africa and Latin America'.[40] A Soviet specialist has even proposed unofficially that global *détente* could be secured through 'Non-Alignment Pacts', which would guarantee the non-alignment of specific countries or regions (see Chapter 3).

One form of conflict in the Third World which Soviet leaders have for many years expected to favour their interests over those of Western states has ensued from current or former colonial disputes. Since the mid 1970s Soviet officials have voted more consistently alongside the non-aligned states in the United Nations on 'colonial' issues to reinforce the image of an identity of interest of the 'socialist community' and the Non-Aligned. By the early 1980s colonial controversies were mostly residual or historical, but Soviet diplomats pressed the Non-Aligned towards a 'complete and final eradication of all vestiges of colonialism'. For one Soviet commentator this entailed support for 'the national liberation movement in Southern Africa, the demand to give Namibia its independence, the struggle of Arab countries against Israel's aggression and its imperialist patrons in the Middle East, the support of revolutions in Iran and Nicaragua, and of the determination of the Latin American states to free themselves from the political and economic domination of American imperialism'.[41] This catalogue includes a number of regional conflicts which involve the United States. Soviet spokesmen worked to isolate the United States for criticism during the extraordinary sessions of the Non-Aligned Coordinating Bureau held in the 1980s on the Palestinian question, Namibia, Lebanon and on conditions in Latin America. Soviet representatives pointed out, for example, that only two states voted against a resolution on Lebanon proposed by the Soviet bloc and the non-aligned states at a session of the UN General Assembly in October 1982 – the United States and Israel.

In the 1980s Soviet leaders have urged the Non-Aligned Movement and its leading members such as India to assume a special role alongside the Soviet Union in resuscitating *détente* and in averting and settling regional conflicts involving non-aligned states in various parts of the world.[142] In his message to the Non-Aligned Foreign Ministers' Conference in Delhi in 1981 Brezhnev exhorted joint efforts by 'all peace-loving states' to 'divert the course of events from increasing international tension to strengthening *détente*, from aggravating conflicts to settling them'.[43] A declaration adopted by the Warsaw Pact early in 1983 identified the 'growing contribution' by the Non-Aligned Movement in 'the elimination and averting of crises', and noted that its practical steps in this direction 'deserve the recognition and support of all countries'.[44]

The most significant conflict in this period involving non-aligned states and engaging the interests of the superpowers followed Soviet military intervention in Afghanistan. It became apparent that Moscow in fact expected the Non-Aligned to play only a limited role in the resolution of this conflict. After a visit to Pakistan by the Cuban Foreign Minister, Malmierca, in March 1980 the Soviet media observed that rumours were spreading in Islamabad that Castro as chairman of the Non-Aligned 'was acting in a mediatory role for the normalisation of relations between Pakistan and Afghanistan'.[45] Soviet leaders may have expected that Cuban action could lead to direct state to state talks between the DRA and Pakistan. However, it was difficult for Cuba to present herself as an even-handed broker and this undercut attempts to build cohesion around Cuban-led mediation efforts on the Afghan question. Castro explained to the non-aligned countries later that once Soviet troops entered Afghanistan 'we established the necessary contacts' through the Cuban Foreign Minister and other leaders. Efforts were formalised towards 'an honourable and acceptable settlement for all parties concerned'. But in his view 'conditions were not ripe then for fruitful results'. Castro argued that once it was realised that the United Nations' mediation efforts 'could advance in an already favourable climate, we discontinued our efforts and supported the UN endeavours'.[46] Cuba thereby absolved itself of the need to act over Afghanistan which could highlight its conflicting loyalties between the Non-Aligned Movement and the USSR.

Before the Delhi Non-Aligned Summit in 1983 Moscow sought to divert the attention of the Non-Aligned from Afghanistan. A Soviet statement described a suggestion by President Zia of Pakistan early in January that the Afghan problem was an 'issue' for the Non-Aligned Movement as 'an artificial and spurious linkage'. The route to a political settlement of the situation around Afghanistan in the Soviet view was by means of DRA–Pakistan talks through the personal representative of the UN Secretary General.[47] Soviet leaders sought an endorsement of this process of negotiations from the Non-Aligned summit, and it is likely that they favoured the informal contacts the UN Secretary General made with the leaders of the DRA and Pakistan at the summit.[48] Moscow was gratified no doubt by the support extended by the summit for the 'constructive steps' of the UN Secretary General and its approval for the continuation of his mediation efforts.[49] A Soviet specialist maintained that 'the purposeful actions of the Afghan government in search of the means for a peaceful settlement, responding to the resolutions adopted earlier by the non-aligned countries, received approval and support at the [Delhi] Conference'.[50] Another Soviet observer claimed that the summit had exhibited a 'mounting trend towards the recognition of the authority of the DRA in the international arena'.[51]

It appeared that Soviet officials have allotted the Non-Aligned a role in the search for a settlement of the Afghan question, but one ancillary to and in support of the UN-sponsored talks. Moscow has hoped that with the passage of time a greater number of states in the Non-Aligned Movement will come to accept the claims of the incumbent if beleaguered DRA regime and that this acceptance will add diplomatic weight to DRA–Soviet conceptions of a long-term solution of the Afghan question. At the same time Soviet officials are aware that the violation of Afghan non-alignment remains an emotive issue in the Third World. Before the Harare Non-Aligned Summit in 1986 a Soviet specialist noted that 'the Afghan leaders rightly believe that the Non-Aligned Movement could influence Pakistan to start direct talks with Afghanistan in Geneva and persuade the other member countries involved in the undeclared war against Afghanistan to withdraw from it'.[52] But the USSR was keen to avoid any replay of the earlier controversy over Afghanistan which had beset the largest Third World forum and had caused the Soviet Union severe discomfiture. The head of the Soviet Foreign Ministry Department on Questions of Non-Alignment warned the non-aligned states against kindling heightened tensions over the issue of settling the situation around Afghanistan.[53] In fact the resolutions adopted on Southwest Asia in the final documents at Harare merely reconfirmed these adopted in 1983 at Delhi. The United-Nations-sponsored indirect negotiation process remains the only effective multilateral channel towards a resolution of the Afghan conflict.

In the early 1980s Soviet officials also aimed at rallying support among the Non-Aligned representatives on the UN Security Council behind Soviet prescriptions for dealing with potential or actual conflicts. They pointed out that the cooperation of the Soviet bloc states had been necessary for the Non-Aligned to secure their choice of Nicaragua for the Security Council in face of opposition from the United States.[54] During the first meeting of the new Security Council on 13 January 1983 the Soviet delegate, alone among the permanent members, singled out the non-aligned members on the Council for praise. He noted that 'membership on the Security Council for eight states representing the Non-Aligned Movement lays on them a special responsibility and makes it possible for them to play an important role in the Council's activities'. In the absence of similar statements from the Western members on the Council a Western specialist on the United Nations regarded this as further evidence that the 'non-aligned bloc dynamic tends to favour Soviet over Western interests' on the Council.[55]

Soviet diplomats have also backed the Non-Aligned in their wish to apply their campaign for a 'democratisation of international relations' to the United Nations' structure and to the basis of international law itself. 'It is quite natural', a Soviet writer maintained in 1983, that the Non-Aligned Movement 'strives to secure equal participation for the liberated countries in working and carrying out all important international decisions, in a reconstruction of the activities of global organisations.' He observed that efforts were being undertaken to change a 'number of conceptual bases of international law with the goal of taking account of the basic interests of the developing states'.[56]

Such support for the principles of multilateral diplomacy and democracy between states may win Moscow some popularity among smaller Third World nations but it runs counter to the realities of the international power structure which ensure that the role of the non-aligned nations in the resolution of possible confrontations between the superpowers will depend on the goodwill and interests of those powers. Most likely, as in the Cuban missile crisis, the resolution of the dispute will depend on bilateral diplomatic devices between the superpowers. In the case of regional conflicts in the Third World, key non-aligned states necessarily may form part of the settlements eventually achieved. But this will derive from their geographic involvement rather than from any Soviet or American commitment to the need to legitimise the settlement among the non-aligned nations at large. Moscow and Washington are likely to prefer bilateral to multilateral channels in negotiating over conflicts involving strategically located non-aligned states. This appears to be the case even in relation to the Iran–Iraq war, where the Great Powers share certain interests in an early conclusion to the conflict. Despite the unanimous adoption of a UN Security Council Resolution in July 1987 calling on Iran and Iraq to implement an immediate cease-fire,[57] the Soviet Union received the Iranian Deputy Foreign Minister the following month for bilateral discussions on measures to reduce tension in the Persian Gulf and to conclude the Iran–Iraq War.[58] The tendency for the Great Powers to downgrade the potential role of multilateral non-aligned diplomatic efforts to resolve Third World conflicts has been encouraged by the fact that so many regional conflicts have reflected deep divisions between member states of the Non-Aligned Movement.

The superpowers do not deny, however, that in certain cases third party mediation by regional groupings of non-aligned states, such as the OAU, can play a role in the formation of a political settlement. In particular regional conflicts Soviet support for cherished policies and goals of the non-aligned states may help Moscow gain privileged access to key non-aligned states, such as the frontline states in Southern Africa. But such access is not determined merely by declaratory support for Non-Aligned ambitions. This is indicated by the Palestinian dispute. Despite longstanding Soviet support for the Palestinian declarations of the Non-Aligned, Moscow remained excluded until at least 1986–7 from moves towards a Middle East settlement.

The experience of the last quarter of a century shows that the non-aligned states have been comparatively ineffectual as a collective force in resolving conflicts involving the interests of the Great Powers, whether by mediation or by throwing their diplomatic support behind one party. The non-aligned states have proved to be more influential and cohesive in proposing broader measures for averting and diffusing military tensions in Third World regions prior to the outbreak of open conflict. Soviet leaders will continue, therefore, to urge the Non-Aligned as a body to work for the resuscitation of *détente* and for the formation and consolidation of various 'zones of peace' which favour the Soviet reading of the current 'correlation of forces'. Another area of activity for the non-aligned states which Moscow encourages is the whole field of disarmament.

DISARMAMENT

The Non-Aligned group recognised already during its formative years that the dissolution of blocs and alliance systems and the renunciation of the practices associated with them were closely linked to the issue of Great Power disarmament. However, in the mid 1950s Tito regarded disarmament as a secondary objective. He gave priority to the idea of a four-power conference since he considered it futile 'to discuss the question of disarmament if the present problems dividing the two blocs are not settled by peaceful means'.[59] Yugoslavia's overriding concern was its vulnerable position between the blocs and it had committed itself to maintain strong armed forces. Great Power disarmament appeared most pressing for the new Third World states as an issue in European security. Early in 1958, however, the Soviet Premier, Bulganin, highlighted a recent NATO Council decision to establish close ties between NATO, the Baghdad Pact and SEATO (Southeast Asia Treaty Organisation). He called upon countries such as India, Afghanistan and Egypt to join the European neutrals and the states of the two alliance systems in a summit conference to consider 'such questions as the ending of nuclear weapon tests, the renunciation of their use, the establishment of an atom-free zone in Europe'.[60] Such a conference failed to materialise, but by the time the first Non-Aligned summit convened in 1961 the combination of nuclear arms competition and critical political relations between East and West, persuaded the non-aligned delegations to press for immediate steps in the field of disarmament. At the Sixteenth Session of the United Nations General Assembly in 1961 a resolution proposed by a number of non-aligned states was adopted calling for a prohibition on the use of nuclear arms and authorising the UN General Secretary to ascertain the possibility of convening a conference to establish such a prohibition.

The non-aligned states deplored the apparent disregard shown for them by the Soviet decision to detonate the world's largest nuclear bomb in a test on the eve of their summit meeting in Belgrade. The Soviet press admitted that even radicals such as Nkrumah had been shocked by the Soviet resumption of nuclear weapons tests, but quoted him as saying that 'this was the kind of "shock" that would force people to realise the full seriousness of the situation and to take immediate action in the interests of securing peace'.[61] Although the Soviet media claimed at the conclusion of the summit that the non-aligned states 'understand that the Soviet Union was compelled to take this step, a step which serves to preserve peace',[62] they were in fact deeply disturbed by this act and induced into a more cynical appraisal of Soviet declaratory policy on testing. The issue of nuclear testing made disarmament directly pertinent to many non-aligned countries. In particular, nuclear tests in the Pacific and the Sahara had received adverse publicity among these states. The Belgrade Summit consequently appealed for the conclusion of a treaty prohibiting all nuclear tests.

In addition, the Belgrade Conference declared that the Non-Aligned should be represented at all further world conferences on disarmament, and its representatives delivered a letter to Khrushchev and Kennedy calling for the immediate conclusion of a treaty on general and complete disarmament. In reply Khrushchev expressed the Soviet Government's 'great respect' for the Belgrade Conference's 'considerations and conclusions', but maintained that the USSR had been 'compelled to take the measures to strengthen the security of our country with which you are familiar' (an allusion primarily to the Soviet nuclear test) to avoid falling into a 'dangerous position'.[63] This reconfirmed that the USSR would act as a customary Great Power in taking unilateral steps based on its own judgement of its defence requirements regardless of the views of small non-nuclear states.

The atmosphere for arms control markedly improved after the Cuban missile crisis had displayed the real danger of nuclear confrontation. After long negotiations Soviet, American and British delegations signed a (partial) nuclear test ban treaty in August 1963. A large majority of the world's nations followed suit. Soviet leaders recognised this as a seminal accomplishment in the field of arms control. They openly favoured the Non-Aligned group by 1964, despite Yugoslavia's pre-eminent role, in preference to the prospect of a second Bandung dominated by China. Consequently they sought to rally the Non-Aligned behind the test ban treaty as the first step towards more far-reaching measures. On the eve of the Cairo Non-Aligned Conference the Soviet press claimed that 'it is a known fact that the majority of the non-aligned countries share a conviction of the necessity of attaining general and complete disarmament and value highly the enormous constructive work the Soviet Union is doing to solve this most important problem of our time'.[64]

Soviet officials sought to dispel doubts on the Soviet commitment to arms control which had arisen in Belgrade in 1961 and now were only too ready to acknowledge the role played by the non-aligned states in pressing for disarmament and a total test ban. They observed that the Cairo Conference 'gave high appraisal to the Moscow Treaty partially banning nuclear weapon tests' and called on all states which had not yet done so to accede to the treaty.[65] Certain non-aligned countries did not sign the treaty, and a number of them signed but did not ratify it. Contemporary Soviet writers still urge the Non-Aligned to 'broaden the frame of the treaty', although they now present it as a joint achievement of the socialist and non-aligned states in the face of the 'diplomatic subterfuges' of the USA and Britain.[66]

The delegations at Cairo urged an extension of the Moscow Treaty to cover underground tests and requested the 'Great Powers to abstain from all policies conducive to the dissemination of nuclear weapons' among states which do not already possess them. They declared their readiness not to produce, acquire or test any nuclear weapons and called on all countries to enter into a similar undertaking.[67] Although the nuclear powers were not persuaded to renounce their capabilities, Soviet and American leaders, and a large number of leaders of non-aligned states, recognised a common interest in averting nuclear proliferation. During the joint Soviet–American diplomatic efforts towards a non-proliferation treaty the United Nations' membership was divided into those countries which could be influenced by the Soviet Union and those which could be persuaded by the United States.[68] Chinese opposition to the treaty led to further competition between the two largest communist states for influence among radical non-aligned and Third World states. When the treaty was finally concluded in 1968 Cuba strongly criticised it, and a number of non-aligned states, including India, refused to sign it. In later years some non-aligned states even succeeded in taking significant steps towards acquiring a nuclear capability.

Moscow has had to recognise since 1968 that the perceived national interests of distinct members of the Non-Aligned group continue to prevent the emergence of a consensus among them on the non-proliferation issue. For this reason the Lusaka Non-Aligned Summit in 1970 failed to endorse or refer specifically to the Non-Proliferation Treaty and the issue has been avoided during Non-Aligned conferences. The NPT question remains a source of contention between certain non-aligned states and the USSR, although India escaped direct Soviet criticism when it succeeded in exploding a nuclear device in May 1974.[69] Soviet officials point out that India adheres to a policy of not producing or acquiring nuclear arms. But they still criticise a group of non-aligned states, including Ghana, Morocco, Nepal and Nigeria, for hindering the strengthening of the NPT regime. These countries justify their recalcitrance on this issue with the claim that the system of international legal guarantees of the security of non-nuclear states is insufficient. Soviet writers have responded to this objection by stressing that the USSR is prepared to conclude a special agreement with any non-nuclear state that it will never employ nuclear weapons against states that abstain from the production and acquisition of nuclear arms and from locating them on their territory.[70]

The Cairo Conference in 1964 also approved the declaration of the African states on the denuclearisation of Africa, the aspirations of the Latin

American states to denuclearise their continent and 'various proposals pertaining to the denuclearisation of areas in Europe and Asia'. Since 1958 Khrushchev had been pushing for the formation of nuclear-free zones in Europe. Soviet spokesmen from the early 1960s had argued that the 'neutralists' were obliged to support the idea of an African nuclear-free zone. In later years Soviet spokesmen frequently stressed the common stand of the Soviet bloc and the Non-Aligned on the formation of nuclear-free zones and the denuclearisation of distinct regions (see below).

The Cairo Summit additionally urged the convention of a world disarmament conference under United Nations auspices. The Lusaka Summit more cautiously noted that such a conference 'may be useful... at an appropriate time', while the Algiers Non-Aligned Conference appealed again for its speedy convocation. In the 1960s Soviet officials were reticent on this proposal since they regarded the invitation of all countries to a world disarmament conference as an undesirable concession to China. But by 1973 during the Algiers Conference they accepted that 'what will be of great importance will be the support of the conference for the idea of holding a world disarmament conference and solving the issue of placing a total and final ban on testing and using nuclear weapons'.[71] In the new atmosphere generated by superpower *détente* and the European Security Conference Moscow considered this proposal more attainable.

Soviet statesmen simultaneously urged the non-aligned states to recognise the significance of the Basic Principles Agreement signed by Nixon and Brezhnev in May 1972. Among other provisions this committed the superpower parties to 'do their utmost to avoid military confrontations and to prevent the outbreak of nuclear war'. Like China, however, many non-aligned states were not fully convinced that they would derive direct benefits from *détente*, and they referred to the continued vertical proliferation of nuclear weapons among the Great Powers. The Non-Aligned favoured linking the idea of banning the use of nuclear arms with the principle raised at the Bandung Conference in 1955 of the inapplicability of force in international relations. A corresponding resolution was adopted at the Twenty-Seventh Session of the UN General Assembly in 1972 with the support of the USSR and many developing countries. At the Algiers, Colombo and Havana Non-Aligned conferences the non-aligned states urged the rapid adoption of a resolution on the inapplicability of force in international relations. The opposition of the Western states to these proposals stemmed from their view that such initiatives were hollow, used cynically by the USSR, and unrelated to the real needs of security. But the Soviet Union tended to benefit from the continued interest displayed by the non-aligned states in such declaratory statements of policy.

The efforts of Soviet officials to rally the Non-Aligned behind their disarmament initiatives grew as *détente* soured towards the end of the 1970s. An official of the USSR Supreme Soviet, V. Kudryavtsev, observed in 1979 that 'some non-aligned countries may wonder: how can one talk of disarmament when the national liberation movement calls for arming the peoples who are subjected to armed aggression...or when they are fighting for their freedom and independence'. To counter this 'armed liberation' left-wing critique he accepted that 'the countries and peoples who fight for their freedom and independence have the sacred right to wage all types of struggle, including armed struggle'. But he underlined the long-standing Soviet contention that while Warsaw pact proposals on disarmament primarily concern Europe 'they also embrace the interests of the non-aligned countries'. Kudryavtsev took as examples the proposals for the non-expansion of military–political groupings in Europe and the extension of confidence-building measures to the Mediterranean. These were relevant since 'the tendency towards expanding the NATO bloc directly affects the newly independent countries...and a number of countries belonging to the Non-Aligned Movement are situated on the coast of the Mediterranean'. In his view the proposal to conclude an agreement committing every state not to be the first to use nuclear and conventional arms was aimed at preventing Europe from becoming the epicentre of a new war 'and Europe is a continent that has a strong influence on the Third World'. He emphasised that the lethal effects of a nuclear war could not be confined to one part of the world.[72]

Soviet writers welcomed the initiative taken by the non-aligned countries on the question of disarmament at the 1978 Special Session of the UN General Assembly and the interest they expressed in convening a universal conference on disarmament. They noted that in June 1979 the Non-Aligned Coordinating Bureau had stressed the urgency of measures leading to such a conference and had welcomed the progress achieved by the United States and the USSR in concluding the SALT II treaty. The USSR hoped for further 'moral' pressure from the non-aligned states on American leaders to ratify this treaty. Soviet writers observed that in May 1979 a group of non-aligned states presented a document to the UN Commission on Disarmament on a 'universal programme of disarmament', which stressed the need for universal and full disarmament under effective international control and emphasised the 'tight mutal relations between disarmament and the establishment of a new international economic order'.[73] The latter consideration, which engaged the direct interests of the Non-Aligned, may have acted as more of a compulsion for them to press for disarmament than some of the Soviet arguments presented above. Regardless of motivations, the Soviet view at the close of the 1970s was that on questions of the 'struggle for peace, security, *détente*, curtailing the arms race and disarmament' the Non-Aligned Movement maintained as a whole a 'positive' position and opposed the line of the Western powers.[74]

By 1983, despite the onset of a new Cold War in superpower relations, Soviet leaders had unleashed a barrage of new initiatives and proposals in the field of disarmament. Western statesmen dismissed many of these as pure propaganda. The new Soviet leadership was intent on creating a common front of non-aligned and Soviet bloc states in favour of these proposals while simultaneously negotiating with the West on specific missile systems. Soviet writers claimed that the 'overwhelming majority' of non-aligned states supported Soviet political initiatives to avert nuclear war and strengthen peace at the Thirty-Seventh Session of the UN General Assembly. Some fifty resolutions aimed at stimulating efforts to limit the arms race and for disarmament were ostensibly approved 'thanks to the joint action of the socialist and non-aligned states'.[75] Moscow noted that the great majority of the Non-Aligned had supported a Soviet proposal for an international convention to strengthen the security of non-nuclear states. A coincidence of Soviet and Non-Aligned views on banning the threat or the use of nuclear arms against states which do not possess nuclear arms was stressed. Soviet officials once again commended the Non-Aligned Movement for supporting the creation of nuclear-free zones and 'zones of peace'. A large group of non-aligned countries were praised for their participation in the preparation of documents jointly with the USSR condemning the creation of neutron arms by the United States and urging negotiations for a convention forbidding the production, deployment and use of such arms.[76]

Soviet spokesmen now maintained that the contribution of the non-aligned states towards disarmament not only improved their developmental prospects but strengthened the authority of the Non-Aligned Movement and its overall significance in the system of international relations. This significance was a function of the Movement's support for Soviet-sponsored measures. 'In assessing the attitude of the non-aligned countries as a whole to the struggle for disarmament', a Soviet writer concluded, 'the majority of them occupy a constructive position which corresponds to the position of the USSR and other socialist states or is close to it.'[77] This implied much tighter links than Soviet writers had done a few years previously.

Soviet officials paid close attention to the course of the Delhi Non-

Aligned Summit in 1983. They detected support from the statements of a whole number of delegations at the conference for the proposals adopted at a recent meeting of the Political Consultative Committee of the Warsaw Pact aimed at checking the arms race and reducing tensions. The proposals of the Delhi Conference in this area were described as 'in essence' in conformity with the concrete proposals of the socialist bloc. More specifically, the appeal by the Non-Aligned for the abandonment of 'concepts of limited nuclear war' won Soviet praise.[78] This appeal was clearly directed at the United States, although the Reagan administration soon publicly renounced the notion of a limited nuclear war. Soviet spokesmen were also gratified by the idea advanced by the non-aligned countries at the Thirty-Eighth Session of the UN General Assembly to establish a binding legal obligation for the nuclear powers of no first use of nuclear arms. Soviet support for this idea, which remains contrary to NATO policy, was traced back to its original expression in the resolutions of the Thirty-Fourth Session of the General Assembly.[79]

The urgency expressed in the resolutions adopted at Delhi was justified by the breakdown of Soviet–American negotiations on European nuclear arms in autumn 1983. The Non-Aligned refrained from blaming the USSR for pulling out of the talks or the Western states for their avowed intention to 'modernise' their intermediate range missiles in Europe. But Soviet writers encouraged the non-aligned states in the UN to consider that the new missiles in West Europe could be aimed not only at the USSR and East Europe but also at numerous Middle Eastern and African countries. India and other Asian non-aligned states were also presented as endangered by the American policy of 'saturating' their military bases in Asia and the Pacific Ocean, such as Diego Garcia, with nuclear arms.[80] The European members of the Neutral and Non-Aligned Group remained impartial, however, and did what they could to encourage the preservation of some channels for Great Power dialogue on European security.

Under Indian chairmanship the non-aligned states opposed all plans for the militarisation of space. Since the reversal of American plans for a 'Strategic Defence Initiative' became the central Soviet strategic objective the multilateral support of the Non-Aligned Movement on this issue was highly significant. Soviet writers traced back the opposition of the non-aligned states to the extension of the arms race into space to the 1961 Belgrade Conference. Soviet diplomats were encouraged by the adoption of resolutions at the Thirty-Seventh Session of the UN General Assembly, drafted jointly by the Soviet bloc and non-aligned states, on activating negotiations to work out an international treaty to ban the arms race spreading into space. On the occasion of the thirtieth anniversary of the Bandung Conference in 1985 a Soviet writer stressed that 'in the spirit of Bandung Conference' the ministers of foreign affairs and heads of delegations of non-aligned countries at the Thirty-Ninth Session of the UN General Assembly in October 1984 had opposed the Reagan administration's plans for 'Star Wars' and appealed for the adoption of measures to prevent the militarisation of outer space.[81]

Soviet officials were gratified that the Conference of Non-Aligned Foreign Ministers in Luanda in September 1985 clearly condemned the programme of preparations for 'Star Wars' for threatening an 'unprecedented escalation in the nuclear arms race' and firmly stated that 'outer space should be used exclusively for peaceful purposes', and 'not be transformed into a theatre of the arms race'.[82] When the Zimbabwean Prime Minister, Robert Mugabe, met Soviet leaders during an official visit to Moscow in December 1985 their talks probably focussed on the future of the Non-Aligned Movement and its attitude to the American SDI project, since Mugabe had been chosen as the future chairman of the Movement. Although Mugabe spoke in Moscow only of the alarm and concern of the developing countries over 'the tense relations between the two world blocs', a Tass report of this visit observed that 'like all non-aligned countries, Zimbabwe is resolutely against the arms race being carried into space and does not accept the concept of "Star Wars"'.[83]

The Coordinating Bureau of the Non-Aligned which met in April 1986 called on the superpowers to adhere to the limitations on space weapons in the Outer Space Treaty and the 1972 Anti-Ballistic Missile Treaty since it feared that measures aimed at developing, testing or deploying weapons and weapon systems in outer space would 'dangerously enhance the likelihood of the outbreak of nuclear conflict' and make 'the pursuit of disarmament extremely difficult'.[86] The Political Declaration of the Harare Non-Aligned Summit in August–September 1986 spelt out these views in greater detail, appealed for a strengthening and extension of the ABM Treaty 'as necessary in the light of recent technological advances', and called for negotiations towards an agreement preventing the extension of the arms race into space.[85] Such views paralleled the current declaratory position of the USSR.

Although Soviet leaders can hardly expect appeals by the non-aligned states to strongly influence the American commitment on space-based systems, they will continue in their attempts to diplomatically isolate the United States from the greater majority of Third World states over 'Star Wars' and will use this question to reinforce their claims that the Western states harbour malign strategic intentions. This is made easlier by the tendency of the non-aligned countries to underestimate the anti-satellite and anti-ballistic missile research programme of the USSR itself. A related issue, which Soviet officials no doubt hope will also assume an anti-Western character, is the increasing awareness of the Non-Aligned that military satellites are not simply part of the *East–West* nuclear equation. The Harare Summit in fact raised the issue of exploring 'the ways and means of bringing satellites for military purposes under international control, particularly when it puts at stake the security of the non-aligned countries'.[86]

In the 1980s Soviet officials have encouraged non-aligned states to take initiatives on nuclear disarmament not only within Non-Aligned conferences and as a group within the United Nations but also separately in smaller groups. A group of six countries, four drawn from the Non-Aligned Movement (India, Tanzania, Argentina and Mexico, the latter with the status of observer in the Movement), one European neutral state (Sweden) and one NATO member (Greece), made an appeal in a joint declaration in the UN in May 1984. This appeal called for the nuclear powers to cease all work on, to cease the production and dissemination of nuclear weapons and their means of delivery, to freeze nuclear arsenals and to take immediate steps to curtail them. It was unanimously approved by the Non-Aligned Movement in the Final Declaration adopted at the Luanda meeting in September 1984. India followed this with an initiative drawing together the heads of state and government of the six countries in Delhi in January 1985. This meeting called upon all nations and governments to adopt firm measures to bring the arms race to an end, to prevent it entering space and to conclude a treaty totally banning nuclear tests. Soviet spokesmen praised these initiatives and the new Party Chairman, Gorbachev, declared that the thoughts expressed in the documents of the Six and Soviet proposals proceeded in the same direction.

Soviet specialists interpreted the programme reflected in the documents of the Six as 'the result of a dialogue between the Non-Aligned Movement and the Socialist International on problems of disarmament which was begun already in the mid 1970s'. They anticipated that recognition of common ground between the two bodies could 'contribute to the formation of a broadly composed international anti-war coalition', tending to support Soviet stands. Soviet writers now explicitly approve of a tendency for the Non-Aligned Movement to broaden its sphere of international cooperation to include West European states. Such cooperation in their view should be directed not only at global issues but should also concern questions of European security. The interest of the non-aligned states in cooperation within the 'N and N Group' is explained by their wish not to leave the resolution of important military–political questions purely to agreements between the United States and the USSR, or NATO and the Warsaw Pact. Soviet writers assert that the West European neutral countries in turn consider cooperation with non-aligned states as a means of strengthening their role in European affairs. They refer in particular to the possibility of joint support by the West European neutrals and the Non-Aligned for the creation of nuclear-free zones. Soviet leaders wish to extend the traditional support of the Non-Aligned for such zones within Europe and to encourage the neutral states, especially those in North Europe, to seek support from the Non-Aligned for proposals such as that for a Northern nuclear-free zone.[87]

The current Soviet efforts to extend the involvement of the Non-Aligned in the field of disarmament have given the most prominent member of this group an additional role in Soviet policy. India, as the chairman of the Non-Aligned Movement in 1983–6 was entitled to mediate between the Non-Aligned and the nuclear powers on questions of disarmament. Already in September 1982 when Gromyko and Indira Gandhi met in Moscow the Soviet Foreign Minister welcomed 'India's initiative at the disarmament debate in the United Nations as constructive'. He reportedly wished the Non-Aligned Movement to 'put pressure on the United States of America to resume the arms limitation talks which have been suspended'.[88] India, on behalf of the Non-Aligned, preferred disinterested appeals for superpower negotiations on nuclear arms rather than unrealistic attempts at mediation. These were directed at the USSR, especially after the Soviet walk-out from the Geneva negotiations in 1983, as much as at the United States. But in May 1985 during talks in Moscow between Mikhail Gorbachev and Rajiv Gandhi India was again encouraged to adopt a partial stance. Gorbachev expressed his confidence that India 'as one of the most prestigious leaders and the present chairman of... [the Non-Aligned] Movement would continue to promote its further activisation in the struggle for peace and disarmament and against the nuclear threat and the aggressive aspirations of imperialism'.[89]

On certain arms control and disarmament issues India has been distinctly more sympathetic to the position of the Soviet Union than to that of the United States. This is reflected in a message sent from the Indian Non-Aligned Movement Institute to the USSR in autumn 1985 welcoming the unilateral moratorium on nuclear weapons tests the Soviet Union had assumed in August. In reply Gorbachev thanked the institute for what he chose to regard as its 'ardent expression for the Soviet Union's peaceable foreign policy initiatives, aimed at lessening international tensions and eliminating the threat of nuclear war'. He praised India's efforts in this area as the leader of the Non-Aligned Movement, but also emphasised that there exists a bilateral Indo-Soviet dimension for maintaining peace in a nuclear world. He declared the Soviet conviction that 'the dynamically developing friendship and cooperation between the USSR and India and their commitment to peace are an important factor in averting the threat of thermonuclear war'.[90] This aspect of Indo-Soviet relations was indicated by an announcement by Prime Minister Rajiv Gandhi after returning from a surprise visit to Moscow in October 1985 that recent Soviet proposals on disarmament deserved serious attention. He denied, however, that he had played the role of mediator between the United States and the Soviet Union during his stopover in Moscow.[91] The prospects for such mediation are uncertain. It is likely, however, that the Soviet leadership will continue to use its bilateral relationship with India at least as a channel to influence Third World opinion in favour of Soviet proposals on issues of disarmament and arms control, despite the transfer of the chairmanship of the Non-Aligned to Zimbabwe in autumn 1986.

When Gorbachev was received by Rajiv Gandhi in November 1986 the two leaders signed the Delhi Declaration on Principles for a Nuclear-Weapon Free and Non-Violent World. Soviet spokesmen described this document as 'a powerful impetus to the debate on a comprehensive international security system'. India clearly was conceived as a medium through which the USSR could attract support from non-aligned states for the principles of this system which had first been mooted by Soviet leaders at their Party Congress earlier that year. Soviet commentators claimed that many non-aligned countries displayed a 'positive response' to the idea of such a system when it was discussed at the Forty-First UN General Assembly Session. The principles of this initiative were linked to the political declaration of the Harare Non-Aligned Summit and the appeals of the 'Delhi Six'.[92]

Soviet proposals for disarmament in 1986 were unprecedented in scope and they resulted in further coordination in the declared objectives of the USSR and the Non-Aligned. In January Gorbachev formulated a state-by-state general and complete elimination of nuclear weapons by the year 2000. Soviet spokesmen were gratified by the declaration of the Coordinating Bureau of the Non-Aligned in April that 'the objectives and priorities of this programme ... are largely in consonance with the position that the non-aligned countries had consistently taken on these issues'.[93]

On this occasion the non-aligned states also called on the United States to follow the Soviet example of a moratorium on testing, noted that the 'Delhi Six' group of states had offered 'to lend their good offices to establish verification mechanisms to monitor such a moratorium' and reaffirmed the need for a comprehensive test ban treaty. This was consonant with current Soviet policy. Soviet commentators had stressed that only three states, the United States, Britain and France had voted against a resolution supported by the non-aligned and Soviet bloc states and adopted at the Fortieth Session of the UN General Assembly calling for the cessation of all nuclear tests.

In August 1986 Gorbachev responded favourably to a further initiative by the 'Delhi Six' calling for a meeting of experts from these countries with Soviet and American experts to work towards a comprehensive ban on nuclear weapon tests. He noted that the USSR had already expressed its readiness 'to take advantage of your offer of assistance in verifying the end of nuclear explosions, including on-site inspections, provided it is accepted by the other side too'. He accepted that the new proposed meeting could make a valuable contribution in initiating 'an active and business-like multilateral dialogue on these matters' and explained that the Soviet Union was prepared to send experts to such a meeting. He also pointed out that the Soviet leadership had decided to extend its moratorium on nuclear explosions until the beginning of 1987.[94] The favourable reception of the Soviet moratorium on nuclear testing among the non-aligned states, and therefore their receptivity to broader Soviet-sponsored security initiatives, had certainly been a political influence encouraging its extension despite military pressures to resume testing. Gorbachev told the 'Delhi Six' in August 1986 that the decision to extend the moratorium had not been easy.

In his message of greetings to the Harare Non-Aligned Summit a week later Gorbachev anticipated that all the conference participants would 'appreciate the quiet at the Soviet nuclear testing sites and will make efforts to ensure that nuclear test explosions no longer reverberate in the world'.[95] Soviet commentators detected a 'high appraisal' of the Soviet decision to extend its moratorium among many of the speakers at Harare; they emphasised the summit's call for the United States to join the unilateral Soviet moratorium.[96] Moscow also appreciated the appeal issued at the summit for the United States to reconsider its announcement that it no longer regarded itself bound by SALT II. The Soviet Union now presented this treaty as a pillar of strategic stability. For the Soviet press the backing of the summit for the recent initiative of the Delhi Six, 'just as the approval of Soviet proposals' showed that the Non-Aligned had 'reiterated their readiness to march in the same ranks as those who are concerned about the destiny of peace'.[97] The head of the Soviet Foreign Ministry's Department on Questions of Non-Alignment, Sergey Sinitsyn, also laid stress on the common approach of the Soviet bloc and the Non-Aligned Movement on issues of nuclear disarmament.[98]

On 8 October 1986 the Zimbabwean Foreign Minister was received in Moscow as the special representative of Mugabe, the new chairman of the Non-Aligned Movement, to present the appeal of the Harare Conference. During joint discussions with the Soviet Foreign Minister, Shevardnadze, 'particular attention was paid to matters of strengthening peace and international security, including the issues under discussion at the current Forty-First Session of the UN General Assembly' – a clear indication of Soviet attempts at coordination with the Non-Aligned in this sphere. Shevardnadze praised the 'major contribution' of the Harare Conference in efforts to prevent a nuclear catastrophe and curb the arms race.[99] Gorbachev described the document of the Harare appeal, which was addressed to both the USSR and the United States, as 'in harmony with the Soviet Union's line aimed at eliminating the nuclear threat'.[100]

The Soviet leadership expected firm declaratory support from the larger part of the Third World for the unprecedented Soviet arms concessions tabled at the superpower summit in Reykjavik. Gorbachev replied to the Harare appeal on 3 November, soon after this crucial meeting. His reply took the form of a careful attempt to persuade the non-aligned states of the far-reaching potential of the Soviet platform at Reykjavik, of its conformity with the principal aspirations of the Non-Aligned in the disarmament field, and of the obstructive nature of the American stand. He informed Robert Mugabe that the real possibility of major agreements had been frustrated by the American efforts to implement 'the militarist programme of SDI and thus launch a race in new types of arms'. He asserted that the United States 'did not even show readiness to conduct talks on the issue of halting and banning of nuclear tests, which also caused concern at the summit conference of non-aligned countries'. He presented this issue as the touchstone of the seriousness of the nuclear powers towards disarmament, international security and peace in general and argued that the American refusal to join the Soviet moratorium on testing indicated a striving to achieve military superiority.[101]

In the aftermath of Reykjavik Gorbachev informed the Delhi Six that it was 'essential for us jointly to preserve the historic landmarks on the path to a nuclear-free world' achieved at this summit. He shared his anxiety with this group over 'the possibility of the wrecking of the whole structure of accords on limiting strategic weapons' and claimed that the results of Reykjavik had 'become the common property of all countries and peoples'. Gorbachev acknowledged the 'regret' with which the recommencement of Soviet nuclear testing early in 1987 had been received among the Six but as a palliative reaffirmed Soviet support for the proposals by the Six to help monitor a halt to nuclear tests. He judged it possible now to engage in 'a joint specific search for mutually acceptable solutions which might subsequently form the basis of a reliable monitoring mechanism for a treaty on a complete and universal ban on nuclear weapons tests'.[102] In reply to the Six in June 1987 Gorbachev explained that the Soviet Union was now prepared to reach agreement with the United States on staging the relevant calibration experiments at each other's test sites with the aim of substantially lowering the thresholds for power of nuclear explosions provided for by the unratified Soviet–American treaties of 1974 and 1976 and simultaneously limiting their quantity. But he was careful not to exclude the seismic monitoring services of the Six from this process; they could be used alongside the seismic apparatus of the two superpowers.[103]

The technical assistance of the Delhi Six is less important to Gorbachev, however, than the favourable publicity which their backing for the more sweeping proposals on disarmament made by the Soviet leader in 1986–7 may generate for the USSR. The group of Six called for an INF agreement to be just the initial step towards the goal of the complete elimination of nuclear arms. This objective has been advanced officially by Soviet leaders. Soviet commentators have drawn parallels between the current Soviet foreign policy and military doctrine, premised they claim on the absolute priority of preventing nuclear war in any form and on the need to establish this as a norm of international conduct for all nuclear powers, and the declarations of the Delhi Six.[104]

The West European powers retain the capacity to lobby for revisions in American nuclear policy. Since the non-aligned states do not possess the political influence on American policy which membership in NATO endows Moscow may expect other dividends from their opposition to current American nuclear policy. Moscow may anticipate a more sympathetic hearing for those Soviet security initiatives which are more directly applicable to the Third World. Moral support for Soviet disarmament proposals and for the grander vision of a denuclearised world from the greater part of the United Nations may also help to stave off pressure against Soviet concessions and Gorbachev's radical proposals from more conservative or cautious figures in the higher echelons of the

Soviet Party and military establishments. Gorbachev told the Delhi Six after the Reykjavik Summit that their aspirations on disarmament 'strengthen our confidence in the final triumph of human reason and spur us on to ever more energetic actions for the dream of a nuclear-free world'.[105] Furthermore, at a time when the Non-Aligned Movement is racked by internal divisions and frustrated in the pursuit of its economic objectives, nuclear disarmament is the field above all others in which Soviet leaders currently expect a consensus may develop among the Non-Aligned.

Soviet officials anticipate that such a consensus opposed to Western strategic policy could in some measure overcome the political polarisation of the Non-Aligned Movement, reconfirm its inherent anti-Western thrust, and offset the political influence of the increasing integration of the non-aligned states into the Western-controlled system of international finance and trade. Consequently Soviet writers maintain that the 'difference in socio-economic and political outlook' of those forming the Non-Aligned Movement should not adversely affect their position on 'questions of war and peace'. They call to task certain non-aligned states in Latin America and Africa which, through lack of experience of the consequences of open military action or owing to their location in isolated regions of the world, 'are inclined to underestimate the global character of the dangers of war' and to limit their 'basic moral support' for peace initiatives.[106] Soviet writers now argue that a third stage of the Non-Aligned Movement is underway (after the periods of struggle against military alliances and of demands for a new international economic order) characterised primarily by efforts directed at banning nuclear weapons.[107] Attempts to mobilise the non-aligned states in opposition to Western strategic policies will continue to characterise Soviet conduct later in the 1980s.

The non-aligned states may be prone to pass resolutions and issue appeals but there is little that they can directly undertake to reduce the risks inherent in the existing arsenals of nuclear arms except observe the non-proliferation regime. The Non-Aligned Movement certainly remains committed to the goal of general and complete disarmament, although the definition of this notion by the non-aligned states has become less extensive over the years and it has been biased in favour of prohibiting nuclear weapons. It could be argued, however, that the security of all Third World states, aligned and non-aligned, is more immediately threatened by the conventional arms race than the nuclear arms race, and that disarmament in this field should be the absolute priority of the leaders of these states.

It is revealing that Kudryavtsev, the Soviet official who exhorted the Non-Aligned to work for disarmament on the grounds of self-interest in 1979, stressed the tendency of NATO military activities to extend outside Europe, and noted the existence of a relationship between nuclear and non-nuclear arms strategies. He accepted that disarmament should include conventional disarmament but endorsed the 'sacred right' of armed struggle for countries and peoples fighting for their independence. The non-aligned states had already made this qualification in 1972 in relation to the UN resolution they supported on the inapplicability of force in international relations. Soviet officials also stressed that states subject to foreign aggression were entitled to seek military assistance from abroad. They used this argument to legitimise the large-scale transfer of arms, and the deployment of Cuban troops and Soviet advisers in Africa in the 1970s. Soviet troop deployments in Afghanistan in the 1980s were justified on similar grounds.

Nevertheless, as conventional arms were amassed further in the Third World and wars between non-aligned states became more damaging and frequent, and their extra-regional consequences more threatening, Soviet specialists expressed increasing frustration and criticism over the arms expenditures of non-aligned states. In an article written in 1983 and intended for a broad readership among such states Evgenii Primakov, who later became the director of the influential Institute of World Economy and International Relations in Moscow, stressed that the developing states bear a disproportionately large share of global military expenditures. He detailed the adverse effects of this on their economies. Primakov deplored the fact that the arms race on the global level 'inspires the "miniraces" in the developing world, which are motivated by factors totally alien to the security interests of the newly free countries'.[108]

At their conferences in the mid 1980s the non-aligned states recognised this problem and urged states to adopt measures at the regional level 'with a view to stregthening peace and security at a lower level of forces through the limitation and reduction of armed forces and conventional weapons'. They commended recent unilateral as well as regional and subregional initiatives taken by non-aligned countries to limit the acquisition of conventional arms and reduce military expenditures'.[109] These declarations have failed to impress Soviet specialists. An authoritative Soviet work stated bluntly in 1985 that 'although the non-aligned countries also declare themselves in general forums for the curbing of the conventional arms race, as a whole at present they show clearly insufficient activity in this important area of struggle against military dangers'.[110] This kind of criticism has a particularly sensitive aspect since it could imply indirect criticism also of the Soviet policy of arms sales in the Third World. It is probable that the credibility of appeals by the Non-Aligned for Great Power disarmament is reduced in Moscow by the evidence of soaring arms imports by these states themselves.

The Soviet approach to the accumulation of conventional arms in the Third World reveals a paradox. Soviet statements currently underline the importance of 'curtailing the conventional arms race, limiting it on a global scale, as well as on a regional basis, in particular in those regions where large stocks of arms are accumulated or where situations threaten international peace and security'. This is probably a genuine sentiment. Yet the USSR clearly has political and economic interests in maintaining substantial exports of arms to certain Third World states and in retaining the option of militarily assisting radical regimes. Soviet spokesmen assert, therefore, that Moscow favours 'limiting the international trade in conventional arms and their delivery, naturally taking account of the legal right of states opposing aggression and people struggling against colonial-racist domination'.[111] Unfortunately the qualification contained here obviates any possible Great Power understanding limiting conventional arms transfers to non-aligned and Third World states, since according to the Soviet interpretation it would justify Soviet military 'assistance' in the form described above. The Western powers would not accept restraints on the military assistance they may wish to render their allies or clients in the Third World while Moscow retains a free hand to assist 'national liberation movements' militarily.

A NEW INTERNATIONAL ECONOMIC ORDER

The central concern of the non-aligned group of states in the 1960s had been the eradication of Great Power conflicts which stemmed from bloc divisions and bloc mentalities and the elimination of colonialism. By the early 1970s the commencement of *détente* and the successful decolonisation of much of the world reduced the urgency of these objectives. Soviet leaders trusted that the enlarged Non-Aligned Movement would concentrate its energies on encouraging the process of *détente* and supporting Soviet measures in this context. But as the international environment became more secure militarily for the Great Powers the non-aligned states turned their attention to the underlying source of their insecurity – their economic dependence on the developed Northern states, their structural weakness in international economic and monetary systems and the general backwardness of their economies. This economic debility and the ambition to reconstruct the international economic order was common to the Third World as a whole and the Non-Aligned have pressed their demands on the developed Northern states in this field on a common platform and in joint forums with other Third World states. The response of Soviet leaders reveals the clash in priorities between Soviet bloc and inherently Third World Non-Aligned goals and the limits of any structural coordination in policy between these two groups of states.

During the 1960s Soviet officials became more broadly convinced of the benefits to be gained from the diversion of Soviet resources to build up the state sector of distinct non-aligned states, although this remained a contentious issue among the Soviet political elite. The authors of the first Soviet work on neutralism in Africa and Asia argued in 1964 that the Soviet bloc should render 'concrete, real assistance' in the economic and technological fields to the new sovereign states, that it should allot significant material and financial resources to help liberate these countries from poverty, economic backwardness and colonial exploitation. They attacked 'dogmatists and sectarians', implicitly in the communist world, who did not wish to understand that in rendering this assistance the USSR proceeded from the view that rapid economic progress in these countries met the interests of socialism.[112] Although Soviet outlays could not compete with those of the West, Soviet commentators maintained that the principles underlying the economic relations of the Western and the Soviet bloc states with the countries of the Third World were entirely different. At the end of the 1960s they still promised that the 'large-scale, all-round assistance' of the Soviet bloc states to the developing countries directed at social and economic progress would 'undoubtedly increase as the economy of the socialist community develops and its power grows'.[113] However, Soviet economic assistance remained selectively targeted and did little to remedy the structural weakness of the developing states in the international economic order.

In 1973 the Algiers Non-Aligned Summit effectively adopted the economic platform of the Group of 77. The Group of 77 had been set up at the first United Nations Conference on Trade and Development (UNCTAD) in 1964 as a kind of Third World lobby on economic issues, although its views had had little impact on the developed Northern states until they were compelled to react to the Arab oil embargo of 1973–4 and the OPEC price increases. Soviet leaders hoped to direct such Third World radicalism over economic issues against the Western states but they had to overcome the suspicions of the Non-Aligned that through the policy of *détente* the USSR was colluding with the West to the economic detriment of the Third World. Before the Algiers Summit a Soviet specialist argued that *détente* would develop 'discrimination-free economic cooperation between the socialist and capitalist states', a factor which would assist the establishment of 'normal worldwide economic relations and the overcoming of all manifestations of inequality in these relations'.[114] In their message to the conference Podgorny and Kosygin noted that *détente* was opening up favourable prospects 'for reducing military expenditures and increasing, at their expense, allocations for developing the economy...for expanding aid to developing countries'.[115] These assurances notwithstanding, the Algiers Summit, under the genuinely non-aligned radical leadership of Algeria, brought economic issues to the forefront of the agenda of the Non-Aligned. The summit called for a new international economic order (NIEO), and demanded the convention of a special session of the UN General Assembly to discuss it.

In the years following the Algiers Conference the non-aligned states consolidated their platform for the NIEO in the United Nations and brought Moscow under growing pressure to withdraw from its aloof position on the North–South dialogue. The Sixth Special Session of the UN General Assembly in spring 1974 passed a Declaration on Establishment of a NIEO calling for substantial reforms aimed at inequalities in the existing international economic order. But Gromyko's speech at this session avoided any concrete proposals.[116] Soviet leaders were prepared to give a very general endorsement of the NIEO programme, but at UNCTAD and UN General Assembly sessions devoted to discussing it they made persistent attempts to broaden the agenda to include their current security and disarmament proposals. Soviet officials maintained that progress towards economic self-determination in the non-aligned and developing countries should follow on progress in a joint non-aligned and Soviet bloc struggle to consolidate *détente*. This implied that the non-aligned states needed to support Soviet initiatives on East–West matters.

The link between *détente* and the creation of the NIEO was emphasised again in a statement by the socialist countries at the UNCTAD IV Conference in Nairobi in May 1976. This statement also attempted to interlace the demands of the USSR and the developing states into a separate programme, standing as an alternative to the existing world order dominated by the capitalist powers. The conference came three months after the Group of 77 worked out an 'Action Programme' in a meeting in Manila, which devoted an entire section to relations with the communist countries. The Manila Programme called specifically for expanding trade, removing discriminatory exports and imports to and from the Third World and increasing economic and technical assistance to one per cent of their GNP. At the UNCTAD Conference in May the Soviet Minister of Foreign Trade, Patolichev, responded by promising substantial increases in Soviet technical assistance to the Third World. But Third World representatives remained critical of Soviet trade practices and its refusal to accept any responsibility for the state of the world economy.[117] In support of this disclaimer Soviet officials could point out that the USSR was not involved in the institutions of the international economic and monetary systems, and they argued that the current economic plight of the developing states was the legacy of Western colonial plunder. Correspondingly the right of non-aligned states to equal participation in expanding international economic cooperation was set alongside a 'duty clearly to distinguish the real perpetrators of their backwardness and unequal position in world trading and economic relations'.[118] More pragmatically, Soviet leaders felt that the Soviet economy despite the promises of the 1960s still could not provide aid in the quantities that the developing states might eventually demand.

By the mid 1970s it had become apparent that international economic issues would have a lasting impact on the Non-Aligned Movement as the most prominent Third World diplomatic forum. Soviet observers noted that recognition of the common goals of economic development had led many leaders of the Movement into interstate solidarity. This was evident from the Lima Programme of Mutual Assistance and Solidarity, issued after the Lima meeting of Non-Aligned foreign ministers in August 1975. In the Soviet view a growing crisis in the bloc strategy of the West coupled with the influence on the developing states of shocks in the currency-financial and energy markets engendered by world capitalism had altered the principles of non-alignment. New economic factors of non-alignment were considered 'notable for their more fundamental and lasting character' compared to earlier plainly political ones such as non-participation in blocs.[119] Soviet spokesmen maintained that a qualitative evolution in the nature of non-alignment has taken place reflecting changes in the global correlation of forces. While they accepted that a striving towards economic independence had always been at the basis of non-alignment, they considered that in conditions of *détente* the centre of gravity in the strategy of the Non-Aligned Movement had moved from the slogan 'to survive' to that of 'to develop'. This was then accompanied by political changes which made the Movement more attractive to a broad circle of states and led to a growth in its membership.[120]

While Soviet officials now accepted the primacy of international economic issues for the Non-Aligned they continued to foist all responsibility for the resolution of these issues on the West. In his report to the Twenty-Fifth Congress of the CPSU Brezhnev viewed the 'liberated countries' as 'fully capable of standing up to imperialist diktat and achieving just – i.e., equal – economic relations'.[121] But in an attempt to counteract growing cynicism among the Non-Aligned over the Soviet position a Soviet statement on the day the Colombo Non-Aligned Summit opened in 1976 promised 'effective solidarity from the socialist community' for the Third World struggle for a new global economic order. It claimed that this solidarity was 'manifested in concrete political moves and in the daily practices of economic relations' and even that it was 'precisely in these practices' that the NIEO principles advocated by the developing states had first been reflected. Correspondingly, the struggle for the restructuring of international economic relations on a 'democratic progressive basis' would further strengthen the cooperation of the developing and socialist countries.[122]

This optimistic note was dampened by the outcome of the Colombo Summit itself. The Soviet press quoted the argument of the Vietnamese Prime Minister, Pham Van Dong, that the 'neo-colonial' powers would never voluntarily give in to the non-aligned countries in their struggle for economic independence and that to destroy the old economic order and inaugurate a new just one the Non-Aligned should strengthen mutual cooperation and develop relations with socialist states. It stressed that the developing states suffer serious losses from price fluctuations in Western markets and inflation in the Western world. Nevertheless, the Soviet Party organ recognised that the emphasis of the speakers at the summit was on cooperation amongst the non-aligned states themselves to overcome their economic problems, and it decried a tendency in the speeches of the delegates 'to blame capitalist and socialist countries equally for the difficulties of the developing world'.[123]

Soviet dissatisfaction with the approach of the Non-Aligned to the NIEO at the Colombo Summit became more apparent when Moscow for the first time set down objections to items in the NIEO programme in a Declaration on the Restructuring of International Economic Relations submitted to the Thirty-First Session of the UN General Assembly in October 1976. The programme was criticised not only for its stress on 'equal responsibility' but for failing to draw a connection between disarmament and increased aid, and for failing to address the issue of discrimination generally in international trade. The Soviet proposal to the fifth UNCTAD session held in Manila in May 1979 confirmed the divergent approaches on international economics of the Soviet bloc and the Third World. This proposal was founded on different assumptions to the one presented by the Soviet bloc to the previous UNCTAD session; it reflected Soviet views on the globally interdependent character of the international economy, 'which in turn dictates a more universalistic approach based on economic coexistence, not on confrontation'. For the overarching aim of restructuring the global economic order it introduced the principle of non-discrimination, which was intended to benefit more nations than the principle of eliminating 'exploitation'. The Soviet proposal admitted for the first time the difficulties the Soviet bloc faced in expanding its economic activities in the Third World, but it still argued that further joint action of the socialist and developing states was necessary to ensure the latter a truly equitable place in the international economy.[124]

Towards the end of the 1970s Soviet spokesmen pressed for a more universalistic conception of a NIEO, they tried to present the NIEO as the economic component of a broad struggle between the systems, and they sought to dispel any illusions that activity towards the NIEO could replace political and economic transformations within the developing states. In relation to the first area Soviet writers began to accept that the non-aligned countries were developing economically basically within the 'world capitalist economy', although in political and ideological terms they were still considered to be located 'in conditions of struggle between the two world socio-economic systems of states'.[125] A Soviet specialist stressed, however, that the purpose of a NIEO could not be 'confined to a correction of obvious anachronisms in the economic sphere within the capitalist system'. He demanded additionally the 'creation of conditions precluding the continuation of exploitation on an international scale' for an 'entire epoch' in the period of transition from capitalism to socialism. The elaboration of the NIEO was presented as an important economic link in the overall struggle for the democratisation of international relations, a link complementing the efforts of the Soviet bloc towards *détente* and disarmament.[126] This link between ending the arms race and the creation of a NIEO was again underlined by Soviet press reports following the Havana Non-Aligned Summit.[127]

Encouraged by the presence of new radical regimes at Havana the Soviet media claimed that the conference had demonstrated the 'disillusionment of the overwhelming majority of developing countries with respect to the capitalist path of development' and their growing interest in the experience of the socialist countries.[128] This optimistic tone conflicted with the growing appreciation among Soviet specialists that on an international level the non-aligned and Third World states were predominantly located in the global capitalist economy and even that this association was becoming firmer. In this respect a Soviet writer warned that 'in place of global restructuring of international economic relations the Western powers are trying to set up closed economic groupings which include a number of developing countries'. They were seeking 'to push many non-aligned countries along a different path of development and to tie their economies more closely with those countries of West Europe'. To enable the non-aligned and other developoing countries to overcome opposition to their struggle to construct a NIEO he recommended that the unity of the Non-Aligned Movement should be strengthened and all its 'progressive forces' be mobilised, that there should be mutual support between the Movement and world socialism, and crucially that progressive social and economic reforms should be undertaken within the developing countries. He maintained that without such domestic reforms 'even the most favourable terms in foreign economic relations will not help provide a positive solution to problems of national development'.[129] Another Soviet Third World specialist went further to argue that without a 'social and economic renovation inside the Afro-Asian countries', the removal of 'reactionary elements from the economic and political structures', the elimination of 'the remnants of feudal and pre-feudal relations and the extraction of the deep roots of neo-colonialism, the effectiveness and usefulness of a new international economic order for the developing countries will be reduced to a minimum'.[130] This was tantamount to denying the validity of Non-Aligned and Third World efforts towards a NIEO in the absence of domestic transformations in the states concerned along lines ideologically desirable to the USSR.

By the time of the Delhi Non-Aligned Summit in 1983 Soviet objections to the Non-Aligned presentation of the NIEO were fully developed. An authoritative study on the Third World identified certain 'conflicting positions' accounting for the 'basic weakness' of the NIEO. In the first place it noted that the elimination of the injustices existing in the economic relations of the developing states was conceived of within the bounds and the categories of the international economic relations of capitalism. Secondly, the flaws of the world capitalist economy were proclaimed to be universal, with the result that analagous demands and claims were wrongly made on the Soviet bloc states. Thirdly, the subsidising of development from abroad was conceived of in isolation from internal transformations, of internal processes of development.[131] A substantially similar list of complaints was presented before the Non-Aligned Summit in Harare in 1986.[132]

With respect to the first objection, Soviet specialists blamed the socio-political heterogeneity of the movement for the NIEO for its failure to set itself any radical aims which go beyond the framework of capitalism. They rejected the possibility which was implicit in the NIEO concept of transforming capitalism in international relations without eliminating capitalist production relations.[133] At the same time they noted with concern that regional and sub-regional 'power centres' were arising in the Third World which were dependent on the industrially developed Western states and which revealed 'tendencies towards economic expansion in the less developed regions'. Soviet writers were equally critical of views advanced in the United States which conceived of the non-aligned and Third World states as a repository of 'peripheral capitalism'.[134] With such unsettling developments in mind they still accepted that an implementation of the principal premises of the NIEO 'would mean substantial progress as compared with the present state of affairs in the world economy'. The NIEO was viewed as part of a general process of change in the global 'correlation of forces', as a long-term phenomenon which in the future will exert 'an ever greater influence on the formation of the concepts and strategy of the economic development and international cooperation of the newly free countries'.[135]

At the same time Soviet commentators noted that 'many principles of the international socialist division of labour are not confined just to the framework of the socialist community: they are also applied, to some extent, to the relations with the developing states'. This was supposedly borne out by the relations of COMECON (Council for Mutual Economic Assistance) with 'a fairly large group group of countries'.[136] Indeed, by the early 1980s the USSR appeared to be offering a socialist variant for the NIEO as an optimal international economic strategy. This was aimed at solving domestic problems in the Eastern bloc and enhancing the role played by the Soviet Union on the world market. Soviet specialists began to treat Soviet–Third World relations as complementing East–West exchanges, that is, as 'fitting into a global three-way relationship in which the USSR occupies the middle ground'. This ideal scenario of global cooperation fitted into the significance now attached by Soviet writers to the notion of a single world economy and global interdependence.[137]

This outlook also induced Soviet scepticism of Non-Aligned and Third World plans for regional economic cooperation and 'collective self-sufficiency', which were advanced at the Colombo Non-Aligned Summit in

1976. Those Soviet specialists who believed that some states in the developing world had become 'sub-imperialist centres' were already doubtful of the benefits of such self-reliance. An important Soviet study in 1985 accepted that the slogan of collective self-reliance is aimed at 'economic decolonisation' but maintained that the non-aligned states could anticipate great difficulties and even harm in realising the programme set out at the Havana and Delhi conferences. Soviet writers questioned how it would take account of and secure the interests of the more developed Third World countries and they predicted that it would clash with the process of differentiation taking place in the Third World. They also anticipated that this programme could be frustrated by local conflicts and the opposition of the Western countries.[138] They claimed that such self-reliance could create barriers to a free flow of trade which, as shown below, they now accepted as necessary.

This Soviet scepticism was reinforced by the Chinese commitment to 'South–South cooperation' which forms part of the broader Chinese effort to woo the Third World. At the meeting commemorating the thirtieth anniversary of the Bandung Conference in 1985 the Chinese Premier maintained, for example, that such cooperation could effectively promote the struggle to establish a NIEO and he proclaimed the Chinese determination to contribute their effort to promoting South–South cooperation.[139] In contemporary conditions China may be closer than the Soviet Union to Non-Aligned conceptions of how to proceed on this aspect of their agenda. But the Soviet Government adopted a conciliatory line towards an extraordinary conference of the non-aligned countries on South–South cooperation held in June 1987 in Pyongyang. In a message to this body the USSR expressed its 'understanding' and 'sympathy' with 'the processes of development of all-round cooperation among the non-aligned countries' aimed at speeding up economic development and strengthening self-sufficiency.[140] This appears to reflect the current Soviet determination to cut back personal economic commitments to the weaker Third World states.

Soviet writers still proclaim that the Soviet bloc countries 'support the principles and trends of the NIEO programme in the belief that the vital interests of the socialist and developing states in improving the system of international economic relations coincide in the main'. In their view progress in this direction depends on a 'firm alliance' between the two groups of states, but they reject all demands 'resting on the thesis of "universal solidarity"'.[141] This is the basis of the second main objection of contemporary Soviet officials to the Non-Aligned conception of the NIEO, and it is intended to deflect demands to burden the ailing Soviet economy with more long-term aid commitments to Third World states. As previously noted, since the Non-Aligned first adopted the NIEO programme Soviet officials have insisted that the 'imperialists' carry the sole responsibility for providing aid to the developing countries as recompense for their history of colonial exploitation. For the benefit of those 'who like to talk about the allegedly "selfish" economic aims of the Soviet Union and who try to equate Soviet aid with that of imperialist countries' Soviet specialists claim that the commencement of large-scale cooperation between the Soviet bloc states and the non-aligned countries in the mid 1950s had originally forced the Western states to revise their aid strategy away from simply an emphasis on military aid to military allies.[142] Soviet aid is presented as a kind of bonus, which should be mutually advantageous to the economies of the USSR and the recipient developing states. On these grounds Soviet commentators objected to the demands made at the sixth UNCTAD session for preferential or concessional treatment of the developing countries. After this meeting Soviet specialists criticised the notion of an automatic distribution of income from the developed to the developing countries for contradicting all the laws of international trade.[143]

Soviet aid has traditionally been concentrated in the public sector of the non-aligned states and this leads to the third Soviet objection to the NIEO programme – its tendency to exaggerate the role of external factors in solving urgent economic tasks. In the context of the NIEO Soviet specialists now lay emphasis on 'international cooperation in the sphere of production on a long-term basis, including that with the use of planning instruments'. They identify the key to a fuller implementation of the NIEO principles in the organisation of the productive forces of underdeveloped countries on a modern basis, which is considered 'unthinkable without the most active participation of the state and the creation of a powerful public sector representing the majority's interests'.[144]

Thus domestic socio-economic reforms should precede any effective realisation of the NIEO principles and the more conservative non-aligned states are considered outside the field of operation of these principles despite their proclaimed support for them in Third World forums. These conservative regimes are attacked for exploiting the NIEO programme as a source of enrichment and for using it as a 'lightning conductor', as a general pretext, in the event that their domestic economic and social policies fail. The 'local bourgeoisie' in turn are accused of using the NIEO as a political 'battering-ram' to penetrate the 'club of the rich'. Soviet specialists describe the NIEO programme as a means for both groups to conclude deals with the 'monopoly bourgeoisie' of the former metropoles. For 'democratic and progressive regimes' it is characterised instead as an instrument for strengthening national independence and creating 'external conditions favourable for progressive internal transformations'.[145] As Soviet economic commitment to such radical 'progressive' regimes diminishes in the 1980s and as the United States persuades more non-aligned states to constrain the public sector of their economies Moscow's merely lukewarm support of the NIEO programme as the economic platform of the Non-Aligned is likely to decline further.

Soviet spokesmen in the mid 1980s were in the vexed position of urging a more global interpretation of international economics on the Non-Aligned out of economic self-interest while remaining uncertain about the political acceptability of views on global economic interdependence. The somewhat contradictory statements of Soviet specialists on this issue have reflected a broader debate in the USSR on global interdependence, which has been expressed more openly under the Gorbachev leadership. One collective work argued bluntly that the NIEO programme of the Non-Aligned Movement is not universal in essence since it requires the reconstruction of international economic relations only in the North–South sector while the problems which demand changes exist also 'in other international trade flows'. This principally concerned '"East–West" trade, where the imperialist countries on their part conduct multilateral political discrimination against the socialist states'. The leaders of the Group of 77 were accused of concentrating 'more on advancing their own demands on the socialist community than on constructive participation in working out measures for the normalisation of trade between East and West' despite the 'correct statements' in their documents on the 'interdependence [*vzaimosvyas'*] of all flows of trade'.[146]

Despite this assessment Soviet analysts have been unhappy about the implications of admitting a structural interdependence of the economies of the West and the South. They have noted that in recent years there has been a stronger emphasis in the documents of the Non-Aligned on the idea of global interdependence in contrast to earlier views on the dependent character of development of the Third World states in the world capitalist economy. However, Soviet specialists currently assert that those in the West and within the Non-Aligned Movement itself who argue that the economies of the West and the developing countries are mutually dependent, that any radical reform of international trade may lead to its disorganisation and harm all the countries participating in it, aim at the gradual removal of the more radical economic demands of the non-aligned countries. In this context Soviet writers have accused the Non-Aligned of having transferred their attention to 'short-term measures' to ease their difficulties in a period when the economic position of the developing countries is deteriorating.[147] They have pointed out that it was the dissatisfaction of the African states – comparatively more deprived and radical over the NIEO – with the UNCTAD discussions which led the heads of state and government of the Organisation of African Unity in the Monrovia Declaration of July 1979 and the Plan of Action approved in April 1980 to specify their own measures towards estabishing a NIEO.[148]

The economic programme adopted at the Delhi Non-Aligned Conference in 1983 was considered by Soviet analysts to indicate a definite turn by the Non-Aligned Movement towards 'reformism' and a more conciliatory approach to transnational corporations. This was blamed on the increased number of non-aligned states following a 'capitalist path of development' and the greater integration of the developing countries over the previous decade into the 'world capitalist economy'. Despite these admissions, leading Soviet specialists on non-alignment rejected the interdependence thesis in 1985 for ignoring the fact that the current economic crisis 'itself developed in the imperialist centres, and the developing countries became its unwilling sacrifices, that if their economies are threatened by disorganisation then this again proceeds from the preservation of the old order in the international capitalist division of labour and not from its breakdown'.[149] This line is clearly open to reformulation in the USSR in the late 1980s. This is indicated by the fact that current Soviet international economic plans in practice accept a more interdependent world and a greater degree of dependence by Third World states on the West as the source of external economic aid.

One form of interdependence has already been warmly approved by Soviet spokesmen. They have maintained that in recent years there has been a noticeable evolution of the Non-Aligned Movement in favour of 'recognition of the organic interdependence of *détente* and development, which was underestimated in the original variant of the NIEO programme'. This is an admission of the strain that existed between the Non-Aligned plans for a NIEO and *détente* in the 1970s. As in this period, Soviet officials remain critical of the fact that Non-Aligned documents in talking of the 'Great Powers' and the 'developed countries of the industrial world' fail to identify the West as the source of threat to peace and stability and consequently to development. The documents of the 1983 Delhi Conference were also criticised for their assertion that the threat to peace stems not only from the intensification of military–political tensions but also from the preservation of the backwardness of the developing countries as a 'possible autonomous cause of global conflict'.

Soviet commentators accept as evident the 'interdependence between overcoming backwardness and strengthening international stability'. However, they are adamant that it would be quite incorrect to consider 'the immediate danger of nuclear war and the possible consequences of failure in resolving the problems of development' as 'sources of equal significance and danger' in their threat to peace. They point out that peace is the primary precondition for the realisation of the ideas of the NIEO.[150] The formula 'at first development then *détente*' advanced by certain non-aligned states and supported by 'bourgeois-liberal circles of the West' is strongly refuted by Soviet analysts. They also criticise the behaviour of a further group of non-aligned states, which tend to be more developed or burdened with a significant foreign debt, whose emphasis is not on the struggle against military dangers and the need to adopt a complex of measures on disarmament but on manoeuvres to maximise their receipt of additional development assistance.[151] All this reveals a conflict of priorities between the USSR and a large number of non-aligned states.

It is true that at the Harare Non-Aligned Summit in 1986 the Non-Aligned as a body accepted that removing the threat of nuclear war constituted 'the most acute and urgent task of the present day' and urged the convention of an International Conference on Disarmament and Development. Pro-Soviet views were also heard before the summit from radical politicians. In an interview for the Soviet press a leading figure in the Zimbabwean ruling party praised Soviet support for a NIEO and argued that 'the Soviet Union's persistent efforts to put an end to the arms race and achieve disarmament...aim at making available huge resources for social and economic development and providing much greater assistance to economically backward countries than is being done at present'.[152] The majority of non-aligned states remain unprepared, however, to suppress their development priorities while the Great Powers deaf to all appeals continue to build up their arsenals. Yet they admitted at the Harare Summit that the prospects for the establishment of a NIEO 'continue to diminish' and that the North–South dialogue is in a 'state of paralysis'. This induces the non-aligned to adopt more pragmatic, piecemeal measures. In an article on the Harare Summit the influential Soviet political commentator A. Bovin noted that the economic declaration of the conference had concentrated on what the participants considered was possible and practically realisable. But he criticised this approach for divorcing economics from politics and 'considerations of principle'.[153] This betrayed Moscow's concern that in place of a commitment to radical long-term international economic objectives, which remain blocked, the non-aligned are succumbing to pressure to adjust further to Western economic strategies.

Moscow is faced with the prospect of the majority of the non-aligned states becoming more entrenched in the capitalist world market and fears that this economic dependence will be translated into new forms of political dependence. In 1984 the authoritative Soviet spokesman on the Third World Karen Brutents argued on these lines that the United States was evidently trying 'to draw the states composing the "centre" of the [Non-Aligned] Movement closer to itself' by 'using the difficult economic position of the developing countries'.[154] At the time of the Harare Summit a Soviet press release deplored the American initiative known as the Baker plan, announced in autumn 1985, which made the position of economic aid to the non-aligned countries conditional upon the latter's consent to curtail the public sector, stimulate an inflow of private investment and liberalise foreign trade. The debtor countries were conceived to be particularly vulnerable to American 'economic blackmail' as a means to divide the Non-Aligned Movement.[155]

Soviet spokesmen will continue to support the overarching concept of a NIEO sponsored by the non-aligned states as part of still more general ambitions towards a 'democratisation of international relations'. The NIEO like 'non-alignment' is a concept which can be used to mobilise the heterogeneous Third World as a whole and coordinate its objectives. It is also in keeping with the notion of an 'international society' which to an increasing extent appears to underlie aspects of Gorbachev's international outlook. In his message to the Non-Aligned conference on South–South cooperation in June 1987, Nikolai Ryzhkov stressed the Soviet Government's conviction that the restructuring of international economic relations on a just and democratic basis and the establishment of a NIEO is 'an urgent and completely feasible matter'. He urged the unity of the efforts of all countries in the 'struggle to guarantee international economic security' and create 'equal and broad economic cooperation among all states regardless of their social structure'. He perceived this as in harmony with the tenets of the economic declaration of the Harare Summit.[156]

There remains, however, a distinct lack of enthusiasm in the Soviet Union for many of the strictly economic aspects of the NIEO as advanced in meetings of the Non-Aligned. In his message to the Non-Aligned in June 1987 Ryzhkov stressed again the interrelationship between disarmament and development. It is very probable that Soviet officials will continue to argue that cooperation to establish a new international economic order should take the form of pooling the efforts of the Soviet bloc and the developing states in the drive to curb the arms race, avert military conflicts and improve the international political climate, with a view to curtailing global military expenditures.

3 Soviet policy and neutralisation in the Third World

The Soviet attitude to neutralisation in the Third World has a direct bearing on Soviet policy. Neutralisation has an established legal pedigree and in contemporary conditions it remains a possible political formula to resolve or dampen down certain regional conflicts or to stabilise regional conditions which otherwise could escalate into a superpower confrontation. In this sense the neutralisation of a distinct country or region would be intended to lead to its withdrawal from the contest of interests between the Great Powers, at least in the military sphere, and would require assurances or guarantees from these powers to this effect. It would require specific restraints on Great Power conduct with respect to the neutralised country or region. Most Third World states would prefer these to be formulated at an international conference with the blessing of the United Nations. From their perspective this would be the most 'democratic' procedure. Neighbouring states and international bodies could also be brought into the settlement which would preferably be enshrined in a treaty.

Alternatively, in a more traditional diplomatic style, a country could be neutralised, preferably with its own consent (if a viable political force which can speak on behalf of the nation or territory concerned can be identified) through arrangements arrived at by the superpowers, perhaps at summit discussions, with or without the involvement of other Great Powers or regionally influential states. This procedure would best suit states torn by civil strife which is fuelled by the support of the superpowers (or China) for rival political or military factions or by the involvement of superpower 'proxy' forces. One Western analyst recently suggested political solutions based on neutralisation on these lines for Afghanistan, Nicaragua and Kampuchea.[1] Naturally such an arrangement would be politically most acceptable to Moscow and Washington where the balance of local forces which bear upon a conflict appear to be stalemated and where the interests of the superpowers are not greatly asymmetrical. American and Soviet leaders might also feel compelled to reach an understanding over a country/territory where the risks of direct military confrontation do not appear worth the pursuit of particular local or regional interests.

The regime established by the neutralisation of an entire region could be based on a framework of obligations undertaken by the Great Powers to desist or refrain from particular forms of military involvement in that region, in particular the maintenance of military bases, facilities and alliance systems. Another requirement could be the removal of nuclear weapons from the specified region – denuclearisation. The process could be halted here or it could be linked to a more comprehensive attempt at demilitarisation. Certain guarantees could also be laid down. This kind of regime involving broad mutual restraints in the military field would be the opposite of a superpower condominium. It would be more attractive and viable in the late twentieth century, therefore, at least from the perspective of the Third World states involved, than the neutralisation regimes imposed on European states such as Switzerland, Belgium and Luxembourg in the last century.

The Soviet and American interest in schemes for regional neutralisation, like their promotion of the neutralisation of disputed states, is likely, however, to depend on an assessment of the regional balance or 'correlation' of political and military forces and interests in each case. This accounted for Washington's disparaging view of various 'zones of peace' advocated by Soviet leaders in the 1950s and 1960s, which were intended for regions where the Western states remained militarily preponderant. During the *détente* years of the 1970s when the USSR appeared as a revisionist power in the Third World its interest in neutralisation slackened. Neutralisation still had conservative connotations; it would encourage the stabilisation of the political status quo in the country or region concerned and impose restraints on the unilateral pursuit of Soviet interests at a time when national liberation movements were achieving success with Soviet assistance.

In contrast the breakdown of *détente* and the new assertiveness characteristic of American policy in the 1980s induced Soviet leaders and foreign policy specialists to adopt a more *realpolitik* appraisal of the international scene. The USSR had acquired substantial assets in the Third World, which for the first time were threatened by a combination of internal rebellion and external pressure. These considerations and the increasing deideologisation of Soviet foreign policy in this decade encouraged Soviet officials to pay greater attention to more status quo oriented categories in their security thinking. One reflection of this shift was a renewed if selective Soviet interest in neutralisation and demilitarisation schemes for Third World regions. At a time of Soviet retrenchment in the Third World such schemes could constrain American attempts to proclaim new Third World regions as zones of vital interest for the United States. However, any arrangements which acted to endorse the Soviet presence in distinct Third World regions were likely to be resisted by the United States. The Reagan Doctrine expressed an American unwillingness to legitimise Soviet interests or involvement in the Third World. The American view of neutralisation in the Third World will continue to determine the efficacy of this concept for the resolution or limitation of conflict as much if not more than the Soviet view.

The Soviet view of neutralisation in the 1970s and 1980s has evolved from the legalistic and Eurocentric notion of neutralisation which Eastern and Western statesmen held in common in earlier decades and sought to apply to particular disputes. The concept of neutralisation has often been used to describe the process establishing the neutrality or even non-alignment of an area through international guarantees or a multilateral treaty. But under international law neutralisation originally referred to a more specific regime and it was in this sense that Soviet international lawyers in the 1950s understood it.

A Soviet legal specialist wrote in 1958, for example, that the neutralisation of a certain territory was formed by an agreement between two or more states not to transform the territory concerned, which was generally of strategic significance, into a theatre of military operations or a base for such operations. The treaty neutralising a given territory would stipulate rights and conditions pertaining to wartime. But in peacetime if the neutralisation were not accompanied by demilitarisation the states signing the treaty would not have any rights and obligations with respect to this territory. The act of neutralisation would not depend on the will of the neutralised state.[2]

Soviet studies underlined that historically neutralised and demilitarised territories had often been created on the basis of unequal treaties and had resulted from the inability of the colonial powers at a given period to agree to the direct partition of a colony. Nevertheless, Soviet specialists accepted that in the past these zones had to a certain extent acted as a means of averting war.[3] But they regarded the simple wartime orientation of the neutralisation regime as insufficient in the post-Second-World-War era.

Soviet spokesmen began instead to identify peacetime benefits from neutralisation, to link this regime more explicitly to that of demilitarisation and the Soviet doctrine of peaceful coexistence, and correspondingly to advocate the creation of broad 'peace zones'.

'In the contemporary period', a Soviet specialist asserted in 1963,

neutralised zones and zones of disarmament, which the socialist states and the neutralist states of Asia and Africa propose in Central Europe, in the region of the Mediterranean Sea, in the region of the Baltic Sea, in the Far East and on the African continent, are one of the means of securing the peaceful coexistence of states with different socio-economic systems.

Such zones were expected also 'to assist the spread of political, economic, scientific, cultural and other contacts' between states.[4] Numerous Soviet proposals for regional disarmament or nuclear-free zones were advanced in the late 1950s and 1960s, although generally these did not envisage the formal neutralisation of the regions concerned.

The Soviet interest in the demilitarisation of Central Europe was expressed in more explicit proposals. In March 1952 Soviet statesmen suggested a unification of Germany in exchange for its non-participation in coalitions or alliances directed against any of the former wartime allies and in 1954 Molotov more clearly presented the idea of neutralising Germany. Instead an agreement on Austria was concluded between the Great Powers in 1955 which provided the best European example of regulated neutrality, of a modern version of neutralisation. However, since Austria voluntarily adopted this status she was not neutralised in the traditional sense.

The Soviet proposal in the early 1960s to turn Berlin into a 'free city' was closer to traditional concepts of neutralisation. According to a Soviet legal specialist this status could be established by international agreements and would require the demilitarisation and neutralisation of the city. Neutralisation in this context was understood as non-participation in military groupings and alliances, and the conduct of a policy based on good-neighbourly relations with all states. But this proposal to transform Berlin into a 'free city' was politically loaded since according to Soviet interpretations it required the agreement of the government of the state on whose territory the free city would be created (the GDR). Such an agreement in the Soviet view would include understandings over granting Berlin communications if necessary with the outside world. The proposed arrangement did not concern Berlin alone since there were Soviet specialists who argued that 'the creation of a neutralised and demilitarised city of West Berlin is estimated by the government of the GDR as the first link in a chain of measures, the sum total of which should lead to a united, democratic, peace-loving Germany'.[5]

In fact the prospects for some form of neutralised Germany, whether divided or united were no longer realistic in the 1960s. Soviet leaders continued to encourage neutralism in West Europe (as a form of dissociation from the military policies of the Western alliance) but their formal proposals suggested the demilitarisation rather than the neutralisation of regions or states on this continent. The two regimes have become difficult to distinguish in Soviet statements. The Soviet Military Encyclopedia in 1978 defined a neutral or neutralised zone as a defined geographical region in which by international agreement (or the unilateral decision of a state to which this region belongs) 'the preparation of military operations' is prohibited, and which 'cannot be used as a theatre of military operations or a base for the conduct of war'. This arrangement could be temporary or permanent. But apart from the Antarctica Treaty of 1959 no examples were provided from the post-Second-World-War years. The authoritative Soviet Diplomatic Dictionary published in 1984 provides no separate entry for neutralisation, but notes that demilitarisation 'is frequently employed jointly with neutralisation' to exclude the use of a territory as a theatre of military operations. Demilitarisation is considered as the 'international legal regime of a distinct territory forbidding its use for military goals in peacetime'. While full demilitarisation prohibits military installations, the maintenance of armed forces, the conduct of manœuvres or undertaking other military activity, partial demilitarisation either forbids a distinct form of armed activity or establishes a limited level of armaments. This source observes that although demilitarisation generally extends over a limited zone with the goal of separating potentially hostile parties it may also cover regions and even continents, such as the Åland and Spitzbergen archipelagos and Antarctica.[6]

If by neutralisation is meant establishing Great Power guarantees for the neutrality of states or regions, then Soviet interest in this process or regime certainly was not confined to Europe in the 1950s and 1960s. Soviet leaders were prepared to confirm the neutrality of Cambodia and Laos in this way. Soviet specialists approved of a statute adopted by Cambodia in 1957 which stipulated that it was a neutral state.[7] At the Belgrade Non-Aligned Summit in 1961 the Cambodian leader Prince Sihanouk proposed the creation of a 'neutralised or buffer zone' in the areas 'most directly exposed to the confrontation of the two blocs', which would require 'persuading the two blocs to admit the usefulness of a chain of countries, whose neutrality they would solemnly recognise and guarantee, in order to eliminate the risk of conflict'.[8] This example of Third World interest in schemes for the neutralisation of regions between the blocs followed on Soviet acknowledgement of the legitimacy of neutrality and the desirability of 'buffer zones' in Central Europe in the 1950s. But Soviet leaders had not yet conceived of extending such formally guaranteed zones, as opposed to the looser idea of 'zones of peace', to Third World regions.

Following the Cambodian example the government of Laos adopted a declaration of neutrality on 9 July 1962. This had a greater impact on Moscow since it was followed by the declaration on the neutrality of Laos on 23 July adopted by the states which participated in the Geneva Conference. In the Soviet view this created obligations to ensure and defend the neutrality of Laos.[9] Soviet legal specialists maintained that the neutralisation of Laos created a code of conduct applicable more broadly to neutralist states (see Chapter 1). The Soviet interest in undermining Western military influence in the Southeast Asian states also ensured a positive Soviet reception for a proposal by Prince Sihanouk at the end of 1962 for an agreement on international guarantees of the neutrality of Cambodia on the model of Laos. Cambodia suggested that an international conference be convened analagous to the Geneva Conference on Laos which would fix Cambodian neutrality in a multilateral treaty and would provide recognition and guarantees for this status from the participants. Moscow characterised the proposal for a neutralisation of Cambodia as 'an important contribution to reducing international tensions and strengthening peace in Southeast Asia'.[10] The USSR and other Eastern bloc states declared their readiness to take part in such a conference on Cambodia but the Western powers opposed the idea. Although Sihanouk had no communist sympathies Soviet leaders were prepared to provide the assurances he needed against the right-wing regimes in South Vietnam and Thailand in the form of multilateral neutrality guarantees. The USA, however, would not respond in kind.

Soviet criticisms of American 'violations' of the neutrality of Laos and Cambodia persisted later in the 1960s. Soviet writers claimed that the Western states were employing a whole range of devices to undermine the neutralism or proclaimed neutrality of the new states. Cambodia was regarded as under pressure from offers of 'assistance', interference in its affairs and the organisation of incidents against its borders. In July 1966 the Soviet Government specifically declared its recognition and respect for the 'independence, neutrality and territorial integrity of Cambodia'.[11] The United States was accused similarly of conducting a subversive policy towards Laos despite the guarantees on the neutrality of this country. The

American struggle against neutralism was presented as one of the objectives behind its involvement in the 'dirty war' in South Vietnam. Soviet spokesmen underlined in this context the proposal by the National Front for the Liberation of Vietnam for the neutralisation of this region.[12]

The neutrality of Cambodia and Laos certainly did not resolve the security problems of these states. It was undermined by civil war and the ensuing involvement of the Great Powers. But Soviet support for the neutralisation of Cambodia and Laos helped to stimulate a regional interest in neutrality in Southeast Asia which was developed by the ASEAN states in the 1970s. It also created a possible precedent for Soviet conduct in other Third World regions. Nevertheless, as the following studies indicate Soviet officials have regarded neutralisation in the Third World as a pragmatic compromise at best. They have viewed the option of neutralisation cautiously, selectively and with an eye to the political and strategic implications of each particular scheme. In those cases when Soviet leaders have favoured neutralisation it has been advanced as part of a broader Soviet strategy of political and military denial to the Western powers.

THE NEUTRALISATION OF SOUTHEAST ASIA

The idea of neutralising Southeast Asia originally developed in Malaysia. It had been raised in international conferences in the late 1960s but was first officially presented by a Malaysian diplomat in April 1970 at the preparatory meeting of the non-aligned states in Dar-es-Salaam. He expressed the Malaysian hope that the non-aligned countries 'will be able to endorse the neutralisation of not only the Indo-China area but of the entire region of Southeast Asia, guaranteed by the three major powers, the People's Republic of China, the Soviet Union and the United States, against any form of extenal interference, threat or pressure'. This appeal was repeated at the Lusaka Non-Aligned Conference in September 1970 by Tun Razak shortly before his appointment as Malaysian Prime Minister. But he specified later that the Five-Power Defence Arrangements, involving Malaysia, Singapore, the United Kingdom, Australia and New Zealand, which had been formalised in London in April 1970 were 'in no way incompatible with our neutralisation proposal or our non-aligned policy' since the Arrangements were intended for current defence needs and were entirely defensive in nature, whereas the neutralisation was a 'long-term solution'.[13]

Malaysia sought support for its initiative in various forums and in

November 1971 succeeded in gaining a cautious endorsement for it from ASEAN in the form of a declaration issued by a meeting of ASEAN foreign ministers in Kuala Lumpur. The so-called ZOPFAN Declaration agreed that the neutralisation of Southeast Asia was a desirable objective and committed Indonesia, the Philippines, Singapore and Thailand to 'exert initially necessary efforts to secure the recognition of, and respect for, Southeast Asia as a Zone of Peace, Freedom and Neutrality, free from any form or manner of interference by outside Powers'.[14]

The initial lukewarm Soviet reaction to the ZOPFAN proposal turned to qualified support within a year. A Soviet official leading an AAPSO mission to Kuala Lumpur in the spring of 1971 affirmed that the USSR welcomed all policies of neutrality and non-alignment if they were 'directed towards all countries'.[15] In November *Pravda* still viewed the ASEAN declaration for neutralisation as denoting a 'far from easy task' since it presupposed an end to US 'aggression' in Indo-China, to China's 'hegemonistic aspirations' and contradictions among Southeast Asian countries, and the removal of foreign military bases and foreign troops from the area.[16] Early in 1972 *Izvestiya* described the position of the ASEAN states in their declaration of the previous April as lacking in 'consequences' and observed that neutralisation was particularly difficult to equate with the Philippine and Thai adherence to Western military blocs. But a few days later the Soviet Government organ admitted that 'possibly neutralisation would be conducive to the creation of a system of collective security in Asia' and that 'the proposal for this system is cherished by all those who seek the normalisation of the situation in Asia'.[17]

This uncertain response stemmed from initial Soviet concern that the ASEAN scheme would tend to counteract or displace Brezhnev's recent appeal for establishing a collective security regime in Asia; the Southeast Asian countries suspected the Soviet plan was intended to draw the Asian countries into a defence system with the USSR directed primarily at China. By mid 1972 Soviet spokesmen adopted a more conciliatory tone. One such writer considered the declaration on the neutrality of Southeast Asia to sound 'in common with the Soviet proposal on setting up collective security in Asia'. He referred to the opinion of the Indonesian Minister of Foreign Affairs, A. Malik, that the ASEAN initiative 'echoes the Soviet proposal of Asian security in many respects'.[18] By September, a few weeks before an official visit to Moscow by the Malaysian Prime Minister, Tun Razak, the Soviet press described the ZOPFAN initiative as 'an idea that cannot be underestimated'. Malaysia was praised for following 'an independent and realistic' foreign policy course, in which the scheme to neutralise Southeast Asia had evoked 'an extensive response the world over'.[19] This raised Malaysian hopes that they could secure formal Soviet approval for the neutralisation idea during Tun Razak's visit to the USSR.

Speaking in Moscow Tun Razak denied that he had arrived to obtain the official approval of the USSR for the neutralisation of Southeast Asia 'because the responsibility for this rests with the countries of Southeast Asia themselves, acting on a collective basis' but he hoped that 'according to the extent of progress of the countries of Southeast Asia on this path towards our goal the Soviet Government will show sympathy and understanding towards us'. He informed Prime Minister Kosygin that the ZOPFAN proposal was 'not directed at anyone and no one is excluded', that its essence lay in the recognition and harmonisation of the legal interests of all the parties in Southeast Asia, of both the countries actually located in the region and of other powers. But in meeting with Kosygin it became clear to Razak that the Soviet Union would prefer its own larger collective security agreement, which would embrace Japan, Pakistan and India as well as the smaller states. Kosygin expressed his understanding of 'the interest of Malaysia in the normalisation of conditions in Southeast Asia' and told Razak that the USSR 'respected many of the considerations contained in this plan'. But he reiterated the Soviet scheme for collective security in Asia and underlined the Soviet readiness to cooperate with all states, including Malaysia, towards its realisation.[20]

The final joint communiqué of Razak's visit to Moscow contained an agreement to differ. While the Soviet side presented views on ensuring security in Asia on a collective basis the Malaysians 'acquainted the Soviet side with the essence of the proposal on the neutralisation of Southeast Asia'.[21] Razak said afterwards that when Soviet officials told him that neutralisation was similar to collective security he replied that 'he appreciated this, but added that Malaysia preferred a neutrality plan which would be applicable to a smaller region such as Southeast Asia'. He was concerned that to include the large Asian countries in such a scheme would introduce problems that the small nations could find difficult to resolve.[22] Razak seemed to accept that the ZOPFAN and the Soviet proposals supplemented each other to some extent. But Soviet leaders were primarily interested in the former as a means to promote the latter among the ASEAN states. They favoured ZOPFAN as the kind of indigenous initiative they had hoped to stimulate under the umbrella notion of collective security, but in the absence of clear agreement in ASEAN over neutralisation they were loath to become committed to a proposal which could be turned against themselves.[23]

As a contemporary writer observed, Moscow had no interest in an ASEAN-sponsored neutralisation that could act as a smokescreen for continued US control and influence or create a vacuum from which the Soviet Union is excluded but China, because of its location and ambitions is not.[24] Yet Soviet diplomats had to consider that should their collective security fail to gain acceptance neutrality would be preferable to them to a series of regional alliances in which the Western powers play even a marginal role. In this respect some form of neutralisation could be 'only the first step toward final acceptance of collective security Soviet style'.[25] The development of neutralist tendencies in Asia, along the lines of Malaysian policy, could act to nullify any defence component of regional organisations such as ASEAN and in the medium term reduce their resistance to the Soviet collective security scheme. This could serve to bolster the Soviet 'containment' of China.

The Chinese were cautious in their initial approach to the ZOPFAN proposal, but by June 1973 a Chinese Foreign Ministry official welcomed it. He considered it in harmony with the Chinese wish to keep Southeast Asia free of interference, to prevent any power from dominating it. During a visit by Razak to Peking in 1974 Chou En-lai appears privately to have 'accepted and supported' neutralisation, 'provided foreign bases...were dismantled in good time'. China may not have been unsympathetic towards the neutralisation of the region, but may have been doubtful about her capacity to act as a guarantor of such a regime.[26] In later years China sought to present her credentials as a regional power and encourage an interpretation of neutralisation which would be directed against the USSR as an external power and would underline the illegitimacy of Soviet support for Vietnamese actions in Indochina. The ZOPFAN idea was also used to promote China's own acceptability in Southeast Asia.

Already by the mid 1970s it appeared, however, that neutralisation under Great Power guarantees as elaborated by Malaysia was acceptable neither to the majority of Southeast Asian states nor to the external powers that count. There was agreement among the ASEAN states on the broad ZOPFAN principles, but they were reluctant to accept the limitations on their actions that being neutralised would entail. The case has been made that neutralisation is potentially attractive only to relatively minor states that by virtue of their strategic position or symbolic political value have become or threaten to become the focal points of contests for control or dominant influence between principal regional or global rivals.[27] Kampuchea and Laos would correspondingly have welcomed Southeast Asian neutralisation in the early 1970s, while Indonesia regarded itself too grand for a neutralised status. Thailand and the Philippines had reservations stemming mainly from the disharmony between the Zone concept and their alliance relationships with the United States. Singapore's doubts with the Zone idea reflected the view that its interests and the interests of Great Power equilibrium would be best served by the involvement of all major powers in the region so as to enhance the prospects for a balance.

Singapore has also been concerned about the role of Vietnam in Southeast Asia. It could be anticipated that a new united Vietnam might regard neutralisation as a useful device to effect the transition from wartime dependence on external allies to a peacetime independent regional or subregional role. But in the long term it could be predicted that Vietnam also would lose interest in a South Asian neutralisation since it was an ascending regional power. A neutralisation would act to perpetuate the balance of forces that formalised the agreement to neutralise, which would not be in the interest of those parties to the agreement who expect to upgrade their relative involvement in the region over their current level. Naturally, this consideration could also apply to China or other Great Powers external to the region whose military or political presence in Southeast Asia appeared likely to increase.

In fact, the failure of the ASEAN countries to issue a neutralisation blueprint in early 1975 resulted from the communist victories in Indo-China, which changed the political and social balance of forces in Southeast Asia. When the heads of government of the five ASEAN countries held their first meeting for eight years in February 1976 in Indo-China they failed to agree on regional security and the communiqué of the meeting did not mention neutralisation. The proclaimed 'non-alignment' of Vietnam, Kampuchea and Laos may have been reassuring to a certain extent to the non-communist five, but neutralisation as a strategic concept had been anchored on the assumption that the Indo-Chinese war would end with the survival of non-communist, neutral regimes in South Vietnam, Kampuchea and Laos and that the overall balance of forces in Southeast Asia would remain decisively in favour of the non-communist states. Nevertheless, in the wake of the retreat of American power and the demise of SEATO neutralisation remained the regional strategic stance of Southeast Asia, if only because it was considered by the region to be the only plausible defence against becoming a Chinese sphere of influence. The Malaysians hoped in particular that, once relations between Hanoi and Bangkok were normalised, the concept of neutralisation would gather new momentum because ASEAN would recognise the importance of detaching

Indo-Chinese communism from the communism of China and the USSR, and of merging it in the mainstream of Southeast Asian nationalism.[28]

Vietnam gave greater emphasis to its regional diplomacy from about mid 1976 after the withdrawal of the United States' military forces from Thailand. A programme to guide Vietnam's foreign policy was announced in March 1976, which included a point similar to the ZOPFAN Declaration on developing cooperation among the countries of the region 'for the cause of independence, peace and genuine neutrality in Southeast Asia'. In July after touring the states of the region Vietnam's Deputy Foreign Minister reportedly said that Hanoi was not interested in joining ASEAN or subscribing to the Zone of Peace proposal 'for the moment'.[29] In his address to the Colombo Non-Aligned Conference Premier Pham Van Dong expressed support for 'the Southeast Asian peoples in their efforts to achieve genuine independence, peace and neutrality'.[30] but Vietnam joined Laos to torpedo Malaysia's attempts to have the conference renew the endorsement of ZOPFAN previously made at the Algiers Summit Conference. Laos was particularly opposed to the terms 'ASEAN proposal' and 'the Kuala Lumpur Declaration' in the draft resolution.[31]

Over the winter of 1977-8 the Vietnamese Foreign Minister, Trinh, visited the region again and raised the idea of a new and broader organisation to that of ASEAN, which would embrace all the countries of Southeast Asia based on the principles of 'peace, independence and neutrality'. In July 1978 Vietnam pressed a proposal on the ASEAN states first made in New York in May of that year for discussions on the concept of a 'zone of peace, independence and genuine neutrality'. The idea was not elaborated and ASEAN leaders showed suspicion about what was meant by 'genuine neutrality'.[32] This suspicion was enhanced by the close links which were developing between Vietnam and the Soviet Union. Indeed, it is precisely this relationship between a Third World 'socialist' state and the USSR which makes an examination of Vietnam's view of a neutral or neutralised zone interesting. This may shed light on Soviet views of such zones. It does appear that the Soviet approach to a neutralisation of Southeast Asia has been strongly influenced by Vietnamese proposals and Vietnamese regional policy. These proposals may illustrate the independent interest of a regionally influential pro-Soviet Third World state in some forms of neutralisation. Alternatively, they could themselves reflect Soviet policy priorities.

In this vein a Soviet commentator maintained that Vietnamese initiatives advanced by Prime Minister Pham Van Dong during talks in the ASEAN countries in autumn 1978 were supported by Soviet diplomacy.

He noted that these talks showed that 'the difference in social systems cannot be an obstacle in establishing in the region a zone of peace, independence, freedom and neutrality, a zone of stability and prosperity'.[33] At approximately the same time the Soviet Deputy Foreign Minister, Nikolay Firyubin, carried out official talks and consultations in three ASEAN states: the Philippines, Indonesia and Thailand. Although he failed to endorse ZOPFAN, from the Soviet perspective this tour 'confirmed once again the Soviet Union's readiness to treat any proposal prompted by the concern for peace and security in Asia with all attention, and to strive to ensure them by joint efforts'.[34] From 1978 Soviet officials began to show greater interest in the Vietnamese concept of a Zone of Neutrality in Southeast Asia despite their former lack of enthusiasm for the ZOPFAN proposal. This change was reflected in Soviet publications.

An authoritative Soviet study on the diplomacy of the developing states, prefaced by Firyubin a couple of years before his ASEAN tour, had arrived at a definition of neutralisation on the basis of declarations by the statesmen of Southeast Asia. Such neutralisation should provide for 'the elimination of military blocs and foreign military bases, the withdrawal of foreign armed forces, the respect for sovereignty and the territorial integrity of the countries of the region, refraining from acts threatening the security of neighbours, the protection of economic interests against the interference of foreign monopolies'.[35] This was the kind of neutralisation which Soviet leaders could find attractive in Third World regions like Southeast Asia where the Western military presence considerably outweighed that of the USSR. But this maximal definition went beyond the framework of the ZOPFAN scheme and assumed an anti-Western colouring in its talk of foreign monopolies.

In the late 1970s Soviet officials did not consider the ZOPFAN plan, however, to be realistic. This was apparent from the views of the head of the Far East section (which covers Southeast Asia and Japan) of the International Department of the Soviet Central Committee, Ivan Kovalenko. He observed initially that there were people 'who believe that a neutral foreign policy would guarantee the security of the Asian peoples, and that it would at first stabilise the situation and then ensure peace and security on the Asian continent'. He accepted the 'desire to remain neutral', interpreted as 'the reluctance of one or other state to participate in military–political blocs set up by the imperialist powers' as a 'favourable phenomenon'. He stated furthermore that 'the Soviet Union supports the aspirations of the Afro-Asian countries to peace and neutrality and views neutrality *in its modern interpretation and in practical policy* as an important factor of peace and international security' (my emphasis). This was an unusually specific Soviet comment in the 1970s on neutrality in the Third World. It implied that the USSR did not favour transplanting the more passive, traditional and legalistic forms of neutrality found in Europe into the Third World.[36]

Kovalenko cast doubts on the ASEAN proposal for a neutral zone since he imagined it 'wrong to think that the ASEAN countries have already managed fully to break away from the influence of the imperialist powers and that they are free to pursue their own foreign policy'. He pointed out that only Indonesia was not 'affiliated with blocs' and had 'no foreign troops and military bases on her territory'. He acknowledged the interest the Zone idea had raised in Southeast Asia, indicated by the fact that 'representatives of the most diverse social groups advance many ideas concerning the organisational forms of translating the idea of neutrality into practice', and by the regular meetings of a special ASEAN committee to formulate recommendations that could form the basis of a plan for neutralising Southeast Asia. But he judged the search for means to ensure security on the basis of neutrality 'in such a complex region as Southeast Asia' as a 'very difficult matter'. Kovalenko concluded that it was 'highly improbable that the five ASEAN countries, which lack adequate political, economic and military strength to force the imperialist powers to withdraw from Southeast Asia and thus make it possible for its people independently to determine their future, will be able to solve this question on their own'. In this sense he presented the Soviet proposal 'that collective security be established on an all-Asia basis' as 'all the more realistic and feasible', since this envisaged 'the participation of all countries of the continent, including socialist and non-aligned'. This larger group would 'have the ability to turn the whole of Asia into a zone of durable peace and universal security'.[37]

This Soviet tendency to downgrade the ZOPFAN scheme for Southeast Asia in favour of their Asian collective security plan was a legacy of the early 1970s. By the end of the decade it was clear that the Soviet initiative would not win the support of the major Asian states. Even India, despite her animosity towards China would not countenance the Soviet plan, and Soviet intervention in Afghanistan dashed all remaining hopes of rallying the Asian states in a broad Soviet-sponsored security arrangement. As tensions increased in Southeast Asia in 1978–9 in response to the Vietnamese occupation of Kampuchea and the confrontation between China and Vietnam Soviet leaders began instead to favour the less ambitious task of drawing conflict-prone Asia in the *détente* process. The indigenous Southeast Asian interest in neutralisation could be incorporated into this process. Thus during a visit to Moscow by the Malaysian Prime Minister, Datuk Hussein Onn, in September 1979 Kosygin expressed support for the ZOPFAN resolution since its implementation 'would establish a precondition for the widening of the process of *détente* over all the Asian continent'.[38]

Two further developments had favoured the Zone of Neutrality scheme. In the opinion of Soviet writers, a decisive influence had been exerted on the process of working out the ASEAN Zone concept by the 'victory of the Peoples of Indo-China' and the consequent 'weakening position of imperialism'. The new socialist regimes in Vietnam and Laos had undermined the military and political pre-eminence of the Western states in Southeast Asia and this counteracted Kovalenko's objections to the ZOPFAN idea, provided that Vietnam and Laos were included within its ambit. The second development was the readoption of the ZOPFAN idea by the Non-Aligned Movement. In the Soviet view 'new aspects in the idea of neutralisation' of Southeast Asia involved an emphasis on its 'full conformity with the policy of non-alignment and the decisions of corresponding conferences on this problem'.[39] These two developments were fused in the actions of the Non-Aligned as a group and Vietnam separately towards a settlement of the tensions and hostilities in Indo-China.

The foreign ministers of the three Indo-Chinese regimes met on 5 January 1980 just before a visit to Hanoi by the Malaysian Foreign Minister. The foreign ministers, naturally under dominant Vietnamese influence, met to discuss the establishment of 'a region of peace, independence, freedom, neutrality, stability and prosperity', and they issued their first joint communiqué since 1975. This copied Soviet descriptions of Vietnam's Zone proposal in 1978, but in 1980 the proposal was specifically concerned with the crisis in Indo-China. In the wake of the entry of Soviet troops into Afghanistan, Vietnam's first priority in Southeast Asia was to legitimise its role in Kampuchea and normalise its relations with the ASEAN states to offset renewed pressures as a result of the new hostility to the Soviet Union in international forums. The Indo-Chinese ministers warned the ASEAN states that they would do well to accept the reality of Indo-China and offered to sign non-aggression treaties with them on a bilateral basis.[40]

In 1981 the three Indo-Chinese regimes presented a joint initiative aimed at normalising conditions in Southeast Asia and creating a zone of peace, stability and good neighbourliness. The Soviet Union considered the essence of their proposals as an attempt to resolve the problems and differences in relations between the ASEAN and Indo-Chinese states 'by means of a direct dialogue between them and without any outside interference'.[41] This was supported by the Political Declaration of the Conference of Non-Aligned Foreign Ministers in February 1981, which called for a dialogue between the Southeast Asian states to resolve their differences and eliminate the involvement and threats of intervention by outside powers. The Non-Aligned also approved 'the efforts being made for the early establishment of a zone of peace, freedom and neutrality in the region' and called on all states to support these efforts.[42] Contemporary Soviet commentators were reticent on this reference to the Zone but they praised the Non-Aligned for condemning the attempts of 'external forces...to aggravate tensions in the region and set one group of countries against the other' and for stressing the need for 'a comprehensive political solution of the problems of the present tensions in Southeast Asia'.[43]

The Soviet priority had become the stabilisation of the Indo-Chinese regimes under Vietnamese control. The establishment of a 'zone of peace and stability' in Southeast Asia was promoted in the 1980s as a means towards this end, as a diplomatic device to legitimise these regimes. The Zone plan supported by Vietnam and the USSR would incorporate the Indo-Chinese states. It would require direct negotiations between the ASEAN and Indo-Chinese states towards a resolution of the Kampuchean problem and the provision of guarantees against further external (interpreted as Thai and by extension American) attempts to unseat the Vietnamese-installed regime in Kampuchea.

Soviet and Vietnamese officials could not, however, simply replace the ZOPFAN proposal with one of their own since the Third World confirmed its support for a zone of peace, freedom and neutrality at the Delhi and Harare Non-Aligned Summits in 1983 and 1986. Soviet writers tended to stress rather that, although this was not specified in the ZOPFAN declaration, it was clear from its 'context' that 'the zone of peace, freedom and neutrality should be extended to all the states of Southeast Asia and not only to the members of ASEAN'.[44] They claimed that the ASEAN states which initiated the Zone plan intended it also to embrace other states located in the region. Moreover, since the early 1980s they have tended to gloss over the 'neutrality' component of this plan.

The Soviet Union has failed to win ASEAN or general Third World support for the broader Zone concept. The Vietnamese occupation of Kampuchea has been the primary stumbling block. By the mid 1980s Soviet writers were stating bluntly that 'the real way towards the adoption of true security measures' in Southeast Asia requires 'setting into motion equal cooperation between the ASEAN countries and Indo-China, without which the existence of any viable regional system of security is inconceivable'. They decried the fact that the Non-Aligned Movement in its approach to the creation of a zone of peace in Southeast Asia 'is very one-sidedly oriented to the initiative of the ASEAN member states'. They blamed this on those circles who obstructed 'the restoration of the legal rights of the Peoples' Republic of Kampuchea as a participant of the Movement' and therefore an 'objective approach' to the 'zone of peace'. The Non-Aligned were urged to adopt a 'constructive role' in creating this zone. This required in particular a 'correction' of the word 'neutrality' appearing in the ASEAN proposal, which was deemed incompatible with the goals and principles of the Non-Aligned.[45]

The current Soviet aversion to the 'neutrality' component of the formula for a zone of peace in Southeast Asia follows the development of Vietnamese opposition to this aspect of the Zone scheme. Since the beginning of the 1980s Vietnam has considered that its future policy in relation to the Zone idea would merely be a continuation of its course as a 'non-aligned' state. Kampuchea, under the Vietnamese-installed regime, is also presented as a non-aligned state. Since Vietnam and Kampuchea are heavily dependent politically and militarily on external sponsors such a concept of 'non-alignment' involves a very different emphasis to that of neutrality or neutralisation. Soviet specialists argue that the Vietnamese believe that the insistence on neutralisation in the ASEAN Zone proposal is intended to isolate Vietnam, since it could not obtain sufficient guarantees against being isolated as a participant in a neutral zone. This can be understood to mean that Vietnam is not prepared to renounce or emperil her close ties with the Soviet Union. Soviet specialists also maintain that neutrality or neutralisation would anyway be a regression for a 'socialist' state such as Vietnam.[46]

The Soviet Union and Vietnam oppose the idea of a separate neutralisation of Kampuchea on similar grounds. In September 1979 the Vietnamese Prime Minister Van Dong told the participants of the Havana Conference that 'the victory of the Kampuchean people' (Vietnamese occupation) had created the conditions 'for the construction of a peaceful, independent, neutral and non-aligned Kampuchea'.[47] But Kampuchea failed to acquire this status. A Soviet initiative issued on 21 February 1981 called for an international conference on Kampuchea, including the permanent members of the United Nations Security Council, which would be held after ASEAN and Indo-China signed non-aggression pacts.[48]

ASEAN rejected the 1981 Soviet *démarche*, which was directed at ASEAN acceptance of the Heng Samrin regime in Kampuchea, despite the call in the same month by the Twenty-Sixth Soviet Party Congress for Asian participation in the settlement of regional disputes.

The ASEAN states presented their own plan in summer 1981 at the United Nations Conference on Cambodia convened at their instance. It envisaged the disarming of all the Kampuchean factions and the creation of a neutral interim administration to organise free elections. But it was opposed by Beijing since it required the Pol Pot group supported by China to lay down its arms.[49] An alternative proposal presented by the Indonesian Foreign Minister to his hosts during a visit to Moscow in April 1984 went to the heart of the matter in suggesting a phased withdrawal of Vietnamese troops from Kampuchea and the establishment of a neutral Kampuchea acceptable to the Great Powers including the Soviet Union. Moscow did not change its standard position; it merely repeated its willingness to guarantee any agreement concluded between ASEAN and Indo-China alongside the other members of the UN Security Council.[50]

In May 1984 and in March 1985 Sihanouk called for a neutralised Kampuchea with an international peacekeeping force guaranteed by the superpowers, ASEAN, Vietnam or Australia/New Zealand. China was conspicuously omitted from this scheme since it had already rejected it.[51] Soviet leaders regarded this as an attempt to displace their initiative of February 1981. Sihanouk's plan was unacceptable to Soviet leaders anyway since like the proposal for a neutralisation of contemporary Afghanistan it would emperil the retention of the socialist structure of government in the neutralised state. From the Soviet perspective a socialist government in Kampuchea has remained a *sine qua non* of any settlement of the Kampuchean issue, although Soviet resolve on this issue may weaken in the face of the current ASEAN commitment to a neutral Kampuchea (see below).

Soviet officials can not countenance any neutralisation of Indo-China. But since the Vietnamese Zone of Peace and Stability has won little support they have been reluctant to reject out of hand the ZOPFAN proposal if this eventually could provide the basis of a long-term settlement of the disputes between Indo-China and the ASEAN states and encourage a military disengagement of the ASEAN states from the West. In 1983 a Soviet writer listed the basic features of the ZOPFAN neutralisation idea on the basis of his reading of the documents and declarations of ASEAN statesmen. These included recognition and respect for the zone of peace, freedom and neutrality by all states, in particular the Great Powers;

abstention by the ASEAN states from participation in conflicts between the Great Powers; guarantees for the zone from the Great Powers – the United States, the USSR and China; securing the legal rights of Great Powers in the region; and observance of the obligation of the peaceful settlement of all disputed questions between the states participating in the zone. The author noted that the zone should be extended to all the states of Southeast Asia and raised the question of its full demilitarisation. But he noted that there had been great differences over the issue of securing international guarantees for the zone, and concluded that the practical realisation of the zone idea was a long-term task.[52]

A recent specialist Soviet study on Southeast Asia argued that the term 'neutralisation' as distinct from the related terms 'neutrality' and 'neutralism' contained the idea of activity over a more or less defined period of time; it implied a process of gradual and progressive development. In his view neutralisation as a concept concerned not only the attainment of the final goal but also the path towards it. He identified the 'main positive significance of the concept of creating a zone of peace, freedom and neutrality', despite 'its contradictions determined by the social-class nature of its ideologues', in the gradual advance towards the accepted goal and in the realisation of the principle of peaceful coexistence which corresponds to it.[53] This emphasis on neutralisation as a process is intended to keep the notion alive as a long-term objective for Southeast Asia.

In the short term Soviet spokesmen need not feel that general support for the Zone idea will harm Soviet–Vietnamese relations or act to isolate Vietnam. Despite the Soviet interpretation cited above, the ZOPFAN proposals still have not been defined with any precision by the ASEAN states and the mechanism by which they would limit Great Power involvement in Southeast Asia remains vague. Malaysia continues in general to place most emphasis on the scheme despite its continued participation in the Five-Power Defence Arrangements; Singapore and Malaysia retain New Zealand and Australian air and army bases. Thailand and the Philippines remain reluctant to abrogate their formal security alliances with the United States in current conditions of regional instability. The United States still has two of its largest overseas air and naval bases in the Philippines, and the Pentagon decided recently to establish an arms stockpile in Thailand. Nevertheless, the concept of a zone of peace continues to represent a potential significant area of shared interest between the ASEAN states and Vietnam and this ensures that it will remain on the agenda for both parties although the terminology they use and the objectives they pursue may differ.

The emphasis will be less on the mechanics of neutralisation and more on the means to exclude certain forms of involvement in Southeast Asia by outside powers. One possibility lies in the proposal for a nuclear-free zone in Southeast Asia, which has been promoted in particular by Indonesia and Malaysia. Speaking before the ASEAN standing committee in September 1984, the Malaysian Foreign Minister declared that it would be a mistake to wait for a solution to the Kampuchean problem before making attempts to implement the idea of the zone of peace, freedom and neutrality. In his view it was high time ASEAN made a serious study of proclaiming Southeast Asia a nuclear-free zone as a first step towards implementing the zone concept. A Soviet writer regarded this as evidence of 'positive elements' in Malaysian foreign policy.[54] In contrast, before meeting ASEAN leaders in June 1986 the American Secretary of State, Shultz, stressed the need to maintain a balance of power against Soviet might and asserted that he could see no reason for a partial or regional ban on nuclear weapons.[55]

The nuclear-free zone proposal was reportedly in the annual ASEAN discussions in 1986, and Soviet spokesmen underlined press reports at the close of the following annual ASEAN Conference in June 1987 that specific plans were being worked out to set up such a zone which would be examined at a summit level meeting of the ASEAN states in Manila in December. The Soviet media noted that this meeting would also raise the issue of American military bases in the Philippines 'where it is supposed the Pentagon has already been able to site nuclear weapons secretly'. According to Soviet commentaries the United States' commitment to these bases underlay its warnings to the ASEAN countries against pursuing the idea of a nuclear-free zone in Southeast Asia.[56] The USSR perceived the zone proposal alternatively as directed against the creation of a nuclear weapons stockpile in Thailand. It is not surprising that Moscow has pronounced its strong support for a nuclear-free Southeast Asia. This new, specific ASEAN zone concept is also supported by Vietnam, Kampuchea and Laos, and the 'convergence of views' of the Southeast Asian states on this issue has inspired Soviet hopes that 'the existing positive process' in favour of the zone 'can be further developed'.[57]

The emphasis on the exclusion of outside powers from Southeast Asia could also be linked to the search for a comprehensive political settlement of the Kampuchean dispute, which would enmesh Indo-China into the arrangement reached. This has become more of a priority under the Gorbachev leadership since the Kampuchean conflict continues to obstruct a normalisation of Sino-Soviet relations, a process which otherwise could be expected. But Moscow remains unwilling to depart from the Vietnamese conception of a settlement. Hanoi's view was outlined recently by Foreign Minister Co Thach in March 1987 at a dinner to mark the close of an Asian tour by his Soviet counterpart Eduard Shevardnadze. He expressed his intention to seek talks with both China and ASEAN on a political solution to the war in Kampuchea through establishing a zone of peace, stability and friendly cooperation in Southeast Asia.[58] When General Secretary Nguyen Van Linh visited Moscow a couple of months later Gorbachev praised Indo-Chinese efforts to create such a zone.[59] This reaffirmation of Hanoi's scheme was given despite the lobbying of the Thai Foreign Minister, Sitthi Sawtsila, who visited Moscow on behalf of ASEAN a week prior to Nguyen Van Linh.

Soviet Foreign Minister Shevardnadze showed that the USSR had not forgotten the ZOPFAN impulse in informing Sitthi that 'there can be no calm or stability in a region in which there exist foreign military bases and which is not protected from the military rivalry of non-regional powers'. But Sitthi had a more specific brief. He expressed his conviction that the USSR could play a leading role in the resolution of the Kampuchean conflict. This settlement should entail 'an early withdrawal of foreign troops from Kampuchea, the exercise of the fundamental right of the Kampuchean people to self-determination and the emergence of an independent and neutral Kampuchea which poses no threat to her neighbours'. Sitthi explained that the ASEAN countries had instructed him to communicate these principles for a settlement to the Soviet leadership. But Shevardnadze failed to endorse this neutral formula for Kampuchea for fear of straining Soviet–Vietnamese relations. Moreover he had doubts about the Soviet ability to press a settlement upon a reluctant Vietnam. He merely reaffirmed Soviet readiness 'within its capabilities and together with other states, including the countries of ASEAN and Indo-China' to promote a settlement of the situation relating to Kampuchea and to guarantee 'generally acceptable accords' with other permanent members of the UN Security Council.[60]

In the late 1980s the ZOPFAN notion appears to have turned into a more abstract ambition for the ASEAN states, into a long-term goal. In current conditions it is likely to be displaced by the search for arrangements to resolve the immediate destabilising conflict around Kampuchea. This is the priority for ASEAN, Vietnam and the Soviet Union. But the process of negotiation over the conflict around Kampuchea will keep the broader notion of neutralisation on the Southeast Asian agenda. The ASEAN states are committed to a limited neutralisation of Kampuchea. The Soviet Union may eventually accept a loosely formulated neutralisation of this country if Vietnam proves tractable. In this sense parallels may develop between the regional negotiation processes over the Kampuchean and Afghan conflicts.

THE NEUTRALISATION OF THE PERSIAN GULF AND THE MEDITERRANEAN SEA

In the 1980s Soviet leaders have proposed the neutralisation or demilitarisation of two specific regions involving Third World states: the Persian Gulf and the Mediterranean Sea. As observed in the previous chapter, Moscow also set on record its continued interest in the demilitarisation of the Indian Ocean although this scheme had lost momentum by the turn of the decade. In 1982 the Soviet Third World specialist Primakov asserted that 'an understanding on the military neutralisation of a number of regions where an accumulation of armed forces and armaments is taking place would be of great significance'. He specified such regions as the Indian Ocean, the Persian Gulf and the Mediterranean Sea.[61] The Soviet initiatives on the Gulf and the Mediterranean are the best statements of what neutralisation on Soviet terms implies for Third World regions, although the Mediterranean proposal was intended also to include European states. In both cases they were related to earlier initiatives by the non-aligned states. The Persian Gulf proposals were an outgrowth of the sponsorship of a zone of peace in the Indian Ocean by the Non-Aligned, while the Mediterranean proposals were similar to ideas developed by the Mediterranean non-aligned states.

The Soviet leadership chose an official visit by Brezhnev to New Delhi in December 1980 to proclaim a set of principles to neutralise and demilitarise the Persian Gulf. This venue enabled Brezhnev more effectively to link his proposals on resolving tensions in the Gulf and containing the Gulf War with the Indian interest in the Indian Ocean zone of peace idea. During Brezhnev's discussions with Indira Gandhi both leaders condemned the buildup of military activity in the Indian Ocean and the Persian Gulf and spoke in favour of dismantling all foreign military bases in the former region.[62] In an address to the Indian Parliament on 10 December Brezhnev went further. He accused 'powers which are situated many thousands of kilometres from this region' of having 'concentrated a naval armada' in the Persian Gulf and Indian Ocean and of 'intensively building up armaments, expanding the network of their military bases and pressuring

147

and threatening small countries that do not follow their lead'. He rejected attempts to justify these actions 'with talk about the "Soviet threat" to that region's oil wealth' and underlined that 'we are not indifferent to what takes place in this region, which is so close to our borders'.

Brezhnev went on to propose a 'doctrine of peace and security' with respect to the Persian Gulf countries which would require the United States, the other Western powers, China, Japan and 'all states showing an interest' to reach an agreement on a number of mutual commitments. These were specified as follows:

- not to create foreign military bases in the Persian Gulf or on adjacent islands; not to deploy nuclear weapons of mass destruction there;
- not to use force or threaten the use of force against the Persian Gulf countries, and not to interfere in their internal affairs;
- to respect the non-aligned status chosen by the Persian Gulf countries; not to draw them into military groupings to which nuclear powers are party;
- to respect the sovereign right of the states of this region to their natural resources; and
- not to create any obstacles or threats to normal trade and the use of the sea lanes linking the states of this region with other countries of the world.

In Brezhnev's opinion an accord of this kind involving the states of the region as 'full-fledged parties', would act as a 'reliable guarantee' of their security.[63]

The individual principles in Brezhnev's five-point doctrine were familiar to numerous Soviet proclamations on Third World regions. Several of them had already been contained in a draft proosal in 1957 on the principles to determine Great Power conduct on questions of peace and security in the Near and Middle East.[64] Nor did they differ essentially from the principles contained in Brezhnev's 1969 proposal on Asian collective security. But it was the first time these five principles had been drawn together and proclaimed specifically for the Gulf. Brezhnev's proposal could be viewed as an East–West non-aggression pact for the region in the form of a partial neutralisation and demilitarisation of the Gulf, which would also indirectly guarantee the Gulf's oil links with the West. The region's arms purchases and commercial links with the Western states, Japan and the Soviet Union would not be affected. Brezhnev's plan did not preclude regional defence agreements among the Gulf states. Nor did it necessarily require the Great Powers to act as the guarantors of the regime established.

148

Soviet spokesmen expected the Third World states to form a strong constituency of support for Brezhnev's plan and they chose their arguments accordingly. One commentator explained that this plan would enable the Persian Gulf states 'to choose their foreign policy course and the means of resolving their internal problems in conformity with their needs and traditions, free of all outside pressures'. The plan envisaged 'the equal participation of these states in all agreements relating to the Persian Gulf'.[65] The Soviet proposal was presented as a means to ease tension not only in the Persian Gulf 'but also as a result of that in a much bigger area where militaristic actions aimed at the Gulf region have already increased tension', especially in the Horn of Africa. Moscow described the new Soviet initiative as 'fully in line' with the position of the Organisation of African Unity.[66]

Soviet officials hoped to tap the broad Third World commitment to the Indian Ocean zone of peace scheme. Brezhnev's proposals for the Gulf were characterised as an 'extension of the conditions which the Soviet Union set earlier on the normalisation of conditions in the basin of the Indian Ocean, on transforming it into a zone of peace'. For states located in the Indian Ocean the Gulf plan would open out 'new perspectives, strengthening their independence, safeguarding them against involvement in the arms race'.[67] At the conclusion of his speech in New Delhi on 10 December Brezhnev had called for understanding and support for his initiative in India. It is plausible that on one level this new *démarche* was directed at Indian reservations about Soviet intervention in Afghanistan and the intensified tensions which ensued in the Indian Ocean. Brezhnev's scheme for the Persian Gulf may have been intended to reassure India of the Soviet desire for peace in India's vicinity.

The primary object of Brezhnev's speech remained the United States and other Western states rather than India. Moscow may have been concerned in particular about the global and regional repercussions of a prolonged Iran–Iraq war and the opportunities this provided the West. Brezhnev had expressed unease in Delhi that 'foreign military penetration' in the Middle East was intensifying in the wake of this conflict. A Soviet commentator explained that the Soviet programme unveiled at Delhi would provide 'reliable guarantees of the legitimate interests, and only the legitimate interests of all countries, including the industrial capitalist countries'.[68] Soviet leaders were prepared to enter a broad-ranging understanding with the West over the Gulf, which would recognise Soviet interests in a region close to Soviet borders and of equal importance would help preclude an expansion of unilaterally proclaimed American interests in this volatile area. This reflected a Soviet awareness that a fundamental strategic reappraisal of this part of the globe was underway in the United States.

In his memoirs President Carter's National Security Adviser, Zbigniew Brzezinski, relates that he had urged Carter already in February 1979 to abandon earlier plans to demilitarise the Indian Ocean and to adopt a new 'security framework' to reassert American power and influence in the region. By June 1979 Brzezinski was arguing in favour of American military preponderance in the Indian Ocean–Persian Gulf region. On 23 January 1980 Carter finally committed the United States to the security of the Persian Gulf region by proclaiming that: 'any attempt by any outside force to gain control of the Persian Gulf will be regarded as an assault on the vital interests of the United States of America and such an assault will be repelled by any means necessary, including military force.' Brzezinski considered the President's words to represent 'a formal recognition of a centrally important reality: that America's security had become inter-dependent with the security of three central and interrelated strategic zones consisting of Western Europe, the Far East and the Middle East–Persian Gulf area'.[69]

The combination of the 'Carter Doctrine', the outbreak of the Iran–Iraq war and the proclaimed American intention to establish a rapid deployment force for the Middle East added appreciably to the dangers of a superpower confrontation in the Persian Gulf. On the day Brezhnev issued his proposals for this region in Delhi a Soviet statement condemned a speech by Brzezinski for setting forth 'a large-scale programme for the further buildup of the US military presence in the Persian Gulf'. Moscow claimed that Brzezinksi was planning a new military bloc in the region based on his proposed 'structure of regional security' composed of conservative regimes in the Near and Middle East. Under these conditions Moscow predicted that 'the Washington strategists are not going to respect the non-aligned status of the Persian Gulf states'. The American administration was accused of 'striving to draw those countries into a military grouping with the United States, which is a nuclear power, with little consideration for the threat this represents to the security of the Persian Gulf countries, to stability and peace in the region'.[70] If these were genuine Soviet apprehensions Brezhnev's proposal to neutralise the Persian Gulf can be understood as a crisis prevention regime on Soviet terms.

Some weeks after Brezhnev's initiative a Soviet statement quite explicitly linked it with the new American 'arc of crisis' strategy. 'The Transatlantic strategists', it was claimed, 'do not conceal the fact that from a military point of view their aim is to create in the Persian Gulf a third centre – in addition to Western Europe and the Far East – of military might outside the USA and covered by an atomic umbrella.' This meant from the Soviet perspective that 'large-scale military manœuvres are being carried out near the Soviet borders, and the threat of a still greater proliferation of nuclear weapons and of expansion of the zone of confrontation arises'. The USSR correspondingly 'counterposed to that dangerous game an extensive programme of neutralisation and demilitarisation of the Persian Gulf area'. This neutralisation regime was intended to meet the interests of both the oil-producing and the oil-consuming countries, 'the interests of ensuring security and tranquillity in such a sensitive part of the world'.[71]

These Soviet statements imply that the neutralisation scheme for the Gulf was largely a defensive reaction to newly perceived insecurities issuing from the volatile region to the south of the Soviet borders. Soviet leaders wished to contain local conflicts in the Gulf and Middle East to their region of origin and avoid the risk of escalation towards a nuclear threshold. They sought to define the limits of permissible conduct in an area where calculated ambiguity in policy carried too high risks. But since the political and military access of the Soviet Union to the core Gulf states remained limited, the implementation of Brezhnev's proposals would have had clearly asymmetric strategic consequences for the Great Powers, to the detriment of the West. Any arrangement for the Persian Gulf involving superpower guarantees would also legitimise a Soviet involvement in this region, a development which American officials have remained loath to accept. These considerations ensured that the Soviet plan would be rejected by the West, a rejection confirmed once the new American administration under Reagan was installed on 20 January. They also underlay the scepticism of other states such as Japan over such a neutralisation.

The Soviet media explained Washington's rejection of Brezhnev's proposals as a reflection of its intention 'to continue to maintain its strategic military presence in and around the Gulf'. This was manifested in the development of bases in the Indian Ocean and the Gulf region and the creation of new ones.[72] Western, in particular American, statesmen were not prepared to forgo the strategic benefits derived from bases and military facilities in the Gulf region while the Soviet Union retained a military presence in the peripheral countries of South Yemen (PDRY), Ethiopia and Afghanistan. Western strategists maintained that the proposal not to deploy nuclear weapons in the Persian Gulf would leave it under the umbrella of Soviet nuclear weapons deployed in the Soviet

Union. Brezhnev's third proposal would require the Americans to renounce plans to sign bilateral security agreements with the Gulf states. This again was unacceptable to the Western states since they were aware that the Soviet Union had little chance anyway of concluding such agreements. The USSR had signed a Friendship and Cooperation Treaty with Iraq in 1972. But the security provisions of this treaty had been translated into little more than cautious Soviet–Iraqi arms deals. Although the USSR established diplomatic relations with Oman and the UAE in autumn 1985, only Kuwait of the Gulf Cooperation Council states had an ambassador in Moscow in the early 1980s. A Western specialist concluded that Brezhnev's 1980 proposals 'were a call for America to abandon the region, leaving the Soviet Union victorious in the field'.[73]

The Soviet neutralisation plan for the Persian Gulf may have been intended to open up a strategic dialogue on a broad front to enable Soviet diplomats to introduce Western military preponderance in the Gulf region tacitly or explicitly into the negotiation process for the limitation of Soviet military influence in other regions. This could apply specifically to negotiations on the proposed withdrawal of Soviet troops from Afghanistan. The Western states had already linked Soviet intervention in Afghanistan with Soviet intentions towards the oil wealth of the Persian Gulf countries. In his speech before the Indian Parliament in December 1980 Brezhnev denied that the Soviet Union posed a threat to the Gulf. Soviet leaders proposed sureties for Western interests in Gulf oil and by 1981 expressed their readiness 'to take part in a settlement of the situation around Afghanistan...linked with matters of Persian Gulf security'.[74] It became the standard Soviet line that an arrangement on the Gulf could be discussed 'in connection with questions linked with Afghanistan'.[75]

The new Soviet-dominated Afghan regime also linked its predicament with Persian Gulf security. In a statement on 14 May 1980 the DRA Government asserted that it was necessary 'in the process of a political settlement [around Afghanistan] to take into account the military–political activity in the region of the Indian Ocean and the Persian Gulf on the part of states not belonging to this region'.[76] DRA officials strongly supported Brezhnev's Gulf initiative. At the Delhi meeting of the Foreign Ministers of the Non-Aligned in February 1981 Foreign Minister Dost declared that these 'realistic peace proposals concerning the demilitarisation of the Persian Gulf...deserve the greatest attention and thorough examination'. However, he refrained on this occasion from explicitly linking them to the situation around Afghanistan.[77]

Brezhnev's initiative for the Persian Gulf in all probability was also linked to the broader stalemated negotiations over the demilitarisation of the Indian Ocean. The Soviet media drew a connection between these two regions when elaborating the Gulf proposal. Directly after Brezhnev outlined this proposal in Delhi he reiterated the Soviet readiness 'to work actively with other interested states' to transform the Indian Ocean into a zone of peace. In this context a Soviet writer observed with chagrin that the United States administration, in calling into question the right-of the USSR to take part in measures to guarantee the freedom of navigation in the Persian Gulf in the aftermath of Brezhnev's initiative, had forgotten that America had for many years carried out negotiations with the USSR over the Indian Ocean, 'of which the Persian Gulf is a component part'.[78]

This link between the Indian Ocean and Persian Gulf regions has been a consistent theme in Soviet statements. More recently in May 1987 the Soviet Deputy Minister of Foreign Affairs V. F. Petrovskiy held talks with the leaders of Iraq, Kuwait, the UAE and Oman during a tour of the Gulf. He subsequently claimed that the Soviet Union had received great support during these meetings for its readiness to take part 'in multilateral talks among all states which use the waters of the Indian Ocean with a view to formulating guarantees of the safety of maritime lines of communication, including the Persian Gulf and the Strait of Hormuz, as well as guarantees of the littoral states' sovereignty over their natural resources'. The Soviet Government still promotes the convention of an international conference on the Indian Ocean in this context.[79] The contemporary Soviet emphasis, therefore, is on more pragmatic, piecemeal negotiations on the Gulf and Indian Ocean which address the immediate dangers which the increased naval presence of the superpowers in this region entail.

Brezhnev's neutralisation scheme for the Gulf in 1980 may have had an additional, more specific objective. It could have been intended to foment differences between the Western powers over the American intention to set up Rapid Deployment Forces in the Middle East, and over the suggestion that the area of responsibility for NATO be extended outside Europe. This is apparent from a Soviet broadcast a couple of days after Brezhnev's Delhi speech. The commentator claimed that 'most British papers agree that the Soviet peace plan...deserves due consideration'. He expressed disquiet, however, over strong British government support for the 'Carter Doctrine under which any part of the world can be proclaimed a sphere of vital American interests' including 'the oil-rich Persian Gulf region'. This was indicated by the dispatch of British warships to the region, the construction of a major base on Diego Garcia, and the desire of the British cabinet 'to set up its own rapid deployment corps, which will be used to support the convenient regimes in that region and suppress the national liberation movements there'. The Soviet broadcaster underlined that the most recent session of the NATO committee of military planning had decided on 'an expansion of military activities outside Europe'. In his view it was 'in this general context that one has to consider the latest proposals advanced by the Soviet President'.[80]

The Soviet initiative on the Gulf may also have been conceived as an inducement for the key countries of the Persian Gulf and the Arab world to take measures to limit Western military involvement in the region. A Soviet commentator anticipated that Brezhnev's 'positive programme' could 'only find the widest echo in the Arab world, especially in the Gulf'.[81] Soviet sources referred to a Kuwaiti Minister of State who 'called on all Gulf countries to support the Soviet proposal', to Syrian official circles where 'the Soviet proposals were received with satisfaction', and to the approval of the head of state and government of the PDRY for 'the constructive Soviet initiative'. According to Soviet claims the Brezhnev plan was also directed at Egypt's intention to establish its own rapid deployment force with American and Israeli assistance to be deployed against Libya.[82] Libya did not regard this claim as fully convincing. The Libyan leader, Gaddafi, expressed his support for Soviet proposals to safeguard international peace during a visit to Moscow in April 1981. But instead of openly endorsing Brezhnev's initiative he called for 'more details of the ways to neutralise the Arabian Gulf and keep it out of international conflict'.[83]

Soviet leaders anticipated that the Brezhnev plan could stimulate interest among certain key Red Sea states for their own 'zone of peace' aimed at excluding the Western military presence. The USSR and South Yemen (PDRY) examined the situation in the Persian Gulf during a visit by the PDRY leader to Moscow in May 1980. In their joint communiqué the two states 'spoke out resolutely against the creation of military–political blocs and military bases in the region' and expressed themselves 'in favour of making the Red Sea region a zone of peace'.[84] Ethiopia's concern over Western bases in Somalia ensured its support for this scheme. By 1984 North Yemen (YAR) was also in agreement with the USSR on the need to preserve the Red Sea region as a 'zone of peace'.[85] Soviet leaders could not realistically anticipate a broader endorsement of this idea from Red Sea littoral states. Many Third World states regarded it as a blatantly unbalanced proposal since it did not include an offer by Soviet leaders to close down their military and naval facilities in South Yemen and Ethiopia.

Soviet officials were gratified by the reaction of the radical Arab states to their plan for the Persian Gulf but they could anticipate a less forthcoming response from the conservative Gulf states. Indeed Saudi Arabia openly opposed Brezhnev's proposals; the Saudis apparently wished to retain the option of an American presence in the Gulf. The UAE were also critical of the Soviet plan, while a Foreign Ministry spokesman for Oman rejected it outright. Muscat described it as 'interference' in the internal affairs of the Gulf states and portrayed the Soviet invasion of Afghanistan as a demonstration of Moscow's hostile intentions toward the area. Oman has also complained about the presence of Soviet naval vessels and aircraft in the vicinity of the Straits of Hormuz.[86]

The Soviet plan was received more favourably in Kuwait. It had been a deeply held tenet of Kuwaiti foreign policy that the military presence of one superpower in the Gulf will lead to the presence of the other as well, which could threaten a conflict between them injurous to all the Gulf states. Soviet naval forces have been present in the Gulf but they have by no means matched the American military presence in the form of a small naval force permanently stationed there and facilities in Oman and sometimes Bahrain. Kuwait had been particularly concerned about the plans for an American Rapid Deployment Force.[87] When Kuwait's Foreign Minister visited Moscow in April 1981 he found 'positive points' in Brezhnev's proposal 'to remove foreign military forces from the Gulf region and to neutralise the region'. But even he objected to the idea of a security arrangement imposed by foreign powers.[88] Moscow could also expect Iraqi interest in Brezhnev's initiative since Baghdad had floated a 'Pan-Arab Charter' early in 1980, which *inter alia* had asserted the need to keep the Gulf free from all superpower bases.

The attitude of Iran to the Soviet plan was crucial. Soviet Persian language broadcasts described the Soviet Gulf plan as aimed at the defence of the Persian Gulf countries against any foreign intervention and at securing the self-determination of the regional nations, including Iran. Revolutionary Iran responded with the familiar accusation that the superpowers were uniting at the expense of Iran to secure their own interests. The Soviet media observed with chagrin that the official spokesman of the Iranian government referred to 'completely false facts' and 'assessed the Soviet proposals on the Persian Gulf negatively'.[89]

These negative or unenthusiastic reactions from the primary Gulf states showed that the prospects for involving them in the proposed neutralised area were poor. However, since Brezhnev's proposals for the Gulf were linked to the broader issue of the Indian Ocean 'zone of peace' Soviet officials still made an effort to gain support for them from the Indian Ocean Third World states and the non-aligned nations in general. Soviet writers contended that the Gulf initiative had been 'positively appraised by the statesmen of the series of countries of the region of the Indian Ocean as corresponding to the vitally important interests of the developing and non-aligned states'. They referred to the opinion of the Indian Foreign Minister that 'the Soviet initiative deserved the most fixed and serious attention'.[90] Soviet officials also expected positive references to Brezhnev's Persian Gulf plan at the meeting of the non-aligned states in Delhi in February 1981. The Soviet media linked the concern of the conference delegates over international tension in the 'Arab Gulf and the Arabian Peninsula' to ostensible American plans to set up a new military alliance in the Red Sea area.[91] Soviet writers claimed that the Non-Aligned 'displayed significant interest' at Delhi in the Soviet scheme for the Gulf.[92]

In reality the non-aligned states could not agree on any formula endorsing the Soviet proposals to neutralise the Persian Gulf since the primary Gulf states remained opposed to any security arrangement imposed by foreign powers. The Arab Gulf states were already working towards a mutual security arrangement to pool the forces indigenous to the area against internal and regional threats. This was eventually formalised in February 1981 in the form of the Gulf Cooperation Council (GCC), a body which was regarded initially with deep suspicion by Soviet officials (see Chapter 4). The GCC was not originally intended as a military security organisation but it created the framework for non-bloc security cooperation which in principle meant rejecting both Western offers of military protection and the Soviet scheme for an international conference to transform the Gulf into a neutral zone. In July 1981 the Secretary-General of the GCC specified that 'the neutrality of the Gulf cannot be separated from the neutrality of the adjacent areas – the Arabian Sea, the Indian Ocean and the Red Sea'. In his view 'it would be futile to neutralise the Gulf while Soviet troops are in Afghanistan and Soviet naval forces cruise the Indian Ocean or maintain facilities in various Red Sea and Arabian Sea ports'.[93] This broader regional or extra-regional appraisal of the Soviet military presence underlies the consistent opposition of the Western powers and the core Gulf states to any renewed Soviet proposals for a neutralisation of the Persian Gulf.

In these circumstances the Soviet Union has pressed more recently for a more limited regime for the Gulf involving restrictions on the naval presence of the Great Powers in the region. A Soviet Government statement on 3 July 1987 suggested that 'all warships not situated in the region be shortly withdrawn from the Gulf and that Iran and Iraq in their turn should keep from actions that would threaten international shipping'.[94] This proposal addressed the contemporary American naval buildup in the Gulf region to protect Kuwaiti oil tankers placed under the American flag. In fact a more limited regime of this kind has been on the Soviet agenda for the Mediterranean for many years.

Soviet intiatives for the Mediterranean in the guise of denuclearisation or the creation of zones of peace date back at least to the Soviet 'Draft Declaration on Non-Intervention in the Middle East' presented in February 1957. Since the Soviet Union had no forces in the region, or only token forces in the 1950s and 1960s it is likely that Soviet leaders did not expect the Western allies to take these early proposals altogether seriously. As in the case of Soviet proposals for zones of peace elsewhere they contributed, however, to the creation of inhospitable local conditions for the Western military presence and formed part of the Soviet policy of military denial. In June 1971 Brezhnev called for mutual naval withdrawals by the Great Powers and he mentioned the Mediterranean Sea and the Indian Ocean specifically as regions of interest. Soviet diplomats had already sounded this issue out earlier in the year. This proposal received greater attention in the West. The Mediterranean was no longer so necessary for Western strategic submarine deployments while the Soviet military presence in the region had grown substantially. Some believed indeed that the original intention of Soviet Mediterranean deployments had been to induce a negotiated withdrawal of the United States' Sixth Fleet.[95]

A Western specialist suggested a regime for the Mediterranean in 1973 which would involve restrictions on naval vessel deployments, the elimination of naval bases and facilities belonging to or operated by the signatories on the territory of littoral states and constraints on the land-based forces of the superpowers in the area. He noted that this would reduce the risk of accidental or inadvertent conflict between the superpowers, aid the depolarisation of regional conflicts, and raise both states in the eyes of the non-aligned nations. But he noted that the USSR would probably evaluate the military concessions granted by the United States as a result of such disengagement as greater than those conceded on their own part. While the United States would yield a constant strategic threat to the Soviet homeland the USSR would yield only a first strike threat to the American fleet. The United States would reduce its ability to impose pressure close to Soviet borders while the USSR would renounce rights far from American shores. Moreover, the United States would be withdrawing a force with stated missions in support of NATO ground forces while the Soviet fleet had only a derivative role in defending the Warsaw Pact. Nevertheless, such an agreement on the Mediterranean would involve risks for the USSR. For example, if the treaty breaks down and the Soviet Navy wishes to return to the Mediterranean rapidly it would have to bypass potentially hostile chokepoints at both ends of the Mediterranean. In addition, the terms of the treaty would probably enable the Mediterranean to be dominated militarily by American forces based in Europe or by allies of the United States.[96] This equation of costs and benefits also applies to more recent Soviet proposals for the demilitarisation or neutralisation of the Mediterranean.

No progress was achieved on a superpower military and naval regime for the Mediterranean in the 1970s. However, since the 1976 Colombo Conference the non-aligned states issued numerous appeals to transform the region into a zone of peace and cooperation. When the foreign ministers of the Non-Aligned met in 1981 they deplored the buildup of foreign arms and military forces in the area. They resolved that the idea of a European conference on disarmament should take into account the Mediterranean dimension and should involve 'concrete measures which will lead not only to confidence building but also to the initiation of steps to lessen forces in the region'.[97] The Mediterranean non-aligned states held their first regional conference in Malta in 1984 (see Chapter 2). Malta had proclaimed itself a neutral state with a policy strictly founded on principles of non-alignment in 1981. At the Delhi summit in 1983 the non-aligned states described the recognition of this status by Mediterranean and other states and their undertakings not to jeopardise it 'as an effective means of lessening tension and strengthening security in the Mediterranean, which could be further extended in future'.[98] This fell short of an appeal for the Mediterranean states to follow Malta's example, which would have implied a neutralisation of the Mediterranean. But the non-aligned states remain interested in a demilitarisation of the Mediterranean. Malta endorsed a series of proposals in this field in the 1980s, which originated in the Soviet Union. This reflected the successful Soviet cultivation of this small state and it helped the Soviet Union legitimise a number of its cherished initiatives for the Mediterranean.

In October 1981 when the USSR recognised Malta's new international status the two states agreed on a series of measures to reduce tensions in the Mediterranean. Both states were in favour of an international conference to extend confidence-building measures to cover the region and an agreement to reduce armed forces in the region. They proposed the withdrawal of ships carrying nuclear arms from the Mediterranean and called for all countries to abstain from deploying such weapons in the territories of non-nuclear Mediterranean countries. They also professed themselves in favour of the nuclear powers assuming a commitment not to use nuclear weapons against any Mediterranean country that does not permit them to be stationed on its territory.[99] In the early 1980s Soviet leaders repeated this call for a nuclear neutralisation of the Mediterranean, for the creation of a nuclear-free zone in this region, on a number of occasions. But Western statesmen would not countenance the Soviet proposals since their implementation would require the withdrawal of the primary nuclear strategic asset of the West in the Mediterranean, the American Sixth Fleet, with no equivalent strategic loss to the USSR.

Early in 1986 the strategic sensitivity of the Mediterranean region was brought into sharper focus in East–West exchanges. In March Spain voted to remain within NATO, which confirmed the status of the Mediterranean as a 'NATO lake'. Later in the month American aircraft carrier groups operating off the Libyan coast clashed militarily with Libya. This highlighted Soviet naval facilities in Libya and Syria. Against this background the Soviet leader Gorbachev chose a visit to Moscow by the Algerian President to seize the diplomatic initiative by calling for superpower talks on the nuclear and naval demilitarisaiton of the Mediterranean Sea, for the transformation of this region in a military sense into a neutral zone for the naval forces of external powers.

In his speech on 26 March Gorbachev reiterated the Soviet proposals for the Mediterranean which had been issued previously following discussions with Malta. He then conceded that 'in principle there is no need for the Soviet Union to have its fleet in the Mediterranean on a permanent basis'. He argued that the USSR 'has to keep its ships there permanently for this sole reason: the US Sixth Fleet, armed with nuclear missiles and threatening the security of the USSR, its allies and friends, is in the immediate proximity of our borders'. Gorbachev proposed that 'if the USA, which is situated thousands upon thousands of miles from the Mediterranean, withdrew its fleet from there, the Soviet Union would simultaneously do the same'. He stated that the Soviet Union was prepared to enter into talks on the issue without delay. According to Gorbachev's proposal 'at this first stage' there would be no restrictions imposed on the 'naval activities and naval arms of the coastal Mediterranean states themselves'. Further steps to strengthen security in the region could, in his opinion, be determined by taking into account Soviet proposals on the abolition of weapons of mass destruction. Finally, Gorbachev proposed the convention of a broad conference on the Mediterranean, similar to the

CSCE, which could be attended by the Mediterranean states, 'the states adjoining the region', the United States and 'other interested countries'.[100]

As in the case of the Soviet intiative to neutralise the Persian Gulf this Soviet proposal for the Mediterranean was justified by a stated need to remove a strategic threat to the southern borders of the USSR. But the implementation of both proposals would require the United States to renounce established military and naval capabilities and forgo a future expansion of these capabilities. The Soviet Union in comparison would suffer no equivalent military loss. The American Sixth Fleet is more powerful than Soviet naval groupings in the Mediterranean and as previously observed it fulfils a strategic role which is denied the Soviet navy in this region. Soviet leaders could count on the support of most states in the region for a general demilitarisation and limitation of superpower military presence in the Mediterranean. But such support was qualified since there remained ambiguity over whether the Black Sea and Soviet naval forces in those waters should be included within the ambit of the Soviet proposal for the Mediterranean.

It is likely that Gorbachev's Mediterranean initiative was not intended for serious negotiation. Senior American officials were quick to dismiss it as propaganda which would not even warrant a formal reply since it had been issued through. Tass.[101] A briefing by spokesman for the Soviet Foreign Ministry on the Algerian President's visit to Moscow repeated Gorbachev's proposals 'aimed at turning the Mediterranean into a zone of stable peace and cooperation' but failed to elaborate them.[102] The Soviet media was no more forthcoming. Indeed it made very few references to the Mediterranean initiative unlike the heavy coverage of the Soviet scheme to neutralise the Persian Gulf.

The bombing of Libya by the United States followed soon after Gorbachev's offer for the removal of the Sixth Fleet. The American administration also began to impose pressure on Syria – a state which had concluded a friendship and cooperation treaty with the USSR. These events showed that the danger of superpower confrontation in the Mediterranean was far from illusory. Since the early 1970s Soviet leaders had placed greater emphasis on the role of the Soviet navy as an instrument to deter Western intervention in the affairs of non-aligned and pro-Soviet countries. Of course it could be argued that the unhindered American action against Libya indicated the ineffectiveness of this role and reinforced the benefits perceived by the USSR and the Non-Aligned in an agreement on superpower naval and military withdrawal from the Mediterranean. However, given the clearly expressed strategic interests of the United States in the region it is probable that the latest Soviet 'neutralisation' proposal was not a serious attempt to bring the Western states to the negotiating table. Its primary function was to generate goodwill among the Mediterranean non-aligned states for Soviet policies and to encourage these countries in their search for effective measures for the demilitarisation of the Mediterranean region.

THE NEUTRALISATION OF AFGHANISTAN

If Third World states and the Soviet bloc promoted their ideas on the neutralisation of countries or territories in the Third World through their respective plans for Southeast Asia and the Persian Gulf, then the Western powers indicated the conditions under which they believed neutralisation was most appropriate in the Third World when they proposed the neutralisation of Afghanistan at the beginning of the 1980s. An examination of Soviet attitudes to Western schemes to neutralise Afghanistan in the wake of Soviet military intervention in that country is particularly revealing since such Soviet attitudes are sharply at variance with those expressed in connection with the Soviet-sponsored Persian Gulf plan. Soviet leaders have not accepted that the essence of the Brezhnev initiative for the Gulf could be applied to the different strategic and military environment in which Afghanistan lies. This is the more paradoxical as Soviet leaders have expressed their readiness since the Twenty-Sixth Soviet Party Congress in February 1981 to discuss issues linked with the international aspects of the Afghan problem in connection with questions on the security of the Persian Gulf.[103]

Afghanistan has had a long history of neutrality and non-alignment which Soviet leaders have assiduously fostered. A treaty of neutrality and non-aggression was concluded between the young Soviet state and Afghanistan on 31 August 1926. It bound the parties to observe neutrality in the event of war between one of them and a third state and to refrain from any kind of aggression against each other. This treaty was enlarged and extended on 24 June 1931 and it was given material expression in Afghan neutrality during the Second World War. According to Soviet legal specialists in the 1950s and 1960s the conditions of this treaty determined the peacetime foreign policy of Afghanistan, 'which in essence differs in no way from a policy of non-alignment'. They regarded it as necessary for Afghanistan to conduct a strictly neutral policy requiring non-participation in blocs and refusal to permit foreign military bases on its territory. Soviet writers acknowledged, however, that the

1931 treaty only bound Afghanistan contractually to pursue such a policy in relation to the Soviet Union. Afghanistan did not have a comparable legal obligation to third states predetermining its conduct in peacetime or war.[104] In addition, there existed no third party guarantors of Afghanistan's neutrality or non-alignment. This meant that Afghanistan was not covered by a multilateral neutralisation regime.

Soviet spokesmen accepted that Afghanistan need not be neutral in relation to third countries engaged in a war which did not involve the Soviet Union as a party. But they sought to argue that Kabul had an obligation to Moscow to pursue a policy of non-alignment in peacetime. The ambiguity in Soviet interpretations of the 1931 treaty partly derived from Article 6 which permitted both parties full freedom of action to establish any relations and alliances with third parties provided that such links do not contradict the other provisions of the treaty.[105] Soviet–Afghan communiqués in the 1960s referred to Afghanistan's 'policy of non-alignment and neutrality'. Protocols prolonging the 1931 treaty for ten-year periods were concluded by Soviet and Afghan leaders in December 1955 and August 1965.[106] The Afghan President Mohammed Daoud described the most recent adoption of such a protocol in December 1975 as indicating the 'vitality' of the 1931 document which remained 'the stable basis of friendship and fruitful cooperation' between the neighbour states.[107] The 1931 treaty is automatically prolonged from year to year and each party has the right to terminate it after six months' notification. The treaty appears to remain valid although no official protocol to extend it was adopted in 1985. It has been referred to only rarely in official Soviet and Afghan statements in the 1980s since the Soviet–Afghan Friendship and Cooperation Treaty of December 1978 has replaced it as the contractual charter determining the relations between the two states. After the coup by the Marxist PDPA in Kabul in April 1978 Soviet officials grew reluctant to acknowledge Afghanistan's legal status of neutrality in relation to the USSR. They regarded the political category of neutrality similarly as inappropriate for a 'socialist-oriented' country.

Afghan neutrality was openly discounted in Moscow following the entry of Soviet troops into Afghanistan at the end of 1979. In April 1980, for example, Andrei Gromyko noted that the word 'neutral' was sometimes used in relation to resolving the question of Afghanistan. In his view 'to be accurate one must say "non-aligned" state' since 'both we and the Afghan leadership proceed from the premise that Afghanistan should be a non-aligned state'.[108] In the 1980s Soviet and DRA leaders have persistently claimed that Afghanistan remains non-aligned whatever its bilateral links with the Soviet Union (and this is meant to imply more than just membership in the Non-Aligned Movement). In February 1980 the Afghan Foreign Minister argued that 'the presence of foreign troops in a country, especially when it is requested by that country, is basically not against the principles of non-alignment'.[109] Such Soviet and DRA claims that Afghanistan can meaningfully still be described as non-aligned have been ridiculed by Western statesmen. Various proposals have been made aimed at creating a legal framework to enable Afghanistan to revert essentially to its pre-1978 international status. These proposals have generally assumed the need for international guarantees of this status. But Moscow has consistently disparaged any initiatives for the formal neutralisation of the country.

When the Soviet Union intervened militarily in Afghanistan the British Foreign Secretary, Lord Carrington, rapidly proposed a plan for Afghanistan which was approved by the Council of Ministers of the EEC and adopted as a joint EEC declaration on 15 January 1980. This plan provided for the withdrawal of Soviet troops in exchange for 'guarantees of the neutrality' of Afghanistan by the Great Powers and its neighbours and the creation of peace-keeping forces. At a conference of the Foreign Ministers of the EEC states in Rome the following month Carrington made a general proposal for the conclusion of an international treaty guaranteeing Afghanistan's status as a 'neutral' state, which in his view would provide the Soviet Union the possibility of withdrawing its troops on a legal basis in light of the United Nations' resolution on this issue. This idea was acknowledged in a declaration of the European Council on 30 June 1981 and subsequently adopted at an EEC conference in Luxembourg.

The reaction of the new Afghan regime to the West European initiative was unequivocally negative. A discussion of this initiative was undoubtedly on the agenda of Soviet–DRA talks when the DRA Foreign Minister, Dost, visited Moscow in mid March 1980. Dost accused the 'imperialists' of concocting 'various "plans" with respect to Afghanistan, such as its "neutralisation"', and promised to administer a firm counter-blow to 'this outside interference'.[110] During this visit Gromyko defined the 'political solution' preferred by Moscow as one that would not 'affect the state sovereignty of Afghanistan or ignore its lawful government'. In the Chinese opinion this amounted to 'telling those advocates of neutrality for Afghanistan that any political solution must conform to the Soviet condition of recognising the accomplished facts of the Soviet military invasion and the "legitimacy" of the Karmal regime'. The Chinese echoed Western views that the USSR had 'in effect turned down the proposal of some Western countries for the neutralisation of Afghanistan'.[111]

The Soviet–DRA rejection of neutrality for Afghanistan was confirmed by the Afghan leader Babrak Karmal in an appearance on Afghan television on 21 March. He roundly condemned the Carrington Plan and stressed that a full and unconditional end to 'foreign interference and aggression' against Afghanistan was a precondition to the withdrawal of Soviet troops. In an interview for *L'Humanité* published on 5 April Karmal rejected 'any plan aimed at the adoption of decisions in our stead', including efforts 'to bind us to a so-called "neutralisation", which represents in fact only one of the forms of neo-colonialism'.[112] Soviet articles during spring 1980 confirmed Karmal's views. One Soviet journal questioned why people 'in certain Atlantic capitals...want to fasten the word "neutrality" to Afghanistan's non-aligned policy' and concluded that 'the "neutralisation" label conceals a course aimed at the elimination not only of the government now in power but also of the very system established by the April [1978] revolution'. The 'authors of the "neutralisation" idea' were accused of trying to decide the Afghan people's fate for them 'without asking the government of that country what its position is and what it thinks on this score'. A normalisation of the situation in Afghanistan, according to this Soviet report, would require the United States and 'those acting in concert with it' to ensure the 'complete cessation of outside interference in the affairs of Afghanistan and, together with that country's neighbours, effectively guarantee that such interference will not be resumed'.[113] This proposal for foreign guarantees against external interference in Afghanistan was intended to strengthen the current regime in that state by sealing off the contesting forces in Afghanistan from Western and Pakistani 'assistance' while legitimising the continuation of Soviet 'assistance'. It had nothing in common, therefore, with the much publicised Western idea of imposing a form of neutrality on Afghanistan.

In an attempt to maintain pressure on Soviet leaders Carrington explained his proposal to neutralise Afghanistan to President Ceausescu during an official visit to Romania in mid March 1980. Romania had not in fact recorded a vote on the crucial resolution on 14 January in the United Nations' General Assembly on the withdrawal of foreign forces from Afghanistan. Soviet leaders were concerned lest this Warsaw Pact state sanction the neutralisation of a state which had a socialist-inclined regime and was upheld by Soviet troops. The Soviet media did not openly rebuke Ceausescu for his reception of Carrington. But they argued on the basis of British press reports that despite the considerable identity of views of the participants to the talks 'the Romanian leaders do not wish to be involved in any Western plan for the establishment of a "neutral" Afghanistan'.[114]

An additional source of pressure on the USSR was its southern neighbour Iran. After discussions with the Soviet Ambassador to Iran in March the Iranian Minister of Foreign Affairs, Ghotbzadeh, made a statement on the organisation of multilateral negotiations on Afghanistan, which aroused a strong Soviet protest. Soviet sources charged that Ghotbzadeh had made 'the totally unsupported claim that he had obtained Soviet concurrence in his proposal' and had maintained that 'an understanding had allegedly been reached between Iran and the Soviet Union on some kind of principles for a settlement in Afghanistan, including the imposition of "neutrality" on that country'. The Soviet press stressed that during the Soviet–Iranian talks 'no agreement resembling what the Iranian Minister is now saying was or could have been reached'.[115] This was probably true. It was a priority for Soviet leaders to limit the damage their intervention in Afghanistan had wrought on Soviet–Iranian relations. But they would not countenance the replacement of the pro-Soviet Marxist regime in Afghanistan by a regime that proclaimed itself 'neither East nor West' in a fashion similar to the Iranian theocracy.

Soviet officials believed that an EEC-style neutralisation formula would anyway be unaccepatable to the 'counter-revolutionaries'. A Soviet writer pointed out that this was the reaction of even a figure such as Sayyid Gailani, the head of the National Front for the Islamic Revolution, who was far more cosmopolitan than other resistance leaders and recognised the necessity of coexistence with the USSR.[116] Gailani reputedly stated in an interview in March 1980 that 'as regards the West European initiative we support that part which provides for a withdrawal of Soviet troops' but 'we do not agree with the proposed neutrality of Afghanistan because it is imposed from outside'.[117] The impracticability of gaining the acceptance of the fractious Afghan groups opposing the DRA regime for a compromise formula based on the neutrality of Afghanistan certainly further discouraged Soviet leaders from taking proposals of this kind seriously. Apart from this consideration, Soviet spokesmen implied that there was little difference between Gailani's stand and the essence of the Carrington Plan: both were directed at a thorough recomposition of the Marxist DRA government.

One Soviet writer argued in this vein that the EEC proposal was not directed at the neutralisation of Afghanistan at all but at hiding the 'undeclared war against the Afghan people'. 'The formal words about the necessity of the "neutrality" of Afghanistan contained in the Carrington Plan' were described as 'no more than a screen for the creation of conditions in which it would be possible to achieve a restoration of the regime overthrown by the Afghan people'. Afghanistan, it was argued, was anyway actively conducting a policy of 'positive neutrality' among the g.)up of non-aligned countries, which was fixed in the 'Basic Principles' of the DRA.[118] Afghan non-alignment remained unimpaired in Soviet eyes. Soviet officials failed to respond, therefore, to Western attempts in 1980 to broaden support for the idea of creating a 'neutral and non-aligned Afghanistan' by enlisting the ASEAN states behind the proposal.

The framework of the Soviet-sponsored settlement of the 'situation around Afghanistan' was enshrined in a political programme advanced by the DRA government on 14 May 1980. This established that a political settlement had to precede agreements between the Soviet and DRA governments on the withdrawal of Soviet troops from Afghanistan. The non-renewal of 'intervention' against Afghanistan also had to be reliable and guaranteed.[119] For Soviet officials such international guarantees should become a component part of a political settlement. Soviet writers raised the idea that the guarantor countries, which should include the USSR, the United States, and other states acceptable to both Afghanistan and its neighbours which were negotiating with the former, could adopt an obligation to observe the sovereignty, independence, territorial integrity and non-aligned status of Afghanistan. The DRA in turn would 'confirm its adherance to a policy of peace and non-alignment, its desire to develop friendly relations with all countries, in the first place its neighbours'. The DRA was not expected to object to 'a discussion of issues connected with the working out of international guarantees', which would be initiated simultaneously and proceed parallel to bilateral or trilateral negotiations between Afghanistan, Pakistan and Iran.[120] This Soviet–DRA scheme for guarantees of non-intervention in and the non-alignment of Afghanistan sounded like a form of neutralisation of that country on Soviet terms. In fact it was intended to legitimise the incumbent DRA regime whose genuine political non-alignment was not credible in the West and many Third World states. Such non-alignment was far from the EEC proposals on Afghan neutrality.

On 30 June 1981 an EEC declaration formally approved the Carrington Plan. Its essence lay in a proposal to create an international conference to resolve the Afghan problem by political means. At the first stage this presumed the participation of the permanent members of the UN Security Council, Pakistan, India, the General Secretary of the UN and the Organisation of the Islamic Conference or their representatives. Certain 'representatives of the Afghan people' would be admitted only at the second stage of the conference and they would need to accept the decisions of the conference. At this stage the future status of Afghanistan as an independent state would be discussed. In particular, guarantees would be provided for the non-alignment of the country.

Both the American Secretary of State, Alexander Haig, and the Pakistani Foreign Minister, Agha Shahi, welcomed the EEC initiative. But the Ambassador of the DRA to the Soviet Union, Habib Mangal, in reply to questions on the EEC initiative on 1 July underlined that his government did not accept 'any policy, any manœuvres, any political subterfuges aimed at making the prob.em of Afghanistan international'. In his view the events in Afghanistan were 'entirely our internal affair, that can be resolved by our people under the guidance of our party'.[121] A Soviet statement three days later made it 'absolutely clear' that the proposal of the EEC states 'cannot serve as a basis for talks and no-one intends to hold such talks with them'.[122] In the Soviet view 'any proposal excluding the principal party, the DRA government, from the search for a solution to the problem cannot provide a foundation for any serious agreement and is quite unrealistic'.[123] This line was confirmed by Gromyko in a meeting with Habib on 10 July[124] and echoed by the DRA Foreign Minister, Mohammad Dost, a couple of weeks later. Dost stressed that 'so far the Government of the DRA has not received from the EEC or from any other organ any proposal in connection with the so-called "conference on Afghanistan"'.[125]

The uncompromising Soviet attitude on the question of the representation of the DRA regime in negotiations on Afghanistan predetermined the outcome of an attempt by Carrington to convince Soviet leaders of the merits of the EEC plan during a visit to Moscow in early July. After Carrington's visit the prominent Soviet commentator Alexander Bovin set down two further Soviet objections to the plan. He maintained that 'the composition of the conference [on Afghanistan] arouses doubt since most of the proposed participants are clearly hostile to the present government'. He also found it unacceptable that 'although this has not been set down in black and white, the West is clearly inclined to have the conference discuss the regime existing in Afghanistan, and the character of Soviet–Afghan relations'. Bovin believed that in place of such a conference 'Afghanistan should conduct direct negotiations with its neighbours, above all with Iran and Pakistan'.[126] Soviet leaders had been prepared to consider international arrangements and guarantees only on the external aspects of the Afghan problem. They were not prepared to subject Soviet–DRA relations and the legitimacy of the DRA regime, which they defined as an internal matter, to international scrutiny. They realised that they would be diplomatically isolated on these issues in any representative convention of the Great Powers and regional Third World states.

After a meeting of the leading Western industrial states in Ottawa approved the EEC initiative on Afghanistan the Soviet press described the idea that the DRA requires some kind of 'neutralisation' as 'blasphemous'.[127] This hardening Soviet response ensured that further diplomatic activity by Britain on behalf of the EEC plan, such as during a visit by Prime Minister Thatcher to Pakistan in October 1981, made no progress. The prospects of multilateral talks on Afghanistan including the Great Powers became dim. Soviet officials in fact had expressed their suspicion all along, however, that the EEC scheme for Afghanistan had a strong propaganda function. Soon after the EEC had adopted the plan a Soviet statement anticipated that this 'patently unrealistic "initiative"' would be used 'to launch another round of propaganda attacks on the USSR' by Westerners who simultaneously strike 'a pose of peacemaker and champion of a settlement'.[128] Soviet writers subsequently argued that the EEC policy on the Afghan issue, coordinated in the neutralisation plan, 'served as an additional factor strengthening the inconsistency of the policy of Pakistan in the "Afghan question" and, consequently, postponing the prospects of a real settlement of the situation around Afghanistan'.[129] It is likely that Soviet leaders regarded the EEC plan as a frustrating obstacle to negotiations on their own terms. They were unprepared to accept the structure of the initial conference proposed since it excluded and therefore tended to outlaw further the DRA regime. Still less acceptable was the idea of introducing Afghan 'representatives' at the second stage of the conference since this would act to legitimise the resistance groups within Afghanistan.

Soviet leaders may have been more amenable to a plan for negotiations on Afghanistan developed in France, which did not incorporate the neutralisation element of the EEC scheme. In January 1981 the French President, Giscard d'Estaing, proposed the creation of a 'conference on non-interference in Afghanistan'. Besides the permanent members of the UN Security Council he proposed to invite to the conference Iran, India and representatives of the Islamic community. He did not envisage the participation of representatives of the Afghan government in such a conference, which he emphasised would be devoted not to the status of Afghanistan but to 'terminating interference in Afghanistan' as a condition for restoring its character as a non-aligned state. Since France did not receive any substantial support for this scheme it did not try to propose it on behalf of the EEC. In autumn 1981 France associated itself instead with the EEC initiative on the neutralisation of Afghanistan. Soviet reports on the French idea were factual rather than critical.[130]

Alternative plans to neutralise Afghanistan surfaced in the early 1980s in the West and the Third World among academics and diplomats. One of the least realistic was an Iranian proposal, the implementation of which would in all likelihood have turned Afghanistan into a pro-Iranian Islamic state distanced from both East and West. In October 1981 Iranian leaders suggested the creation of 'peace-keeping forces' recruited from the armed forces of Pakistan, Iran and a third Islamic country, the construction of a 'Constituent Council' formed of representatives of 'responsible and militant clergy' of the Islamic world, and general elections in Afghanistan. Iran wished all this to come under quadripartite negotiations between Iran, Pakistan, the Afghan *mujahidin* and the USSR. Soviet officials were relieved when the Iranian government replaced this extremist plan in July 1982 with the view that a settlement of the situation around Afghanistan should be based on 'the principles of Islam and non-alignment'.[131]

In winter 1980–81 a Western specialist on South Asia, Selig Harrison, suggested that a formula involving the emergence of a provisional government in Afghanistan might win Soviet acceptance if could provide for arrangements under which Moscow could withdraw from that country in a phased fashion over several years and if the new Afghan government could return to the pre-1973 Soviet-tilted brand of neutralism. He envisaged a regional security arrangement with firm guarantees of a timetable for Soviet force withdrawals from Afghanistan and of the functions of residual Soviet forces in this country. Harrison argued that an enduring Afghan settlement would have to be accompanied by parallel understandings between the United States, the USSR and China designed to neutralise Pakistan and Iran as arenas of Great Power conflict, which would rule out military alliances and special military relationships.[132] A former Indian Foreign Secretary, J. S. Mehta, supported this contention in an article in 1982. He argued that 'the Kremlin's attitude toward withdrawal from Afghanistan will depend on whether Pakistan becomes a heavily armed, pro-Western ally or a neutral state between the superpowers'.[133]

Both Mehta and Harrison referred to the historical example of Soviet troop withdrawals from Finland (the Porkkala base), and to the security pledges that Finland gave the Soviet Union. In their view this Soviet withdrawal, and the policy of 'Finlandisation' which Finland ostensibly embarked on, had been enabled by Sweden's decision to remain neutral after the war. In light of this, Mehta proposed a series of diplomatic steps intended to create an outer belt of neutrality as a precondition for the 'Finlandisation' of Afghanistan. Like Harrison, he expected that an earlier form of Afghan neutralism could still be resuscitated. He believed that Soviet leaders in retrospect probably recognised that a genuinely non-aligned Afghanistan pursuing non-radical policies was a better guardian of Soviet security interests.

Mehta proposed initially the convention of a regional conference of countries 'closely affected by the present situation in Afghanistan'. Pakistan, Iran, India and the Gulf states having mostly refused military bases to the superpowers could in his view credibly affirm their opposition to the permanent presence of Soviet troops in Afghanistan and endorse the objective of returning Afghanistan to a non-aligned status. Since the conference would not initially focus on the problems inside Afghanistan Kabul need not be invited. The meeting would seek specifically an agreement by which all countries reaffirm their neutrality and detachment from military blocs, as the first step towards the eventual 'Finlandisation' of Afghanistan. Once this non-aligned buffer is established and had gained credibility in Mehta's view the conference could seek the addition of selected non-aligned countries from other regions to enhance its international standing. This larger group would then choose an observer group of given countries to perform a peace-keeping role in Afghanistan, which would involve defusing the insurgency and surpervising general elections. Mehta believed that the Afghan regime and the USSR would have a strong incentive to accept the group in Kabul. Mehta's final proposal was that the newly elected government conclude an Afghan–Soviet treaty along the lines of the Soviet–Finnish treaty and negotiate the withdrawal of the remaining Soviet forces. He believed that the treaty could be endorsed by the United Nations so that in the final instance all major powers would be committed to respect Afghan neutrality and non-alignment.[134]

Unfortunately there are weaknesses in both Harrison's and Mehta's proposals to neutralise Afghanistan. Their parallels with the case of Finland are unconvincing since Soviet policies towards Afghanistan and Finland have operated in quite dissimilar political and strategic environments. Soviet leaders never committed themselves ideologically and politically to Finland in the manner they did in Afghanistan. The USSR had limited military–strategic objectives in Finland; the country was never occupied by Soviet troops, except in the case of the lease of the Porkkala base, and this was returned once it became strategically redundant. It was crucial that Soviet leaders came to trust non-Marxist and not necessarily pro-Soviet Finnish political forces to abide by the military provisions of the 1948 Finnish–Soviet Friendship and Cooperation Treaty which met Soviet security needs in the direction of Finland comprehensively and permitted the expression of the Finnish brand of neutrality.[135]

In contrast Soviet leaders committed themselves, at least until the late 1980s, to the maintenance of a Marxist dominated pro-Soviet regime in Kabul, to the 'irreversibility' of the process of 'revolutionary development' in Afghanistan, with the future political and strategic implications this entailed for South Asia and the Persian Gulf. For this reason the Soviet Union and the DRA regime were unwilling to accept an observer group in Kabul as proposed by Mehta, however worthy its non-aligned credentials. Soviet leaders were interested only in a kind of 'non-alignment' for Afghanistan comparable with that of the radical pro-Soviet members of the Non-Aligned Movement; they did not hanker for Afghan neutralism of the pre-1973 variant. Mehta's idea for a new Afghan–Soviet treaty comparable to the Finnish–Soviet treaty (presumably meaning the 1948 treaty) which eventually encouraged the withdrawal of Soviet troops from Porkkala is unlikely to impress Soviet officials since the USSR has already signed a bilateral security-oriented treaty with Afghanistan in the form of the 1978 Treaty of Friendship, Good-Neighbourliness and Cooperation.[136]

Harrison and Mehta are more convincing when they argue that one precondition for a long-term settlement in Afghanistan based on a stricter interpretation of non-alignment could be a broad Great Power or regional understanding on the neutralisation of Southwest Asia. The former Pakistani Foreign Minister, Agha Shahi, suggested similarly in December 1984 that the strict non-alignment of the countries spanning the Persian Gulf and South Asian regions, together with American willingness to concede the Soviet Union a role in a comprehensive Middle East settlement, might create a situation congenial to the withdrawal of Soviet forces from Afghanistan. According to a Pakistani commentary, Shahi appeared to be suggesting that once the neutrality of the area was ensured by the regional states pursuing a policy of strict non-alignment, the superpowers could perhaps be persuaded to work towards some sort of mutual accommodation.[137]

A quid pro quo arrangement of the latter kind could prove attractive to Soviet leaders. During an official visit to Moscow in April 1981, the Libyan leader, Gaddafi, spoke of the need to ensure the 'independence and neutrality' of Afghanistan alongside a halt in all forms of outside interference in its affairs. Brezhnev responded with an appeal for the Great Powers to adopt certain norms in relations with Third World states including respect for the status of non-alignment chosen by them and abstention from attempts to draw them into military–political blocs of powers.[138] So far Soviet officials have failed to link the notion of some form of neutralisation of Afghanistan specifically with understandings on the neutrality of the states around it. But for many years Soviet statements have considered the DRA's 'peaceful initiatives' on settling the situation around Afghanistan (such as the regime's political programme of 14 May 1980) 'in the context of normalising the situation in the region as a whole'. Moreover, the USSR has expressed itself ready to take part in such a settlement 'linked with matters of Persian Gulf security'.[139] This could imply a link with Brezhnev's scheme in 1980 to neutralise the Gulf.

In this context it is interesting to note the unauthorised proposals advanced by an anonymous Soviet specialist on international and defence affairs in autumn 1984. 'Colonel X' proposed the establishment of 'Non-Alignment Pacts'. These would constitute treaties which 'for each Third World country currently or potentially the focus of dangerous conflict, would guarantee the non-alignment of that country'. He suggested that the signatories of the Pact 'be all those world and regional powers with an interest in the particular country concerned'. An '"outside power"', whose objectivity could be equally trusted by all involved parties, would implement and supervise each Pact'. The Colonel proposed that the signatory powers would form a 'consortium, guaranteeing the non-alignment of the country'. He accepted that each country presents different problems, requiring special solution, but believed that the problems of one country are linked to those of other countries in the same region. He proposed Pacts, therefore, to cover regions as well as countries. Examples given were Central America, the Horn of Africa (Ethiopia, Somalia), Pakistan, Afghanistan and Iran, Kampuchea, Korea, and the Middle East (Israel, Palestine, Lebanon).

This Soviet specialist, whose views remain unofficial, proposed a Non-Alignment Pact for Afghanistan, 'which would both guarantee the West against our continued presence there and guarantee us against a Western presence'. The Pact would provide for the withdrawal of Soviet forces following the formation of a coalition government in Kabul. The need to halt Pakistani aid to the insurgents in Afghanistan indicated the regional dimension to any neutralisation of this country. 'Colonel X' claimed that it would first be necessary to implement a Non-Alignment Pact for Pakistan, which would 'create the preconditions of a Pact for Afghanistan'.[140]

It is difficult to judge how far the views of this anonymous source diverged from the mainstream of Soviet official thought reflected a more conciliatory approach to the Afghan problem among Soviet foreign policy specialists, an approach which is less dogmatic about the nature of the internal regime in Afghanistan and more appreciative of the benefits which the USSR derived from Afghan non-alignment in the past. Such an approach may have become more widespread among the Soviet political elite since the death of Brezhnev. Earlier Soviet statements in the 1980s only rarely referred to the Soviet interest 'in having Afghanistan remain a *neutral* and non-aligned state and its good neighbour' (my emphasis).[141] In April 1983, however, the main features of a draft agreement on a comprehensive settlement of the Afghan question were worked out for the first time during the United Nations-sponsored talks in Geneva.

It was implicitly understood in this agreement that a political solution would ultimately involve the emergence of a coalition regime within the framework of a settlement; the Soviet Union indicated to a number of non-aligned states including India that it was not averse to such a development.[142] The views of 'Colonel X' become pertinent in tnis context. He argued that to implement a 'Non-Alignment Pact' in a civil war between an incumbent government supported by one Great Power and insurgents supported by another Great Power 'a coalition government must be formed comprising those elements of both Government and insurgent forces which are prepared to come to a compromise and work together in the context of non-alignment'. He believed that the Great Powers would be 'in a position to exert the pressure on their clients necessary to induce them to accept such arrangements'.[143] This foreshadowed the trend of Soviet policy towards Afghanistan pursued by Gorbachev. In 1983, however, it seems that Pakistan did not seriously test Soviet terms for a withdrawal of forces from Afghanistan, and in May the Pakistani Foreign Minister failed to obtain the concurrence of the United States for the draft settlement reached the previous month.

The American Secretary of State, Shultz, would not accept the UN agreement without the prior replacement of the existing regime in Kabul by a more representative one. This effectively destroyed any chance of progress at a crucial stage in the negotiations, it meant the collapse of the so-called 'Finlandisation' option. The USSR had given the appearance of supporting the plan of the United Nations' negotiator. Until this stage 'it had been clearly understood and implicity accepted during the entire process by all parties involved that the recomposition of the regime in Kabul would occur in parallel with the phased withdrawal of Soviet forces'.[144] Little progress was achieved during the UN-sponsored negotiations over the next two years. In June 1985 there was a renewed effort to advance these talks. Certain Western journalists claimed on the basis of Soviet sources that 'Moscow would much prefer a negotiated settlement which would involve the "Finlandisation" of Afghanistan along neutral lines' to a large increase in Soviet troops deployed in Afghanistan. One Soviet specialist on Afghanistan reputedly maintained that 'the option of "Finlandisation" is still possible' and 'it is to be preferred', but 'if the Geneva negotiations are obstructed, then Soviet policy will be one of "Mongolization"'.[145]

Not too much should be read into this kind of loose terminology, since it is greatly at variance with the vocabulary customarily employed by Soviet diplomats, officials and academics. Moreover, the descriptive value of the term 'Finlandisation' and even more the historical parallel with Finland, as previously observed, are questionable. It is misleading to regard the Soviet withdrawal from the Porkkala base in 1955-6 as the final stage of a phased withdrawal of Soviet troops from Finland when Soviet troops had at no stage occupied Finnish soil. This act certainly constituted a legal precondition to the proclamation of Finland's neutrality, but it coincided with a period in the mid and late 1950s when for various reasons the notion of neutrality in Europe suddenly gained a positive image among Soviet leaders. These circumstances are not comparable to those which determine the Soviet outlook on Asia in the mid 1980s. In addition, the Porkkala base was relinquished many years after Finland re-established the independent operation of her internal political processes. It was not paralleled by any externally influenced recomposition of the political forces in Finland,[146] and in the Afghan case it is precisely the issue of the internal composition of the Afghan regime which will determine whether Afghanistan will eventually embark on a more truly non-aligned path.

Influential Western figures encouraged a revival of plans to neutralise Afghanistan in the mid 1980s. In autumn 1985 the former American National Security Adviser, Brzezinski, proposed the external neutralisation of Afghanistan combined with a Soviet military withdrawal, the introduction of Islamic peace-keeping forces for an interim period, and self-determination for the Afghans.[147] In a television interview in late December 1985 the British Prime Minister, Thatcher, suggested that a revival of the Carrington initiative for international guarantees for Afghanistan's neutral status 'would perhaps be a possible way forward that might be pursued again'. British Foreign Office officials were quick to caution, however, that these remarks did not mean that Britain was set to launch a new peace initiative. In their view a Soviet troop withdrawal remained the key to a settlement and the possibility of a 'neutral Afghanistan' could only arise consequent to that.[148]

The new Soviet leadership under Gorbachev has evidently been more intent on extricating itself from Afghanistan through political accommodation. In an address to foreign ambassadors at the end of 1985 Gorbachev underlined the Soviet readiness to search for 'just solutions jointly with other countries' to conflicts in various regions and 'to participate where necessary, in respective guarantees'.[149] Greater Soviet flexibility on the nature of the Afghan regime was indicated by the decision of the DRA in December 1985 to admit a group of non-party (non-PDPA) figures into the DRA government.[150] The replacement of Karmal as head of the PDPA by Major General Najibullah (or Najib) on the eve of the reopening of the UN-sponsored peace talks on Afghanistan in Geneva on 5 May 1986 was intended *inter alia* to encourage the Kabul regime to broaden its power base as Moscow considered politically necessary.[151] In August Najibullah claimed that the PDPA would even countenance 'settling up a government that would include representatives of the political forces now outside the country, but who sincerely want to participate in the nationwide process of building a new Afghanistan'.[152] In a New Year's Day report he told the PDPA that he did not wish 'to exclude from the process of national reconciliation the various political groupings of a centrist or monarchist persuasion or the leaders of armed anti-government groupings operating abroad'. He suggested the discussion of a draft constitution 'so that representatives of the opposing side could express their proposals'.[153]

In November Gorbachev for the first time conceded that Moscow stood not only for a 'non-aligned, independent, sovereign Afghanistan' but a 'neutral Afghanistan'.[154] This term was also used by Najibullah. Flexibility on the Pakistani side was shown by the Pakistani Foreign Minister's recognition of the Soviet Union's 'legitimate interest in expecting that any Government in Kabul should be friendly towards it and should be mindful of its security interests'. This meant in his view that the Afghan Government had to be 'such as does not maintain a hostile attitude towards the Soviet Union and does not join anti-Soviet alliances'.[155] The Iranian attitude has also become more accommodating. During talks in Moscow in February 1986 the Iranian Foreign Minister proposed a second conference on Afghanistan, independent of the Geneva conference, which would be attended by Iran, Pakistan, the Soviet Union and the Afghan *mujahidin*. Previously Iran had sought an unconditional withdrawal of Soviet troops as a precondition of any discussion on Afghanistan. Soviet interest was aroused by the Iranian view that 'there will have to be guarantees that neither the Americans nor American surrogates substitute for the departing Russians', that the problem of Afghanistan should not be solved in the East/West context.[156]

The difficulty in obtaining the compliance of the United States to an agreement on Afghanistan between the regional states involved in the conflict stemmed from a continued American reluctance to accept an unrepresentative pro-Soviet and Marxist-inclined (if not dominated) government in that state. But in December 1985 United States' officials indicated that they could accept a United Nations' agreement if it led to a 'comprehensive and just settlement', involving a short time frame for Soviet withdrawal and self-determination. They showed greater flexibility over the regime which Pakistan could accept.

Real progress was made at the UN-sponsored talks on Afghanistan in May 1986 since it was agreed that Soviet troop withdrawals should begin simultaneously with the cessation of external interference and not after it as Soviet officials had previously insisted.[157] In November Moscow agreed on United Nations monitoring on both sides of the Afghan border. A (Soviet) DRA proposal at the Geneva talks in February 1987 for the first time made public a time frame for Soviet withdrawal, eighteen months, with no conditions attached to the process of 'national reconciliation' in Afghanistan. Pakistan countered with a proposal for a seven-month time frame. Soviet officials calculated that a longer time frame would assist the USSR to stabilise a viable and desirable regime in Kabul.[158]

In January–February 1987 separate talks were held in Moscow with Pakistan, Afghanistan and Iran. The discussions dealt not only with a Soviet withdrawal but with the structure of the government to remain behind in Kabul. The United Nations' mediator, Diego Cordovez, admitted for the first time that a Geneva agreement on a Soviet troop withdrawal would only be the starting point for a settlement. It would serve 'as a catalyst to produce another process, which will be the post-settlement arrangement'.[159] Moscow was operating within the United Nations' scenario which would leave the present regime in place after the departure of Soviet troops. Soviet leaders have given no indication, moreover, that they are prepared to abandon the PDPA and apparently expect its apparatus to be retained in post-settlement Afghanistan even if its role is reduced and its monopoly of power relinquished. But this issue is an area of tension between Moscow and the PDPA leadership. An interim regime could reduce the role of the PDPA but the USSR has not made the establishment of an interim government a precondition of a settlement.

It is precisely the role of the PDPA which frustrates a superpower accommodation over Afghanistan. American policy on Afghanistan has been reactive and government spokesmen have been reluctant to define the permissible political bounds of the Afghan regime after a Soviet withdrawal. More recently, certain United States government figures have ruled out a settlement which would leave the PDPA as the 'backbone of the Kabul Government' and they have indicated the unacceptability of the continuation of a 'communist front government' in Afghanistan. This leaves open the possibility of the inclusion of the PDPA in some format in a future settlement on Afghanistan, even though the principle of representation of the PDPA in an eventual settlement has not yet been accepted by Washington. American and Soviet leaders could arrive at a compromise over the composition of the future Afghan regime, perhaps at a summit meeting, which would pave the way for subsequent international guarantees of Afghanistan's formal non-alignment. But this would still fail to resolve the outstanding obstacle which to a greater or lesser extent was incorporated in earlier Western neutralisation plans – the attitude of the indigenous Afghan resistance groups.

In August 1985 the Supreme Council of the Afghan *mujahidin* Alliance, based in Peshawar, reiterated that its goal was the establishment of an independent Islamic state and declared that no power had the right to impose a political solution or a leadership on Afghanistan that did not satisfy the resistance fronts.[160] In May 1986 the spokesman of the resistance coalition proclaimed that any form of international guarantee which directly or indirectly recognises the Kabul regime would be unacceptable. He promised that the resistance would not lay down its arms until the last Soviet soldier had left Afghanistan and that if a deal was made over their heads the guerrillas would continue fighting even if foreign help were withdrawn.[161] In March 1987 the Hizb-e-Islami party accepted that Afghanistan should be a truly neutral and non-aligned state after a Soviet withdrawal. Its primary spokesman suggested that guarantees could be given that Afghanistan would not become a base for foreign powers. But he reaffirmed that no 'Finnish solution' or 'conspiracy of accommodation' made by the superpowers from outside would be acceptable to the *mujahidin* or considered binding on them.[162]

This uncompromising line by the main resistance groups implies that the USSR would need to maintain a political and military commitment to any Afghan regime which includes a PDPA component and emerges out of an international settlement. This would be incompatible with any form of neutrality or Western conceptions of non-alignment. However, more recently there have been indications that the *mujahidin* are moderating their expectations. In March 1987 the seven-party *mujahidin* alliance indicated its readiness to consider a settlement formula as evolved in the UN-sponsored negotiations. A spokesman pointed out that the alliance had agreed to the idea of an interim government in Afghanistan pending elections, and he observed that this could include 'neutral' personalities.[163] In April reports appeared that both the superpowers and Pakistan were actively promoting the idea of including Zahir Shah, the exiled former monarch, in a future coalition government in Kabul, although the *mujahidin* alliance were split on the issue.[164] Washington appeared to believe that Zahir Shah could act as a bridge between the *mujahidin* and the marxists in Kabul.

The recent terminology of Soviet and DRA leaders confirms the impression that some form of neutralisation of Afghanistan has become more acceptable to Moscow. On the eve of the Geneva talks in February 1987 the DRA Foreign Minister claimed that Afghanistan was ready to reach a settlement leading to the establishment of a 'free, neutral, non-aligned Afghanistan'.[165] The Pakistani Prime Minister, Mohammad Khan Junejo, and Prime Minister Margaret Thatcher of Britain agreed in April 1987 that a peace settlement for Afghanistan should include a commitment to establish 'a neutral non-aligned' regime in Kabul. In response to this meeting a Soviet newscaster asserted that 'more than anyone else, the Soviet Union comes out in favour of an independent, neutral, non-aligned Afghanistan which maintains relations of friendship and good-neighbourliness with our country'.[166] In an interview in May, Gorbachev underlined that Moscow favoured Afghanistan remaining independent, sovereign and non-aligned and if it 'also decided to be a neutral state, then that is the Afghan people's affair too'. He described the view that 'the Soviet Union would only accept a political settlement of the Afghan problem which would leave Afghanistan in its "sphere of influence"' as 'very mistaken'. He denied that the Soviet Union had or sought spheres of influence and implied that Zahir Shah could be brought into an Afghan coalition government.[167]

The following month Najib conceded that the Marxist authorities of the DRA were ready for contacts with supporters of Zahir Shar to promote a settlement. He declared that 'it is necessary to use the possibilities for entering into contact with monarchist forces, political activists of former regimes, and well-known and authoritative clergymen'. In describing a future coalition government he promised that 'we will not give representatives of the other side just two or three armchairs'. He accepted that 'we will have to share power'. Najib said the authorities were prepared to tolerate a multi-party system in Afghanistan provided that the new parties agreed *inter alia* on a policy of non-alignment and 'the strengthening of the traditional historic friendship with the Soviet Union'.[168] Gorbachev underlined this proviso in discussing the Afghan problem with the UN Secretary General, Javier Perez de Cuellar. He declared that 'our only wish is that Afghanistan should be a neutral and independent state developing in its own right and friendly to the USSR, and not a base for hostile activity threatening the security of neighbours'.[169] A few days later a Soviet commentary from Kabul indicated the limits of such 'neutrality' in asserting that the PDPA 'will remain the chief mobilising and guiding force in the [Afghan] government of national unity, even after it becomes a coalition'.[170]

A loosely formulated neutralisation of Afghanistan, involving super-power guarantees of that country's non-aligned status, mutual DRA and Pakistani pledges of non-interference and non-intervention, the with-drawal of Soviet troops (though perhaps not military advisers) combined with the cessation of external assistance to the *mujahidin*, and the retention of the PDPA as an important Afghan political force in a future coalition government, appears in principle acceptable to Soviet leaders. Indeed, in a major speech on 8 February 1988, Gorbachev declared explicitly that the Soviet Union no longer expected agreement on the nature of any interim or coalition government before commencing the withdrawal of its troops from Afghanistan. He accepted that it was not the business of the Soviet Union to participate in talks on the issue of a coalition government, and announced a ten-month timetable for troop withdrawals. However, it remains unclear how far the Soviet leadership may seek to influence the internal composition of the post-settlement Afghan regime in order to safeguard the minimal security and strategic needs of the USSR which, Moscow asserts, originally compelled the intervention of Soviet troops in Afghanistan.

4   Soviet policy and military alignment in the Third World

For many years Soviet leaders have anticipated military–political and strategic benefits for the Soviet Union from the shift in the global 'correlation of forces' represented by the spread of non-alignment in the Third World. They understood that neutralism and non-alignment could impede or restrain the development of close military relations between many newly independent states and the Western powers. In the 1950s and 1960s the American strategy of containment sought to integrate key Third World states in anti-Soviet (and anti-Chinese) coalitions and alliances in regions close to the Soviet borders. In response Soviet officials strove to convince third World states that entry into such alliances and the concession of military bases and facilities to Western states were counterproductive. The developing countries were urged to renounce such military links and embrace a policy of neutralism or non-alignment. This Soviet strategy is analysed in the first section of this chapter.

The continent where coordination in questions of military security between the Western powers and Third World states aroused the greatest concern among Soviet leaders was Asia. To counteract Western influence Soviet officials advocated a system of collective security. The idea of collective security had emerged as a theme in Soviet policy in the 1950s. Western statesmen had perceived it as a Soviet device to prise the United States and Western Europe apart. A Soviet statement in March 1958 had called for the establishment of collective security in both Europe and Asia as a basis for destroying the Western-inspired pacts, NATO and SEATO. In the 1970s Soviet promotion of the notion of collective security among Asian states was intended *inter alia* as a means to undermine SEATO, CENTO, ANZUS and the bilateral pacts the United States had concluded with South Korea, the Philippines and Japan. Moscow characterised it as a concrete response to Asian concerns about the vulnerabilities resulting

180

from close military association with the United States. No doubt Soviet leaders hoped that a Soviet-inspired collective security regime could underwrite the decline of the American military presence in Asia, but the primary Soviet target was China. As an organising principle collective security was expected to underpin an Asian 'coalition' of states under the Soviet aegis, which would constitute a barrier against the emergence of Chinese influence in the 1970s.[1] However, the Soviet initiative attracted only marginal support from the states in the region.

Soviet leaders were unsuccessful in their efforts to mobilise Asian states around the ill-defined principles of collective security. However, they developed a measure of security coordination with non-aligned or pro-Soviet Third World states in the 1970s through the conclusion of bilateral treaties of friendship, cooperation and assistance and through the acquisition of new military facilities overseas. Officials in Western and some non-aligned states have decried the tendency in the Non-Aligned Movement to criticise Western military bases and facilities located in Third World states whole glossing over the concession of military facilities to the Soviet Union. This chapter outlines the Soviet characterisation of Great Power military bases and facilities on foreign territories and analyses Soviet efforts to implement a strategy of 'base denial'.

Soviet friendship and cooperation treaties with Third World states were intended to displace or counteract the existing alignments and alliances between these states and the Western powers. As the number of states contractually linked to the Soviet Union in this manner increased, it became apparent that Moscow hoped to construct a network of loose understandings on military security with Third World states and establish Soviet relations with them on a firmer institutional basis. This could act to some extent as a rival system to the more traditional system of alliances and pacts in the Third World upheld by the Western powers. Western analysts have frequently regarded Soviet friendship and cooperation treaties as defining relations of alignment between the treaty parties. Soviet officials have denied that these treaties have prejudiced the pursuit of non-alignment by the Third World states involved. The final section of this chapter examines these contrary claims.

The primary intention of this chapter is to assess the Soviet strategy of military denial in the Third World in relation to the forms of military alignment outlined above.

In the decade following the conclusion of the Second World War the Western powers, and in particular the United States under the Truman and Eisenhower administrations, negotiated a whole series of bilateral and multilateral security treaties with Asian states, which in certain cases took the form of formal alliances. These succeeded the foundation of the NATO alliance in Europe and were intended to constrain the influence of Soviet and Chinese communism. (The collusion of the two communist powers was formalised by Moscow's conclusion of an alliance with the newly victorious Chinese communists in late 1949.) The United States concluded bilateral mutual defence treaties with the Philippines in 1951, South Korea in 1953 and Taiwan in 1954. Australia, New Zealand, Pakistan, the Philippines, Thailand, Great Britain and France came together additionally to sign the South East Asia Treaty Organisation (SEATO) Pact in Manila in September 1954. SEATO was intended primarily to cordon off Communist China and North Vietnam.

The instrument chosen to contain the Soviet Union in Asia was the Baghdad Pact. This military pact, signed in February 1955, included Iraq, Turkey, Iran, Pakistan and Great Britain. When Iraq withdrew in 1958 the Pact was succeeded by the Central Treaty Organisation (CENTO), which was reinforced by the conclusion of bilateral military agreements between the United States and respectively Iran, Turkey and Pakistan early in 1959. The United States was not a signatory in the CENTO arrangement, but it became involved in CENTO planning and some of its military committees and virtually committed itself to a military response to an attack on any of its members. Pakistan acted as a link between SEATO and CENTO, while Turkey performed the same function between CENTO and NATO.

The SEATO and CENTO pacts brought certain Asian states into pro-Western blocs and set them apart from a larger neutralist group. But the political and military efficacy of the pacts was always open to doubt. SEATO established no combined military comand or joint military force and relied merely on joint military manœuvres for regional defence. Its member states had joined for diverse reasons, and of the regional states perhaps only Thailand took the Pact seriously. By the late 1960s Pakistan had ceased to participate in military exercises within the framework of SEATO and CENTO and it eventually withdrew from SEATO. The SEATO Pact effectively became moribund in the wake of the American military withdrawal from Indo-China in the mid 1970s, and was not reinvigorated.

The Soviet Union initially regarded the ASEAN community as an American-devised SEATO-type alliance, but growing understanding of ASEAN led to a reversal of this stand (see below). CENTO had already ceased to be a threat to the Soviet Union in the Middle East with the assumption of power by the Ba'ath Party in Iraq. Much of the continuing Soviet obsession with CENTO was directed against Iran, whose position in CENTO was reinforced by the effective military guarantee from the United States contained in the bilateral agreement of 1959. However, even Iran's interest in CENTO dwindled in the 1970s and the Pact finally collapsed at the end of the decade when both Iran and Pakistan withdrew.

Soviet leaders responded to the creation of the Baghdad Pact and SEATO with a vigorous campaign among the states of the Middle East and Asia in favour of neutralism and neutrality. They were gratified by Egypt's resistance to Western pressures to enter the Baghdad Pact and by Iraq's withdrawal. In his report to the Twentieth Congress of the CPSU in 1956 Khrushchev branded these two pacts as 'not only aggressive military and political alignments but also instruments of enslavement; a new colonial-type form of exploitation of the underdeveloped countries'. He considered it 'obvious to everyone that neither Pakistan nor Thailand in SEATO, nor Iraq, Iran or Turkey in the Baghdad Pact set the policy'. In his view these blocs were part of a Western policy of 'divide and rule' in the Arab East and Southeast Asia. As an alternative to this bloc policy Khrushchev offered to conclude treaties of non-aggression and friendship with the states concerned.[2] In February 1957 the Soviet Government sent the Western powers a note proposing the adoption of mutual obligations towards the Near and Middle East including an abstention from 'all kinds of attempts to draw these countries into military blocs with the participation of the Great Powers'.[3] In January 1958 the Soviet Premier, Bulganin, deplored a NATO Council decision to establish close ties between NATO, the Baghdad Pact and SEATO. He urged states such as India, Afghanistan and Egypt to join the European neutrals and the states belonging to the Warsaw Pact and NATO in a summit conference to end international tension.[4]

Soviet leaders cited the examples of Afghanistan, Burma and India in Asia to urge Turkey, Iran and Pakistan to withdraw from multilateral and bilateral military pacts. The former group of states was encouraged to campaign against these pacts. A Soviet Government statement in March 1959 on the bilateral pacts the United States had concluded with Iran, Turkey and Pakistan claimed that military cooperation with the United States stimulated certain circles in Pakistan to prepare against India and

Afghanistan. Prime Minister Nehru and Prime Minister Daoud, it was observed, had publicly admitted such concerns. Moscow claimed that these agreements enabled the United States to take measures to prepare 'the territories of these countries as a theatre of military operations in accordance with the plans of the American military'.[5] It followed that a *de facto* neutralisation of the Soviet southern flank was a primary strategic objective for the USSR. At the beginning of the 1960s Soviet spokesmen expected dividends from indigenous neutralist opposition to CENTO and SEATO. They claimed that 'voices demanding Pakistan's withdrawal' from these pacts were 'increasing', and that 'the Iranian people are effectively campaigning for Iran's withdrawal from the aggressive CENTO bloc, the abrogation of the military treaty with America and for Iran's return to a policy of neutrality'. Support for 'neutrality' was also detected in Turkey. The Turkish leader General Gursel told journalists in 1961 that he favoured neutrality but because of Turkey's geographical position it could not remain neutral. The Soviet media responded with the assertion that 'this is evidently not inevitable' and pointed to official Turkish neutrality during the Second World War.[6]

In advance of the Belgrade conference of the Non-Aligned group in 1961 Soviet officials dwelt on the threat the existence of CENTO and SEATO posed to all neutralist states. They asserted that the pacts were involved in plans for fighting a thermonuclear war. At the Twenty-Second Congress of the CPSU Khrushchev attacked the Shah of Iran for having agreed 'to turn almost half the country into a zone of death in the interests of the aggressive CENTO bloc'.[7] The Soviet media published ostensible 'top secret CENTO documents' proving that the authors 'want to transform into zones of death not only their two allies in CENTO, Iran and Pakistan, but also the territory of neutral Afghanistan'. A Soviet commentator speculated on the existence of 'another top secret CENTO and SEATO plan which determines zones of death in the territories of India or Indonesia or Burma or other neutral countries'.[8] Soviet spokesmen naturally used various arguments to encourage the neutralists to work for the dissolution of CENTO and SEATO, but Soviet leaders may have recognised already in the 1960s that these alliances were operating more effectively as political symbols than as military structures.

The President of Pakistan, Ayub Khan, held discussions with Soviet leaders in April 1965 and explained that Pakistan's presence in CENTO and SEATO 'was serving as a moderating influence, and in any case the pacts were not hurting the USSR'. In response Kosygin admitted that 'they may not be hurting us, but they give us no pleasure either'. He told Ayub

Khan that before this meeting 'all we knew about you was that you were a member of certain pacts – even though paper pacts – and we were doubtful and cautious about you'.[9] Soviet leaders interpreted participation in SEATO and CENTO as a political commitment to the West and to anti-Sovietism. At the same time the USSR managed to cultivate reasonable neighbourly relations with the Asian CENTO states and used this to dilute further the military cohesiveness of the CENTO Pact. In the case of Turkey a further objective was a weakening of Turkish commitment to NATO membership. There is some evidence that in pursuit of a 'decoupling' of Turkey from CENTO and NATO Moscow attempted to negotiate a Soviet–Turkish treaty of friendship and cooperation in 1976.

In the 1970s Soviet commentators accepted that despite Turkish participation in 'imperialist blocs', which acted to restrict joint Turkish actions with the non-aligned states in resolving international problems, such as over the Middle East and disarmament, Turkey and the non-aligned countries faced 'very many similar problems'.[10] Turkey achieved observer status at the Algiers Non-Aligned Conference in 1973, but was unable to retain this status. Rumours that Turkey and Pakistan would be proposed as candidates at the 1976 Non-Aligned Summit proved groundless. However, Pakistan was accepted into the Non-Aligned Movement once it formally withdrew from CENTO in 1979. This followed the example of Iran and confirmed the dissolution of CENTO. At his first appearance in the Movement the Pakistani President, Zia Ul-Haq, accepted its general principles, including 'opposition to hegemony or domination in any guise or form', and was careful to avoid anti-Soviet expressions.[11]

Soviet leaders considered the withdrawal of Pakistan from CENTO as long overdue. They doubted that this act represented any substantial change in policy and did not regard it as sufficient to confirm Pakistani non-alignment in light of the continuation of strong military links between Washington and Islamabad. The Afghan regime under Taraki, which was under military pressure from Pakistan and Iran, expressed its own doubts during the 1979 Havana Non-Aligned Summit. President Taraki pointed out that 'some of the countries joining the Movement as full-fledged members may have come after their dissociation from aggressive regional military pacts and alliances'. In his opinion this entitled the Movement 'to have as a matter of principle, assurances with regard to such countries, to the effect that they have no lingering military commitments with the major partners of these pacts against third countries'.[12]

In light of such assertions, claims by the USSR and the new DRA regime that Afghanistan remained non-aligned after the Karmal regime was installed by force of Soviet arms a few months later are disingenuous. It was true that Afghanistan refrained from assuming open multilateral military commitments but the character and scale of Soviet–Afghan bilateral military relations could not be ignored in this context. Indeed, the Soviet press supported a query by the Indian Foreign Minister, N. Rao, in May 1981 about whether to permit Pakistan to remain in the Non-Aligned Movement with the assertion that 'Islamabad's policy of all possible military rapprochement with Washington and the huge shipments of American arms that have been promised cannot help but raise legitimate doubts among many member countries of the Non-Aligned Movement as to whether Pakistan is legally entitled to remain in their ranks'.[13] This played directly to Indian susceptibilities; Soviet spokesmen have not queried the prominent Indian position among the Non-Aligned when large-scale Indo-Soviet arms agreements have been concluded. Nor did Moscow raise the principles of non-alignment when it transferred arms on a large scale to radical 'non-aligned' African states in the 1970s or to Afghanistan in the 1980s.

Soviet leaders considered Iran's renunciation of the CENTO Pact in early 1979 when the Shah was overthrown as a seminal event. Soviet commentaries lauded the new 'progressive' policy of Iran which had resulted in its withdrawal from CENTO.[14] In an interview with *Pravda* in March 1979, the Iranian Minister of Information and Propaganda drew attention to measures such as 'the establishment of control over bases from which the Pentagon was carrying out electronic intelligence observations of the territory of the Soviet Union, the termination of the services of American military advisers in the armed forces, and a sharp cut-back in the military budget'.[15]

Moscow chose initially not to stress Soviet–Iranian relations at the expense of Iranian independence and non-alignment. When the Iranian government abrogated its CENTO membership it branded any neighbouring country that remained in CENTO as a lackey of imperialism and as hostile to Iran. As a result Iranian–Turkish relations deteriorated. The preferred approach of Soviet officials was to confirm Iran's abandonment of a pro-Western political and military policy by encouraging its association in the Non-Aligned Movement. The Soviet media observed in March 1979 that 'the policy which Iran is pursuing today in many respects resembles the programme formulated by the Non-Aligned Movement which is being implemented successfully'. The USSR noted 'with satisfaction' that 'Iran is expressing its support for the world-wide democratic international Non-Aligned Movement'.[16] Iran took part in the summits of the Non-Aligned in 1979 and 1983, and the new Iranian constitution defined the basis of the

country's foreign policy *inter alia* as 'ending any kind of domination,...practicing non-alignment with respect to the dominating powers
and maintaining mutual peaceful relationships with non-belligerent
nations'.[17]

Despite Iran's avowed non-alignment Soviet officials in all likelihood
expected that the tide of anti-Western sentiment which swept Iran out of
CENTO would open the way for a closer political affiliation with the USSR
as practiced by other radical states in the Non-Aligned Movement.
However, Iran came to regard the need for closer identification with the
Third World as the counterpart to a progressive de-emphasising of ties
with both superpowers. At the Conference of Foreign Ministers of the Non-
Aligned in February 1981 Iran pressed for a purist conception of non-
alignment, which involved a rejection of all forms of dependency on the
superpowers, an emphasis on self-reliance, and a purge of those who did
not live up to this ideal.[18] This outlook emboldened Iran to repudiate the
military provisions of the 1921 Soviet–Persian Treaty at the time it
abrogated Iranian membership in CENTO. In the 1980s Soviet leaders
have remained unable to alter the Iranian posture of 'neither West nor
East' in their favour. The case of Iran has shown Soviet leaders that a
Third World state may withdraw comprehensively from a Western-
sponsored military alliance in a strategically sensitive area and avoid
subsequent alignment with the USSR. It has underlined that Third World
nationalism may frustrate zero-sum calculations by the superpowers.

The dissolution of CENTO left ASEAN as the primary multilateral body
of states in Asia predominantly oriented towards the Western powers in its
security outlook and ties. At the time ASEAN was created in August 1967
Soviet officials had been anticipating an American attempt to construct a
broader alliance to replace the decrepit SEATO. In their view this new
alliance would incorporate the neutral states of the region such as
Malaysia and Indonesia, which refused to join SEATO. Moscow expected
that as in the case of the Baghdad Pact it would not include the United
States by formal association. Soviet observers interpreted the proclamation
of the Nixon Doctrine as confirmation that the long-term American
ambition was to create a larger military grouping embracing the entire
region, and to employ ASEAN as a substitute military alliance.[19] However,
ASEAN's promulgation of the proposal for a zone of peace and neutrality
in 1971 and the effects of Vietnamese successes in the mid 1970s induced
a change in the Soviet evaluation of ASEAN. 'Neutralist' tendencies were
discerned among the ASEAN states, and these were regarded as long-term
historical trends.[20]

After 1975 ASEAN downgraded its security links with the West in order to adapt to the new regional constallation of forces. Soviet officials began to accept that ASEAN was not an American- or Western-controlled body, although they remained ambivalent about the developing emphasis on regional political cooperation within ASEAN. Their primary concern was the possibility that the decline of American influence in Southeast Asia could still precipitate an American-sponsored military pact of ASEAN states directed at the Soviet Union. The ASEAN states decided in 1976 not to form a multilateral security relationship but to confine security cooperation within ASEAN to the bilateral level. However, ASEAN claims that this body is not a military organisation have failed to dispel Soviet suspicions. These suspicions have some basis since the network of security relationships that were developing under ASEAN auspices increasingly amounted to a low-profile military association in effect, if not in name.[21] The goals of this association, like former SEATO and CENTO goals, include the maintenance of the existing political status quo and the containment of Communism. From the Soviet perspective, therefore, ASEAN already displays certain of the features of a *de facto* security alliance. It remains a Soviet priority to dissuade the ASEAN states from taking the final step that would transform ASEAN into a Western-sponsored security system.

The Soviet Union has been eager to support the demands of the non-aligned states for the dissolution of multilateral military alliances in the Third World such as CENTO and SEATO. But Soviet leaders have consistently and unsuccessfully tried to convince the Non-Aligned majority of the difference in principle between the alliances in Europe, NATO and the Warsaw Treaty Organisation. Before the first Non-Aligned Summit in Belgrade, the Soviet media tried to persuade the Yugoslavs that the Warsaw Pact member countries 'have no military, naval or air bases in the territories of foreign states', and that they 'exert constant efforts for the relaxation of international tension and the suppression of the hotbeds of military conflict created...by imperialist states' such as Suez. It was considered incorrect, therefore, 'to measure all the military groups by the same yardstick'.[22] During the Lusaka Conference in 1970 a Soviet commentary described NATO as a 'collective coloniser' which was used on many occasions 'for reprisals against the liberating peoples'. This was contrasted with the 'defensive character' of the Warsaw Pact.[23] Such assertions were developed in the 1970s into an onslaught on the theory of 'equidistance between the blocs'.

Soviet leaders strove to convince the non-aligned states that Moscow had no objection to the dissolution of the Warsaw Pact or the imposition of restraints on it so long as these measures applied equally to NATO. In his message to the Havana Non-Aligned Summit in 1979 Brezhnev stressed the Soviet opposition to 'the division of the world into military–political blocs opposed to each other'. He pointed out that the USSR had repeatedly confirmed its readiness to disband the Warsaw Pact alongside a simultaneous dissolution of NATO. This could be preceded by a mutual reduction of military activities.[24] A Soviet official argued at the same time that Warsaw Pact proposals on the non-expansion of military–political groupings in Europe and on limiting the scale of military exercises also involved the interests of the non-aligned countries since 'the tendency towards expanding the NATO bloc directly affects the newly independent countries'.[25] The Soviet message to the Delhi Non-Aligned Summit in 1983 stressed recent initiatives by the Socialist countries 'proposing that the zones of responsibility of NATO and the Warsaw Treaty should not be extended to any new parts of the world'.[26] This reflected the Soviet fear that even as CENTO collapsed the United States was preparing the construction of new alliance structures in the Third World and working for an extension of the geographic responsibilities of NATO.

Soviet commentaries pointed out that the foreign ministers of the non-aligned states had expressed their concern during a meeting in February 1981 over the aspirations of NATO to extend its activities outside Europe. Moscow speculated over Western efforts to draw together new 'groupings' in various regions of the world such as Southeast Asia, the South Atlantic and the Red Sea. Soviet spokesmen warned the non-aligned states against succumbing to Western attempts to secure their support for American Rapid Deployment Forces. Reports were cited to the effect that during a visit to Argentina in January 1981 the Egyptian Foreign Minister handed the Argentine President, Videla, a message from President Carter proposing the creation of a South Atlantic Alliance of the NATO type involving Egypt.[27] Following the break with Moscow and the Camp David Accords the USSR also appeared anxious that Egypt could be drawn into a new Western-sponsored and Chinese-backed military bloc of conservative Middle East states.

Soviet commentators in the late 1970s warned Asian and African countries against Chinese pronouncements in favour of creating regional military blocs and alliances of Third World States to combat 'hegemonism'. Chinese support for CENTO activities in the Middle East was linked to its support for the idea of a 'Red Sea bloc' involving countries such as Saudi Arabia and Egypt as members.[28] Soviet officials considered the formation of this bloc to be a primary objective of the more assertive American policy in the Persian Gulf which followed the dissolution of CENTO and Soviet intervention in Afghanistan. When the foreign ministers of the non-aligned states assembled in February 1981 a Soviet commentary linked their concern over tensions in the 'Arab Gulf and the Arabian Peninsula' to the expansion of the American military presence in Oman and American arms sales to Somalia and Egypt. These acts were described as part of a chain of military moves aimed at setting up a new alliance in the Red Sea area with the direct and active participation of the United States. This alliance would ostensibly be used to suppress 'national liberation movements' in the Middle East and to exert political and military pressure on South Yemen (PDRY) and Ethiopia. American strategists were accused of plans to involve Egypt, Oman, Somalia, Israel and if possible Saudi Arabia in this alliance. Moscow exhorted the non-aligned states of the Middle East and Africa to resist these designs.[29]

Such Soviet commentaries revealed deep unease about the implications of growing anti-Soviet sentiments in Southwest Asia early in the 1980s. Moscow interpreted statements by Brzezinski on the need to construct an anti-Soviet Islamic coalition as proof of American intentions 'to bring together reactionary regional coalitions on a religious basis'. Soviet commentators accepted, however, that religion could also hinder American plans in the Middle East. They have argued that the 'contradictions' between Israel and Arab states have for many years frustrated the attempts of American strategists to construct an alliance between Israel and the more conservative Arab states. Washington has been accused of striving towards this objective by means of aligning Saudi Arabia, Jordan, Lebanon and other states to the Camp David process on a Middle East settlement.[30]

The Soviet fixation on Western-sponsored alliance formation in the Middle East induced great scepticism in the USSR towards regional plans for security coordination developed among the Gulf states at the beginning of the 1980s. A Soviet statement at the end of 1980 accused the 'reactionary regimes' of the Gulf, 'obviously promoted by Washington' of 'nurturing plans of forming a certain "mutual security pact", in other words a military alliance to fight against the national liberation movement'. The USSR was unwilling to condone an arrangement primarily directed at preserving the conservative status quo among the Gulf regimes. Nor did it believe in hopes expressed by Saudi Arabia that the six countries involved could become militarily self-sufficient, since it characterised all these states as 'military clients of Western states'. The former Shah's advocacy of a collective security pact was a further black mark against the Gulf scheme.[31] However, on 4 February 1981 the foreign ministers of Saudi Arabia, Kuwait, Bahrain, Qatar, the UAE and Oman decided to establish the Gulf Cooperation Council (GCC). In response *Pravda* cited American press reports that the United States and its NATO allies were making active preparations towards 'creating a security pact in the Persian Gulf zone, prepared to cooperate with the West'. The Soviet press nevertheless refrained from describing the GCC as a military alliance and conceded that regional economic cooperation in the Gulf could be useful.[32]

Although the USSR has hinted at the possibility of cooperation with the GCC over issues of Gulf security, its attitude to this body, especially over GCC plans for coordinated security arrangements, remained negative in the early 1980s.[33] This was influenced by Oman's wish for the GCC to act as a military alliance in conjunction with the West against a perceived Soviet threat. In contrast Kuwait wished the GCC to remain neutral. In the Kuwaiti view Moscow's greatest objection to the GCC has been the participation of Oman, which has strong military links with the West.[34] The USSR may become more tolerant of GCC security arrangements following the establishment of Soviet–Omani and Soviet–UAE diplomatic relations in autumn 1985.

Soviet spokesmen have characterised Western attempts to construct new military alliances and alignments in the Middle East since the end of the 1970s as part of a broad front of measures in different regions of the globe. In Southeast Asia they attacked Western and Chinese support for the addition of military clauses to the ASEAN instruments. Plans for an Asian Common Market, which would include Iran, India, a number of South Asian and possibly Southeast Asian countries, were described as reactionary. They claimed that the Western states hoped to use this scheme 'to establish a new regional bloc, which would be torn away from the mainstream of non-alignment'.[35] Soviet spokesmen vehemently opposed American plans to establish a new strategic command, CENTCOM, which would include nineteen African and Asian countries in its zone of operation. All these states were members of the Non-Aligned Movement. CENTCOM formally came into operation in 1983. Soviet accusations followed that Washington was trying to create the basis for a military alliance through strengthening mutual dependence between its regional partners in an arrangement over which it presided. An underlying objective was perceived as the attainment of a 'strategic understanding' between the United States, Israel, Saudi Arabia and Pakistan.[36]

Soviet spokesmen have remained aware of the existence of indigenous constraints on such American ambitions. Religion, as noted above, would limit the association of the Arab states with Israel. In Africa, American attempts to construct blocs would be undercut by the fact that even the most pro-Western states in the region 'in every way avoid tight (particularly formally established) association with the racist regime' of South Africa. Moreover, Soviet specialists point to the unresolved disputes and mutual claims over territory, and to the existence of national, tribal, religious, economic and other issues within and between the states of the Indian Ocean basin. But they argue that since the leadership of President Carter the United States has sought to circumvent these constraints on formal alliances through the looser concept of 'strategic understandings' with key Third World states (see below).[37] In their view this approach does not preclude continued American attempts to construct new blocs.

The current Soviet contention is that 'the USA has worked out a plan of knocking together an Indian Ocean Defence Organisation, INODO, that will include [at least] Pakistan, Egypt, Somalia, Kenya and Oman'. A Soviet commentator explained that 'officially the USA will not take part in the new military bloc, but it promises its participants all-round assistance by supplying them arms and training their military personnel'. The Pentagon is still accused of organising attempts to construct 'military coalitions of the littoral states of the Indian Ocean' in place of the demilitarisation of this region.[38]

Beyond Asia Soviet officials continued to attack American and South African attempts in the 1980s to construct a South Atlantic Treaty Organisation. They were gratified by the communiqué issued in January 1983 after a meeting of foreign ministers of the Non-Aligned in Managua which warned Latin American states against involvement in this plan. Indeed, Moscow entertained some hopes that the growth in interest in non-alignment in Latin America, a phenomenon which had induced Soviet writers in the mid 1970s to talk of a 'Latin American stage' of the Non-Aligned Movement, could weaken or even undermine the military treaty system which bound this continent to the United States. This system was formed by the Rio Treaty of 1947 and the related Charter of the Organisation of American States. A Soviet writer argued in 1979 that the growing participation of Latin American states in the Non-Aligned Movement directly affected the character of relations in the inter-American system and set the question of its 'basic restructuring' on the agenda. He maintained that Washington feared that the gradual shift of the states of the region into the political orbit of the Non-Aligned Movement could draw them away from the system of 'inter-American treaties of mutual assistance'.[39]

Soviet specialists believed that the shift towards non-alignment in Latin America was hastened by the political situation in the region after the Falklands War which resulted in 'an open crisis of the inter-American system, including its military–political mechanism'.[40] At the conference of the Non-Aligned held in Managua in January 1983 the Cuban Foreign Minister, Malmierca, argued that the Falklands War 'proved to Latin Americans that their instruments and means of collective defence with the United States, which were supposedly for protection against extra-hemispheric powers, are nothing but mechanisms to be used when Washington's interests are threatened by pro-independence actions in any of our states'. In place of the Organisation of American States and the Inter-American Treaty for Reciprocal Assistance he proposed that the Latin American and Caribbean states establish an agency of their own that would 'create mechanisms for [mutual] consultation and cooperation in the political field' and allow them 'to join our efforts in the defence of our common interest'.[41] This proposal was stillborn. The financial and economic hold of the United States retarded fully independent steps by the majority of the Latin American states in the security and defence fields. By 1985 Soviet specialists acknowledged that taking into account the fact that the Latin American states were being 'drawn into the inter-American system ever more significantly' through 'their economic and political dependence on the United States' the issue of their 'full "dissociation" from this system, of the creation of their own intergovernmental organisation independent of the United States, will be difficult to resolve'.[42] Soviet officials have had to recognise that there is no immediate prospect of a major modification of the structure of alignments and alliances in their favour in Latin America.

The numerical growth of states participating in the Non-Aligned Movement in the 1970s reinforced the Soviet perception that the global 'correlation of forces' was shifting away from the West and that Western-sponsored multilateral military alliances and alignments in the Third World were fragmenting or weakening. The breakdown of CENTO and SEATO were regarded as part of a historical process which paralleled the emergence of the Soviet Union as a superpower with its own 'legitimate interests' in the Third World. It was believed that Western military preponderance throughout most of Asia and Africa had been undercut by the balancing effect of the Soviet Union, which made formal American military alignment with Third World states both more hazardous and anachronistic. Evidence of American interest in drawing together new alliances in areas of regional tension in the Third World in the early 1980s and of extending the competence of existing ones came, therefore, as a shock to Soviet leaders. In spring 1981 Brezhnev responded with his formal proposal for the West to accept certain norms in relations with the Third World, including respect for their status of non-alignment and 'abstention from attempts to draw them into military–political blocs of powers'.[43] Similar understandings for specific regions such as the Persian Gulf were proposed by Soviet leaders. In the Indian Ocean basin they sought to rally the non-aligned states against existing blocs being activated or the composition and spheres of responsibility of these blocs being broadened. Moscow tried to encourage the non-aligned states to commit themselves in this region to the 'gradual curtailment of distinct forms of military–political cooperation...the non-creation of new forms of multi-lateral and bilateral alliances, the non-adoption of military functions by non-military regional organisations'.[44]

It became a Soviet priority in the 1980s to prevent a whole series of Third World states from reverting back to military alignment or alliance with the West. Soviet spokesmen accused 'NATO circles' of distorting the idea of non-alignment through relegating 'to the number of the "non-aligned" states those few newly free countries whose leaders are presently...regarded as "friends of the West" and share the concept of the "strategy of a united front", that is are in favour of setting up alliances with imperialist powers, first of all the United States'.[45] To some extent this accusation mirrored Soviet policy towards the Non-Aligned since Moscow had worked towards a 'solidarity front' with the Non-Aligned Movement, especially with the radical states participating within it. Soviet spokesmen have interpreted such Western 'alliances' as 'a system incorporating a "range of economic, political and strategic policies and understandings (which) may...be extended to the demand for military or communications bases"'.[46]

Soviet specialists maintained that partnership based on 'strategic understanding', in distinction to the blocs and alliances of earlier decades, was offered by Washington in the 1980s to the broadest possible circle of states. Such partnership was based not exclusively on military integration. It presumed that the 'partners' of the United States, especially non-aligned countries, could also make a non-military contribution 'in the common cause'. This could take the form, for example, of 'rejecting cooperation with the socialist states and curtailing relations with them, adhering to the capitalist path of development, broadening links with imperialist powers, and approving geopolitical concepts propagandised by the West'. A Soviet writer recognised that there existed no obligation formally to codify such understandings. In his view, Washington reasoned that the absence of direct military alliances between Third World states and the West meant that the non-aligned status cherished by the majority of such states was not undermined in the formal sense and their participation in strategic partnerships with the United States was facilitated. Nevertheless, this analyst concluded in 1984, the partnership of the United States with Israel, Egypt, Saudi Arabia, Oman, Pakistan and Thailand was constructed on *de facto* alliances.[47]

Soviet spokesmen claim that American ambitions in the 1980s are not confined to cultivating relations of 'alignment' on a bilateral basis. They accuse Washington of exploiting regional trends among Third World states, of attempting 'to emasculate the positive basis of such processes, to militarise the activity of regional organisations created by the developing countries, transforming them ultimately into pro-Western military blocs'.[48] This underlying concern still shapes Moscow's attitude to bodies such as ASEAN and it expresses a growing resentment over the limitations of Moscow's policy of military denial in the Third World in this decade. Soviet spokesmen could argue that although the USSR had for decades proselytised the notion of a national liberation or solidarity 'front' of Third World states, aligned at least politically to the Soviet bloc, it had not created regional groupings or coalitions of states militarily tied to the USSR or the Warsaw Pact and it had supported the opposition of the non-aligned states to military blocs. There has been an artificial element to such 'restraint' by Soviet leaders since the USSR has remained poorly placed to openly compete with the West in forming coalitions or alliances in the Third World. However, as indicated by certain recent Soviet writings on the non-aligned states examined in Chapter 1, such closer multilateral East–South military integration is not a prospect the USSR would necessarily be averse to if the required opportunities arose.

The Soviet Union, with Cuban assistance, experimented with the idea of a left-leaning confederation of states in the Horn of Africa in spring 1977. But intra-regional conflict destroyed this initiative and made Moscow reluctant to repeat this kind of experiment. It is true that a military coalition of sorts has existed in Indo-China since the Vietnamese occupation of Kampuchea and Laos. During an official visit by the Vietnamese leader to Moscow in May 1987 Gorbachev still hailed 'the strengthening of the fraternal alliance of Vietnam, Laos and Kampuchea'.[49] However, Soviet leaders have not shared the Vietnamese interest in a *de facto* Indo-China federation under Vietnamese control. The Soviet aversion to this multilateral arrangement and the apparent Soviet preference to deal bilaterally with Vietnam, Laos and Kampuchea reflects the Soviet opposition to the creation of blocs outside Soviet control, even if the blocs are constituted of states they accept as 'socialist'.[50] The USSR influences, often rather ineffectually, rather than controls Vietnamese military policy in Indo-China.

It could be argued that the Soviet Union has offset the lack of pro-Soviet military blocs or coalitions in the Third World in some degree by the creation of a mutual strategic support system based on a network of bilateral treaties of friendship (see later in this chapter). These treaties may well be perceived by Soviet strategists as fitting into the structure of collective security originally proposed by Brezhnev in 1969. More recently the Soviet leadership under Gorbachev has attempted to revive the framework of Asian collective security through promoting a range of interlocking initiatives addressing military and security issues in the Asian-Pacific region. This was the central theme of Gorbachev's renowed Vladivostok speech in July 1986. A year later the Soviet Deputy Minister of Foreign Affairs, Ivor Rogachev, called for movement towards this objective through 'bilateral accords, sub-regional accords and finally, in the last analysis, if this becomes realistic with the passage of time, through the conclusion of a regional agreement on issues of security'.[51]

In a discussion of Asian security on Soviet television a *Pravda* writer denied that Soviet initiatives for 'pan-Asian security' were intended by Moscow 'to draw the countries of the region into some kind of Asian-Pacific pact, to make allies of them in its conflict with Washington'. He admitted, however, that there had been 'some people in countries such as India to whom it has occurred to ask whether this [Soviet policy] is in keeping with the principle of non-alignment, with a non-bloc policy'. He claimed that such 'unclear matters' had been eliminated following recent high-level Soviet–Indian talks, and cited Rajiv Gandhi to the effect that the principles of non-alignment 'provide a legal and political framework for an analysis of the complex and particular problems of peace and security in the Asian-Pacific region'.[52] But even if the majority of Asian states recognise a link between the *political* aspirations of non-alignment and the broader goals of the revived Soviet 'pan-Asian security' scheme they are unlikely to permit themselves to become drawn into a new structure of strategic accords in Asia presided over by Moscow which could enable the USSR to press for more direct relations of military alignment in the future.

BASES AND MILITARY FACILITIES

The Hague Conventions of 1907 explicitly prohibited the creation of military bases on the territory of neutral states. In the period since the Second World War certain states in multilateral alliances also made commitments not to permit foreign military bases on their territory in peacetime. Norway, for example, has assumed such a commitment since the mid 1950s despite its membership in NATO. The renunciation of foreign military bases also became a *sine qua non* of neutralism and non-alignment in the 1950s and 1960s. The neutralist and non-aligned states associated military base rights with bloc alignment and alliance structures and they were encouraged in their opposition to these rights by the Soviet Union which since the mid 1950s has consistently denied the existence of Soviet bases on foreign territories. This question is complicated by the reluctance of host countries to acknowledge Soviet military and naval support arrangements of any kind. Donor states are aware that by providing support for the armed forces of one superpower their territory could become a target in the military operational planning of the other superpower.

It is misleading to use the terms 'military facilities' or even 'base facilities' simply as synonyms for military bases. A base acts as an installation supporting the operations of a military force and serves as its point of origin. In the case of overseas bases, the right of access for a specified period is secured by a treaty between the host state and the lessee. In general the latter is conceded a judicial right of access and rights concerning the operation and security of the base. Bases may be used for purposes such as naval and aerial reconnaissance, storing ammunition and supplies, training and the collection of intelligence and communications. In distinction a 'facility' connotes 'non-contractual, less extensive and *ad hoc* privileges'. The nature of access may merely involve regular authorised visits by warships or it may include the permission to conduct repairs in port, without the use of onshore installations, and to load on fuel and supplies. It is essentially the denial of access to extensive facilities on land and the need to seek permission prior to each naval visit that distinguishes these limited concessions from bases.[53]

In the years following the Second World War the European colonial powers retained control over a large number of military and naval bases among their colonies. The United States had entered the Second World War with a very limited overseas basing system, but by the close of the war had acquired a massive global basing network 'derived from a combination of conquests, agreements with allies, and temporary arrangements with neutrals and exile regimes that had at least the potential for post-war renewal and extension'.[54] The Soviet Union acquired and developed a structure of ground and air installations in Eastern Europe which were integrated in the Warsaw Pact. Elsewhere the only substantial bases Stalin acquired out of the post-war settlement were those at Porkkala, Finland, and at Port Arthur in Chinese-controlled Manchuria. Stalin's perception of the Soviet Union as encircled militarily was aggravated by the gradual development of an American policy of military containment of the USSR. In the 1950s this involved the creation of a ring of military bases around the Soviet perimeter. The Soviet Union had no equivalent forward bases for strategic deterrence or any other purpose until the Cuban revolution provided an opportunity at the beginning of the 1960s. Until the mid 1950s, however, Soviet leaders were reluctant to engage in blanket denunciations of military bases since this could complicate their own policy in Eastern Europe.

The Soviet leadership openly proclaimed the illegitimacy of military bases on foreign territories only after the death of Stalin. The principles of Soviet foreign policy were re-examined in the mid 1950s as was Soviet strategic thinking in Europe. In autumn 1955 the decision was taken to withdraw Soviet troops from the military and naval base at Porkkala which the Soviet Union had leased from Finland under the terms of the 1947 Finnish–Soviet Peace Treaty. In the same year Moscow also reached an accommodation over Austria with the Western powers which resulted in joint troop withdrawals from that country. The issue of abandoning Soviet bases was disputed in July 1955 at a Central Committee meeting in the Soviet Union. Molotov was opposed to the evacuation of any Soviet military bases for fear of setting a dangerous precedent which could apply to other similar and more important issues. He may have had in mind the possible loss of East Germany as a military base area. Khrushchev saw no objection to the withdrawal of Soviet troops from a non-Sovietized country as a part of a compromise agreement and he overruled Molotov on both Austria and Porkkala.[55] He regarded Porkkala as strategically redundant and politically burdensome.[56] Political considerations simultaneously led to the Soviet decision to abandon its rights, derived from the Yalta Agreements and specified in the Chinese–Soviet treaty of friendship of August 1945, to exclusive use of the naval base in Port Arthur and shared use of the port of Dairen in the Chinese People's Republic.

When Prime Minister Bulganin declared Soviet readiness to abandon Porkkala in September 1955 he suggested that 'the removal of military bases situated on foreign territory by other states also would significantly assist the further relief of international tension and assist the creation of conditions to end the arms race'.[57] In a statement on disarmament on 17 November 1956 the Soviet Government proposed the elimination of foreign military, naval and air bases over a two-year period. This proposal was advanced as an important measure towards disarmament and the creation of zones of limited arms, but it was not taken seriously by Western leaders since it required in effect wholly asymmetrical concessions by East and West. However, Soviet leaders continued to urge West European countries, such as Iceland and Italy, to renounce American or NATO bases. In February 1957 Moscow suggested that the Great Powers accept certain principles to cover their behaviour in the Near and Middle East, including the elimination of foreign bases and the withdrawal of foreign troops from the region. The following year when Eisenhower first proposed a ban on the use of outer space for military purposes the Soviet leadership insisted that such a measure be accompanied by the removal of foreign military bases from Europe, the Middle East and North Africa.

It was a Soviet strategic priority to prevent pro-Western Third World states from conceding new military bases to the Western powers in proximity to Soviet borders. The United States acquired few significant military facilities between Southeast Asia and the Mediterranean during the buildup of its global basing system in the 1950s and early 1960s. The American position in Turkey was an important exception. Turkey had a critical location, along the Black Sea, astride the Bosporus and along the Soviet border. In 1959–60 intermediate range ballistic missiles were located on sites in Turkey pending the development of reliable American ICBMs. Bases for American fighters and facilities for American U-2 planes, surveillance and communications were also established in Turkey.

In 1957–60 U-2 flights also operated out of an American base at Peshawar, Pakistan. In a note presented to the Pakistani Prime Minister in April 1958 Moscow accused Pakistan of constructing launching pads for guided missiles and airfields for strategic bombers on its territory. A warning was given of 'the grave consequences for Pakistan if military bases to be used for aggression against the Soviet Union and other peace-loving countries are created on its territory'. Any aggressive actions against the USSR, the Soviet Government promised, would meet 'a retaliatory blow at the aggressor, including the bases of the aggressor that are situated on foreign soil'.[58] Pakistan denied that any missile sites were under construction on her soil and pointed out that the Soviet Union had herself been supplying arms and building airfields and other military installations in countries in the neighbourhood of Pakistan. However, Moscow described Pakistan's military agreement with the United States of 1959 as turning it into a 'foreign war base'. After the 'U-2' American spy-plane incident in 1960 Pakistan was warned again that the USSR 'possesses means to render harmless in case of need the war bases used for aggressive actions against the Soviet Union'.[59]

The Soviet contention that military bases in the Third World could generate dangerous East–West tensions was forcibly and unexpectedly underlined by the crisis initiated by Soviet attempts to establish a nuclear missile base on Cuban soil in 1962. The Cuban revolution had provided the USSR with numerous technical facilities, especially electronic listening posts which could to some degree counteract similar American installations which had encircled the Soviet Union since 1945. The creation of these facilities was followed by a Soviet attempt to rectify the unfavourable strategic balance it faced through the introduction of intermediate range missiles into Cuba. This tactic failed but the crisis was followed by the American withdrawal of IRBMs from Turkey. The United States presented this as a quid pro quo for the Soviet failure to establish a missile base in Cuba. In September 1962 the USSR was also gratified by a pledge given by the Shah of Iran not to permit the establishment of foreign missile bases of any sort on its territory. But technological advances by this stage had altered the strategic planning of the United States; nuclear missile bases close to the territory of its adversary were no longer necessary. The Cuban débâcle dissuaded Moscow from further attempts to restore a nuclear strategic balance cheaply through basing agreements. Soviet leaders resolved instead to develop ICBM technology.

In the 1960s Soviet specialists reinterpreted international law to bolster Moscow's declared opposition to foreign military bases. M. I. Lazarev, the author of a comprehensive analysis in 1963, described 'imperialist' military bases as an important instrument for the preservation of colonialism or the maintenance of neo-colonialism, for interference in the domestic affairs and foreign policy of the states on whose territory they are located. These bases were alleged to be incompatible with the principles of the peaceful coexistence of states with different social systems, to constitute an 'international crime' and to contradict the 'most important principles of international law'. Lazarev declared foreign military bases as illegal on the grounds that they violated the 'criterion of the will of the people' by which the legality of international agreements and foreign policy acts should be judged. In his opinion the phenomenon of bases required 'special defensive measures, not only of a military and political character but also of an international legal character'. He stressed the need to defend the 'independent' countries in this context.[60] This appeal to outlaw the military bases of external powers was issued largely for the consumption of Third World countries and the emergent group of non-aligned states. Since there were few Third World states in the 1960s willing to offer the USSR the military facilities it desired it had little to lose from supporting the principled opposition of the non-aligned group to foreign military bases.

At the first summit of the non-aligned nations in 1961 the Cuban President had declared that 'the peoples reject the installation in their territory of foreign military bases implying an imminent danger of war' not only for reasons of principle 'but by mere instinct of self-preservation'. He had maintained that 'some of these bases do not even answer to strategic necessities in connection with the possibility of a world war, but simply serve for the imperialist domination of the peoples concerned, the subjection of nations and the combating of movements of national liberation'.[61] The Cubans particular grudge was over the United States' retention of the Guantanamo base on Cuban soil against Cuban wishes. The Belgrade Summit appealed to 'those countries maintaining foreign bases to consider seriously their abolition as a contribution to world peace' and referred specifically to Guantanamo.[62] In light of this appeal it was ironic that a superpower crisis developed from subsequent Soviet efforts to establish a missile base in Cuba.

In the 1960s the Non-Aligned Movement remained uncompromising on the issue of military bases conceded 'in the context of Great Power conflicts'. The Cairo Summit in 1964 described foreign bases more forcibly as 'a threat to freedom and international peace', strongly condemned the 'expressed intention of imperialist powers to establish bases in the Indian Ocean', and called upon 'all states maintaining troops and bases in other countries to remove them forthwith'.[63] Soviet writers observed that these resolutions corresponded with resolutions on eliminating foreign bases in the Third World adopted in the UN General Assembly (for example at the Twenty-First Session in December 1965) and described them as part of the broader 'struggle against imperialism'.[64] Moscow wished to cultivate this strand of the policy of the non-aligned states to strengthen their political dispute with the Western powers.

At the Twenty-Third Congress of the CPSU in March 1966 Brezhnev attacked the Western states for scattering 'numerous military bases throughout the world' and deploying 'contingents of their armed forces on the territories of other countries'. He committed the Soviet Union to a policy directed at removing the military bases and armed forces of outside powers from foreign territories.[65] Soviet spokesmen brushed aside Western references to Soviet bases in Eastern Europe and stressed their clean record on bases in the Third World. In the early 1960s the American containment ring around the Soviet bloc had been seriously breached only by the Soviet acquisition of military facilities in Cuba. Soviet capabilities for the long-range projection of power in the Third World were comparatively ineffectual. It followed naturally that in the absence of an effective base network Soviet leaders would adopt a *base denial strategy* directed against the West's military assets.[66] This strategy involved proposals for formal arrangements for joint Great Power elimination of bases and the encouragement of neutralist and non-aligned sentiment in the Third World against Western bases.

By the early 1970s it became apparent that the Soviet Union had become engaged in a much more competitive effort to acquire overseas facilities for similar functions to American ones. The USSR had successfully cultivated military relationships founded on arms sales with a number of radical pro-Soviet or friendly regimes and states in the Middle East and South and Southeast Asia. Western states had lost valued military facilities in the Middle East and Indo-China and were seeking new concessions to offset these losses. To counteract these attempts and to shift the 'correlation of forces' further away from the West in these regions the USSR was tempted to seek facilities in the Third World to enhance its development of long-range air and naval capabilities. At this point it should be underlined that there is no evidence that Soviet military access arrangements in this decade were 'codified by anything resembling the leasehold treaties invariably associated with bases'. This meant that the USSR did not have the security of tenure stipulated by such treaties. This enabled Somali and Egyptian leaders unilaterally and abruptly to terminate Soviet access to their installations in the 1970s. However, while Moscow has not possessed *de jure* foreign bases since the mid 1950s it has obtained at times such extensive control over certain installations that they have resembled extraterritorial enclaves and *de facto* bases.[67]

Following the 1967 Six-day War the Soviet Union developed substantial military facilities in Egypt. Nasser gave Soviet warships access to the port of Alexandria for servicing, and facilities for storage and repair were constructed ashore. The USSR also began developing a second major naval support complex at the port of Mersa Matruh. These facilities enabled a permanent Soviet presence in the East Mediterranean. Nasser rejected the idea of granting the USSR bases in Egypt and he denied Soviet requests for permanent staging and overflight rights. But Soviet piloted aircraft operated, at times on an exclusive basis, from airfields at Cairo West, Aswan and elsewhere on reconnaissance flights.[68] Up to 15,000 Soviet personnel were stationed in Egypt. In the case of these privileges the distinction between facility and base was blurred. However, in 1972 Egypt retook control of all Soviet military facilities in the country and in 1975–6 the Soviet naval facilities were first curtailed, then closed down. This followed clear indications, at least since 1974, that Sadat had attempted to use Soviet port privileges as leverage to obtain arms.[69] Moscow's main response to such attempts to apply reverse influence was to intensify its search for access elsewhere, especially in Syria. But the denouement of the Soviet military presence in Egypt proved at least that the concession of military facilities to the USSR was unlikely in itself to induce a dependent alignment on that power.

In the 1970s Soviet leaders publicly denounced Western military bases in the Mediterranean, although this tended to undermine the legitimacy of their own military presence in Egypt. Soviet spokesmen sought credit from the non-aligned states by attacking Western efforts to turn Cyprus into a NATO military base and by calling for a withdrawal of all foreign forces from the island.[70] Such attacks may have been counterproductive. In 1973 the Libyan leader, Gaddafi, indirectly attacked Egypt for the concessions it had made. He pointed out that his country had 'liquidated the military bases which were in the Mediterranean Sea and...forbidden the entry of Soviet naval ships into its harbours'. He characterised the denial of such access to both superpowers as 'an act of non-alignment'.[71]

Soviet leaders were willing to support such a conception of non-alignment when it hindered the Western states. After the Egyptian leader, Sadat, granted the United States rights to use certain of Egyptian military facilities at the beginning of the 1980s, notably at Ras Banas on the Red Sea, Soviet writers described his 'preparedness to allow military bases for the armed forces of the United States of America on his territory' as being 'in violation of the basic principles of the Non-Aligned Movement'.[72] This development particularly concerned Soviet leaders, although Egypt reserved for itself the right to exercise sovereign control over these facilities. The strategic position of Egypt in relation to the Arabian Peninsula was decisive for American crisis planning under the Carter Doctrine. Moscow hoped to rally the opposition of the Non-Aligned against these developments by linking them to the Camp David Agreement and to Israeli policy.[73]

By this time, however, the USSR itself had gained non-permanent access to Libyan ports and airfields in return for the provision of arms. Moscow still has not acquired extensive onshore facilities in Libya, despite strong rumours that a Soviet delegation sought military bases from Libya during Soviet–Libyan talks in April 1981. This was implied in Gaddafi's declaration that Libya 'resists any attempt to reduce or cancel out its international role by imposing a situation which might oblige it to relinquish neutrality in compelling circumstances'.[74] A Soviet statement vigorously denied that a demand for bases in Libya had been made or that the Soviet Union strove for 'concessions or military bases on foreign territories, including the African continent'.[75] But there is evidence that Soviet officials have unsuccessfully requested Algeria several times for permanent access to ports and short installations and for combined military exercises. In return for military and economic assistance the Syrians, however, have provided the USSR access to the ports of Latakia and Tartus for the servicing of ships as well as to the airfield at Tiyas. Tartus has become the primary maintenance facility for Soviet submarines operating in the Mediterranean.

Even non-aligned Yugoslavia enacted new legal regulations in 1974 which permitted within limits the provision of support services to any 'non-aggressor' navy. Yugoslavia sought to reconcile the economic interest involved in supporting a foreign navy with the political injunction of the non-aligned world against granting base rights to foreign powers. For the first time a non-aligned state provided not only support for Soviet warships on a commercial basis but did so without in the process tarnishing its non-aligned credentials. Soviet leaders unsuccessfully attempted to gain greater access to Yugoslav facilities in 1976. But Yugoslavia maintained restrictions which prevent the Soviet navy from coming ashore in Yugoslavia as it had in Egypt. Since Yugoslav support for the Soviet navy is based less on coordination in security policy than on commercial interest it is not regarded by Belgrade as likely to lead towards a form of alignment with Moscow. In this sense it could act as a model for 'non-aligned naval support' for the USSR.[76]

Soviet officials have considered it necessary, however, to gloss over their search for naval facilities in the Mediterranean to encourage neutralism and maintain pressure on Western bases in other countries in the region.[77] Malta finally eliminated Western military bases from its territory in spring 1979 and the renunciation of bases became a principle of Maltese foreign policy. Malta turned down the offer of an American security guarantee in 1981 for fear that this would require the concession of a military base. The Soviet Union proposed instead an agreement on consultations on Maltese security, which would not involve the establishment of a base and would include Soviet recognition of Malta's status as a neutral country pursuing a policy of non-alignment.[78]

Soviet officials regard such an agreement as ideal also for Greece. They are well aware that the status of the military bases leased by the United States on Greek territory has been a bone of contention in Greek–American and Greek–NATO relations in the 1980s. In 1983 the Soviet media cited a *New York Times* report that in the absence of an agreement with the United States on the bases Greek officials were prepared simply to liquidate them and were 'seriously considering taking up a position of neutrality similar, for example, to that adhered to by Sweden'.[79] This prospect had particular significance to the Soviet Union on account of Greek membership in NATO. In fact a Greek–American agreement was concluded in 1983 governing the status of the United States bases in Greece until December 1988. With this deadline in mind Gorbachev wrote to the Greek Prime Minister, Andreas Papandreou, on the issue of the American bases in May 1987. He informed Papandreou that 'we share your view that these bases, in accordance with the Greek people's unanimous demand, should be removed from the country'. Gorbachev linked this to a broader requirement for states to reject 'any military presence outside national frontiers'.[80]

Soviet leaders have expressed no readiness, however, to withdraw Soviet base facilities in neighbouring Eastern bloc states to compensate for those they wish removed from Greece or for the adoption of neutrality by Greece. Instead Soviet officials have called upon the other NATO country in the region, Turkey, similarly to renounce the United States' military presence. In July 1987, for example, the Soviet Foreign Ministry expressed concern over the new Turkish–American 'agreement on economic and defence cooperation' which defines the American military presence in that country until 1990. Moscow noted that the United States 'was given the right to further use of some sixty military facilities, including big air force bases, nuclear arms depots and radio surveillance centres located close to the southern borders of the USSR'. The Turkish leadership were urged to take 'a fresh look at the situation'.[81]

As in the Mediterranean region the Soviet Union has tried to ride the tide of hostility expressed by non-aligned nations to military bases in South Asia and the Indian Ocean. This has been facilitated by the principled opposition of India, which developed firm political ties with the USSR, to Western bases in this region. Nevertheless, the Soviet Union itself conducted tentative probes for military access in South Asia. For example, in 1969 after a warming in Soviet–Pakistani relations the USSR was willing to help Pakistan construct a naval base for submarines at Kwadar, which was near the Pakistani–Iranian border and the developing Iranian naval base at Chah Bahar. Some Indians interpreted this as a response to India's refusal to offer bases to the Soviet Union. But the project was dropped and reports began to appear in the Western press in the early 1970s of Soviet use of Indian port facilities, especially the naval base at Vishakapatna. In reality the USSR did not ask India for bases but only sought limited facilities for berthing and recreation.[82] This has remained the case despite close Indo-Soviet military links in other respects.

In the early 1970s the United States decided to construct a large naval and air base on the Indian Ocean island of Diego Garcia. This plan was initiated despite strong opposition from the nations bordering the Indian Ocean, which was expressed for example in a joint statement issued in 1974. Western statesmen were inclined to link the military and naval facilities in the Indian Ocean to those found in its littoral states. This tended to complicate the negotiations on the demilitarisation of the region and any development of the Indian Ocean zone of peace proposal. The Soviet Union in turn demanded the elimination of Western military bases in the Indian Ocean as a price for naval arms control accords in this region. In the Soviet view foreign bases in the Indian Ocean should be dismantled as the first step towards the establishment of a zone of peace in the region. At the Twenty-Fifth Congress of the CPSU in 1976 Brezhnev stated categorically that 'the Soviet Union has never had and has no intention now of building military bases in the Indian Ocean' and he called on the United States 'to take the same stand'.[83]

Already in 1975, however, the American Defence Secretary, Schlesinger, had justified the need for the Diego Garcia base as a response *inter alia* to an extensive naval 'facility' built by the Soviet Union at the Somalian port of Berbera. This facility allegedly commanded the strategic approaches to the Red Sea. In 1972 Moscow had gained access to the ports and airfields at Berbera and Mogadishu as well as the airfields at Uanle Uen. Schlesinger additionally alleged that storage facilities for Soviet missiles existed at Berbera. This claim remained unresolved. Although both the USSR and Somalia downplayed the Soviet presence in Berbera, there existed at least a long-range communications station for submarines at Berbera, which formed part of the Soviet nuclear strategic infrastructure. This may have been a Soviet response to the American nuclear war base facilities under construction at Diego Garcia (and to a lesser extent to those at the Kagnew Communications Station near Asmara in Ethiopia which had declined in strategic significance and were slowly being wound down).[84] These Somalian concessions certainly substantially strengthened the Soviet ability to support its permanent naval presence in the Indian Ocean. However, the Berbera facility and Soviet access to Somalian ports, airfields and shore installations was lost in 1977 when the Soviet Union eventually sided with Ethiopia in the Somali–Ethiopian conflict. Somalian pragmatism had already been indicated in October 1974 when the Somali leader Siad Barre had offered the United States naval-base facilities at Kismayu in the south, to balance the Soviet facilities at Berbera in the north. The American administration turned down this offer for fear of weakening the case for constructing the new Diego Garcia base.

In August 1980 the United States assumed control of the naval facilities at Berbera for its Rapid Deployment Force. Both the Soviet Union and the new Ethiopian regime denounced the use of these facilities, but the USSR simultaneously developed facilities off the Ethiopian mainland at the Dahlak Archipelago, including a floating dry-dock, and used Asmara to stage reconnaissance flights over the Red Sea. The agreement on the Dahlak facilities apparently was reached in November 1980 during a visit to Moscow by the Ethiopian leader, Mengistu Haile Mariam. It was not acknowledged in the joint Soviet–Ethiopian statement following this visit. Instead the two countries asserted that 'the creation of military bases in Somalia by the United States administration poses a direct and serious threat to Ethiopia as well as to the peace and security of the countries in that region'. Although the USSR had originally developed the military facilities in Somalia the Soviet and Ethiopian leaders now condemned 'the creation of such bases' and called for their speedy removal.[85]

This denouement in Somalia, following the débâcle in Egypt, further discouraged the Soviet Union from seeking and constructing substantial military and naval facilities or bases in Third World states with a record of instability. The concession of such facilities to the USSR had been shown as no reliable indication of genuine alignment with that power. The establishment of more temporary and flexible facilities, such as floating docks entailed fewer risks when dependent on volatile regimes. The Soviet Union became still more reliant on her facilities in solidly pro-Soviet 'socialist' regimes in the Third World. Cuba hosts numerous Soviet facilities encompassing a large range of military functions. Cuba's proximity to the United States has given it great value for Soviet intelligence, surveillance and communications operations. Intelligence information is gathered by the USSR at the Lourdes installation near Havana, Moscow's largest and most valuable base of this kind outside the USSR. Cuba also grants the Soviet Union facilities for deploying the Soviet

BEAR D long-range reconnaissance aircraft and naval combatants along the United States' East Coast and throughout the Caribbean. In 1970 and again in 1979–80 there were diplomatic skirmishes between the United States and the USSR over Soviet attempts to emplace support barges at Cienfuegos clearly intended to allow for the operation of Soviet nuclear submarines out of Cuba. These Soviet moves were frustrated, but facilities for a 2,800-man Soviet military brigade and 2,800 Soviet military advisers exist in Cuba.[86]

In Vietnam the Soviet Union acquired the use of the former United States' naval and air facilities at Cam Ranh Bay and Danang under a military cooperation agreement which apparently accompanied the signing of the Soviet–Vietnamese Friendship Treaty in November 1978. The Chinese attack on Vietnam in March 1979 gave the USSR the leverage to activate this agreement; a gradual extension of Soviet facilities in Cam Ranh Bay took place over the following years. There is a tendency among American officials to classify Cam Ranh Bay as a fully oprational Soviet military base, and the Reagan administration has used this definition of the Soviet presence in Vietnam to press for increases in American naval deployments and military access in the Far East. Even when American analysts admit that the USSR has access rather than base rights in Cam Ranh Bay and Danang they argue that the apparant permanency of its presence in these ports means that this access has effectively provided the USSR with its only operating military base between Vladivostok and the East coast of Africa. Cam Ranh Bay is regarded as having developed into the largest Soviet naval forward-deployment base outside the USSR. Various Soviet military assets in Cam Ranh Bay are currently listed to support this contention. These include a naval base, a composite air unit, a growing communications, intelligence collection, and logistics support infrastructure. Attention is also drawn to the fact that since late 1984 a Soviet air unit composed of BADGER and BEAR aircraft and a squadron of FLOGGER aircraft have been deployed at Cam Ranh airfield.[87]

It is prudent, however, to describe Cam Ranh Bay as a 'permanent facility' for the USSR. Although reports indicate that the Soviet Union has exclusive control over Cam Ranh Bay there remains a difference in size between it and the Soviet 'base' in Alexandria until 1972 or the American base in the Philippines. Moreover, the Soviet Union has constructed only limited installations and relied upon temporary docking facilities in Cam Ranh Bay. In November 1982 two floating piers and a floating dry-dock were added. As in the case of Soviet facilities in other Third World states these indicate a reluctance to make permanent investments or a major military commitment. This self-imposed limitation by the Soviet leadership probably reflects its unwillingness to subject a major base in Vietnam to the vicissitudes of Sino-Vietnamese relations; the lessons derived from Soviet experience in Egypt and Somalia have not been forgotten. Moreover, for geographic reasons the strategic benefits of Cam Ranh Bay in peacetime are likely to turn into a liability during war.[88]

The Vietnamese themselves do not accept Cam Ranh Bay as a Soviet 'base', although in 1982 Vietnam's Foreign Minister claimed that Vietnam was 'leaving the door open' to the possibility of Soviet bases on its territory if China continued to confront Vietnam.[89] This possibility conflicts with the nationalistic, independent strain in Vietnamese policy. Vietnamese nationalism will probably act as a brake on further unrestrained Soviet development of Cam Ranh Bay and Danang. The Soviet tendency to gloss over its military presence in Vietnam has been accompanied by denunciations of the agreement which permits the Americans to lease their most significant bases in Southeast Asia, Clark Air Base and Subic Bay in the Philippines. Soviet spokesmen claim that the revised conditions governing American access to these bases since 1983 still permit the Americans 'unlimited possibilities to use the bases for their operational goals'.[90] Most recently, however, Admiral Nikolay Amelko, the Deputy Commander-in-Chief of the Soviet Navy and a former Commander of the Soviet Pacific Fleet, has been more frank about Cam Ranh Bay. He described Cam Ranh port as a 'material and technical supply point' used jointly by Vietnamese and Soviet ships rather than a 'naval base in the accepted sense with a full intrastructure'. He contrasted this with Subic Bay where there exist 'weapon stores, and big repair enterprises, docks, and...rented territory which Filipinos are not allowed to enter'.[91]

In the Persian Gulf Soviet leaders have long demanded that an extensive American naval base in Bahrain be dismantled and argued that no comparable Soviet base exists in this region. It is true that Moscow has failed to gain access to military facilities in Iraq, despite some ambiguity over the Soviet status in the port of Umm Qasr. However, the Marxist regime in South Yemen has permitted the USSR the use of port facilities at Aden and numerous airfields for reconnaissance missions over the Indian Ocean and the Horn of Africa. Moscow has also sought military access to port and air facilities in the Seychelles and built the Angolan port of Luanda into the main support facility for the Soviet Navy's West Africa Patrol. Soviet assets in Luanda now include a floating dry-dock, a communications station and access for BEAR D aircraft which patrol the

South Atlantic sealanes. But further concessions from these states to Soviet military requirements will in fact be difficult to justify while Soviet officials routinely castigate other developing states for their military concessions to the West. Indeed, the Angolan constitution contains a provision prohibiting the installation of foreign military bases.

In the 1980s Moscow has endeavoured to expose new American basing networks and strategies. At the beginning of the decade Soviet spokesmen sought to highlight the possibility of new NATO bases being established in connection with alleged plans for a South Atlantic Alliance. They warned ASEAN against granting new bases to the United States. They have also worked to rally Third World opinion, especially in the United Nations, against various island dependencies which remain in the American and Western orbit. Much attention has been paid to Diego Garcia as an anti-American rallying point among the Non-Aligned. The Soviet Union has concentrated its attacks on American military bases located in the Indian Ocean and its littoral states. A detailed Soviet study of American policy in the Indian Ocean published in 1984 identified over thirty American military bases in the Indian Ocean basin. The author defined the three primary tasks of American base policy in this region as follows: to help carry out plans for American rapid deployment forces in crises, to secure a permanent United States' military-naval presence in this region, and to transform this zone into a potential front of strategic nuclear war.[92]

In January 1980 a Soviet commentator noted that according to the admissions of the American State Department 'the leaders of Egypt, Oman, Somalia and Kenya have agreed to grant the Pentagon the right to use the ports and a number of military installations in their countries'. Eschewing strategic analysis in favour of a more polemical approach he argued that these concessions were to be used as 'trans-shipping points for American combat units that are to carry out punitive operations against the peoples of the Near and Middle East, as well as in Africa'. In assisting the implementation of these Western plans these developing countries were 'demonstrating their disregard for the principles of the Non-Aligned Movement'.[93] An appeal to the principles of non-alignment had formed one strand in the Soviet strategy of base denial. But this tactic was seriously undermined by Soviet military intervention in Afghanistan at the end of 1979, which was widely deplored among non-aligned states. A number of Third World states reacted to this assertion of superpower force against a weak non-aligned state by accepting the need for counter-vailing American military power. Soviet spokesmen acknowledged that Washington explained the consent of Egypt, Oman, Somalia and Kenya 'to give in to the American military' by 'their concern for some kind of threat which allegedly comes from the decision of the Afghan leaders to rely on Soviet aid in repulsing outside intrigues'. The American media, Moscow admitted, 'claim that such a decision allegedly runs counter to the principles of non-alignment'.[94]

It was precisely the massive Soviet military presence in Afghanistan, and the creation of a military infrastructure in that hitherto non-aligned country enabling a protracted Soviet 'occupation', which cast the principled Soviet opposition to foreign military bases in Third World countries under a cloud of cynicism. In December 1978 the Premier of the new Marxist regime in Afghanistan, Taraki, declared on Soviet television that 'Afghanistan and the Soviet Union resolutely condemn the creation of military bases on the territories of other countries'.[95] At the Non-Aligned Summit the following year in Havana he demanded 'the termination of all imperialistic foreign military bases in the territory of others' and described them as 'being inconsistent with the sovereignty and territorial integrity of the countries concerned'.[96] Soon after this statement, in November 1979, Taraki's successor Hafizullah Amin reportedly rebuffed a Soviet request to establish an air base at Shindand near the Iranian border. The USSR had linked this request to the developing situation in Iran and the danger of United States' intervention to rescue the American being held hostage.[97] Twelve days before Soviet troops entered Afghanistan Amin gave his word that 'no Soviet military bases will be built in Afghanistan because we do not need them'.[98] But even before the establishment of the Karmal regime the USSR had acquired some control over the major military air base at Bagram near Kabul; this was the base Soviet troops were initially airlifted into at the end of 1979. It is likely that Amin's known opposition to the idea of establishing Soviet military bases on Afghan soil influenced the Soviet decision to remove him from power.

After Babrak Karmal replaced Amin further construction began on an infrastructure and airfields for Soviet military operations within Afghanistan. These may not have constituted bases in the fullest sense nor been intended as permanent strategic installations, but Western statesmen have focussed on their potential and the capabilities they give the Soviet Union. Particular concern has been expressed over the construction of an air base at Shindand in western Afghanistan. One scenario Western strategist feared was the possibility of the USSR basing Backfire bombers in Afghanistan, which could range widely across the Indian Ocean. It is true that Soviet-controlled airfields at Bagram, Kabul, Kandahar and Shindand have runways long enough for long-range strategic aircraft. But these facilities were built before 1980 with earlier Soviet and American military and economic assistance. Since then the USSR has not substantially lengthened their runways. Soviet officials have been unwilling to specify the nature or duration of Soviet-constructed military installations in Afghanistan.

Western statesmen have accused the USSR of intending to turn this country into a forward military base aimed at the Persian Gulf and the Indian Ocean. The typical Soviet response has been that 'the Soviet Union did not and does not intend to turn Afghanistan into a base against other countries'.[99] The broad definition of a 'base' contained in such statements left open the possibility that a settlement of the Afghan conflict along Soviet lines would involve not only the retention of Soviet military advisers but a Soviet–DRA agreement on granting the USSR some form of military base rights in Afghanistan following the withdrawal of Soviet troops from that country. Soviet sources allegedly aired the idea that Kabul should be prepared to grant Moscow such rights 'possibly patterned after the Porkkala naval base precedent in Finland'.[100] This idea has not publicly been advanced by Moscow, and in November 1986 during a visit to India Mikhail Gorbachev told his hosts specifically that 'we are not going to have any bases in Afghanistan'.[101]

Moscow has attempted, rather unsuccessfully, to shift the attention of the Third World from Soviet forces in Afghanistan to the alleged use of Pakistani territory for military purposes by the United States and China. The USSR has derided Pakistan's 'non-bloc policy' on this basis. Soviet leaders have sought to exploit Indian hostility to Pakistan and Indian influence among the Non-Aligned to persuade the latter to denounce 'American bases' on Pakistani soil. But only the radical pro-Soviet regimes in the Non-Aligned Movement were prepared to engage in such attacks. Moscow has publicised a secret agreement allegedly signed between Washington and Islamabad in June 1982 which offered the United States the right to use Pakistani naval and air bases. Pakistan ostensibly kept such 'strategic cooperation' secret to avoid the charge that it was violating the status of a non-aligned country.[102] Such Soviet claims have been consistently rejected by Pakistani officials. In an address to the Pakistani National Assembly and Senate in December 1985 President Zia formally denied that his country had given any bases to the United States.[103]

Despite the controversy surrounding Soviet military action in Afghanistan, Soviet spokesmen in the mid 1980s still try to direct the principles of non-alignment against Western military links with Third World states.

A Soviet specialist observed in 1984 that recent American agreements on bases scarcely mentioned the term 'base'. In order to hide the true extent of military–political cooperation the parties used instead formulations which would attract less attention such as 'understandings on access to facilities'. Washington had agreements with a number of states in the Indian Ocean basin, he claimed, on the joint use of local military bases and installations by American and national armed forces.[104] Another Soviet writer specified that 'United States and NATO military bases exist on the territory of distinct non-aligned states'. He noted that 'Somalia, Kenya, Oman, Zaire, Morocco, and Pakistan tightly cooperate with the USA and all of these continue to remain participants of the [Non-Aligned] Movement'.[105] In his view 'one of the levers of pressure on the policy of the new states by the West is military cooperation, which expresses itself in rendering military assistance, the sale of modern arms, the dispatch of a significant number of Western military advisers to the developing countries and, finally, the creation of military bases on the territory of a series of non-aligned states'. Although such military cooperation equally characterised Soviet–Third World relations it was described as 'incompatible with both the principles and the criteria of non-alignment'.[106] However, by these Soviet standards of judgement not only Afghanistan but a number of African and Asian states in the Non-Aligned Movement have breached the principles of non-alignment in the 1980s through various forms of military cooperation with the Soviet Union.

Despite Soviet action in Afghanistan Soviet leaders believe that the 'Non-Aligned World' still associated the notion of military intervention in the Third World primarily with the Western powers. With this assumption in mind Gorbachev told the Indian Prime Minister Rajiv Gandhi in May 1985 that 'the newly independent countries do not want to be regarded any longer as objects for profit-making and for installing military bases and strongpoints in their territories'. He stressed that in this matter 'these countries can and must be understood'.[107] The Western states have always possessed a more extensive range of military bases and facilities in the Third World than the Soviet Union, and American strategists have relied on such facilities more than their Soviet counterparts to sustain regional and global commitments and military contingency plans. The USSR lent its declaratory support to the principled opposition of the Non-Aligned to foreign military bases and this diplomatic aspect to the Soviet strategy of 'base denial' enabled Moscow to gain credit among non-aligned states. An illustration of the arguments underpinning this strategy was provided by a Soviet commentator who compared the Soviet abandonment of its naval base at Porkkala in 1955 with the American retention of its base at Guantanamo in Cuba. He claimed that the military significance of Porkkala for the USSR had been similar to that of Guantanamo for the United States. But he described the Soviet abandonment of bases on foreign territories as a demonstration to other countries of a 'real way of alleviating international tension', which had been grounded on the assumption that 'the NATO countries, and the USA in particular, would follow its example'. Instead, he claimed, the United States had access in 1985 to 'forty-three naval bases and over seventy airfields, of which a considerable number are situated close to the Soviet border'.[108]

In 1981 the Soviet military specialist Major-General Slobodenko wrote an exposition on the 'bases strategy' as a component of the post-war military doctrine of the United States. He described the changes in the functions of American bases as corresponding to changes in military doctrine and military technology. Their purpose, he concluded, was 'to prepare and wage aggressive wars against the Soviet Union and other socialist states, and to suppress the national liberation and revolutionary movements in countries of Africa, Asia and Latin America'[109] Slobodenko ignored the fact that Soviet military facilities overseas performed 'a multiplicity of military functions, somewhat but not precisely paralleling similar US requirements'. These were adapted to the needs of the Soviet navy and air force. Haselkorn has argued that the USSR has also established aerial staging networks which were used for the airlift of arms to Angola and Ethiopia in the 1970s and which are of paramount importance for Soviet access strategy in the Third World.[110] Furthermore, in connection with strategic missilry and associated surveillance operations, the Soviet Union has developed growing needs for facilities such as 'telemetry monitoring, ASW, nuclear test detection, communications and satellite tracking – many of which involve interconnected global or regional networks'. Harkavy speculates that, as in the case of the United States, such requirements 'may dictate an ever-escalating quest for new points of access, even if and when those of aerial staging and naval replenishments should reach the point of virtual global redundancy'.[111]

It should be emphasised that unlike the United States the USSR has not made extensive use of overseas 'forward' garrisons in the Third World. These involve the stationing of combat troop units on a large scale and may well infringe upon the sovereignty of the host country. In an assessment of the United States' principle of 'forward basing' Slobodenko observed that since the late 1960s the American leadership began to scale down the numbers of their troops abroad. He argued that 'the stationing of large military contingents on the territory of other countries requires big expenditures and, most important, is connected with political complications caused by the growing dissatisfaction of the peoples of these countries and demands for the withdrawal of American troops from their territory'.[112] The final reference to 'American troops' does not fully disguise this veiled reference to the problems raised by the location of Soviet troops in Afghanistan. The Soviet presence in Afghanistan in the 1980s has further undermined the credibility of Soviet appeals to withdraw military forces from overseas. But since the USSR remains disadvantaged in respect of military facilities in the Third World the Gorbachev leadership may press for general negotiated limitations on superpower military and naval bases and facilities on foreign territories.

In an important speech on disarmament in February 1987 Gorbachev asserted that while it remained best 'to revive the old idea of dismantling foreign bases and bringing the troops home' in the short term it would be desirable to have inspection access to American military bases on foreign territories for verification purposes 'to be sure that there is no activity going on there which is forbidden under an eventual agreement'.[113] This proposal implied a Soviet preparedness to offer its own facilities for inspection. It primarily reflected nuclear strategic concerns. This was confirmed by a further Soviet proposal in May 1987. Gorbachev suggested that Soviet medium-range missiles in Asia could be abandoned altogether in return for the Americans giving up their nuclear bases in the Pacific. Lev Mendelevich, head of the Soviet Foreign Ministry's Planning Department spoke of 'huge American bases in South Korea, Japan and the Philippines'.[114] This initiative implicitly offered the possibility of a Soviet–American arrangement involving mutual restraints on bases on the Asian mainland and in the Pacific. But it was not taken seriously in the West and Moscow did not persist in linking these American bases to the INF negotiations underway.

In the same month, in his letter to Papandreou on the issue of the American bases in Greece, Gorbachev proposed that foreign military presence on the territory of other countries should be renounced everywhere. He accepted that 'appeals for a reduction and, in the final analysis, a rejection of any military presence outside national frontiers concern us too'. He referred to the withdrawal of Soviet units from Mongolia and Soviet preparations to withdraw from Afghanistan. Gorbachev also reiterated his proposal for inspection access to foreign military bases.[115] The Soviet leadership could anticipate diplomatic dividends from these initiatives among the non-aligned countries. But

Washington is not likely to abandon its 'forward garrisons' in the Third World simply in exchange for a Soviet withdrawal from Afghanistan.

These recent proposals reflect Moscow's current priority to retrench economically and militarily in the Third World. Soviet military facilities in Africa and Asia had been acquired and retained only by diverting considerable resources into military assistance programmes and they encouraged demands for open-ended Soviet economic assistance. A recent Soviet report from Kabul stated, for example, that 'the Soviet Union is more than anyone interested in the return home of its soldiers [from Afghanistan]. In the first place this will save huge funds'.[116] In the political sphere Soviet military activism had soured the *détente* relationship with the West by infringing on areas which hitherto had not experienced Soviet military involvement.[117] The USSR had had a long-standing military relationship with Afghanistan but the scale of the Soviet military intervention in that country in the 1980s and the forms it took were quite unprecedented in Soviet–Third World relations. The experience of Soviet military facilities in Africa and the Middle East in the 1970s discouraged Soviet leaders from attempting to invest substantial military commitments in remote and volatile Third World states elsewhere, especially when they were in areas of clearly proclaimed American interest. This was forcibly underlined by the Soviet failure to exert effective military or political control over Afghanistan despite its geographical contiguity with the USSR.

An opinion expressed by Karen Brutents, the senior Soviet official and Third World specialist, is revealing in this context. He described the views of some American politicians that 'Nicaragua threatens US national security and that there are, or shortly will be, Soviet military bases there' as 'too fanciful' to merit much attention. He similarly dismissed a statement by the American Secretary of State, Shultz, that Nicaragua 'could become the source of another crisis similar to the Cuban crisis'.[118] The USSR is not prepared to expose itself in this fashion in Nicaragua. Soviet facilities would be less exposed in bordering states. But when ABC Television reported in March 1987 that the USSR and Iran had reached an agreement 'to set up two super-secret Soviet electronic reconnaissance stations in Iranian territory' to monitor American naval ships in the Persian Gulf Tass rejected this report as 'utterly groundless'.[119] For the USSR broader political calculations currently outweigh the military rationale for attempting to gain a visible military presence in such strategically sensitive countries as Nicaragua or Iran.

Soviet policy towards military facilities overseas will continue to be determined by a fluid assessment of the political and military losses and gains involved. But Soviet leaders are now fully aware that the duration of the military gains achieved through agreements on military facilities in Third World regions is unpredictable. Their experience shows that military facilities may be conceded by a Third World state to the USSR when there exists a coincidence of interests but that such concessions provide leverage on Soviet policy as often as they act as levers for Soviet policy iñ bilateral relations with the Third World party. Such 'alignment' as is achieved will always depend on the vagaries of Soviet–Third World political relations.

FRIENDSHIP, COOPERATION AND ASSISTANCE TREATIES

Soviet leaders have endeavoured to compensate for their exclusion from formal military alliances and pacts in the Third World by entering into a whole series of bilateral security arrangements with Asian and African states through treaties of friendship and cooperation. These have often provided the basis for protracted military relationships between the treaty parties. The implications of the · military and political commitments contained in these treaties for the Third World treaty partner have varied from case to case, but it is clear that in certain cases the consequences of these treaties have compromised the non-aligned policy of the Third World state in question. It has not been politically expedient for either party to admit this.

One of the earliest acts of Soviet diplomacy was the conclusion of treaties with defence provisions in 1921 with Persia, Turkey and Afghanistan. These treaties were intended to insulate Soviet borders from external threats in the aftermath of foreign intervention. After the Second World War Soviet leaders also assumed responsibilities for the defence of certain 'allied' states outside Europe. A treaty concluded with North Korea in 1961 contained specific defence provisions. In 1950 the USSR committed itself to a Treaty of Friendship, Alliance and Mutual Assistance with China, which lapsed in April 1979. The treaty with North Korea effectively constituted a mutual defence pact, while the treaty with China was an actual alliance to coordinate defence against an attack by 'Japan or states allied with it'. Both these treaties were signed during years of acute Cold War tension and they dated from the brief period of political coordination between the Soviet Union and China (China like the USSR signed a treaty with North Korea in 1961). In contrast a defence pact signed by the USSR and Mongolia in 1966 was directed specifically against China. All these treaties fall into a different category to the friendship and cooperation treaties concluded by the USSR in the Third World since the beginning of the 1970s.

The co-signatories of Soviet friendship and cooperation treaties have all been member states of the Non-Aligned Movement, including many of the more prominent moderate non-aligned states. In most cases these treaties have contained general provisions on the cooperation of the parties over certain aspects of their security policies rather than direct commitments to joint military activity. The Soviet assertion has been that such treaties bolster the non-alignment of Third World states. Western officials have challenged this assertion. They have been aware that the unspecific clauses in the friendship and cooperation treaties have often been supplemented by specific agreements on defence and the provision of military facilities.

A further Western concern has been the possibility of these bilateral treaties assuming intra-regional, multilateral characteristics in the field of security. This could enable Moscow to bring considerable influence to bear on regional issues in the Third World while gaining credit for its continued opposition to military blocs in principle. However, national rivalries and other centrifugal forces in the Third World have impeded the transformation of Moscow's network of bilateral treaties and agreements into an effective multilateral structure.

Soviet leaders hoped initially that multilateral arrangements could emerge from an Indo-Soviet treaty of friendship and cooperation. From June 1969 Soviet leaders exhorted the Asian states to draw together in a collective security system. India was reluctant to endorse this blatantly anti-Chinese scheme. Nevertheless, in September 1969 Soviet officials presented India with the draft of a friendship and cooperation treaty; the two countries initiated diplomatic negotiations on the terms of such a security pact well before autumn 1971. India finally accepted the offer of a bilateral treaty with the USSR when it found itself isolated and threatened in its confrontation with Pakistan. This act was precipitated by an announcement by President Nixon on 15 July 1971 that he would visit China before May 1972. On the day the treaty was signed on 9 August 1971 the Indian Foreign Minister tried to convince China that it was 'not aimed at any third country'. He expressed his hope that the treaty would 'provide a pattern for similar treaties between India and other countries in this region'. This reflected the Soviet aspiration that the Indo-Soviet treaty act as an example for other Asian states. When he received Indira Gandhi in Moscow the following month Kosygin repeated that the treaty was 'not directed at any state'. The broader regional relevance of the treaty was implied in his claim that the interest of the USSR and India in the consolidation of security in Asia and the world ran 'like a red thread through the Soviet–Indian treaty'.[120]

The Indian Foreign Minister described the 1971 treaty as a treaty of non-aggression, a reference to Article 8 of the treaty which forbade the parties from participating 'in any military alliance directed against the other party'. This kind of commitment became standard for Soviet friendship and cooperation treaties. He also referred to it as a treaty of peace against war, a reference to the specific obligations of Article 9. This, he noted, provided an assurance that in the event of an attack or the threat of such against either India or the Soviet Union both parties 'shall immediately enter into mutual consultations in order to remove such a threat and to take appropriate effective measures to ensure peace and the security of their countries'.[121] It was under this article that the Soviet Deputy Foreign Minister, N. Firyubin, arrived in New Delhi for consultations with the Indian Government on 22 October 1971. The primary subject under discussion was the mounting crisis in South Asia over East Pakistan. He was followed by the Commander-in-Chief of the Soviet Air Force on 30 October. The consultations provision of the Indo-Soviet treaty did not necessarily require cooperation or collaboration or the formation of an Indo-Soviet bloc. But it was reported in 1971 that the Soviet Ambassador in New Delhi had assured India that in case China took advantage of India's confrontation with Pakistan by mounting an attack across the Himalayas, the Soviet Union would begin diversionary action in Sinkiang. There were some claims that one of the reasons for Chinese inaction militarily during the Indo-Pakistani war at that time was Moscow's fulfillment of its treaty with India through an increased provision of military supplies and timely troop movements along the Chinese border.[122] No doubt India acquired benefits from the Indo-Soviet treaty when the decision was made to impose a military solution to the East Pakistan problem in December, and the existence of the treaty may have encouraged this drastic response. But persistent Soviet attempts to promote a political and peaceful solution in East Pakistan, to avoid an Indo-Pakistani war made it unclear whether Soviet leaders actually wished the treaty to be used in this way.[123]

Article 9 of the 1971 treaty was received with mixed feelings in India. One of India's most prominent papers, the *Statesman*, described it in a lead editorial on 10 August as 'virtually a military arrangement' and identified 'every evidence of alignment in a treaty almost indistinguishable from a defence pact'. The influential *Times of India* also considered that the treaty represented 'a departure from the policy of non-alignment as interpreted all these years'. The Soviet leaderrship certainly had equated Indian non-alignment with her non-participation in defence pacts. Brezhnev made this point, for example, in discussions with President Ayub Khan of Pakistan in April 1965.[124] But it would be mistaken to regard the provisions of this treaty as comparable with those, for example, of the Soviet–North Korean Treaty of Friendship, Cooperation and Mutual Assistance. In contrast to the latter the Indian treaty did not openly oblige the USSR to declare war against any third party that attacked India.

The emphasis of the 1971 treaty in current conditions may be more on military denial to third parties. Article 9 enjoins the two parties 'to refrain from giving any assistance to any third party taking any part in an armed conflict with another party'. In the 1980s Moscow has claimed that Pakistan is in virtual confrontation with the Soviet forces in Afghanistan. This gives a special meaning to Article 10 of the treaty which provides that India and the USSR 'shall not undertake any commitment secret or open with regard to one or more states incompatible with the present treaty'. The commitments of the 1971 treaty tend thereby to preclude India from signing a no-war pact with Pakistan despite the expressed interest of Islamabad in such an arrangement.[125]

Soviet commentators have preferred not to analyse the security mechanism provided by the Indo-Soviet treaty. They have emphasised instead that it enshrined the Soviet respect for the Indian policy of non-alignment (in Article 4). A Soviet legal specialist even described the treaty as an important historical stage in establishing non-alignment as an international legal status and foreign policy course. In his view the Soviet appraisal of non-alignment in this treaty applied not solely to India but to the international legal institution of non-alignment as a whole. He noted that the USSR had expressed its recognition of the non-alignment of a Third World state in an analagous fashion in Article 1 of the Treaty of Friendship signed on 21 March 1964 between the USSR and the Yemen Arab Republic.[126] The Soviet commitment to Indian non-alignment in the context of the Indo-Soviet treaty should not, however, be exaggerated. Soviet 'respect' for Indian non-alignment was simply a concession during the drafting of the treaty in return for Indian respect for the 'peace-loving policy' of the USSR.[127] The Soviet Union signed treaties of friendship and cooperation with the United Arab Republic (Egypt) in 1971 and Iraq in 1972 which contained no comparable reference to non-alignment. After the Algiers Non-Aligned Summit pronounced new radical goals in 1973 Soviet appreciation of Third World non-alignment became a standard component of Soviet friendship and cooperation treaties but this respect was not intended as a restraint on the operation of the security and defence provisions of these treaties.

Contrary to the Indo-Soviet treaty, the treaties Moscow signed with the United Arab Republic on 28 May 1971 and Iraq on 9 April 1972 contained specific articles on the development of cooperation between the parties to strengthen their defence capacity. It has been argued that the Soviet–Iraqi treaty effectively gave contractual authorisation for the stationing of Soviet forces in Iraq or for Soviet use of Iraqi sea and air bases.[128] If this interpretation is valid, there existed still firmer grounds for similar concessions to the Soviet Union under the more detailed terms of the Soviet–Egyptian treaty. Article 8 of the Egyptian treaty stipulated that Egypt would be assisted in training its military personnel to use the arms and equipment it received. The Treaty of Friendship and Cooperation concluded between the USSR and Somalia on 11 July 1974 included a comparable article obliging joint cooperation 'in the field of armed forces' and envisaging Soviet training of Somali military personnel and supply of armaments and equipment.[129]

It became customary for Soviet friendship and cooperation treaties with Third World states to include a Soviet commitment to develop and consolidate the defence potential of her treaty partner. The contractual obligation of cooperation in the military field in these treaties could provide mutual benefits, although the disparity in resources of the treaty parties meant that their contributions in the equation would not be similar in form. In exchange for the Soviet provision of arms and training the smaller and less developed treaty party has usually been expected to provide services to Soviet planes and ships and to permit them to use its military facilities. Such concessions have been greatly valued in Moscow. Third World states in turn have benefited from Soviet military supplies and assistance.

From the Egyptian perspective the Soviet provision of military hardware, especially advanced technology, and Soviet support for Egypt's stand against Israel acted as the very *raison d'être* of the Soviet–Egyptian Friendship and Cooperation treaty. President Sadat regarded Article 8 of the treaty as an important lever in his campaign to acquire open Soviet support for his plans to use 'every means' at his disposal to liberate the occupied territories. It is noteworthy, however, that as in the case of the 1971 Soviet–Indian treaty the Soviet Union did not commit itself in the Soviet–Egyptian treaty to direct involvement in a war involving the other party. Nevertheless, in both cases the USSR undertook a heavy political commitment. Soviet spokesmen were reluctant to elaborate the military aspects of the Soviet–Egyptian treaty. At its conclusion the Soviet press underlined instead the extent to which the treaty would consolidate the advances Egypt had made along the socialist path and serve as a model for future relations between the Soviet Union and the other Third World countries.[130]

This Soviet emphasis served to draw attention away from the implications of the defence provisions of the early friendship and cooperation treaties for the non-aligned policies of the Third World treaty parties. The standard Soviet contention was that the principles of non-alignment were consistent with such treaties since the latter had no aggressive aims and were not intended to draw the non-aligned states into military alliances but to strengthen their independence and to broaden multilateral cooperation.[131] Certain Soviet commentaries accepted that the treaties were directed at creating a political alliance between their signatories but failed to see a contradiction between this objective and a policy of non-alignment. A Soviet broadcast in August 1973 described it as 'contrary to logic and common sense' to equate the Soviet–Egyptian and Soviet–Iraqi treaties, 'which express the inevitability of close alliance between the forces of socialism and national liberation', with 'alignment with imperialist blocs'.[132] However, Iraqi, Egyptian and Somali leaders did not conceive of their treaties with the USSR as charters to encourage general political and ideological coordination with the Soviet Union. They remained primarily interested in using these treaties to bolster their defences by means of Soviet assistance. This proved to be a calculated, and in the case of Egypt and Somalia transitory, form of 'alignment'.

After signing the Soviet–Iraqi treaty Iraq received a large supply of Soviet arms. President Sadat of Egypt had still greater demands and his frustration over the failure of Soviet leaders to deliver the arms he expected helped gradually to undermine the Soviet position in Egypt. Sadat was satisfied with the provision of Soviet arms and technicians in spring 1973. Soviet leaders felt compelled to resupply Egypt on a massive scale during the October Yom Kippur War in order to avoid a total loss of their investment in that country. But over the following years Soviet–Egyptian relations soured over the issue of arms deliveries and the Egyptian debt to the USSR. Finally, on 14 March 1976 Sadat unilaterally abrogated the Soviet–Egyptian Treaty of Friendship.[133] A Tass announcement the following day claimed that this merely placed a 'juridical seal' on a situation in which the operation of the treaty had in fact been 'paralysed' as a result of Sadat's unfriendly policy towards the Soviet Union. It was ironic, however, that only three weeks previously Brezhnev had praised the treaty in a speech to the Twenty-Fifth Party Congress as 'a long-term basis for relations conforming with the interests not only of our two countries but also of the Arab world'.[134] Sadat's action was particularly damaging to the Soviet image in the Third World since Egypt had been the first Third World state to sign such a treaty with the USSR. This blow to Soviet credibility was compounded the following year when Soviet leaders refused to render Somalia the military supplies and support she demanded to press her irredentist claims on Ethiopian territory. Somalia reacted similarly by abrogating her friendship treaty with the Soviet Union on 13 November 1977. Soviet military advisers and technicians were expelled subsequently from Egypt and Somalia and Soviet rights of access to military facilities in these states were terminated. In both cases failure to reach an understanding over the defence provisions of the friendship treaties led to a breakdown in bilateral relations.

Soviet publications written before these setbacks in Soviet policy had adopted an optimistic tone in describing the friendship and cooperation treaties concluded with developing states and had concentrated on their political aspects. An authoritative text of the Soviet Diplomatic Academy described the general security provisions of these treaties but contained no reference to the commitments on developing defence capabilities. It regarded the treaties as evidence of growing understanding among Third World states of the importance of firm cooperation with the Soviet bloc for resolving the tasks of national development. Such treaties ostensibly 'facilitated the conduct of a policy of non-alignment by the liberated countries'.[135] The Soviet–Egyptian treaty had not explicitly expressed Soviet respect for the Egyptian policy of non-alignment, but to remain consistent with this line Soviet recriminations in the aftermath of the break with Egypt included the charge that Sadat had 'refrained from a consistent implementation of non-alignment'. Soviet writers maintained that the separate negotiations with Israel which Sadat subsequently entered into 'greatly harmed the status of Egypt as a non-aligned country' and constituted a blow against the Non-Aligned Movement as a whole.[136] Sadat's allegations of Soviet unfaithfulness as a treaty partner were strongly refuted. Somalia was attacked similarly for colluding with the United States. It was not only Soviet prestige which was at stake during these bitter exchanges since there were figures in the Iraqi leadership in 1978 who strongly advocated following the example of Egypt and Somalia and denouncing their own friendship treaty with the USSR. Although Iraq decided against this course of action the Iraqi treaty lost much of its content.[137]

Despite the dissolution of the Soviet friendship treaties with Egypt and

Somalia Soviet leaders remained convinced of the potential of such treaties as a means of institutionalising security relations and political consultations with Third World states. Indo-Soviet relations remained unaffected by the turmoil in Soviet relations with her other Third World treaty partners in the mid 1970s. In June 1976 Moscow and New Delhi decided in fact to further develop the practice of bilateral political consultations making them 'systematic and substantive and paying special attention to using them in assisting the implementation of agreed measures to strengthen peace, international security and cooperation'.[138] Elsewhere Soviet leaders successfully negotiated friendship and cooperation treaties with the radical regimes in Angola (8 October 1976), Mozambique (31 March 1977), Vietnam (3 November 1978), Ethiopia (20 November 1978), Afghanistan (5 December 1978), South Yemen (25 October 1979) and Syria (8 October 1980). Only the treaty with Vietnam followed the exact formula of the 1971 Soviet–Indian treaty, according to which the parties 'will immediately begin consultations' under the conditions specified. However, the other treaties contained clauses obliging the parties immediately 'to enter contact with each other' in the event that their security or international peace is threatened, or to engage in regular bilateral consultations on important international questions.

All the Third World states which concluded these arrangements had formally entered the Non-Aligned Movement but tended to support the Soviet stand on disputed issues between East and West. Soviet officials regarded them as socialist oriented in their domestic pattern of development. (Egypt had also been included among the Arab states of socialist orientation until the Twenty-Fifth Party Congress in February 1976. It was excised from that category of developing states in Soviet classifications after the cancellation of the Soviet–Egyptian treaty.) This influenced the general Soviet characterisation of friendship treaties with Third World states. By the end of the 1970s a Soviet specialist identified the particular characteristic of these treaties in the fact that they were concluded between a socialist state and countries which were in the process of creating new social structures leading towards socialism. The treaties were described as the international legal expression of a change in the global correlation of class forces. They were believed to provide the contractual basis of a shift in the balance of Third World political loyalties in favour of the USSR. At the same time, Soviet specialists maintained that the legal quality of non-alignment did not prohibit non-aligned states from entering into contractual relations of the form represented by the new treaties with the Soviet Union.[139] In support of this line, which reflected the politicised Soviet perception of non-alignment in the late 1970s, Soviet spokesmen have pointed to the respect Moscow has formally expressed for the non-alignment of her treaty partners in virtually all the friendship and cooperation treaties concluded since 1976.

Officials in many Western countries and West-leaning Third World states have dismissed or regarded rather cynically claims that the new friendship and cooperation treaties are consistent with or even strengthen a policy of non-alignment. In the first place, they contend that the actual operation of these new treaties has appeared to reflect an increasing Soviet reliance on military instruments in its policy towards the Third World. Unlike the Indo-Soviet treaty of 1971, provisions concerning military cooperation and assistance were inserted in all the new treaties (indirectly in the case of the treaty with Vietnam) and were used to justify unprecedented forms of Soviet military involvement in the Third World. Moreover, since the new treaties Moscow concluded were with states economically and politically weaker than Egypt had been, the military dependence of these states on the USSR could more readily be translated into political dependence. The second reason for doubting the non-aligned basis of these new treaty relationships arose from the clear pro-Soviet ideological orientation they expressed for certain Third World states, especially for Vietnam in the Soviet–Vietnamese treaty. In a more general sense Soviet leaders expected that the treaties would also provide the basis for multilateral support in the Third World for Soviet regional and global security initiatives.

The terms of the Soviet–Angolan and Soviet–Ethiopian treaties on strengthening the defence capabilities of the parties and on cooperation in the military field (Articles 10) legitimised the specific agreements which led to the large-scale supply of Soviet arms and equipment to defend the Angolan and Ethiopian regimes against external and internal attack. The Soviet Union responded to the Somali attack on Ethiopia during summer 1977 with an airlift of Soviet arms to Ethiopia in November. Cuban and Soviet military advisers became directly involved in the conflict. However, these measures preceded the conclusion of the 1978 Soviet–Ethiopian Treaty of Friendship and Cooperation by a full year. Soviet officials signed a secret arms agreement with an Ethiopian delegation in Moscow as early as December 1976[140] in full knowledge of the hostility existing between this state and Somalia. This was done notwithstanding the Soviet–Somali treaty of 1974. Similar flexibility characterised Soviet policy towards the Angolan MPLA. This organisation had been receiving Soviet arms years before it won power and concluded the Soviet–Angolan Friendship Treaty of 1976. Egypt had also been a recipient of large quantities of Soviet arms before signing her treaty with Moscow in 1971. Obviously the Soviet decision to provide arms to threatened or beleaguered Third World states stems in the first place from an appraisal of rapidly changing political and military considerations rather than from a scrutiny of broad-based bilateral accords, and there are advantages in not publicising such intentions in advance. The commitment to the development of defence capabilities found in the Soviet friendship and cooperation treaties effectively only expresses the Soviet view that under certain conditions, which depend on Soviet judgement, the USSR will be prepared to act as a supplier of military hardware and assistance to its Third World treaty partners. Since the form of such assistance is not specified in these treaties this is also subject to short-term Soviet calculations of strategic and political losses and gains.

Soviet unwillingness to assume and fulfil broad-based military commitments in relation to such states, as could be expected from a relationship of military alignment, was indicated by Moscow's conduct towards Somalia and Mozambique. Article 4 of the Soviet–Somali Treaty of Friendship and Cooperation of 1974 was unusually specific in explaining that military cooperation between the two states would include the training of Somalian military personnel in the assimilation of armaments and equipment provided. However, when Somalia wished to turn its Soviet trained and equipped army against Ethiopia in 1977 Moscow cut back on its military assistance to Somalia (this officially ended in mid October), and Somali frustration eventually resulted in its renunciation of the friendship treaty with the USSR. In an astute act of *realpolitik* Soviet leaders redirected their military favours towards Ethiopia. Although from the Soviet perspective this shift in loyalties had the benefit of cementing Soviet–Ethiopian relations it underlined a lesson provided by the course of recent Soviet–Egyptian relations: that a Third World recipient of Soviet arms can apply reverse influence when wishing to pursue regional military ambitions. These experiences also indicated the unpredictable outcome for the USSR of becoming embroiled in distant regional conflicts alongside a Third World treaty partner. Loyalty to the spirit of a treaty had to be weighed against a calculation of potential strategic losses and gains. Thus while Mozambique received quantities of Soviet arms in the late 1970s in keeping with the commitment to military cooperation in the 1977 Soviet–Mozambique treaty, Soviet leaders were unwilling to increase qualitatively their military assistance to this state in the early 1980s as it weakened under South African pressure and internal rebellion. This has contributed to a shift towards the West in Mozambique's political and economic ties.

The political imbroglio in the Horn of Africa also demonstrated the problems of converting the bilateral commitments on military and political issues between the USSR and a Third World treaty partner into multilateral regional understandings. In what appears to have been a reaction to Saudi and Sudanese attempts to draw together an Arab bloc of Red Sea states, Fidel Castro presented the idea of a federal union of South Yemen (the PDRY), Somalia and Ethiopia at a meeting with their heads of state in March 1977 in Aden. In this federation of Marxist states Eritrea and Djibouti would receive substantial autonomy. The following month the Soviet Union took up this proposal, but the scheme foundered on the Somali–Ethiopian confrontation and has not been revived.

The flexibility with which Soviet leaders have regarded the military and security components of their friendship and cooperation treaties with Third World states was indicated by the conclusion of such a treaty with Vietnam in November 1978 a few weeks before the Soviet–Ethiopian treaty was signed. While the treaty with Ethiopia was an *ex post facto* expression of the Soviet commitment to this state, the Soviet–Vietnamese treaty was clearly intended as a signal in advance of Soviet support for Vietnam in its developing confrontation with China. Vietnam planned an invasion of Kampuchea, then led by Pol Pot and supported by China, to unify the whole of Indo-China. In this strategic context the security treaty with the USSR could act to neutralise China. There are parallels with the Soviet–Indian Friendship and Cooperation Treaty, which was also signed to bolster the Third World treaty partner before a regional military confrontation. Indeed, Article 6 of the Soviet–Vietnamese treaty, which obliges the treaty parties to enter into consultations in the event that they are subject to an attack or threat of attack is identical to Article 9 on mutual consultations in the Soviet–Indian treaty. As in the wording of the other friendship and cooperation treaties concluded by the USSR in the 1970s the means by which the threat would be met was left unspecified which indicated the Soviet desire to avoid defined commitments. The Soviet–Vietnamese treaty did not itself directly commit the two states to defence cooperation. But it appears that a military cooperation agreement accompanied the signing of the treaty, and press reports claimed that a second secret military protocol (which has never been made public) was added after the Vietnamese–Chinese border war began in February 1979.[141]

The Soviet–Vietnamese treaty converged the interests of the two parties and formalised their security policies on an anti-Chinese basis. For Moscow the treaty was a response to the coalition forming from the normalisation of relations between China and the United States and the Sino-Japanese Treaty of Peace and Friendship signed on 12 August 1978. The latter contained an anti-hegemony clause expressly directed at the Soviet Union. From the Vietnamese perspective the treaty with the USSR acted as a security guarantee against an unrestrained Chinese reaction to Vietnam's subsequent invasion of Kampuchea. Already before this action the Chinese press alleged that the treaty 'represented a military alliance pure and simple and was designed to clear the way for the Vietnamese leaders' military expansion in Southeast Asia'. The Soviet media countered this by arguing that 'it is clearly stated in the document that the two sides will do their utmost to defend world peace and the security of all peoples...What evidence is there to link this treaty with any alleged military alliance... ?'[142] It was also in the Vietnamese interest to tone down the military significance of the treaty in public statements to avoid foreclosing options in her relations with other states such as Japan. Vietnamese officials claimed that Vietnam remained neutral in the Sino-Soviet conflict. In December 1978 the Vietnamese Deputy Foreign Minister specified that Article 6 of the treaty, which provided for joint consulations, did not mean that the parties would support each other militarily. He asserted that 'we have nothing to do with the Warsaw Pact'. This was significant since there were reports that the Soviet Union had made moves to draw Vietnam into a relationship with the Warsaw Pact to establish a basis for controlling Vietnam's defence policy.[143] In the same month Vietnam undertook her final offensive against the Khmer Rouge regime which resulted in the fall of Phnom Penh on 7 January 1979 and the formation of the Heng Samrin regime.

The military basis of the Soviet–Vietnamese treaty was put to the test in February 1979 when China launched a month-long military incursion into Vietnam in retaliation for the Vietnamese occupation of Kampuchea. During this crisis the Soviet Union deployed ten ships from the Soviet Pacific Fleet to the South and East China seas as a warning to China but otherwise acted with great circumspection. Moscow preferred the humiliation of inaction to the danger of confrontation with China and possibly the United States. In fact the Soviet–Vietnamese military relationship was not severely tested; Vietnamese resistance was sufficient to persuade the Chinese to withdraw without undermining Vietnamese control of Kampuchea. However, the Chinese attack resulted in greater Vietnamese military dependence on the USSR. The large-scale supply of

Soviet arms to Vietnam following this attack was balanced by the gradual development of Soviet military facilities on Vietnamese soil. Soviet commentators claimed that the 'effectiveness' of their treaty with Vietnam 'was proven during February and March when the Vietnamese people faced serious difficulties in their fight against 600,000 Chinese invaders'. The 'overall assistance of the USSR and other socialist countries' in this struggle was cited as an important factor in causing China to suffer 'severe setbacks both politically and militarily in that war'.[144]

On the anniversary of the Sovet–Vietnamese treaty Brezhnev and Kosygin sent a message to the Vietnamese leadership proclaiming that: 'True to its international duty and to the spirit and letter of the treaty, the Soviet Union will continue resolutely to side with and support the fraternal Vietnamese people in building socialism and in further strengthening their international position and security'.[145] This sounded very much the language of alignment if not alliance and China certainly interpreted it as such. Since China's military clash with Vietnam the Chinese press maintained that 'though Vietnam has not formally joined the Soviet military bloc, it has in fact become a full-fledged military ally of the Soviet Union by virtue of the Vietnamese–Soviet treaty'. Articles in this treaty were considered to bear 'the nature of a military alliance', and with this in mind the non-aligned states were invited to ridicule Vietnam's pretensions to non-alignment.[146] At the Havana Non-Aligned Summit in September 1979 the Vietnamese leader Pham Van Dong sought to counteract this claim with the categorical affirmation that 'one of our principles is non-participation in any military bloc and not to allow oneself to become an instrument of the aggressive and war-provoking aims of any bloc'. He weakened his case by attacking the view that standing clear of blocs should be the highest objective of the Non-Aligned Movement and underlining the 'great, valuable and effective assistance' Vietnam received from the Soviet Union and other socialist countries.[147] Vietnam did not stand isolated, however, since by the end of the 1970s a series of countries in the Non-Aligned Movement were linked to the Soviet Union by friendship and cooperation treaties containing military clauses and the Movement had endorsed Soviet and Cuban military assistance to Angola and Ethiopia. But within a few months Soviet military intervention in Afghanistan made the whole issue of such military commitments much more controversial.

The Soviet Union had already concluded a Treaty of Friendship, Good Neighbourliness and Cooperation with Afghanistan in December 1978 a couple of weeks after signing a corresponding treaty with Ethiopia. As had become customery in such treaties the Afghan treaty committed the parties, in the interests of strengthening their defence capacity, to 'continue to develop cooperation in the military field on the basis of appropriate agreements concluded between them'. Unlike many of the other friendship and cooperation treaties negotiated by the USSR the treaty with Afghanistan did not contain a specific clause committing the parties to coordinate their positions through consultations or mutual contact to remove threats to peace which may arise. Nor were consultations obligatory to remove the threat of attack against either party as in the Indo-Soviet treaty. Instead, this new treaty contained a weak agreement in Article 4 for the parties to 'consult each other and take by agreement appropriate measures to ensure the security, independence and territorial integrity of the two countries'.[148]

The bilateral military aspects of this treaty were not publicly referred to in Soviet reports on its conclusion and ratification. The day following its conclusion the Afghan Premier, Nur Mohammad Taraki, asserted that the treaty 'is not directed against anyone'. He underlined Afghanistan's policy of non-alignment and the joint Afghan–Soviet condemnation of 'the creation of military bases on the territories of other countries'.[149] During the ratification process for the treaty Brezhnev agreed that the treaty was not directed at any other country and stressed the Soviet understanding of the 'desire of Afghanistan's new leadership to adhere to a policy of non-alignment'. However, Ponomarev cast doubts on this in referring to Article 8 of the treaty. In a fashion novel to such treaties this article committed the parties to work towards 'the creation of an effective security system in Asia on the basis of the joint efforts of all the countries of the continent'. Ponomarev considered this multilateral commitment, which Soviet leaders had conspicuously failed to incorporate into the texts of the friendship treaties with India and Vietnam, 'has special significance these days, when Peking leaders have committed aggression against the heroic people of Vietnam and are providing direct support to anti-government elements in Afghanistan and outside it'.[150] In this sense an anti-Chinese security understanding certainly underlay the treaty.

The Soviet–Afghan treaty to some extent also provided an additional deterrent against an attack on the fledgling Marxist regime from Pakistan or Iran. The former had long been in conflict with Afghanistan over the Pushtunistan issue and both Pakistan and Iran were beginning more actively to support insurgent groups in Afghanistan. But the significance of the military cooperation component of the treaty should not be overstated. The USSR had been a major supplier of military assistance to

Afghanistan for many years. It could have continued these supplies to enable the Afghan regime to combat the very limited counter-revolutionary violence initiated by rebel groups, which existed at that stage, without any such new treaty arrangement. Moreover, during 1978–9 Afghan leaders such as Hafizullah Amin tended to downplay the friendship treaty by linking it to the earlier Soviet–Afghan treaty of 1921 which remained in force.

The 1978 treaty acquired an *ex post facto* notoriety since it was used as one of the main grounds to vindicate the entry of what Moscow described as 'a limited Soviet military contingent' into Afghanistan at the end of 1979. In explaining this military intervention a *Pravda* article on 31 December 1979 stated that 'in making this decision, the Soviet Union proceeded from the community of interests of Afghanistan and our country in security questions, as stated in the 1978 Treaty'. Article 4 of the treaty was then recited. This treaty provision became a standard Soviet reference point to justify Soviet 'military assistance' to Afghanistan. In the view of a leading Soviet specialist on Afghanistan if the USSR had refused the request of the DRA government for such assistance it 'would have broken the obligation which it had assumed [in Article 4], and it did not permit this'.[151] It should be understood, however, that such legal justifications or pretexts are less important in determining the Soviet military presence in Afghanistan and the character of Soviet–Afghan military alignment than an agreement or treaty signed between Kabul and Moscow in March 1980 'on practical questions relating to the conditions of the temporary stay' of Soviet military units in Afghanistan. Although the ratification of this agreement was announced its text remains secret.[152]

The retrospective Soviet interpretation of the military basis of the Soviet–Afghan friendship treaty may have unsettled certain Third World states which were still tied to the USSR by friendship and cooperation treaties. However, for other radical pro-Soviet governments it marked Soviet determination to maintain the revolutionary status quo of friendly regimes (even if this involved their reconstitution), at least in regions proximate to the Soviet Union, and therefore enhanced the value of bilateral treaty commitments with Moscow.

The USSR had concluded a Treaty of Friendship and Cooperation with Marxist South Yemen (PDRY) in October 1979, which like the 1978 Soviet–Afghan treaty committed the parties to the Soviet-sponsored Asian collective security system.[153] At the time South Yemen was the only Arab state linked to the USSR by a friendship and cooperation treaty. In the

Soviet view this new treaty defined a model relationship between an Arab 'non-aligned' state and the Soviet Union. On the day following the conclusion of the treaty a Soviet broadcast in Arabic drew attention to Article 5 which commits the parties to 'continue to develop cooperation in the military field'. The commentator argued that 'to eliminate the consequences of Israeli aggression' a 'strengthening of the defence capabilities of the Arab states which stand in the front lines of this struggle, in cooperation with the Soviet Union, is a vital necessity'. This implied some kind of Soviet assisted defence community. He claimed, nevertheless, that the Soviet–PDRY treaty was not directed at any third party and that its contents made clear that the USSR and South Yemen 'reject the plans to set up closed military–political blocs in the Middle East and in Asia'.[154] Reports that the treaty included secret clauses committing the Soviet Union to support and defend the PDRY regime 'under all circumstances' are implausible, and the PDRY Foreign Minister asserted directly that all its clauses and provisions had been made public.[155] However, if the treaty is considered alongside the presence of Soviet, East German and Cuban military advisers in South Yemen and the Soviet use of PDRY military facilities the overall picture is one of a state 'as closely tied militarily to the Soviet bloc as any state can be without actually being a member of the Warsaw Pact'.[156]

A Soviet–Syrian Friendship and Cooperation Treaty was signed in October 1980. Despite the controversy surrounding Soviet military intervention in Afghanistan this treaty appeared to have a specific military function. Although Syria was not as ideologically close to the Soviet Union as South Yemen the Syrian Minister of Information asserted in advance that the treaty would be 'totally different from those concluded between the USSR and other Arab countries' and would provide for the dispatch of Soviet troops to Syria in case of need.[157] In all likelihood this claim was not based on the conventional provision on defence cooperation in the Soviet–Syrian treaty but on Article 6 which obliges the parties to contact each other in situations threatening their security 'with a view to coordinating their positions and cooperation to remove the threat that has arisen and restore peace'.[158] Apart from the reference to 'cooperation' this consultations clause is very similar to those Moscow had obtained in other friendship and cooperation treaties, such as with Ethiopia and South Yemen. If the assumption is made that the assurance in this article would provide for direct military support to bolster Syrian defences in the event of attack, including the use of Soviet military forces if all else fails,[159] then this either implies a wider scale of commitment by the USSR to other Third World treaty partners or a very specific Soviet policy towards Syria.

The Soviet–Syrian treaty was followed by high-level Soviet–Syrian exchanges and more weapons deliveries. Yet Moscow has been unwilling to accept the broad interpretation of the treaty which the Syrians sought to establish in the early 1980s in relation to events in Lebanon and the possibility of conflict with Israel. Soviet commitment to the defence of Syria was signalled by joint Soviet–Syrian naval manœuvres in July 1981 and by military consultations in June 1982 after Israel sent its troops into southern Lebanon. Soviet leaders were loath, however, to become embroiled in the limited war which developed between Syria and Israel through direct military assistance to their treaty partner. Despite speculation over the implications of the 1980 friendship treaty Moscow confined its role in this conflict to a belated resupply of Syrian weapons' losses.[160]

The limits of such military alignment as Soviet friendship and cooperation treaties may provide has been amply illustrated by the official neutrality of the Soviet Union in the Iran–Iraq Gulf War. Moscow has assumed this stand although the Soviet–Iraqi treaty of friendship and cooperation remains in force. There is no evidence that the Soviet Union was consulted in advance by her treaty partner about the details of Iraq's planned invasion of Iran which began the Gulf War in September 1980. Egypt had similarly kept the USSR uninformed about the details of its planned offensive against Israel in 1973. Despite the understanding on defence cooperation in Article 9 of the Soviet–Iraqi treaty, when the Gulf War began Moscow withheld military supplies from Iraq. Indeed, in the midst of this war the USSR signed a treaty of friendship and cooperation with a rival of Iraq, Syria. By 1982 when Iraq was thrown more on the defensive Moscow resumed arms supplies and by 1985 about eighty per cent of Iraqi military equipment came from the USSR. No clear signal of Soviet alignment with Iraq has emerged, however, even after President Saddam Hussein visited Moscow in December 1985 seeking increased Soviet military and diplomatic support. On this occasion the Soviet press referred only to the general principles underlying the 1972 treaty rather than its military aspects and Gromyko repeated the Soviet characterisation of the Gulf War as 'unnecessary and senseless'.[161]

Another example of moderation in the Soviet perception of its friendship and cooperation treaty commitments is provided by the most recent treaty of this kind concluded with North Yemen (the Yemen Arab Republic) in October 1984. North Yemen had already concluded a treaty of friendship with the Soviet Union in March 1964, but this treaty had not contained any military consultation or assistance clauses as in more recent Soviet treaties with Third World states. In September and November 1979 the

USSR concluded arms agreements with North Yemen. Prime Minister al-Iryani indicated the limits to which military cooperation with the USSR would be pursued in May 1983 when he stated that although the 1964 Soviet–YAR treaty would be renewed on its expiry in 1984 'it is certain that when we renew the agreement...we shall not introduce any articles pertaining to security matters'.[162] The modified Soviet–YAR Treaty of Friendship and Cooperation committed the parties to 'consult with each other on international problems affecting the interests of both countries' (Article 6) but contained no provisions on military assistance or mutual consultations in the event of a military threat.[163] President A. A. Saleh informed his hosts in Moscow that the YAR 'on the basis of the non-aligned policy which it pursues will continue to reject military groupings and alliances and the establishment of military bases'.[164] By all relevant criteria it seems that North Yemen will remain non-aligned despite her treaty relationship with the Soviet Union.

The indications are, nevertheless, that in the 1980s Soviet leaders have continued to rely on the security and defence components of their friendship and cooperation treaties as a means of selective military access to Third World states and of possible military cooperation with the USSR. Soviet military officials appear to have shared this aim. For example, just before the Soviet military intervention in Afghanistan in December 1979 the Soviet military theorist Colonel G. Malinovskiy prefaced a list of Soviet–Third World friendship and cooperation treaties with the claim that 'there is inestimable importance in the support provided by socialist states to peoples who are forced to fight for their independence or defend it with guns in hand'.[165] Whereas Soviet analyses of Moscow's friendship and cooperation treaties in the mid 1970s had tended not to refer to defence cooperation as an obligation for the treaty parties, by 1984 a Soviet specialist clearly identified an obligation for such states 'in the interests of strengthening defence capacities, to develop cooperation in the military field on the basis of corresponding agreements concluded between them'. This consultations obligation specified for Soviet treaty parties was identical to the consultations provisions found in the Soviet treaties with states such as Ethiopia, South Yemen and Syria.[166]

The Indian scholar Zafar Imam has argued that the provisions in Soviet friendship and cooperation treaties are geared towards the indigenous development of the defence potential of the Soviet treaty partners. He accepts that as a short-term measure these treaties commit the USSR to provide its treaty partners with a defensive shield to meet a crisis or threat affecting their security. But he claims that even in the latter

234

case the Soviet arms supply to its treaty partner has been oriented to immediate defence needs and that the treaties do not imply a permanent *locus standi* for the Soviet Union in terms of military facilities and defence arrangements suited exclusively to the Soviet Union.[167] Even disregarding the case of Afghanistan it has become apparent, however, that for many of the states which have concluded friendship and cooperation treaties with the USSR military cooperation has meant in effect an exchange of military assistance received from the USSR for the eventual concession of military facilities to that power. As concluded previously, this has cast a shadow over their non-alignment.

One important and long-term treaty partner of the USSR in the Third World, India, has consistently refused to accept such a military quid pro quo. In an article on the tenth anniversary of the seminal Indo-Soviet Friendship and Cooperation Treaty Gromyko argued that the USSR was giving India 'the necessary assistance in strengthening its defence capability...in full accordance with the spirit of the Soviet–Indian Treaty'.[168] The Indians would not object to this assessment, although the 1971 treaty does not contain a provision on defence cooperation, since they welcome Soviet arms supplies and do not fear for their non-alignment. Many Western officials have believed, however, that a political quid pro quo exists for the military benefits derived from the close treaty relationship with the USSR. They could point to India's studied neutral approach to Soviet intervention in Afghanistan.[169] Soviet spokesmen subsequently drew indirect comparisons between India's behaviour in relation to the Afghan crisis and Soviet support for India during the 1971 crisis over Bangladesh. As mentioned previously, the 1971 treaty may act as a constraint on India against concluding a no-war pact with Pakistan such as proposed by Islamabad in November 1981. Western officials could also underline the benefits Moscow derives from the continuation of New Delhi's adversarial approach to China. India functions thereby as a vital political flank for the USSR.

It should be kept in mind, moreover, that the military and security commitments contained in the treaties analysed above are rather unspecific compared to those the Soviet Union has extracted from some other Third World states, and that the military consequences of such treaties depend on other factors like the geographical proximity and political compatability of the treaty partners. The Treaty of Friendship, Cooperation and Mutual Aid between the Soviet Union and Mongolia, signed in January 1966 and aimed at China, stipulated that the parties 'will jointly undertake all the necessary measures, including military ones, aimed at ensuring the security, independence and territorial integrity of both countries'.[170] In comparison the Soviet–Afghan treaty of 1978 only contained a very general consultations provision and the standard commitment to defence cooperation. Yet Soviet troops were eventually stationed in both Mongolia and Afghanistan. Article 1 of the 1961 Soviet–North Korean Treaty of Friendship, Cooperation and Mutual Assistance (which has been renewed twice) stipulates that should either party be subject to an armed attack and find itself at war the other party 'shall immediately extend military and other assistance with all the means at its disposal'. This constitutes a straightforward defence pact.

The treaty concluded between the nascent Soviet Republic and Persia in 1921 actually included terms for Soviet armed intervention in Persia. Article 6 provided for this radical measure in the event that a threat arises to the USSR from Persian territory and that the Persian government is unable to avert this threat after a Soviet request to that effect. The Soviet Government undertook to withdraw its troops from Persia only once the threat was removed. This article provided the legal basis for the entry of Soviet troops into Persia in 1941 during the Second World War and for their stationing in the northern part of the country. The USSR eventually withdrew from Persia but repeated Persian (Iranian) efforts to secure the annulment or revision of the 1921 treaty on a bilateral basis were blocked by the Soviet authorities. The Shah declared Articles 5 and 6 of the treaty null and void and on 22 January 1980 the Khomeini regime made a similar declaration. Since Iran's unilateral denunciation of these offending articles has met with silence from the Soviet side it appears that Moscow would like them to remain in force to provide for future contingencies. This position may have acted as a deterrent to American intervention in Iran during or after the Iranian revolution. However, in spring 1980 the Iranian ambassador in Moscow informed Soviet foreign ministry officials that 'in the likely event of an attack on Iran by America, we can defend ourselves alone, and we will not allow a single foreign soldier to enter the country on whatever pretext and by virtue of whatever friendship treaty'.[171] Such warnings have encouraged Soviet reticence in the 1980s about the military provisions of the 1921 treaty, although Iranian assistance to Afghan rebel forces could be construed as contrary to Article 5. Moscow has not characterised its relationship with Teheran as one of alignment and has underlined its official neutrality in the Iran–Iraq war.

It is also necessary to consider the political and ideological dimensions of alignment with the Soviet Union, which friendship and cooperation treaties have reinforced for certain Third World states. Such alignment is clearly apparent in Soviet treaties with 'socialist' developing states. The preamble to the Soviet–North Korean treaty affirmed the readiness of the parties to strengthen friendly relations 'based on the principle of socialist internationalism'; the preamble of the Soviet–Vietnamese treaty referred to the solidarity of the parties 'resting on the principles of Marxism–Leninism and socialist internationalism' and to 'their internationalist duty to assist each other in consolidating and protecting socialist gains'. Article 4 of the latter treaty also obliged Vietnam in every way to further 'the unity and solidarity of the socialist countries' and 'actively contribute to the development and protection of socialist gains'. Mozambique's treaty with the USSR avoided such language but referred to the two parties as 'natural allies'. The text of the 1978 Soviet–Afghan treaty was still more circumspect, but similar political expectations emerge from statements made by Soviet and Afghan leaders at the time the treaty was concluded.

A different ideological formula has been used to express the form of cooperation expected between the USSR and all her Third World 'socialist oriented' friendship and cooperation treaty partners in the 1970s. Provisions in these treaties stipulated that the parties would cooperate to ensure conditions 'for the safeguarding and further development of the socio-economic achievements of their peoples' (the Indian treaty contained no such clause but the Syrian treaty repeated the trend in the 1980s). This pledge has been interpreted to imply a possible Soviet commitment to intervene in case such 'achievements' are endangered, as in Afghanistan at the end of 1979, or perhaps in the way the Brezhnev Doctrine was used to justify intervention in Czechoslovakia.[172] But this is misleading, since this formula orginated in Article 2 of the 1971 Soviet–Egyptian treaty as a commitment by Egypt to the goal of a socialist reconstruction of society. Neither in the cases of Egypt, Somalia, or more recently Mozambique have Soviet leaders shown themselves able to prevent a reversal of this commitment to socialist progress. Moreover, the 1978 Soviet–Afghan treaty is the least specific of all these treaties on this commitment; it is contained merely in the preamble of the treaty in a weakened form.

The real substance of political alignment is to be found in the Soviet–Vietnamese treaty. In the Soviet view this treaty served to strengthen the Soviet-led socialist bloc of states as a whole. More specifically it formalised the fundamental anti-Chinese thrust of the Soviet–Vietnamese relationship. In this sense the treaty acted as a symbolic act of commitment by Vietnam to the Soviet Union and registered the change in the relationship between China and Vietnam since 1977.

During the ceremonial signing of the treaty Brezhnev described it as confirming the 'basic direction' of the foreign policy of the parties. They were 'equal members of the mighty family of the socialist community'. He underlined that the establishment of Soviet–Vietnamese relations on a 'firm contractual basis' served 'the interests of all the fraternal countries and the strengthening of their international positions'. The Vietnamese delegation stressed that the treaty 'marked a fresh stage in the strengthening of the militant solidarity and unbreakable friendship between the Soviet Union and Vietnam'.[173] The joint Soviet–Vietnamese communiqué on the visit of the Vietnamese delegation to Moscow referred to the 'complete unanimity' of the two sides on all the international questions discussed, and promised that they would 'contribute to consolidating the solidarity and unity of the world socialist systems'.[174] During the Soviet ratification of the treaty Mikhail Suslov claimed that the main aim of the treaty was to secure favourable international conditions for the peaceful construction of socialism in both the USSR and Vietnam, and this was echoed by Soviet writers.[175]

These statements made abundantly clear that for Soviet leaders the political function of the treaty with Vietnam from the Soviet perspective was to mark the expansion of socialism, to accelerate Vietnam's integration into the socialist world and to hasten the domestic construction of socialism in Vietnam by stabilising the external environment of Moscow's treaty partner.[176] The treaty obliged the USSR and Vietnam to 'do their utmost to further consolidate the world socialist system'. Although Vietnam entered the Non-Aligned Movement the treaty pointedly avoided any description of Vietnam's policy as 'non-aligned'. This term has been used to designate the foreign policy of nearly all of Moscow's other friendship and cooperation treaty partners in their treaties. At the Havana Non-Aligned Summit in 1979 Premier Pham Van Dong urged 'solidarity with the forces of socialism and other progressive forces', and admitted that Soviet–Vietnamese relations were based on 'proletarian internationalism'.[177] Just as in the case of Cuban involvement in the Non-Aligned Movement Soviet commentators believe that in the 'theoretical' event of a clash between the principles of non-alignment and socialist internationalism in Vietnamese foreign policy the former would have to prevail. Soviet comments on the Cuban position strengthen this appraisal since the Cuban ideological link with the Soviet bloc has not even been contractually formalised in a friendship and cooperation treaty with the Soviet Union.

The Soviet treaty with Vietnam was intended to mark the process of integration of Soviet and Vietnamese foreign policies on a long-term basis. On its fifth anniversary in autumn 1983 a new Soviet–Vietnamese agreement was signed in this spirit, which confirmed and updated the principles agreed on in 1978. This agreement was intended specifically to express Soviet support for Vietnamese control of Kampuchea and to reaffirm the joint approach of the two states to their common adversary, China.[178] Despite some friction between Moscow and Hanoi on these issues there has been sufficient congruity in their strategic, ideological and political programmes since 1978 to encourage Western commentators rather generally to describe the relationship of the two communist states as one of 'alliance'. This alliance may weaken as Soviet leaders seek a normalisation of relations with China. This is indicated by the remarkable even-handedness of Soviet commentators in describing the causes of Sino-Vietnamese clashes in the mid 1980s. Both sides are urged 'all the more since they are socialist states to settle their disputes by peaceful means'.[179]

Soviet leaders expected the 1978 Soviet–Afghan treaty to pave the way for closer ideological coordination between the parties, although their Afghan counterparts also wished to set on record their commitment to non-alignment. When the treaty was signed Brezhnev described Soviet–Afghan relations in the aftermath of the April 1978 coup as 'permeated by a spirit of comradeship and revolutionary solidarity' which 'found expression in the Treaty of Friendship'.[180] The DRA Premier, Taraki, accepted that Afghanistan and the USSR were 'participants in the world revolutionary movement'.[181] During the ratification of the treaty Brezhnev noted that the USSR had repeatedly stressed its understanding of the desire of the new Afghan leadership 'to adhere to a policy of non-alignment and to develop cooperation with all states'.[182] At this time the Soviet leadership did not consider that their new treaty with Afghanistan provided for firm ideological alignment between the parties as in the case of the Soviet–Vietnamese treaty. But once the Karmal regime was installed Soviet spokesmen referred to the 1978 Soviet–Afghan treaty to support the process of Soviet–Afghan political integration. One Soviet specialist maintained, for example, that following the conclusion of the 1978 treaty 'regular comradely contacts between Soviet and Afghan representatives were brought into practice'. In his view 'the fruitful exchange of views' 'well served the cause of the drawing together [*sblizheniya*] of the USSR and the DRA [and] fully corresponded to the letter and spirit of the 1978 Treaty'.[183]

Soviet leaders anticipated that the treaties they signed with socialist or revolutionary democratic Third World states would encourage a process of integration between these states and the socialist camp and help shield such a process from international and indigenous pressures. During the ratification of the Afghan treaty Brezhnev expressed his confidence that it would create 'the kind of foreign policy climate that will permit Afghanistan's people to steadfastly follow a path of construction and progress in an atmosphere of peace and security'.[184] However, the events which followed in Afghanistan confirmed that such treaties were not by themselves a sufficient guarantee of the survival let alone consolidation of a pro-Soviet revolutionary regime. They were an insufficient measure of alignment with the USSR. The setbacks sustained in Egypt and Somalia had resulted in Soviet attempts to gain broader acceptance for the second pillar of revolutionary alignment: a ruling Marxist–Leninist vanguard party within the Third World state. But Moscow has no ultimate assurance of continued Soviet alignment even with her treaty partners which meet this condition. Mozambique has increasingly assumed an orientation towards Western states, tribal divisions still beset South Yemen, Angola relies on Cuban troops and the PDPA regime in Afghanistan is likely to be lost without Soviet troops.

The most enduring Soviet political alignment with a Third World state has been in fact with Cuba. Soviet leaders have never sought a treaty of friendship and cooperation with this state despite Cuba's apparent interest in the early 1960s in receiving a security guarantee from Moscow. The absence of a contractual basis to Soviet–Cuban military alignment or even a general Soviet commitment expressed in a friendship and cooperation treaty to consult with Cuba or develop its defence capabilities if a threat arises to its security reflects the geopolitical sensitivity of Cuba's position. This is apparent from the Soviet–American understanding over Cuba following the Cuban missile crisis in 1962. Geopolitics also determined the far-reaching military commitments Soviet leaders were prepared to assume in the 1980s in relation to the Marxist regime located on the Soviet southern borders which had signed a friendship and cooperation treaty with the USSR, Afghanistan.

The foregoing analysis indicates that whatever forms of political or military alignment Moscow has anticipated from its Third World treaty partners the latter have interpreted their friendship and cooperation treaties to suit their own interests. When these interests have not proved compatible with those of the USSR the Third World state has often preferred to break ties with Moscow rather than to conform to the Soviet agenda. Since the Soviet–Syrian treaty of 1980 the USSR has been unable and perhaps unwilling to foster new political or military alignments with

Third World states through such formal contractual means (this is only confirmed by the absence of military commitments in the 1984 Soviet–YAR treaty). This tendency corresponds to a general Soviet retrenchment in the Third World in the 1980s, involving the rationalisation of commitments and the realisation that 'socialist orientation' does not signal a process of progressive alignment with the Eastern bloc to the exclusion of ties with the West. The new Soviet leadership is aware that formalised understandings on security relations between the Soviet Union and most developing states may be undercut by the economic needs of such states, which compel them to enter a network of international economic and trade relations dominated by the leading Western powers.

Conclusion

The emergence of a group of militarily uncommitted, non-bloc states in the early and mid 1950s posed a dilemma for Soviet statesmen and theorists. The orthodox Soviet outlook on international affairs could not accommodate the existence of independent states, free of involvement in the competitive ideological and political struggle between East and West. However, on another level the existence of the non-bloc states conformed to the doctrinal precepts on national liberation which were elaborated in the USSR following the death of Stalin. From this perspective the formation of the new non-bloc states heralded the destruction of Western colonial empires, undermined Western military structures and promised strategic dividends to the Soviet state. Under Khrushchev Soviet statesmen proceeded to encourage the emergent non-bloc neutralist impulse in Europe and the Third World, but sought to harmonise it with Soviet policy. Soviet politicians, scholars and international lawyers employed their specialist skills in an attempt to persuade the neutralist and non-aligned states that a truly autonomous course in international affairs could not be achieved, and that the pursuit of a programme to enhance the security of the new states required coordinated action, which foreshadowed greater integration, with the Soviet-led group of states.

This study has identified a range of Soviet influences and pressures on the strategy of neutralism or non-alignment developed by the non-bloc states. These have varied from abstruse claims about the legal, ideological and political character and obligations of neutralism and non-alignment, to suggestions and requests for non-aligned states to assume particular objectives on conflict prevention, disarmament, international economics and regional problems. The term 'non-alignment' only acquired positive connotations in the USSR in the 1970s. However, for several decades Soviet officials have effectively promoted a very broad conception of non-alignment in different guises which has required political and military dissociation from the Western powers. Soviet leaders have made consistent efforts to capture the motive force of non-alignment and the international security programme of the non-aligned states and to subsume them to the broad Soviet policy agenda. This has formed an important element of the basic Soviet strategy of political and military denial of 'third' areas to the Western powers. Moscow's pursuit of such a strategy forms an underlying theme of this study. It is illustrated more fully by an examination of Soviet policy towards the idea of neutralisation in Third World regions and through an assessment of Soviet policy in relation to various constituents of military alignment in the Third World.

The Soviet leadership under Khrushchev first initiated a diplomatic offensive in the Third World which was designed to undercut the preponderant influence of the Western powers. This was accompanied by a general expectation that political and socio-economic transformations within the developing states would gradually induce them to forge closer relations with the USSR. Soviet leaders remained aware, however, that in all likelihood the USSR would remain militarily dispossessed or disadvantaged in the Third World for many years to come. In these circumstances it appeared both rational and in conformity with Soviet ideological tenets to pursue a strategy directed at prying apart the central military relationships of the Western states with the Third World. The neutralist anti-bloc impulses of many newly independent states confirmed the promise of this approach. The primary objectives of the Soviet leadership were the creation of a buffer zone of friendly or at least militarily uncommitted nations surrounding the USSR, and the denial of lands bordering the USSR to foreign military installations.

The objective of military denial to the West also explained the interest exhibited by Soviet statesmen in the 1950s and 1960s in neutrality as a political issue in Europe. Moscow interpreted the obligations of neutrality in a manner intended to restrict the military potential of the European neutral states and to encourage neutralist tendencies more generally among West European states. However, in this period it remained a high Soviet priority to promote a European collective security system, and Soviet officials regarded the principle of collective security as superior to that of neutrality. Soviet doctrine on international relations sought to accommodate the phenomena of neutrality and neutralism by recognising a 'transitional' phase in the historical development of states towards socialism. In practice this meant that neither neutrality nor neutralism was acceptable as a course for Warsaw Pact states, which remained firmly under Soviet military control. According to Soviet leaders, neutrality or neutralism could not anyway by applied to the Warsaw Pact since it was not a 'bloc'. Molotov claimed: 'the Soviet Union and the other countries of the Warsaw Pact have never created military blocs. Nor will they do so in the future. But they will be obliged to unite their efforts in safeguarding their security.'[1] This claim was fundmental also to the Soviet characterisation of non-alignment.

In the 1960s non-alignment gradually developed into the dominant concept determining the foreign policy outlook of the majority of Third World states. The essence of neutralism had been opposition to Cold War military blocs and relationships. This was not the only basis for the unity of the Non-Aligned group of states since non-alignment had a significant political component. However, Soviet spokesmen tended for many years to refer to non-alignment and neutralism (or 'positive neutrality') interchangeably and this resulted in confusion in Soviet accounts between the principles applicable for European neutral states and those relevant for the Non-Aligned. The association of non-alignment with Yugoslavia retarded Soviet appreciation of this policy since Yugoslav non-alignment was directed against integration with the Eastern bloc. Moscow was also slow to recognise the emerging organisationally distinct Non-Aligned body of states, and unwilling to regard the Non-Aligned Movement as an autonomous intermediate actor in the international order rather than as a potential adjunct to the 'world socialist system'.

Soviet commentators regarded non-alignment in the form espoused by its adherents as the transitional foreign policy expression of a particular domestic stage of economic development. This doctrinal premise discouraged serious Soviet interest in non-alignment as a multilateral international phenomenon until the early 1970s. Even in the 1970s Soviet spokesmen remained strongly opposed to the idea that the Non-Aligned could adopt a policy of 'equidistance' between East and West. They sought to portray the Non-Aligned as the 'natural ally' of the Soviet Union, although this conflicted with the conception of non-alignment held by the great majority of the states participating in the Non-Aligned Movement.

Soviet leaders finally acknowledged the growing organisational cohesion and influence of the Non-Aligned Movement on the world stage in 1973 following the Algiers Non-Aligned Summit. They foresaw a role for this body in promoting Soviet strategic objectives in the Third World. Moscow sought to use the new radicalism of the Non-Aligned on international economic issues to effect a further shift in the military aspect of the 'correlation of forces' in the Third World in favour of the Eastern bloc. A vocal pro-Soviet constituency within the Non-Aligned Movement supported the revisionist and activist policy pursued by the USSR in the Third World during the *détente* years. This had some influence on the broader perception by the Non-Aligned of the legitimacy of Soviet involvement in the Third World in the 1970s. Soviet leaders also aimed to generate broad Third World backing through the Non-Aligned Movement and the Non-Aligned group in the United Nations for Soviet regional and global proposals on international security and disarmament. The Soviet objective was to capture the independent impetus of the Non-Aligned on the promotion of international security and to direct it towards current Soviet strategic initiatives.

In the 1960s and 1970s the Non-Aligned Movement adopted a tripartite strategy to enhance international security: the prevention of dangerous escalatory conflict between the superpowers, and the reduction of tensions between them through various channels and proposed security regimes; global disarmament; and the formation of a new international economic order. Although the success of the non-aligned states in pursuing these objectives has been limited this independent strategy of non-alignment still, in principle, determines their collective agenda on international security.

The record of the past quarter century shows that Soviet leaders have been suspicious of mediation efforts by the Non-Aligned group to defuse conflicts or tensions between the Great Powers or simply unwilling to renounce bilateral channels. However, in line with their policy of military denial, they have supported 'zones of peace' and demilitarisation proposals advocated by the Non-Aligned in various regions where Soviet military influence has been negligible or where Soviet strategic interests would benefit from a stable low level of Great Power military presence. The Indian Ocean and the Mediterranean Sea are two such areas. Moscow has achieved partial success in merging the declarations of the non-aligned states with the proclaimed policy of the USSR on nuclear-free zones in various Third World regions.

Initially in the 1960s, Soviet leaders were unresponsive to the appeals of the Non-Aligned in the field of disarmament. Eventually, however, they sought to acquire the support of Non-Aligned resolutions for cherished Soviet ideas, such as a world disarmament conference. In the 1970s and 1980s it became a primary Soviet objective to rally a broad front of non-aligned states in the United Nations against the current strategic posture of NATO and the United States. A series of joint Soviet bloc and Non-

Aligned proposals and declaratory resolutions on nuclear disarmament were aired in the United Nations. Until the early 1980s Soviet officials were prepared to overlook the escalating build-up of conventional arms among the Third World non-aligned states themselves. Moscow acquired favourable publicity among the Non-Aligned by supporting the initiatives of the Delhi 'Group of Six'. A current Soviet priority is to underline the opposition of the Non-Aligned to the American SDI programme. The convergence of Soviet and Non-Aligned views in these areas has increased the legitimacy of the Non-Aligned Movement in Soviet eyes.

The Soviet failure to create a coordinated front with the non-aligned states has been most glaring in the sphere of international economics. Soviet officials refused to accommodate the structural developmental needs of Third World states, which were specified in the programme of the Non-Aligned for a new international economic order, in any material form. This resulted in widespread disillusion with the USSR among many non-aligned states in the late 1970s, which contributed to a greater polarisation of the Non-Aligned Movement in the 1980s. By the middle of this decade Soviet officials were referring to theories of economic interdependence in place of the NIEO and calling for non-discriminatory trade flows between all states, including East–West trade.

The Soviet policy of military denial in the Third World has been expressed in various initiatives for the neutralisation and demilitarisation of specific countries or regions. These proposals should not be dismissed since neutralisation remains a possible means for the superpowers to regulate their competitive relationship in areas where the risks of confrontation are too high. Initially, in the 1950s, Soviet interest in neutralisation was an adjunct of Soviet policy in Europe, but the neutralisation of Laos illustrated the potential application of this notion for the Third World. Soviet leaders did not display any real commitment to neutralisation as a means to stabilise conflict-prone regions in the 1970s when Soviet policy was apparently successful in pursuing revisionist ambitions in the Third World. However, in the 1980s Soviet officials expressed greater interest in such status-quo-oriented security concepts.

In 1980 Brezhnev issued a 'code of conduct' for the Persian Gulf, which aimed at its neutralisation. The Soviet proclamation of this scheme was in striking contrast to Moscow's rejection of the Western plan, issued in the same year, for the neutralisation of Afghanistan. Soviet attitudes varied in each case according to their regional political and strategic interests and the prevailing military balance. This has also been apparent in the qualified Soviet support for the indigenous ASEAN scheme for a zone of peace and neutrality in Southeast Asia. In this case Moscow sought to subsume the principles of non-alignment and neutrality to those of collective security in Asia. It remains possible that Moscow may accede to a loosely formulated neutralisation of Afghanistan or Kampuchea. In other regions, especially where Western military influence is preponderant, the USSR has continued to call for the withdrawal of extra-regional powers. Neutralisation has not, therefore, been withdrawn from the Soviet diplomatic agenda.

Military denial has additionally been the primary objective behind Soviet diplomatic efforts to engineer the breakup of Western-sponsored military alliances and pacts in the Third World. Since the USSR was deprived of similar strategic assets it supported the non-bloc principles of the Non-Aligned. When it appeared that new military groupings for Third World regions were under consideration by the United States in the 1980s Moscow initiated a diplomatic offensive designed to frustrate such plans. In a similar fashion Soviet leaders fully endorsed the original campaign of the non-aligned states against Great Power military bases on foreign territories; a policy of base denial suited the interests of both groups of states. This convergence of interests was qualified in the 1970s by the more active efforts of the Soviet Union to acquire its own overseas military facilities in sensitive Third World regions.

There is some evidence that Soviet military officials wished to integrate the military facilities they acquired in the Third World into a strategic support system. This system could be reinforced by the military security provisions of a network of friendship and cooperation treaties concluded by the USSR and members of the Non-Aligned Movement. In this fashion Soviet leaders hoped to develop the loose framework of a rival security system to the Western system of military pacts, although the Third World states involved still proclaimed their commitment to non-alignment. In addition the treaty partners of the USSR in the Third World in most cases refrained from direct military commitments to the Soviet Union. Military denial to the West on the basis of a Soviet-oriented security system remains the minimal objective underlying Soviet efforts to revive their scheme for Asian collective security. However, Soviet military intervention in Afghanistan led to a reaction against the USSR among many Third World states that has limited the effectiveness of the broader Soviet strategy of military denial and hampered Soviet efforts to create their own security system in the Third World. Moscow began to suffer from American efforts to undermine established Soviet military strategic and political gains in the Third World.

In the early 1980s there also ensued for the first time a more active competition between Moscow and Washington for influence over the Non-Aligned Movement. President Reagan sent a letter to the Delhi Non-Aligned Summit in 1983 which expressed keen American interest in the activities of the Non-Aligned Movement and commitment to the 'original' principles 'upon which non-alignment is based'.[2] This overture did not materially affect the final declaration of the Delhi Summit which criticised American actions at least eleven times without corresponding criticism of Soviet conduct. Nevertheless, Soviet commentaries began to express concern about the possibility of Soviet influence over the Non-Aligned Movement being progressively supplanted by American influence. For example, an article in *Kommunist* conjectured that the Western powers aimed at the neutralisation of the Non-Aligned Movement on the world arena and the creation of a 'partnership' between this body and the West in all areas of international political and economic relations.[3] The Soviet official Karen Brutents claimed in 1984 that current American strategy was to use the Non-Aligned Movement 'as a channel of influence on the foreign policy positions of a number of liberated countries friendly to the Soviet Union and also of other developing countries conducting an independent policy'. He attacked the United States for using the economic difficulties of Third World states to draw the states composing the 'centre' of the Movement closer to itself.[4]

By the mid 1980s the Soviet leadership was pursuing a policy of retrenchment in the Third World that left the USSR unable effectively to compete with the West for favours from non-aligned countries through economic instruments. Soviet unwillingness to offer economic concessions to these states had already led to a division between them and Moscow in the 1970s over the projected new international economic order. In the 1980s the Soviet Union was thrown onto the defensive by a broad assault on established Soviet positions in the Third World. Incumbent Marxist-inclined regimes were threatened by the Reagan Doctrine, and the prospect of abrupt reversals in the Third World transformed the Soviet Union into more of a status quo power. Moscow had acquired a direct stake in the current political composition of a number of beleaguered Third World regimes. The limits of Soviet material commitment to such radical states had been drawn, however, by the time the Twenty-Seventh Party Congress was convened early in 1986. Current commitments to Afghanistan, Vietnam and Cuba would be maintained but other 'socialist-oriented' and non-aligned states would have to pay their way and could expect few bonuses from the USSR whatever their ideological credentials.

Soviet leaders hoped the Non-Aligned Movement could be mobilised against the Reagan Doctrine. Prominent Soviet officials refrained from statements before the Harare Non-Aligned Summit which could act to further polarise the participants into pro-Soviet and pro-Western factions. However, the Soviet press characterised the American raid on Libya, its support for the contras in Central America and its supply of weapons to 'terrorist' groups in Angola and Afghanistan was 'a broad assault on non-aligned countries whatever the pretext in each particular case'.[5] Soviet commentaries boasted that the political declaration of this forum mentioned the United States 'in anything but complimentary terms ... more than twenty-five times and again contains no criticism of the Soviet Union'.[6] Nevertheless, the ritualised declarations of the Non-Aligned were no substitute for policy coordination between these states.

A clear dissonance existed by the mid 1980s between the formal position the Non-Aligned Movement had assumed in Soviet strategy towards the Third World and growing Soviet recognition that the effectiveness of this body in the contemporary international system, judged by its ability to implement its resolutions and maintain its cohesion, was seriously open to challenge. Soviet spokesmen now openly acknowledged the differential approach of the Non-Aligned to the concept of non-alignment and the existence of centrifugal currents within the Non-Aligned Movement. For certain states, Alexander Bovin observed in 1986, 'non-alignment is a world outlook, a political philosophy and a basic principle in their approach to international affairs'. For others, he admitted, non-alignment may be 'just diplomacy, a practical plan aimed at exploiting international contradictions to bolster their own positions'.[7] After the conclusion of the 1986 Harare Non-Aligned Summit Bovin criticised the ineffectiveness of resolutions adopted by the Non-Aligned on specific situations such as the Iran–Iraq war. He noted despondently that 'the problems of the effectiveness and efficiency of the resolutions adopted by the non-aligned countries – their ability to achieve results – will grow more critical in the coming years'.[8]

This gloomy assessment has not been endorsed by Gorbachev himself. The Soviet leader is astute enough to realise that time-worn attempts to persuade the non-aligned states that they should state their loyalties in the basic clash of international systems have been counterproductive. In current conditions such ideological exhortations could precipitate the fragmentation of the Non-Aligned Movement. In this message of greetings to the Harare Summit Gorbachev sounded a pragmatic note in underlining Soviet opposition to this body 'being viewed through the prism of

East–West confrontation'. He expressed Soviet understanding for the desire of the non-aligned countries 'to stay away from military blocs, to pursue independent policies'.[9] Gorbachev characterised the Movement as 'an authoritative and progressive force of modern times' which was making a 'truly historic' contribution at the 'current crucial stage of world development'.[10]

This effusive rhetoric was derivative of the 'new thinking' on international affairs proselytised by Soviet spokesmen. Gorbachev told his Indian hosts in November 1988 that, in an age when an understanding of interdependence and mutual responsibility was becoming vitally important, international institutions and organisations such as the Non-Aligned Movement and other regional bodies acquired an increasing significance.[11] Moscow appears to consider the multilateral diplomatic channels such organisations could offer as particularly suited for the elaboration or propagation of the Soviet scheme for a 'comprehensive international security system' advanced at the Twenty-Seventh Party Congress. At the Forty-First Session of the United Nations' General Assembly the Soviet bloc states explained that among other objectives this system aimed at the creation of a world 'in which there would be neither a nuclear nor military space club of select powers', where 'efforts in tackling global problems would be pooled'.[12] This grand vision was calculated to appeal to the non-aligned states and to undercut the American SDI programme. Nevertheless, a global perspective on international affairs does appear to inform the policy orientation and outlook of the Soviet leadership to a greater extent than in past years. Consequently, Soviet officials will seek for areas of convergence between Soviet policy and the globalist vision found in many of the appeals issued by the Non-Aligned. A joint Soviet–Syrian statement in spring 1987 asserted that the Non-Aligned Movement had 'an important role to play in the process of establishing the new political thinking'.[13]

Soviet leaders currently attempt to converge the declaratory policy of Moscow and Non-Aligned aspirations through linking the issues of disarmament and development. This was apparent at a United Nations' conference on disarmament and development in August 1987, which the United States boycotted on the grounds that these two issues were not related. Soviet spokesmen also urge the Non-Aligned Movement to step up its activity as a pressure group within the United Nations and to galvanise this body in favour of Soviet proposals on disarmament and international security. Gorbachev informed the Syrian leader Assad that the Non-Aligned Movement was 'exerting a solid influence on world affairs', that 'its influence can be seriously felt at the UN and it has an effect on the character of the decisions being taken there'.[14] In this context it is significant that in September 1987 Gorbachev called for an expansion of the responsibilities of the world body in the nuclear age. He suggested that the UN assume a new role in monitoring international compliance of arms control agreements, and proposed that a direct link be established between the UN headquarters and not only the five permanent members of the Security Council but also the seat of the Non-Aligned Movement.[15]

The new Soviet leadership appears prepared to dispense with much of the ideological rhetoric premised on systemic conflict which formerly characterised Soviet statements on international relations and to downgrade ideological factors and considerations in policy formation in favour of 'realism'. As a result it becomes easier for the Non-Aligned body of states to acquire a legitimacy in the Soviet international outlook which it never truly had in earlier years. Before this new pragmatism began to infuse Soviet policy, in particular policy towards the Third World, the Non-Aligned Movement could only be understood in Moscow as the organisational expression of the national liberation movement on a world scale. As the Gorbachev leadership provides further evidence of its acceptance and promotion of aspects of 'international society', the Non-Aligned Movement assumes a role which it hitherto was denied in Soviet policy. Soviet leaders expect that the Non-Aligned may perform the function of integrating different aspects of international security in global manifestos and appeals which could broaden the agenda for future negotiations between the United States and the Soviet Union.

It is premature to speak of a new orthodoxy in the Soviet characterisation of the Non-Aligned Movement and the non-aligned states. The traditional Soviet outlook on the Third World remains influential in the USSR. This was reflected in the final version of the new Party Programme which, after expressing Soviet understanding of the goals and activity of the Non-Aligned Movement, highlighted 'the alliance of forces of social progress and national liberation'.[16] However, the realisation of this 'alliance' in the form of systemic integration between the majority of Third World states and the Soviet bloc or even in the shape of intimate political and military relations between the two groups of states, remains a long-term Soviet objective. If anything, these desired outcomes have been advanced further into the future like the prospect of 'true' Communism within the Soviet Union. In Soviet thinking it is quite consistent with these optimal long-term goals to accept a variety of 'tactical' measures and compromises in the short term (a period of unlimited duration), which depend on rapidly shifting events, on vicissitudes in international politics and on the prevailing distribution of power (the correlation of forces). From the Soviet perspective this helps to rationalise the greater incrementalism and pragmatism which are characteristic of current Soviet policy towards the Third World.

Soviet leaders will continue their efforts to coordinate policy with the non-aligned states on broad themes and to use the multilateral diplomatic channels of the Non-Aligned Movement to gain support for, or advance, favoured initiatives. Soviet spokesmen will praise non-alignment as the organising principle underlying the programme of the greater part of Third World states. The majority of the Non-Aligned are unlikely to succumb to Soviet blandishments; as in the past they will pursue an autonomous course, despite similarities in outlook with the Soviet bloc in certain areas and on some issues. The Soviet Union will also cautiously continue to proclaim the merits of non-alignment as a policy of military denial in the Third World directed at Western bases, pacts and other Western military relationships. This may be expressed in a selective sponsorship of neutralisation, demilitarisation and other security regimes in Third World regions. The USSR has acquired an appreciable military stake of its own in the Third World, but at a cost in certain regions which exceeds the benefits derived. In these circumstances Soviet and Western statesmen may eventually be able to reach tacit understandings or more formal agreements on security regimes which would involve mutual restraints and reinforce the non-aligned character of the states or regions under consideration.

Notes

INTRODUCTION

1 Speech in Constituent Assembly (Legislative), 4 December 1947, cited in A. Appadoria, 'Non-alignment: some important issues', in K. P. Misra, ed., *Non-Alignment: Frontiers and Dynamics* (New Delhi: Vikas, 1982), p. 5.
2 See P. Willetts, *The Non-Aligned Movement: The Origins of a Third World Alliance* (London: Frances Pinter, 1978), p. 23.
3 See *Ibid.*, pp. 127–32.
4 See *Ibid.*, pp. 22–3.
5 See G. Ginsburgs, 'Neutralism à la Russe', in G. Ginsburgs and A. Z. Rubinstein, eds., *Soviet Foreign Policy Towards Western Europe* (New York: Praeger, 1978).
6 D. Bindschedler-Robert, 'Völkerrecht und Neutralität in sowjetischer Sicht', *Österreichische Zeitschrift für Aussenpolitik*, 5 (1965), 157.
7 G. Ginsburgs, 'Neutrality and neutralism and the tactics of Soviet diplomacy', *The American Slavic and East European Review*, 19 (1960), 538–9.
8 *Ibid.*, p. 544.
9 Report on 14 February 1956, in M. Rush, *The International Situation and Soviet Foreign Policy: Reports of Soviet Leaders* (Columbus, Ohio: 1970), p. 185.
10 Statement on 11 May 1955, *New Times* (Moscow), 21 (1955), Supplement, 9. See also S. Allard, *Russia and the Austrian State Treaty: A Case Study of Soviet Policy in Europe* (University Park and London: Pensylvania State University Press, 1970), pp. 238–41.
11 A. Galina, 'Problema neytraliteta v sovremennom mezhdunarodnom prave', *Sovetskiy ezhegodnik mezhdunarodnogo prava* (1958), 203.
12 *Izvestiya*, 9 March 1955.
13 O. I. Tiunov, *Neytralitet v mezhdunarodnom prave* (Perm State University, 1968), p. 156.
14 *Ibid.*, p. 157.
15 L. A. Modzhoryan, *Politika podlinnogo neytraliteta – vazhny faktor bor'by narodov za mir i nezavisimost'* (Moscow: Znanie, 1956), p. 7.
16 VII Congress of International Association of Democratic Jurists, convened in Sofia, 10–14 October 1960. V. Nesterov, 'Yuristy-demokraty v bor'be za strogoe soblyudenie mezhdunarodnogo prava', *Sovetskiy ezhegodnik mezhdunarodnogo prava* (1961), 459.
17 A. A. Gromyko, I. N. Zemskov and V. M. Khostov, eds., *Diplomaticheskiy slovar*, vol. 2 (1971), p. 373.
18 Tiunov, *Neytralitet v mezhdunarodnom prave*, p. 157.
19 Yu, M. Prusakov, *Neytralitet v sovremennom mezhdunarodnom prave* (Moscow: Znanie, 1972), p. 64.
20 *Ibid.*, pp. 23–4.
21 Joint Soviet–Maltese communiqué issued on 10 October 1981, in *Izvestiya*, 10 October 1981.

22 Yu. Alimov, 'Vazhny faktor mirovoy politiki (K itogam Deliyskoy konferentsii neprisoedinivshikhsya stran)', *Mirovaya ekonomika i mezhdunarodnye otnosheniya*, 6 (1983), 7.

23 B. V. Ganyushkin, *Neytralitet i neprisoedinenie* (Moscow: Mezhdunarodyne otnosheniya, 1965), p. 198.

24 K. Ginther, *Neutralität und Neutralitätspolitik: die österreichische Neutralität zwischen schweizer Muster und sowjetischer Koexistenzdoktrin* (Vienna and New York: 1975).

25 Tass, 9 August 1958; see *Izvestiya*, 11 February 1959, 7 May 1959, 24 April 1965.

26 *Pravda*, 8 February 1958.

27 Interview on 24 March 1958, in N. S. Khrushchev, *For Victory in Peaceful Competition with Capitalism* (London: Hutchinson, 1960), pp. 232–3.

28 V. N. Durdenevskiy and G. A. Osnitskaya, 'Neytralitet i atomnoe oruzhie', *Sovetskoe gosudarstvo i pravo*, 2 (1960), 103

29 See Prusakov, *Neytralitet v sovremennom mezhdunarodnom prave*, p. 18.

30 E. Korovin, 'The problem of neutrality today', *International Affairs* (Moscow), 3 (1958), 39.

31 Galina, 'Problema neytraliteta', 206.

32 *Dokumenty konferentsii Yevropeyskikh kommunisticheskikh i rabochikh partiy v Karlovykh Varakh 24–26 aprelya 1967 goda* (Moscow: Politizdat, 1967), p. 12.

33 See W. B. Bader, *Austria Between East and West* (Stanford University Press, 1966), pp. 204–5.

34 Speech by A. N. Kosygin at dinner in Vienna, 2 July 1973, in *SSSR–Avstriya: Dokumenty i materialy* (Moscow: Politizdat, 1980), p. 112.

35 See, for example, L. A. Modzhoryan, *Politika neytraliteta* (Moscow: Znanie, 1962), p. 23.

36 Prusakov, *Neytralitet v sovremennom mezhdunarodnom prave*, p. 58.

37 E. Korovin, 'Proletarian internationalism in world relations', *International Relations* (Moscow), 2 (1958), 29.

38 Prusakov, *Neytralitet v sovremennom mezhdunarodnom prave*, p. 60.

39 Speech by A. N. Kosygin at dinner in honour of Chancellor B. Kreisky in Moscow, 28 May 1974, in *SSSR–Avstriya*, p. 123.

40 See, for example, the joint Soviet–Austrian communiqué of 8 February 1978, and the joint Soviet–Swedish communiqué of 8 April 1976, cited in *The Role of the Neutrals and the Non-Aligned in the Détente Process* (Vienna: Peace and the Sciences, 2, 1980), p. 21.

41 Report by L. I. Brezhnev on 23 February 1981, in *Pravda*, 24 February 1981.

42 See *Pravda*, 1 May 1983.

43 Statement in *Izvestiya*, 26 March 1987.

44 V. A. Kremenyuk, 'The European neutrals and Soviet–American relations', in H. Neuhold and H. Thalberg, eds., *The European Neutrals in International Affairs*, The Laxenburg Papers, 7, (Vienna: 1984), pp. 93–4, 100–2.

1 THE SOVIET VIEW OF NON-ALIGNMENT IN THE INTERNATIONAL ORDER

1 See A. Rubinstein, *Yugoslavia and the Non-Aligned World* (Princeton University Press, 1970); S. Clissold, ed., *Yugoslavia and the Soviet Union 1939–1973 – A Documentary Survey* (Oxford University Press, 1975).

2 *Pravda*, 5 January 1957.

3 A. A. Gromyko, S. A. Golunskiy and V. M. Khvostov, eds., *Diplomaticheskiy slovar*, vol. 2 (Moscow: 1961), p. 395.

4 *Pravda*, 17 January 1963.

5 G. B. Starushenko, *Neytralizm segodnya i zavtra* (Moscow: Znanie, 1966), pp. 27–8.

6 *Ibid.*, p. 17.

7 B. V. Ganyushkin, *Neytralitet i neprisoedinenie* (Moscow: Mezhdunarodnye otnosheniya, 1965), p. 193.

8 O. I. Tiunov, *Neytralitet v mezhdunarodnom prave* (Perm State University, 1968), p. 115.

9 Report by N. S. Khrushchev in October 1961, in *The Road to Communism. Documents of the 22nd Congress of the Communist Party of the Soviet Union* (Moscow: 1961), p. 41.
10 Ya. Etinger and O. Melikyan, *Neytralizm i mir. Neytralistskaya politika stran Azii i Afriki* (Moscow: Mysl', 1964), pp. 10–11.
11 Ye. I. Selezneva, 'K kharakteristike vneshney politiki neytralistskikh gosudarstv Azii i Afriki', *Narody Azii i Afriki*, 4 (1963), 13.
12 N. S. Khrushchev's report on 12 December 1962, cited in R. K. Jain, ed., *Soviet–South Asian Relations 1947–1978*, vol. 1 (Oxford: Martin Robertson, 1979); *New Times* (Moscow), 9 (1963), 4–5.
13 Starushenko, *Neytralizm segodnya i zavtra*, p. 32.
14 B. V. Ganyushkin, *Sovremmenny neytralitet* (Moscow: Inst. mezhdunarod. otnosheniy, 1958), pp. 26, 29–30; Ganyushkin, *Neytralitet i neprisoedinenie*, pp. 26–9; F. I. Kozhevnikov, chief ed., *Kurs mezhdunarodnogo prava v shesti tomakh. Tom III, Osnovnye instituty i otrasli sovremennogo mezhdunarodnogo prava* (Moscow: 1967), pp. 421–5; Starushenko, *Neytralizm segodnya i zavtra*, p. 17.
15 O. N. Melikyan, *Neytralizm gosudarstv Afriki* (Moscow: Nauka, 1966), p. 143.
16 Tiunov, *Neytralitet v mezhdunarodnom prave*, p. 6; D. V. Baratashvili, 'Pozitivny neytralitet v sovremennom mezhdunarodnom prave', *Sovetskoe gosudarstvo i pravo*, 6 (1963), 95–7.
17 Kozhevnikov, chief ed., *Kurs mezhdunarodnogo prava*, p. 437.
18 See Ganyushkin, *Neytralitet i neprisoedinenie*, p. 97.
19 Ibid., pp. 95–7; O. N. Khlestov, 'Zhenevskie soglasheniya po Laosu – vazhny shag v formirovanii sovremennogo ponyatiya neytraliteta', *Sovetskoe gosudarstvo i pravo*, 5 (1963), 96–7.
20 Khlestov, 'Zhenevskie', pp. 97–8.
21 O. Melikyan and Ya. Etinger, 'Vneshnyaya politika mirolyubivykh stran Azii i Afriki i ee burzhuaznye kritiki', *Narody Azii i Afriki*, 6 (1961), 62.
22 Baratashvili, 'Pozitivny neytralitet', p. 99; D. V. Baratashvili, *Novye qosudarstva Azii i Afriki i mezhdunarodnoe pravo* (Moscow: Nauka, 1968), pp. 197–8.
23 See B. Khabirov, *Mezhdunarodno-pravovoy status i vneshnie funktsii neprisoedinivshiksya gosudarstv*, dissertation resumé, candidate thesis in juridical science (Moscow: 1972), p. 17.
24 Tiunov, *Neytralitet v mezhdunarodnom prave*, pp. 139–40.
25 *Pravda*, 4 February 1963.
26 Tiunov, *Neytralitet v mezhdunarodnom prave*, pp. 117–19.
27 P. Lyon, 'Neutrality and the emergence of the concept of Neutralism', *The Review of Politics*, 22 (April 1960), 266–7. See also P. Lyon, *Neutralism* (Leicester University Press, 1963).
28 Tiunov, *Neytralitet v mezhdunarodnom prave*, pp. 119, 141 and 138.
29 Moscow home service, 21 April 1955 in SU no. 616, 25 April 1955, p. 30.
30 For a Soviet account of the genesis and development of the AAPSO, including an analysis of the Cairo Conference, see K. Kozhakhmetov, *Dvizhenie solidarnosti narodov Azii i Afriki v bor'be s kolonializmom i imperializmom* (Alma Ata: Kazakhstan, 1983); see also A. S. Dzasokhov, *Dvizhenie solidarnosti narodov Azii i Afriki* (Moscow: Nauka, 1977).
31 See P. F. Power, 'The People's Solidarity Movement: evolution and continuity', *Mizan USSR, China, Africa, Asia*, 9: 1 (January/February 1967), 13.
32 Statement by F. Tabeyev, head of Soviet delegation at the Fourth Afro-Asian Solidarity Conference, held 10–16 May 1965, in *Izvestiya*, 6 June 1965.
33 See *New Times* (Moscow), 9 (1967), 4–5.
34 Statement by the Soviet Government to the governments of Afro-Asian countries, in *New Times* (Moscow), 19 (1964), 31–2.
35 Statement by the Soviet Government on the convening of the Second Afro-Asian Conference, in *Pravda*, 14 August 1964.
36 *New Times* (Moscow), 22 (1965), 8.
37 *Pravda*, 12 June 1965.
38 For the Soviet reaction see *Pravda*, 28 June 1965.
39 R. Mortimer, *The Third World Coalition in International Politics* (New York: Praeger, 1980), p. 21.

40 *New Times* (Moscow), 46 (1965), 13–14.
41 *New Times* (Moscow), 36 (1970), 18.
42 *Ibid.*, p. 18.
43 A. A. Gromyko, I. N. Zemskov and V. M. Khvostov, eds., *Diplomaticheskiy slovar*, vol. 2 (Moscow: 1971), p. 379.
44 B. G. Khabirov, 'O mezhdunarodno-pravovykh aspektakh neprisoedineniya', *Sovetskoe gos·:darstvo i pravo*, 12 (1973), 111.
45 R. A. Tuzmukhamedov, ed., *Dvizhenie neprisoedineniya v dokumentakh i materialakh* (Moscow: Nauka, 1975), pp. 14–17; R. A. Tuzmukhamedov, *Neprisoedinenie i razryadka mezhdunarodnoy napryazhennosti* (Moscow: Mezhdunarodnye otnosheniya, 1976), p. 81.
46 Tuzmukhamedov, *Neprisoedinenie i razryadka*, p. 96.
47 *Izvestiya*, 17 October 1964.
48 *Izvestiya*, 30 August 1970.
49 R. A. Tuzmukhamedov, 'Neprisoedinenie: "latinoamerikanskiy etap"?', *Latinskaya Amerika*, (1972), 58; and see Tuzmukhamedov, ed., *Dvizhenie neprisoedineniya* (1975), pp. 35–6.
50 See Khabirov, 'O mezhdunarodno-pravovykh aspektakh neprisoedineniya', pp. 112–16.
51 Tuzmukhamedov, *Neprisoedinenie i razryadka*, pp. 85–6.
52 R. A. Tuzmukhamedov, 'Neprisoedinenie: nekotorye voprosy mezhdunarodnogo prava', *Sovetskoe gosudarstvo i pravo*, 6 (1981), 119.
53 Ya. Ya. Etinger, 'Vazhny faktor mira i mezhdunarodnoy bezopasnosti', *Mirovaya ekonomika i mezhdunarodnye otnosheniya*, 3 (1983), 44.
54 S. M. Nesterov, 'Dvizhenie neprisoedineniya – vazhny faktor mezhdunarodnykh otnosheniy', *Narody Azii i Afriki*, 6 (1977), 47.
55 See, for example, Ya. Ya. Etinger, 'Dvizhenie neprisoedineniya: aktual'nye problemy', *Narody Azii i Afriki*, 6 (1981), 8.
56 Tuzmukhamedov, 'Neprisoedinenie: nekotorye voprosy mezhdunarodnogo prava', pp. 119–20.
57 Etinger, 'Dvizhenie neprisoedineniya: aktual'nye problemy', p. 8.
58 A. I. Petrov, ed., *Vneshnyaya politika stran Azii* (Moscow: Mezhdunarodnye otnosheniya, 1983), p. 160.
59 *Two Decades of Non-Alignment. Documents of the Gatherings of the Non-Aligned Countries 1961–1982* (New Delhi: Ministry of External Affairs, 1983), p. 2.
60 *Diplomaticheskiy slovar*, vol. 2, (Moscow: 1985), p. 278.
61 A. Klimov and V. Laptev, 'On the policy of non-alignment', *International Affairs* (Moscow), 3 (1969), 16–17.
62 Yu. Alimov, 'Dvizhenie neprisoedineniya – vliyatel'naya sila mezhdunarodnykh otnosheniy', *Mirovaya ekonomika i mezhdunarodnye otnosheniya*, 11 (1976), 40; Tuzmukhamedov, *Dvizhenie neprisoedineniya v dokumentakh i materialakh*, pp. 34–6.
63 Tuzmukhamedov, *Neprisoedinenie i razryadka mezhdunarodnoy napryazhennosti*, pp. 35–6.
64 Tuzmukhamedov, 'Neprisoedinenie: nekotorye voprosy mezhdunarodnogo prava', pp. 117–18.
65 Etinger, 'Dvizhenie neprisoedineniya: aktual'nye problemy', p. 6.
66 For example, E. N. Matyunin, *Dvizhenie neprisoedineniya na sovremennom etape* (Leningrad: Znanie, 1981), p. 9.
67 *Ibid.*, p. 10.
68 *Dvizhenie neprisoedineniya* (Moscow: Nauka, 1985), pp. 313–4.
69 Ya. Etinger, ed., *Dvizhenie neprisoedineniya v sovremennom mire* (Moscow: Mezhdunarodnye otnosheniya, 1985), pp. 88–9.
70 See, for example, *Vneshnyaya politika razvivayushchikhsya stran. Obshchie problemy i metodologiya issledovaniya* (Moscow: Mezhdunarodnye otnosheniya, 1983), p. 82.
71 Etinger, 'Dvizhenie neprisoedineniya', p. 6.
72 Etinger, 'Vazhny faktor mira i mezhdunarodnoy bezopasnosti', pp. 41–2.
73 Etinger and Melikyan, *Neytralizm i mir. Neytralistskaya politika stran Azii i Afriki*, p. 117.

74 Moscow home service, 11 October 1964, in su/1681/c2/1, 13 October 1964.
75 For example, G. B. Starushenko, *Natsiya i gosudarstvo v osvobozhdayushchikhsya stranakh* (Moscow: Nauka, 1967), p. 82.
76 V. S. Kotlyarov, 'Neprisoedinivshiesya strany i gegmonizm Pekina', *Problemy dal'nogo Vostoka*, 4 (1973), 163–4.
77 *Vneshnyaya politika razvivayushchikhsya stran. obshchie problemy i metodologiya issledovaniya*, pp. 72–5.
78 Petrov, ed., *Vneshnyaya politika stran Azii*, pp. 150–1, 174.
79 Etinger, ed., *Dvizhenie neprisoedineniya v sovremennom mire*, p. 26.
80 Z. Imam, 'Soviet view of non-alignment' in K. P. Misra, ed., *Non-Alignment: Frontiers and Dynamics* (New Delhi: Vikas, 1982), p. 468.
81 *The Conference of Heads of State or Government of Non-Aligned Countries, Belgrade, September 1–6 1961* (Belgrade: 1961), p. 21.
82 *Second Conference of Heads of State or Government of Non-Aligned Countries, 1964* Cairo. Speeches, p. 111.
83 Commentary on Moscow Radio for Africa by Ye. Primakov, in su/1675/c/3, 6 October 1964.
84 *Izvestiya*, 4 October 1964.
85 *Pravda*, 25 October 1964
86 Kotlyarov, 'Neprisoedinivshiesya strany i gegemonizm Pekina', p. 164.
87 Etinger, 'Dvizhenie neprisoedineniya: aktual'nye problemy', pp. 8–9.
88 *Dvizhenie neprisoedineniya* (Moscow: Nauka, 1985), pp. 9–10.
89 *Ibid.*, p. 102.
90 Speech at International Scientific Conference in Berlin, October 1980, cited in *Kommunist*, 16 (1980), 38.
91 Ye. Primakov, 'Osvobodivshiesya strany v mezhdunarodnykh otnosheniyakh, *Mirovaya ekonomika i mezhdunarodnye otnosheniya*, 5 (1982), 28.
92 *Izvestiya*, 12 September 1979.
93 *Pravda*, 15 February 1981.
94 *Izvestiya*, 16 August 1986.
95 Etinger, 'Vazhny faktor mira i mezhdunarodnoy bezopasnosti', p. 41.
96 Etinger, ed., *Dvizhenie neprisoedineniya v sovremennom mire*, p. 19.
97 *Ibid.*, p. 271.
98 A. Kolosovsky, 'Non-aligned countries in the UN', *International Affairs* (Moscow), 4 (1986), 124–5.
99 For the Soviet reaction, see *Izvestiya*, 18 March 1983.
100 *New Times* (Moscow), 37 (1986), 7.
101 *Izvestiya*, 17 October 1964.
102 Tuzmukhamedov, 'Neprisoedinenie: "latinoamerikanskiy etap"?', 60.
103 *Ibid.*, pp. 60–1.
104 Tuzmukhamedov, *Dvizhenie neprisoedineniya* (1975), p. 14; Tuzmukhamedov, *Dvizhenie neprisoedineniya v dokumentakh i materialakh*, pp. 23–4.
105 Klimov and Laptev, 'On the policy of non-alignment', p. 16.
106 Radio Moscow, 6 September 1979, in su/6215/A1/3.
107 Tuzmukhamedov, *Dvizhenie neprisoedineniya* (1975), p. 46.
108 See Tuzmukhamedov 'Neprisoedinenie: "latinoamerikanskiy etap"?', p. 60.
109 Radio Peace and Progress in English for Africa, 27 October 1978, in su/5957/A1/5.
110 Tuzmukhamedov, 'Neprisoedinenie: "latinoamerikanskiy etap"?', p. 60.
111 See Radio Moscow in Arabic, 8 September 1973, in su/4395/A4/3, and 9 September 1973 in su/4396/A/1; *Pravda*, 13 September 1973.
112 Tass summary of *Pravda* article, 1 September 1973, in su/4388/A1 and 2.
113 *Pravda*, 12 August 1976; Yu. Alimov, 'Dvizhenie neprisoedineniya – vliyatel'naya sila mezhdunarodnykh otnosheniy', *Mirovaya ekonomika i mezhdunarodnye otnosheniya*, 11 (1976), 48; N. Georgiev and I. Klimov, 'Problems and prospect of the Non-Alignment Movement', *Far Eastern Affairs* (Moscow), 2 (1977), 42–3; Tass report, 21 August 1979 of *Sotsialisticheskaya Industriya* article, in su/6204/c1/2.
114 See Radio Peace and Progress in English for Asia, 27 January 1984, in su/7555/c/3; Moscow world service in English, 28 January 1984, in su/7555/c/4; *Izvestiya*, 3

February 1984; V. Sivtsev and V. Seidov, 'Informatsionny imperializm i bor'ba za novy mezhdunarodny informatsionny poryadok', *Mirovaya ekonomika i mezhdunarodnye otnosheniya*, 3 (1983).
115 Reply by Yu. Andropov to letter from Director-General of UNESCO, in *Pravda*, 1 February 1984.
116 *Dvizhenie neprisoedineniya* (Moscow: Nauka, 1985), p. 395.
117 Etinger, ed., *Dvizhenie neprisoedineniya v sovremennom mire*, p. 6.
118 Etinger, 'Dvizhenie neprisoedineniya: aktual'nye problemy', p. 11.
119 *New Times* (Moscow), 6 (1981), 6.
120 Etinger, ed., *Dvizhenie neprisoedineniya v sovremennom mire*, pp. 117–18; *Dvizhenie neprisoedinenie* (1985), p. 8.
121 Etinger, 'Dvizhenie neprisoedineniya: aktual'nye problemy', p. 11.
122 Etinger, ed., *Dvizhenie neprisoedineniya v sovremennom mire*, p. 104.
123 *Ibid.*, p. 5.
124 *Ibid.*, p. 26.
125 K. Brutents, 'Dvizhenie neprisoedineniya v sovremennom mire', *Mirovaya ekonomika i mezhdunarodnye otnosheniya*, 5 (1984), 30.
126 Etinger, ed., *Dvizhenie neprisoedineniya v sovremennom mire*, pp. 19 and 21.
127 Speech on 4 September 1986; Jana in English, 4 September 1986, in *BBC Summary of World Broadcasts* (Part 4 The Middle East, Africa and Latin America), ME/8357/E/17 and 18.
128 Moscow world service report, 5 September 1986, in SU/8358/i.
129 *Dvizhenie neprisoedineniya* (1985), p. 8.
130 *Ibid.*, p. 379.
131 For Gorbachev's address, Tass in English, 31 August 1986, in SU/8353/A1/1. Statement by Boris Pyadyshev, First Deputy Head of the Information Department of the USSR Ministry of Foreign Affairs, on 18 September 1986; Tass in English, 18 September 1986, in SU/8371/A1/11.
132 *Socialist Affairs*, 4 (1980), 92–4.
133 See O. B. Reznikova, 'Sotsintern i dvizhenie neprisoedineniya', *Narody Azii i Afriki*, 3 (1984), 98–102.
134 *Ibid.*, 99 and 102; Etinger, ed., *Dvizhenie neprisoedineniya v sovremennom mire*, pp. 265–6.
135 Interview for *Le Peuple*, 20 April 1955, cited in *Pravda*, 22 April 1955.
136 Diary entry in relation to the Polish crisis, 23 October 1956. V. Micunovic, *Moscow Diary* (London: Chatto and Windus, 1980), pp. 123–4.
137 A. Z. Rubinstein, *Yugoslavia and the Nonaligned World* (Princeton University Press, 1970), p. 313. See also pp. 308–13, and L. Nord, *Nonalignment and Socialism: Yugoslav Foreign Policy in Theory and Practice* (Stockholm: Raben and Sjögren, 1974).
138 *The Conference of Heads of State or Government of Non-Aligned Countries, Belgrade, September 1–6 1961*, pp. 164–5.
139 Rubinstein, *Yugoslavia and the Non-Aligned World*, p. 317.
140 *The Conference of Heads of State or Government of Non-Aligned Countries*, Belgrade, p. 165.
141 Address by Tito on 17 August 1976, in *Tito and Non-Alignment. President Tito's Addresses at Conferences of Non-Aligned Countries* (Belgrade: Socialist Thought and Practice, 1979), p. 100.
142 *Ibid.*, p. 103.
143 Address on 25 July 1978, in *Tito and Non-Alignment*, pp. 114 and 117.
144 Etinger, ed., *Dvizhenie neprisoedineniya v sovremennom mire*, p. 108.
145 Yu. S. Girenko, *Sovetsko-yugoslavskie otnosheniya* (Moscow: Mezhdunarodnye otnosheniya, 1983), p. 149.
146 *Ibid.*, p. 160.
147 Joint communiqué of official visit to USSR by Yugoslav Prime Minister M. Planinc, 3–7 July 1985, in *Pravda*, 8 July 1985.
148 Reports of talks between R. Dizdarevic, Yugoslav Federal Secretary for Foreign Affairs, and E. Shevardnadze, Soviet Foreign Minister, during visit to Moscow, 10 January 1986, in SU/8155/A/2.

149 Speech on 9 January 1986, in su/8155/A2/7.
150 See R. H. Linden, 'Romanian foreign policy in the 1980s: domestic–foreign policy linkages', in M. J. Sodaro and S. L. Wolchik, eds., *Foreign and Domestic Policy in Eastern Europe in the 1980s: Trends and Prospects* (London: Macmillan, 1983), pp. 49–51.
151 Communiqué on meeting of the Political Executive Committee of the Central Committee of the RCP on 26 August 1975, cited in *La Roumanie et les pays nonalignés (Relations de Solidarité et de large coop amicale)*, vol. 1, (Bucharest: Agerpress, 1976), pp. 2–3.
152 Communiqué on meeting of Political Executive Committee of the Central Committee of the RCP on 23 Spetember 1975, cited in *ibid.*, p. 4.
153 Statement in December 1975, and interview in journal *Delo* in February 1976, cited in *ibid.*, pp. 10 and 18.
154 C. Vlad (Director of the Institute of Political Science of the University of Romania, Bucharest) and N. Calina, 'The Non-Aligned Movement, the international system and Romanian foreign policy', *The Nonaligned World*, 2: 2 (April–June 1984), 261–6. Ceausescu's speech was to the enlarged Plenum of the Central Committee of the RCP, 1–2 June 1982.
155 R. Garai, 'Hungary and the developing world', in C. Gal, ed., *Socialist Community and Non-Alignment* (New Delhi: Allied Publishers, 1979), p. 39.
156 See *ibid.*, pp. 5, 43–5.
157 Vlad and Calina, 'The Non-Aligned Movement', pp. 267–8.
158 *Ibid.*, pp. 268–9, 272.
159 Linden, 'Romanian foreign policy in the 1980s', p. 70.
160 See, for example, V. V. Pashuk, 25 *geroicheskikh let: (respublika kuba v bor'be za mir i mezhdunarodnoe sotrudnichestvo)* (Kiev: Politizdat ukrainy, 1983), pp. 126–7.
161 Soviet–Cuban communiqué, 20 September 1961, in su/749/c/3, 22 September 1961.
162 See W. M. LeoGrande, 'Evolution of the Non-Aligned Movement', *Problems of Communism*, 22 (January–February 1980), 40.
163 Declaration on 2 February 1974, in *Pravda*, 2 February 1974.
164 Colombo Summit. *Documents and Selected Speeches of the Fifth Conference of Heads of State or Government of Non-Aligned Countries* (New Delhi: People's Publishing House), 1976, p. 68.
165 See V. Vladimirov and V. Kostin, *Kuba: 20 let novoy vneshney politiki 1959–1979 gg.* (Moscow: Mezhdunarodnye otnosheniya, 1980), pp. 189–90, 166–7.
166 Radio Moscow, 30 August 1979, in su/6208/A5/1.
167 See R. Tuzmukhamedov, 'Vliyatel'ny faktor mirovoy politiki', *Kommunist*, 14 (1979), 120–1.
168 Kh. Kobo, 'Forum neprisoedinivshikhsya stran', *Latinskaya Amerika*, 1 (1980), 9–11.
169 *Beijing Review*, 34 (24 August 1979), 19–20.
170 *Beijing Review*, 38 (21 September 1979), 21–3.
171 Speech on 3 September 1979. *Fidel Castro Speaks: Cuba's Internationalist Foreign Policy 1975–80* (New York: Pathfinder Press, 1981), pp. 165–6.
172 P. Willetts, *The Non-Aligned in Havana* (London: Frances Pinter, 1981), p. 13.
173 See LeoGrande, 'Evolution of the Non-Aligned Movement', pp. 48–9.
174 Willetts, *The Non-Aligned in Havana*, pp. 13–14; see also LeoGrande, 'Evolution of the Non-Aligned Movement', pp. 50.
175 *Final Documents. Seventh Conference of Heads of State or Government of Non-Aligned Countries, New Delhi, March 1983* (New Delhi: India Offset Press), pp. 17 and 22–4.
176 Pashchuk, 25 *geroicheskikh let*, pp. 124 and 136.
177 Speech by Carlos Rafael Rodriguez, *Colombo Summit*, p. 70.
178 Pashuk, 25 *geroicheskikh let*, pp. 124–5, 134.
179 R. L. Jackson, *The Non-Aligned, the United Nations and the Superpowers* (New York: Praeger, 1983), pp. 200–1.
180 M. Komatina, 'Non-alignment: differences and disputes', *Review of International Affairs*, 5 April 1982, cited in *ibid.*, p. 201.
181 Speech on 1 September 1986, Radio Rebelde, Havana 1 September 1986, in *BBC Summary of World Broadcasts (Part 4 The Middle East, Africa and Latin America)*, ME/8356/E/5.

182 A. N. Schevchenko, *Breaking with Moscow* (London: Jonathan Cape, 1985), pp. 142–3.
183 See *The Guardian*, 24 February 1986; see also W. R. Duncan, 'Castro and Gorbachev: politics of accommodation', *Problems of Communism*, 35: 2 (March–April 1986), 48–50, 53–4.

2 THE SOVIET UNION AND THE SEARCH FOR INTERNATIONAL SECURITY
BY THE NON-ALIGNED STATES

 1 *The Conference of Heads of State of Government of Non-Aligned Countries* (Belgrade: 1961), p. 108.
 2 Radio Moscow, 4 October 1964, in su/1675/c/3–4, 6 October 1964.
 3 Interview in France on 20 April 1955, cited in *Pravda*, 22 April 1955.
 4 *Pravda*, 29 August 1961.
 5 Radio Moscow for Germany, 7 September 1961, in su/741/c/6, 13 September 1961.
 6 Radio Moscow, 6 September 1961, in su/741/c/3, 13 September 1961.
 7 Radio Moscow for Germany, 7 September 1961, in su/741/c/6, 13 September 1961.
 8 Radio Tashkent, 17 September 1961, in su/746/A1/9, 19 September 1961.
 9 Letter sent on 16 September 1961, *Pravda*, 23 September 1961.
10 *Izvestiya*, 4 October 1964.
11 *New Times* (Moscow), 9 (1963), 4.
12 Radio Moscow, 6 September 1961, in su/741/c/3, 13 September 1961; su/738/c/1–2.
13 Tass, 1 September 1961, in su/733/c/1, 4 September 1961.
14 Tass, 8 September 1970, in *Izvestiya*, 10 September 1970.
15 For the role of the Non-Aligned generally in Great Power crises see J. K. Baral, 'Role of the non-aligned countries in crisis management', in K. P. Misra, ed., *Non-Alignment: Frontiers and Dynamics* (New Delhi: Vikas 1982), pp. 122ff.
16 K. Brutents in *Pravda*, 30 August 1973.
17 Tass, 27 August 1973, in su/4384/A1/2.
18 *Pravda*, 5 September 1973.
19 Radio Moscow, 6 September 1973; broadcast of *Izvestiya* article, in su/4394/A1/1.
20 Political Declaration of Algiers Conference, in *Two Decades of Non-Alignment: Documents of the Gatherings of the Non-Aligned Countries 1961–1982* (New Delhi: Ministry of External Affairs, 1983), p. 93.
21 *Izvestiya*, 12 September 1979.
22 V. P. Nikhamin, 'Bandung, non-alignment and the Soviet idea of collective security in Asia', in S. Bhushan, ed., *Twenty Years of Bandung and Problems of Peace and Security in Asia* (New Delhi: Allied Publishers, 1975), p. 92.
23 For such a recent definition see Ya. Ya. Etinger, ed., *Dvizhenie neprisoedineniya v sovremennom mire* (Moscow: Mezhdunarodnye otnosheniya, 1985), p. 211.
24 For general surveys of this proposal see relevant chapters in L. W. Bowman and I. Clark, *The Indian Ocean in Global Politics* (Boulder, Colorado: Westview, 1981); D. Braun, *The Indian Ocean, Region of Conflict or 'Peace Zone'?* (London: Hurst, 1983).
25 See, for example, *New Times* (Moscow), 34 (1979), 5.
26 Cited in A. V. Krutskikh, *Politika SShA v Indiyskom okeane* (Moscow: Nauka, 1984), pp. 220–1.
27 Etinger, ed., *Dvizhenie neprisoedineniya*, p. 214.
28 M. Gorbachev in speech to the Indian Parliament on 27 November 1986, in *Stability and Security – A Common Concern. Visit of General Secretary of the CPSU Central Committee Mikhail Gorbachev to India* (Moscow: Novosti, 1986), p. 29.
29 Etinger, ed., *Dvizhenie neprisoedineniya*, p. 214.
30 See *New Times* (Moscow), 35 (1983), pp. 20–1.
31 *Ibid.*, p. 21. For current Soviet views on the zone see I. Lebedev, 'Indiyskiy okean – zona mira ili konfrontatsii?', *Mirovaya ekonomika i mezhdunarodnye otnosheniya*, 8 (1985), 93–5; Krutskikh, *Politika SShA v Indiyskom okeane*, pp. 203–36.

32 See B. Vivekandan, 'The Indian Ocean as a zone of peace: problems and prospects', *Asian Survey*, 21: 12 (December 1981), 1241ff. This is refuted in M. Goryanov, *Two Ways of Looking at the Indian Ocean* (Moscow: Novosti, 1981). For a non-Soviet view sympathetic to the Zone proposal see C. Kumar, 'The Indian Ocean: arc of crisis or zone of peace', *International Affairs* (London), 60: 2 (Spring 1984).

33 For example, V. F. Petrovskiy, USSR Deputy Minister of Foreign Affairs, after a tour of Persian Gulf states, in *Izvestiya*, 28 April 1987.

34 O. Reznikova and Ya. Etinger, 'Neprisoedinivshiesya strany i bor'ba za ustranenie yadernoy opasnosti, uprochenie mira', *Mirovaya ekonomika i mezhdunarodnye otnosheniya*, 2 (1986), 62.

35 See documentation in *Review of International Affairs*, 36: 853, 20 December 1985, 18.

36 NAC/CONF. 8/Doc. 1/Rev. 1, 6 September 1986, paragraph 194.

37 Speech on 26 March 1986, in *Pravda*, 27 March 1986.

38 For example, V. F. Petrovskiy, USSR Deputy Minister of Foreign Affairs, in *Izvestiya*, 28 April 1987.

39 Speech on 27 April 1981, in *Pravda*, 28 April 1981.

40 Speech on 21 May 1985, Tass, 21 May 1985, in su/7958/A3/4.

41 A. Pavlov, 'The Non-Aligned Movement and the struggle against imperialism', *International Affairs* (Moscow), 4 (1981), 78.

42 See joint Soviet–Indian declaration after Brezhnev's visit to New Delhi, in *Pravda*, 12 December 1980.

43 Tass, 8 February 1981, in *Pravda*, 9 Febraury 1981.

44 Political Declaration adopted in Prague on 5 January 1983; cited in Ya. Etinger, 'Vazhny faktor mira i mezhdunarodnoy bezopasnosti', *Mirovaya ekonomika i mezhdunarodnye otnosheniya*, 3 (1983), 50.

45 Moscow home service, 27 March 1980, in su/6383/c4.

46 NAC/CONF. 7/Doc. 12, 9 March 1983, pp. 4–6.

47 Tass, 9 January 1983, in su/7230/A3/1.

48 For the view of the DRA representative, Prime Minister Keshtmand, on the question of direct DRA–Pakistani talks, during his discussion with the UN Secretary General at the Delhi Summit, see Radio Moscow, 11 March 1983, in su/7281/A3/4–5.

49 See points 114 and 115 in *Final Documents. Seventh Conference of Heads of State or Government of Non-Aligned Countries* (New Delhi: 1983), pp. 42–3.

50 V. S. Kotlyarov, 'Dvizhenie neprisoedineniya – nekotorye itogi i perspektivy', *Narody Azii i Afriki*, 5 (1983), 21.

51 E. Rumantsev, 'The Non-Alignment Movement – an important factor in international life', *International Affairs* (Moscow), 6 (1983), 22.

52 R. Tuzmukhamedov, in *The Non-Aligned Movement: Aims, Principles, Practice. Supplement to New Times* (Moscow), 1986, p. 6.

53 Briefing by Sergey Sinitsyn for journalists, Tass in English, 7 August 1986, in su/8332/A1/7.

54 For example, Kotlyarov, 'Dvizhenie neprisoedineniya – nekotorye itogi i perspektivy', 19.

55 R. L. Jackson, *The Non-Aligned, the United Nations and the Superpowers* (New York: Praeger, 1983), p. 196.

56 Etinger, 'Vazhny faktor mira', 46.

57 For the Soviet view of this important resolution see *Izvestiya*, 28 July 1987.

58 For the content of these discussions see Tass in Russian for abroad and in English, 17 July 1987, in su/8624/A4/1–2.

59 Interview in France on 20 April 1955, cited in *Pravda*, 22 April 1955.

60 N. A. Bulganin's message to Jawaharlal Nehru inviting India to support Soviet proposals on summit conference to end international tension, 8 January 1958, in R. K. Jain, ed., *Soviet–South Asian Relations 1947–1978*, vol. I (Oxford: Martin Robertson, 1979), p. 252.

61 *Pravda*, 3 September 1961.

62 Radio Moscow, 6 September 1961, in su/741/c/2, 13 September 1961.

63 Khrushchev's answer on 16 September 1961, in *Pravda*, 23 September 1961.

64 *Izvestiya*, 4 October 1964.
65 *Izvestiya*, 13 October 1964.
66 For example, Ya. Ya. Etinger, ed., *Dvizhenie neprisoedineniya v sovremennom mire* (Moscow: Mezhdunarodnye otnosheniya, 1985), pp. 203–4.
67 The Programme of Peace and International Cooperation of the Second Conference of Heads of State or Government of Non-Aligned Countries, in *Two Decades of Non-Alignment* (New Delhi: Ministry of External Affairs, 1983), p. 23.
68 See A. Shevchenko, *Breaking with Moscow* (London: Jonathan Cape, 1985), p. 141.
69 See commentary in *New Times* (Moscow), 21 (1974), 13–15.
70 See Etinger, ed., *Dvizhenie neprisoedineniya*, pp. 206–7.
71 Radio Moscow, 6 September 1973, broadcast of *Izvestiya* article, in SU/4394/A1/1.
72 V. Kudryavtsev, 'Non-alignment and disarmament', *Soviet Review* (New Delhi), 39 (1979), 23–5.
73 P. Artem'ev and A. Klimov, 'Dvizhenie neprisoedineniya v mirovoy politike', *Mirovaya ekonomika i mezhdunarodnye otnosheniya*, 8 (1979), 15.
74 *Ibid.*, 16.
75 Etinger, 'Vazhny faktor mira', 49.
76 See, for example Etinger, ed., *Dvizhenie neprisoedineniya*, p. 203.
77 V. Sergeev, 'Neprisoedinenie i problema razoruzheniya', *Aziya i Afrika segodnya*, 1 (1983), 6–7.
78 See, for example, Yu. Alimov, 'Dvizhenie neprisoedineniya na vazhnom rubezhe', *Kommunist*, 7 (1983), 106. For the relevant conference resolutions see *Final Documents. Seventh Conference of Heads of State or Government of Non-Aligned Countries* (New Delhi, 1983), pp. 7, 12–13.
79 *Dvizhenie neprisoedineniya* (Moscow: Nauka, 1985), p. 135.
80 *Ibid.*, p. 137.
81 Yu. Alimov, 'Svyaz' vremen i sobytiy (k 30-i godovshchie Bandungskoy konferentsii)', *Mirovaya ekonomkia i mezhdunarodnye otnosheniya*, 6 (1985), 47.
82 See *Review of International Affairs*, 36: 853 (20 October 1985), 8–9; L. Tepinsky, 'Unity on the crucial issues' in *The Non-Aligned Movement: Aims, Principles, Practice. Supplement to New Times* (Moscow), 1986, p. 25.
83 Speech on 2 December 1985, in SU/8125/A5/5.
84 See *Review of International Affairs*, 37: 866 (5 May 1986), 9.
85 See *Eighth Conference of Heads of State or Government of Non-Aligned Countries*, NAC/CONF. 8/Doc. 1/Rev. 1, 6 September 1986, paras. 35–8.
86 *Ibid.*, para. 36.
87 O. Reznikova and Ya. Etinger, 'Neprisoedinivshiesya strany i bor'ba za ustranenie yadernoy opasnosti, uprochenie mira', *Mirovaya ekonomika i mezhdunarodnye otnosheniya*, 2 (1986), 60–2.
88 Meeting on 22 September 1982, in SU/7139/A3/1 and 2.
89 Report of talks held on 21 May 1985, Moscow home service, 21 May 1985, in SU/7958/A3/2.
90 Tass, 6 September 1985, in SU/8051/A3/1.
91 *The Guardian*, 28 October 1985.
92 V. Oleandrov and A. Kozyrev, 'International dialogue on building a secure world', *International Affairs* (Moscow), 4 (1987), 13–14.
93 *Review of International Affairs*, 37: 866 (5 May 1986), 9; for Soviet comment see, for example, report by A. Bovin in *Izvestiya*, 16 August 1986.
94 Gorbachev's reply in *Pravda*, 24 August 1986. The message from the Six was delivered on 7 August.
95 Tass in English, 31 August 1986, in SU/8353/A1/1.
96 *New Times* (Moscow), 37 (1986), 7. See *Eighth Conference*, para. 44.
97 *Pravda*, 7 September 1986.
98 Soviet Foreign Ministry briefing, Tass in English, 7 August 1986, in SU/8332/A1/7.
99 Tass in Russian for abroad, 8 October 1986, in SU/8386/A1/6.
100 Moscow home service and Tass in English, 8 October 1986, in SU/8386/A1/5. For an assessment by Mugabe of the Soviet response to the Harare appeal on disarmament see text of interview with Mugabe, in Tass 28 June 1987, in SU/8608/A5/3.

101 Broadcast text of reply by Gorbachev to Harare appeal, Moscow home service and Tass in English and Russian, 3 November 1986, in su/8408/A5/1 and 2.
102 Message from Gobachev to Delhi Six; Tass in Russian for abroad and Moscow home service, 19 January 1987, in su/8471/A1/1–2.
103 Gorbachev's reply to Appeal by Delhi Six, Moscow home service and Tass in English, 11 June 1987, in su/8594/A1/2.
104 See Moscow home service, 22 May 1987, on anniversary of declaration by Delhi Six; and Tass in English, 24 May 1987, in su/8577/A1/10–11.
105 Moscow home service and Tass in English, 11 June 1987, in su/8594/A1/2.
106 See Reznikova and Etinger, 'Neprisoedinivshiesya strany', p. 63.
107 See, for example T. Tuzmukhamedov, 'Record of a quarter century' in *The Non-Aligned Movement: Aims, Principles, Practice. Supplement to New Times* (Moscow), 1986, pp. 3–4.
108 E. M. Primakov, 'The new states and the opposing socio-political systems', *The Non-Aligned World*, 1: 3 (July–September 1983), 390–1. See also *Aziya i Afrika segodniya*, 1 (1984), 2–5.
109 See conference documents in *Review of International Affairs*, 37: 866 (5 May 1986), 10; *Eighth Conference*, paras. 51–2.
110 *Dvizhenie neprisoedineniya* (1985), p. 141.
111 *Ibid.*, p. 141.
112 Ya. Etinger and O. Melikyan, *Neytralizm i mir. Neytralistskaya politika stran Azii i Afriki* (Moscow: Mysl', 1964), p. 26.
113 A. Klimov and A. Laptev, 'On the policy of non-alignment', *International Affairs* (Moscow), 3 (1969), 18–19.
114 K. Brutents in *Pravda*, 30 August 1973.
115 Tass, 4 September 1973, in *Pravda*, 5 September 1973.
116 See *Pravda*, 12 April 1974.
117 For the Soviet position on specific issues relating to the NIEO and the Soviet response more generally to the NIEO at UNCTAD and other United Nations meetings see R. H. Donaldson, 'The Second World, the Third World, and the new international economic order', in R. H. Donaldson, ed., *The Soviet Union in the Third World: Successes and Failures* (London: Croom Helm, 1981), pp. 363–72; E. K. Valkenier, *The Soviet Union and the Third World: An Economic Bind* (New York: Praeger, 1983), pp. 111–17.
118 R. A. Tuzmukhamedov, *Neprisoedinenie i razryadka mezhdunarodnoy naprazhennosti* (Moscow: Mezhdunarodnye otnosheniya, 1976), p. 86.
119 *Ibid.*, pp. 34–5.
120 R. A. Tuzmukhamedov, ed., *Dvizhenie neprisoedineniya v dokumentakh i materialakh* (Moscow: Nauka, 1979), p. 19.
121 Report on 24 February 1976, in *Pravda*, 25 February 1976.
122 Tass, 16 August 1976, in su/5289/c/2.
123 *Pravda*, 19 August 1976.
124 For the foregoing argument see Valkenier, *The Soviet Union and the Third World*, pp. 113–16.
125 See, for example, Tuzmukhamedov, ed., *Dvizhenie neprisoedineniya v dokumentakh* (1979), p. 18.
126 E. Obminsky, *Cooperation on an Equitable Basis: Problems of Restructuring International Economic Relations* (Moscow: Novosti, 1978), pp. 20, 27.
127 See *Izvestiya*, 12 September 1979.
128 *Ibid.*
129 M. Volkov, 'Non-alignment movement: struggle for a new international economic order', *Soviet Studies* (New Delhi), 39 (1979), pp. 40–1.
130 N. Simoniya, *Non-Alignment: Its friends and Foes* (Moscow, Novosti, 1979), p. 22.
131 Ya. Ya. Etinger, ed., *Vneshnyaya politika razvivayushchikhsya stran. obshchie problemy i metodologiya issledovaniya* (Moscow: Mezhdunarodnye otnosheniya, 1983), p. 110.
132 See *The Non-Aligned Movement: Aims, Principles, Practice, Supplement to New Times* (Moscow), 1986, p. 12.
133 See *New International Economic Order* (Moscow: Social Sciences Today Editorial Board, 1984), pp. 168–9.

134 See, for example, V. S. Kotlyarov, *Dvizhenie neprisoedineniya – aktivnaya politicheskaya sila sovremennosti* (Moscow: Znanie, 1983), pp. 10, 31.
135 *New International Economic Order*, p. 169.
136 *Ibid.*, p. 181.
137 See Valkenier, *The Soviet Union and the Third World*, pp. 122–5.
138 See *Dvizhenie neprisoedineniya* (Moscow: Nauka, 1985), p. 231.
139 Speech on 24 April 1985, in *BBC Summary of World Broadcasts*, Far East (hereafter FE) /7935/A3/7.
140 Text of message of greetings in Tass in Russian for abroad, 8 June 1987, in SU/8590/A1/2.
141 *New International Economic Order*, p. 170.
142 See Simoniya, *Non-Alignment*, p. 59.
143 E. K. Valkenier, 'Revolutionary change in the Third World: recent Soviet assessments', *World Politics*, 38: 3 (April 1986), 424.
144 *New International Economic Order*, p. 171.
145 *Dvizhenie neprisoedineniya* (1985), pp. 221–2.
146 *Ibid.*, pp. 219–20.
147 Etinger, ed. *Dvizhenie neprisoedineniya v sovremennom mire*, pp. 228–9.
148 See L. Goncharov, 'Afrika v bor'be za novy mezhdunarodny ekonomicheskiy poryadok', *Mirovaya ekonomika i mezhdunarodnye otnosheniya*, 6 (1982), 53ff.
149 *Dvizhenie neprisoedineniya* (1985), p. 227; Etinger, ed., *Dvizhenie neprisoedineniya v sovremennom mire*, p. 228.
150 *Dvizhenie neprisoedineniya* (1985), pp. 220–1.
151 Reznikova and Etinger, 'Neprisoedinivshiesya strany', 63.
152 Interview of M. Nyagumbo, Administrative Secretary and Member of Political Bureau of the Central Committee of the ZANU-PF, in *The Non-Aligned Movements: Aims, Principles, Practice, Supplement to New Times* (Moscow), 1986, p. 32.
153 *Izvestiya*, 9 September 1986.
154 K. Brutents, 'Dvizhenie neprisoedineniya v sovremennom mire', *Mirovaya ekonomika i mezhdunarodnye otnosheniya*, 5 (1984), 38.
155 Press Release, Embassy of the USSR, Harare, no. 30, 26 August 1986, pp. 7–8.
156 Text in Tass in Russian for abroad, 8 June 1987, in SU/8590/A1/2.

3 SOVIET POLICY AND NEUTRALISATION IN THE THIRD WORLD

1 E. Luard, 'Superpowers and regional conflicts', *Foreign Affairs*, 64: 5 (Summer 1986), 1016–17.
2 B. V. Ganyushkin, *Sovremenny neytralitet* (Moscow: Inst. mezhdunarod. otnosheniy, 1958), pp. 16–17.
3 M. I. Lazarev, *Imperialisticheskie voennye bazy na chuzhikh territoriyakh i mezhdunarodnoe pravo* (Moscow: Inst. mezhdunarod. otnosheniy, 1963), p. 227. For a full rendering of the earlier Soviet position on these concepts see B. M. Klimenko, *Demilitarizatsiya i neytralizatsiya v mezhdunarodnom prave* (Moscow: 1963).
4 Lazarev, *Imperialisticheskie voennye bazy*, p. 277.
5 L. A. Modzhoryan, *Politika neytraliteta* (Moscow: Znanie, 1962), p. 12–13, 15.
6 *Sovetskaya voennaya entsiklopediya*, vol. 5 (Moscow: Voennoe izdatel'stvo, 1978), p. 570; *Diplomaticheskiy slovar*, vol. 1 (Moscow: Nauka, 1984), p. 299.
7 See *Pravda*, 20 November 1957; Ganyushkin, *Sovremenny neytralitet*, p. 62.
8 *The Conference of Heads of State or Government of Non-Aligned Countries* (Belgrade: 1961) pp. 188–9.
9 See Ganyushkin, *Sovremenny neytralitet*, p. 101; O. N. Khlestov, 'Zhenevskie soglasheniya po Laosu – vazhny shag v formirovanii sovremennogo ponyatiya neytraliteta', *Sovetskoe gosudarstvo i pravo*, 5 (1963), 99.
10 See, for example, Ya. Etinger and O. Melikyan, *Neytralizm i mir: Neytralistskaya politika stran Azii i Afriki* (Moscow: Mysl', 1964), p. 72; B. V. Ganyushkin, *Neytralitet i neprisoedinenie* (Moscow: Mehdunarodnye otnosheniya, 1965), p. 104.

11 *Izvestiya*, 5 July 1966.
12 See, for example, N. Pastukhov, 'Neprisoedinivshiesya gosudarstva i bor'ba za mir', *Kommunist*, 9 (1964), 97–9.
13 A. Broinowski, ed., *Understanding ASEAN* (London: Macmillan, 1982), pp. 24–6.
14 For the full Kuala Lumpur Declaration see *ibid.*, pp. 294–5, and for the discussion preceding it pp. 24–8.
15 Cited in D. Wilson, *The Neutralization of South-East Asia* (New York: Praeger, 1975), p. 112.
16 Cited in *Asia Research Bulletin*, January 1972, p. 566.
17 *Izvestiya*, 2 January 1972, and cited in Wilson, *The Neutralization of South-East Asia*, p. 113; *Izvestiya*, 7 January 1972.
18 V. Pavlovsky, 'Collective security: the way to peace in Asia', *International Affairs* (Moscow), 7 (1972), p. 27.
19 Cited in Wilson, *The Neutralization of South-East Asia*, p. 113.
20 Speeches on 2 October 1972, in *Pravda*, 3 October 1972.
21 *Pravda*, 6 October 1972.
22 Wilson, *The Neutralization of South-East Asia*, p. 113.
23 See L. Buszynski, *Soviet Foreign Policy and Southeast Asia* (London: Croom Helm, 1986), pp. 76–7, 88–90.
24 R. C. Horn, 'Changing Soviet policies and Sino-Soviet competition in Southeast Asia', *Orbis*, 17: 2 (Summer 1973), 526.
25 A. O. Ghebhardt, 'The Soviet system of collective security in Asia', *Asian Survey*, 13: 12 (December 1973), 1079.
26 Wilson, *The Neutralization of South-East Asia*, pp. 126–7.
27 See *ibid.*, p. 192.
28 B. Sen Gupta, *Soviet-Asian Relations in the 1970s and Beyond* (New York: Praeger, 1976), pp. 51–2, 216, 242.
29 Broinowski, ed., *Understanding ASEAN*, p. 130.
30 *Colombo Summit. Documents and Selected Speeches of the Fifth Conference of Heads of State or Government of Non-Aligned Countries* (New Delhi: People's Publishing House, 1976), p. 61.
31 See *Far Eastern Economic Review*, 3 September 1976, 13–14.
32 Broinowski, ed., *Understanding ASEAN*, p. 131.
33 Radio Moscow, 1 November 1978, in su/5959/A3/2.
34 *Ibid.*
35 *Diplomatiya razvivayushchikhsya gosudarstv* (Moscow: Mezhdunarodnye otnosheniya, 1976), pp. 177–8. This work was prepared by the Soviet Diplomatic Academy.
36 I. Kovalenko, *Soviet Policy for Asian Peace and Security* (Moscow: Progress, 1979), p. 159. This work was originally published as *Bor'ba za sovetskogo soyuza za mir i bezopasnost' v Azii* (Moscow: Nauka, 1976).
37 *Ibid.* (1979), pp. 161–3.
38 *Pravda*, 21 September 1979.
39 A. Petrov, ed., *Vneshnyaya politika stran Azii* (Moscow: Mezhdunarodnye otnosheniya, 1983), p. 256.
40 See *Far Eastern Economic Review*, 18 January 1980, 14.
41 See *Dvizhenie neprisoedineniya* (Moscow: Nauka, 1985), p. 195.
42 *Two Decades of Non-Alignment. Documents of the Gatherings of the Non-Aligned Countries 1961–1982* (New Delhi: Ministry of External Affairs, 1983), p. 508.
43 Tass, 16 February 1981, in su/6655/A3/4.
44 Petrov, ed., *Vneshnyaya politika stran Azii*, p. 255.
45 *Dvizhenie neprisoedineniya*, pp. 195–6.
46 Interview of Soviet specialist on the Third World and non-alignment in the Institute of State and Law, Moscow, September 1985.
47 *Izvestiya*, 7 September 1979.
48 See *Pravda*, 22 February 1981.
49 See *New York Times*, 16 July 1981.
50 See Buszynski, *Soviet Foreign Policy and Southeast Asia*, p. 240.
51 *Ibid.*, pp. 241–2, 238.

52 Petrov, ed., *Vneshnyaya politika stran Azii*, pp. 255–6.
53 T. I. Sulitskaya, *Strany ASEAN i mezhdunarodnye otnosheniya v Yugo-Vostochnoy Azii* (Moscow: Nauka, 1985), p. 23.
54 R. Alexeyev, 'The goodwill of the Indochina countries', *International Affairs* (Moscow), 11 (1985), 75.
55 See *The Korea Times*, 25 June 1986.
56 See Tass in Russian for abroad and English, 15 June 1987, in SU/8599/A3/6; Moscow home service, 16 June 1987, in SU/8599/A3/5.
57 Radio Moscow in Indonesian, 3 July 1987, in SU/8612/A3/16.
58 See *The Times*, 13 March 1987.
59 Tass in Russian for abroad, 19 May 1987, in SU/8573/A3/2.
60 Speech by Shevardnadze, Tass in Russian for abroad, 11 May 1987, in SU/8566/A3/2. Speech by Sitthi, in SU/8566/A3/4; and Xinhua in English, 12 May 1987, in SU/8567/A3/2. Joint Soviet–Thai statement on 14 May 1987, Tass in Russian for abroad, 14 May 1987, in SU/8571/A3/1–2.
61 Ye. Primakov, 'Osvobodivshiesya strany v mezhdunarodnykh otnosheniyakh', *Mirovaya ekonomika i mezhdunarodnye otnosheniya*, 5 (1982), 23
62 *Pravda* and *Izvestiya*, 10 December 1980.
63 *Pravda* and *Izvestiya*, 11 December 1980.
64 See *Izvestiya*, 13 February 1957.
65 *New Times* (Moscow), 51 (1980), 9.
66 Radio Moscow, 12 December 1980, in SU/6601/A5/1.
67 *Pravda*, 3 January 1981.
68 *New Times* (Moscow), 51 (1980), 9.
69 Z. Brzezinski, *Power and Principle. Memoirs of the National Security Adviser 1977–81* (London: Weidenfeld and Nicolson, 1983), pp. 443–7.
70 Tass in Russian for abroad, 10 December 1980, SU/6599/A4/1.
71 Tass in Russian for abroad, 2 January 1981; and in English, 3 January 1981, text of *Pravda* report, in SU/6614/A4/1.
72 Radio Moscow, 12 December 1980, in SU/6601/A4/1.
73 A. Y. Yodfat, *The Soviet Union and the Arabian Peninsula* (London: Croom Helm, 1983), p. 143.
74 For example, Tass in Russian, 30 June 1981, in SU/6764/A3/1.
75 Repeated, for example, in Primakov, 'Osvobodivshiesya strany', p. 24.
76 Cited in *The Truth about Afghanistan* (Moscow: Novosti, 1986), pp. 115–16.
77 *Pravda*, 15 February 1981.
78 N. Polyakov, 'Put' k bezopasnosti v Indiyskom okeane i Persidskom zalive', *Mirovaya ekonomika i mezhdunarodnye otnosheniya*, 1 (1981), 73.
79 *Izvestiya*, 28 April 1987 (morning edition).
80 Radio Moscow in English for Great Britain, 12 December 1980, in SU/6601/A4/ 1–2.
81 Radio Moscow in Arabic, 12 December 1980, in SU/6601/A4/1.
82 *Ibid.*, and Polyakov 'Put' k bezopasnosti v Indiyskom okeane i Persidskom zalive', p. 73.
83 Speech on 27 April 1981, in SU/6710/A4/6.
84 Joint communiqué after visit by Ali Naser Mohammed to the USSR, 27–29 May 1980, in *Pravda*, 31 May 1980.
85 Joint communiqué after visit by A. A. Saleh, President of the YAR to the Soviet Union, 9–11 October 1984, in *Pravda*, 12 October 1984.
86 See M. Katz, *Russia and Arabia. Soviet Foreign Policy Toward the Arabian Peninsula* (Baltimore and London: John Hopkins University Press, 1986), pp. 152–3, 121.
87 See *ibid.*, pp. 168–9.
88 Yodfat, *The Soviet Union and the Arabian Peninsula*, p. 143.
89 Radio Moscow in Persian, 25 December 1980, in SU/6612/A4/4.
90 Polyakov 'Put' k bezopasnosti v Indiyskom okeane i Persidskom zalive', p. 73.
91 See Radio Moscow in Arabic, 12 February 1981, in SU/6649/C2/1; *Pravda*, 15 February 1981; see also Chapter 4.
92 For example, P. Artem'ev, *Podlinnye i mnimye druz'ya dvizheniya neprisoedineniya* (Moscow: Nauka, 1982) p. 54.

93 Cited in Yodfat, *The Soviet Union and the Arabian Peninsula*, p. 145.
94 Tass text of Soviet government statement on 3 July 1987, in su/8612/A4/1.
95 B. Blechman, 'Soviet interests in naval arms control: prospects for disengagement in the Mediterranean', in M. MccGwire, ed., *Soviet Naval Developments* (New York: Praeger, 1973), pp. 521–2.
96 *Ibid.*, pp. 522–32.
97 *Two Decades of Non-Alignment. Documents of the Gatherings of the Non-Aligned Countries 1961–1982* (New Delhi: Ministry of External Affairs, 1983), p. 509.
98 *Final Documents. Seventh Conference of Heads of State or Government of Non-Aligned Countries* (New Delhi: 1983), p. 45.
99 Joint Soviet–Maltese communiqué, published on 10 October 1981, in *Izvestiya*, 10 October 1981.
100 *Pravda*, 27 March 1986, in su/8219/A4/5.
101 *The Guardian*, 27 March 1986.
102 Briefing on 28 March 1986, Tass 28 March 1986, in su/8223/A31/7.
103 See previous section on the neutralisation of the Persian Gulf, and P. Artem'ev 'Neprisoedinenie – vazhny faktor mirovoy politiki', *Mirovaya ekonomika i mezhdunarodnye otnosheniya*, 3 (1981), 70.
104 Ganyushkin, *Sovremenny neytralitet*, pp. 63–5; Ganyushkin, *Neytralitet i neprisoedinenie*, pp. 89–91.
105 *Sovetsko-Afganskie otnosheniya 1919–1969 gg. Dokumenty i materialy* (Moscow: Politizdat, 1971), pp. 83–4. This treaty and the other legal bases of Soviet–Afghan relations prior to the April 1978 coup are treated more thoroughly in A. Rakhim, *Dogovorno-pravovoe regulirovanie sovetsko-afganskikh otnosheniy*, thesis submitted for degree of candidate of juridical science, University of Kiev (Kiev: 1978).
106 See *Pravda*, 19 December 1955, 16 August 1965.
107 Cited in L. B. Teplinskiy, *Afganistan – nash yuzhny sosed* (Moscow: Znanie, 1978), pp. 40–1.
108 Press conference held by A. A. Gromyko in Paris, 25 April 1980, cited in *Pravda*, 26 April 1980.
109 Cited in *Kabul New Times*, 2 February 1980.
110 Speech on 14 March 1980, in *Pravda*, 15 March 1980.
111 Xinhua commentary, in *Beijing Review*, 13 (31 March 1980), 9.
112 Cited in L. B. Teplinskiy, *SSSR i Afganistan 1919–1981* (Moscow: Nauka, 1982), p. 243.
113 *Literaturnaya Gazeta*, 12 March 1980.
114 Tass in Russian for abroad, 14 March 1980, in su/6372/C/4.
115 *Pravda*, 28 March 1980.
116 See A. Hyman, *Afghanistan Under Soviet Domination, 1964–81* (London: Macmillan, 1982), p. 132.
117 Teplinskiy, *SSSR i Afganistan*, p. 243.
118 *Ibid.*, p. 244.
119 See, for example, Tass 30 June 1981, in su/6764/A3/1.
120 Teplinskiy, *SSSR i Afganistan*, pp. 246–7.
121 Tass in English, 1 July 1981, in su/6765/A3/2.
122 Tass, 4 July 1981, in su/6767/A3/1.
123 Tass, 6 July 1981, in su/6769/A3/1.
124 Tass, 10 July 1981, in su/6773/A3/2.
125 Cited in *Pravda*, 16 July 1981.
126 Television commentary on 12 July 1981, and Radio Moscow for Great Britain and Ireland, 13 July 1981, in su/6775/A1/1.
127 *Pravda*, 5 August 1981.
128 Tass, 6 July 1981, in su/6769/A3/1.
129 I. D. Savel'ev, 'Protivniki politicheskogo uregulirovaniya polozheniya vokrug Afganistana', *Narody Azii i Afriki*, 2 (1984), 45.
130 See *ibid.*, p. 45.
131 For a Soviet comment on these Iranian proposals see *ibid.*, p. 47.
132 S. Harrison, 'Dateline Afghanistan: exit through Finland?', *Foreign Policy*, 41 (Winter 1980–1), 183–6.

133 J. S. Mehta, 'A neutral solution', *Foreign Policy*, 47 (Summer 1982), 146.
134 *Ibid.*, pp. 144–50.
135 See R. Allison, *Finland's Relations with the Soviet Union*, 1944–84 (London: Macmillan, 1985). For an attempt to construct a 'Finlandisation' solution for Afghanistan see G. S. Bhargava, *South Asian Security After Afghanistan* (Lexington, Mass.: Lexington Books, 1983), pp. 169–84.
136 Several of these conclusions are also arrived at by B. Sen Gupta in *Afghanistan: Politics, Economics and Society* (London: Frances Pinter, 1986), pp. 155, 192–3.
137 Cited in *ibid.*, p. 151.
138 Speeches on 27 April 1981, in *Pravda*, 28 April 1981.
139 See, for example, Tass in Russian, 30 June 1981, in su/6764/A3/1.
140 Interview of Colonel X, an anonymous army officer in the USSR who now works as an adviser on international and defence affairs, in *Detente*, 2 (February 1985), 3–4.
141 For example, *Pravda*, 16 December 1982.
142 According to the detailed account of the negotiations by L. Lifschultz, cited in Sen Gupta, *Afghanistan*, pp. 143–5.
143 *Detente*, 2 (February 1985), 3.
144 Lifschultz cited in Sen Gupta, *Afghanistan*, p. 147.
145 See *The Guardian*, 1 June 1985.
146 See Allison, *Finland's Relations with the Soviet Union*, p. 40; *Pravda*, 28 December 1985.
147 *The New York Times*, 6 October 1985.
148 *The Muslim*, 29 December 1985.
149 *Pravda*, 28 December 1985.
150 See *Pravda*, 21 December 1985, 3 January 1986.
151 See *The Guardian*, 3 May 1986; *International Herald Tribune*, 5 May 1986.
152 *Pravda*, 8 August 1986.
153 Report to PDPA Central Committee, 1 January 1987, in *Pravda*, 2 January 1987.
154 Joint news conference with Rajiv Gandhi in Delhi, 28 November 1986, in *Stability and Security – A Common Concern. Visit of General Secretary of the CPSU Central Committee Mikhail Gorbachev to India* (Moscow: Novosti, 1986), p. 62.
155 Speech by Foreign Minister Sahabzada Yaqub Khan in Parliament on 24 December 1985, in *The Pakistan Times*, 25 December 1985.
156 See *The Guardian*, 21 February 1987.
157 See *The Guardian*, 12 May 1986. For the previous Soviet position see *Izvestiya*, 24 March 1986; and Tass in Russian, 21 March 1986, in su/8222/A3/1–2.
158 For the background to these Geneva negotiations see *The Independent*, 25 February 1987, 28 February 1987.
159 See *The Independent*, 28 February 1987.
160 *The Muslim*, 20 August 1985.
161 *The Guardian*, 3 May 1986.
162 Statement by Nawab Salim, Director of Press and Information, Hizb-e-Islami, 1–2 April 1987, at symposium on Afghanistan held in Oxford, England.
163 *The Times*, 7 March 1987.
164 *The Independent*, 15 April 1987.
165 *The Guardian*, 25 February 1987.
166 See *The Guardian*, 7 April 1987; Soviet television, 7 April 1987, in su/8538/A3/1.
167 Interview for *L'Unita*, text in *Pravda*, 20 May 1987 (first edition).
168 Tass statement quoting Najib at plenum of PDPA Central Committee, in *The Guardian*, 15 June 1987.
169 Discussions on 29 June, reported by Tass 29 June 1987, in su/8608/A1/1.
170 Report from Kabul by Moscow home service, 20 June 1987, in su/8610/A3/5.

4 SOVIET POLICY AND MILITARY ALIGNMENT IN THE THIRD WORLD

1 L. Buszynski, *Soviet Foreign Policy and Southeast Asia* (London: Croom Helm, 1986), pp. 51–2.
2 Report on 14 February 1956, *Pravda*, 15 February 1956.

3 Note delivered on 11 February 1957, *Izvestiya*, 13 February 1957.
4 See message to Jawaharlal Nehru on 8 January 1958, in R. K. Jain, ed., *Soviet–South Asian Relations 1947–1978*, vol. 1 (Oxford: Martin Robertson, 1979).
5 Soviet Government Statement on 25 March 1959, cited in R. K. Jain, ed., *Soviet–South Asian Relations 1947–1978*, vol. 2 (Oxford: Martin Robertson, 1979), pp. 20–1.
6 Radio Moscow in Persian, 7 September 1961 and Turkish, 10 September 1961, in su/ 741/5, 13 September 1961; Radio Moscow in Turkish, 14 September 1961, in su/ 744/A4/2, 16 September 1961.
7 *The Road to Communism, Documents of the 22nd Congress of the Communist Party of the Soviet Union* (Moscow: Foreign Languages Publishing House, 1961), p. 55.
8 Radio Moscow in Arabic, 23 August 1961, in su/725/A1/1, 25 August 1961.
9 Cited in Jain, ed., *Soviet–South Asian Relations*, p. 38.
10 See, for example, Radio Moscow in Turkish, 12 September 1973, in su/4398/A4/2.
11 See *Dawn* (Karachi), 1 and 8 September 1979.
12 Address by Noor Mohammad Taraki: *Addresses Delivered at Sixth Conference of Heads of State or Government of Non-Aligned Countries* (Havana: Editorial de Ciencias Sociales, 1980), p. 82.
13 *Izvestiya*, 6 May 1981, and *Pravda*, 7 May 1981.
14 Radio Moscow in Persian, 18 March 1979, in su/6073/A4/3.
15 Text of interview of Naser Minachi; Tass in Russian for abroad, 28 March 1979, in su/ 6080/A4/3–4.
16 Radio Moscow in Persian, 18 March 1979, in su/6073/A4/3.
17 *The Middle East Journal*, 34: 2 (Spring 1980), 202. This contains a complete translation of the constitution.
18 See S. Zabih, *Iran Since the Revolution* (London: Croom Helm, 1982), pp. 185–8, 190–1.
19 Buszynski, *Soviet Policy and Southeast Asia*, pp. 86–7.
20 *Ibid.*, p. 100.
21 *Ibid.*, p. 127; see pp. 122–7, 131.
22 For example, Radio Moscow in Serbo-Croat, 28 August 1961, in su/729/A1/6, 30 August 1961.
23 In su/3477/A1/3, 9 September 1970.
24 Brezhnev's message on 2 September 1979, *Pravda*, 3 September 1979.
25 V. Kudryatsev (Deputy to the USSR Supreme Soviet), 'Non-Alignment and disarmament', *Soviet Review* (New Delhi), 39 (1979), 25.
26 Message from USSR Supreme Soviet and Council of Ministers to Mrs Gandhi, 6 March 1983, *Pravda*, 7 March 1983.
27 P. Artem'ev, 'Neprisoedinenie – vazhny faktor mirovoy politiki', *Mirovaya ekonomika i mezhdunarodnye otnosheniya*, 3 (1981), 66–7, 69.
28 See Tass in English, 20 May 1978; text of *Izvestiya* report in su/5820/A3/1.
29 See Radio Peace and Progress in Arabic, 12 February 1981, in su/6649/C2/1.
30 A. V. Krutskikh, *Politika SShA v Indiyskom okeane* (Moscow: Nauka, 1984), pp. 189, 193.
31 Tass in English, 31 December 1980, in su/6613/A4/3–4.
32 *Pravda*, 10 February 1981; see also Radio Moscow in Arabic, 6 February 1981 in su/ 6644/A4/2.
33 See A. Yodfat, *The Soviet Union and the Arabian Peninsula* (London: Croom Helm, 1983), pp. 145–6.
34 M. Katz, *Russia and Arabia* (Baltimore and London: John Hopkins University Press, 1986), p. 169.
35 See N. Simoniya, *Non-Alignment: Its Friends and Foes* (Moscow: Novosti, 1979), pp. 38–9.
36 A. D. Portnyagin, *Strategiya SShA v zone Indiyskogo okeane* (Moscow: Mezhdunarodnye otnosheniya, 1985), pp. 104–5.
37 Krutskikh, *Politika SShA v Indiyskom okeane*, p. 193.
38 Radio Moscow in English for Africa, 16 July 1987, in su/8632/A5/1.
39 V. N. Nikolaev, 'Ot Belgrada k Gavane', *Latinskaya Amerika*, 4 (1979), 19.
40 I. N. Zorina, 'Strany Latinskoy Ameriki na deliyskom forume neprisoedinivshikhsya gosudarstv', *Latinskaya Amerika*, 8 (1983), 132.

41 Speech on 13 January 1983, in *Movement of Non-Aligned Countries 1979–January 1983. vol. I Chairmanship. Various Documents* (Havana: 1983), pp. 304 and 308.
42 See Ya. Etinger, ed., *Dvizhenie neprisoedineniya v sovremennom mire* (Moscow: Mezhdunarodnye otnosheniya, 1985), p. 88.
43 Speech on 27 April 1981, *Pravda*, 28 April 1981.
44 Krutskikh, *Politika SShA v Indiyskom okeane*, pp. 219–20.
45 Ye. Tarabin, 'Newly free countries and international relations', *International Affairs* (Moscow), 4 (1986), 32–3; and Portnyagin, *Strategiya SShA*, p. 105.
46 Tarabin, 'Newly free countries', 32, citing *National Herald*, 17 May 1985.
47 Krutskikh, *Politika SShA v Indiyskom okeane*, pp. 195–6.
48 *Ibid.*, p. 198.
49 Text of speech in Tass, in Russian for abroad and English, 19 May 1987, in su/8573/A3/2.
50 L. Rosenberger, 'The Soviet–Vietnamese alliance and Kampuchea', *Survey*, 27: 118/119 (Autumn–Winter 1983), p. 221ff.
51 Soviet television discussion programme, 8 August 1987, in su/8644/A3/1.
52 V. Ovchinnikov, *Pravda* political observer, on Soviet television, 19 February 1987, in su/8504/A3/3.
53 These distinctions are made by Rajan Menon in *Soviet Power and the Third World* (New Haven and London: Yale University Press, 1986), pp. 228–9.
54 R. E. Harkavy, *Great Power Competition for Overseas Bases: The Geopolitics of Access Diplomacy* (New York: Pergamon, 1982), pp. 110–12.
55 See S. Allard, *Russia and the Austrian State Treaty: A Case Study of Soviet Policy in Europe* (University Park and London: Pennsylvania State University Press, 1970), pp. 216–18.
56 See *Khrushchev Remembers II: The Last Testament*, trans. and ed., S. Talbott (London: Penguin, 1977), pp. 268–70.
57 *Helsingin Sanomat* (Helsinki), 18 September 1955.
58 *Pravda*, 25 February 1956.
59 Soviet Protest Note on 13 May 1960, cited in Jain, ed., *Soviet–South Asian Relations*, p. 24; see also pp. 16–19.
60 M. I. Lazarev, *Imperialisticheskie voennye bazy na chuzikh territoriyakh i mezhdunarodnoe pravo* (Moscow: Inst. mezhdunarod. otnosheniy, 1963), pp. 207–8, 252–3.
61 Speech by President Osvaldo Dorticos Torrado, in *The Conference of Heads of State or Government of Non-Aligned Countries* (Belgrade: 1961), p. 124.
62 *Two Decades of Non-Alignment* (New Delhi: Ministry of External Affairs, 1983), p. 7.
63 *Ibid.*, p. 24.
64 For example, D. V. Baratashvili, *Novye gosudarstva Azii i Afriki i mezhdunarodnoe pravo* (Moscow: Nauka, 1968), pp. 221–2.
65 Report on 29 March 1966, *Pravda*, 30 March 1966.
66 Harkavy, *Great Power Competition For Overseas Bases*, p. 154.
67 R. Remnek, 'The politics of Soviet access to naval support facilities in the Mediterranean', in B. Dismukes and J. M. McConnell, eds., *Soviet Naval Diplomacy* (New York: Pergamon, 1979), pp. 360–1. Although Remnek refers to the Mediterranean region his argument applies more generally to Soviet access arrangements. For a full list of Soviet military facilities in the early 1980s see Harkavy, *Great Power Competition for Overseas Bases*, pp. 176–81.
68 Remnek, 'The politics of Soviet access', pp. 369–73, 396 fn 54.
69 *Ibid.*, pp. 366–7.
70 For example, S. R. Rashidov, candidate member of Soviet Politburo, in S. Bhushan, ed., *Twenty Years of Bandung and Problems of Peace and Security in Asia* (New Delhi: Allied Publishers, 1975), p. 33.
71 *Review of International Affairs*, 24: 564, 5 October 1973, 14–15.
72 P. Artem'ev, 'Neprisoedinenie – vazhny faktor mirovoy politiki', p. 69.
73 See, for example, Krutskikh, *Politika SShA v Indiyskom okeane*, pp. 136–7.
74 Speech on 27 April 1981 during visit to Moscow, in su/6710/A4/7.
75 Tass in Russian for abroad, 29 April 1981, in su/6712/A4/7.
76 Remnek, 'The politics of Soviet access', pp. 384–6, 390.

77 For references to a number of articles in the early 1980s by Soviet military representatives on Western bases in the Near and Middle East and Mediterranean see Menon, *Soviet Power and the Third World*, p. 41.

78 See speech by Maltese Prime Minister, Dom Mintoff, in AFP report in English, 27 September 1981, in su/6841/A1/6.

79 Moscow home service, 16 January 1983, in su/7235/A1/20.

80 Text of letter from Gorbachev delivered on 14 May 1987, in su/8613/c/3. See also *The Guardian*, 6 July 1987.

81 Press briefing by USSR Ministry of Foreign Affairs, Tass in Russian and English, 16 July 1987, in su/8624/A1/1–2.

82 See B. Sen Gupta, *Soviet–Asian Relations in the 1970s and Beyond* (New York: Praeger, 1976), pp. 123–4; A. Haselkorn, 'The Soviet collective security system', *Orbis*, 14: 1 (Spring 1975), 250–1.

83 *Documents and Resolutions 25th Congress of the CPSU* (Moscow: 1976), p. 28.

84 Sen Gupta, *Soviet–Asian Relations*, p. 119. For the controversy over the Diego Garcia base see pp. 113–14.

85 Statement in *Pravda*, 12 November 1980.

86 W. R. Duncan, 'Castro and Gorbachev: politics of accommodation', *Problems of Communism*, 35: 2 (March–April 1986), 46. See also Harkavy, *Great Power Competition for Overseas Bases*, p. 196.

87 See *Soviet Military Power*, fifth edn, (Washington: US Govt Printing Office, March 1986), p. 138; Rosenberger, 'The Soviet–Vietnamese alliance and Kampuchea'; J. G. Whelan and M. J. Dixon, *The Soviet Union in the Third World: Threat to World Peace?* (Washington, New York, London etc.: Pergamon, 1986), pp. 114–17.

88 Buszynski, *Soviet Foreign Policy and Southeast Asia*, pp. 204–6; for a good analysis of the strategic character of Cam Ranh Bay see pp. 202–6.

89 *Ibid.*, p. 203.

90 V. S. Rudenev, *Politika SShA v Yugo-Vostochnoy Azii* (Moscow: Nauka, 1986), p. 135.

91 Admiral Nikolay Nikolayevich Amelko, Deputy Commander in Chief of USSR Navy and Deputy Chief of the General Staff, in Soviet television discussion on 19 February 1987, in su/8504/A3/11.

92 Krutskikh, *Politika SShA v Indiyskom okeane*, p. 124. For a map of such installations see pp. 4–5. For an analysis of Diego Garcia see pp. 125–31.

93 Radio Peace and Progress in English for Africa, 14 January 1980, in su/6320/c/2.

94 *Ibid.*

95 Text of report on Taraki's statement during official visit to USSR by Tass in Russian for abroad, 6 December 1978, in su/5989/A3/1.

96 *Addresses Delivered at Sixth Conference of Heads of State or Government of Non-Aligned Countries* (Havana: Editorial de Ciencias Sociales, 1980), p. 81.

97 According to A. Mascarenhas of the *Sunday Times* who interviewed a number of former intimates of Amin in early 1980; cited in S. Harrison, 'Dateline Afghanistan: exit through Finland?', *Foreign Policy*, 41 (Winter 1980–1), 173.

98 *Kabul Times*, 17 December 1979.

99 For example, *Pravda*, 16 December 1982.

100 See S. Harrison, 'A breakthrough in Afghanistan', *Foreign Policy* (Summer 1983), 13.

101 Interview for Indian journalists on 21 November 1986, in *Stability and Security – A Common Concern. Visit by General Secretary of the CPSU Central Committee Mikhail Gorbachev to India* (Moscow: Novosti, 1986), p. 14.

102 Krutskikh, *Politika SShA v Indiyskom okeane*, p. 142.

103 See *The Muslim*, 24 December 1985.

104 Krutskikh, *Politika SShA v Indiyskom okeane*, p. 119.

105 Etinger, *Dvizhenie neprisoedineniya v sovremennom mire*, p. 51.

106 *Ibid.*, p. 243.

107 Speech in honour of visit to Moscow by Rajiv Gandhi, 21 May 1985, in su/7958/A3/4.

108 Radio Moscow in Finnish, 19 September 1985, in su/8064/A2/3–4.

109 A. Slobodenko, 'The "bases strategy" – a strategy of expansion and diktat', *International Affairs* (Moscow), 7 (1981), 75–84.
110 Haselkorn, 'The Soviet collective security system', and *The Evolution of Soviet Security Strategy 1965–1975* (New York: Crane Russak and Co. Inc., 1978).
111 Harkavy, *Great Power Competition for Overseas Bases*, pp. 200–2.
112 Slobodenko, 'The "bases strategy"', pp. 77–8.
113 Address to Moscow international forum, Soviet television and Tass, 16 February 1987, in SU/8494/C1/10.
114 See *The Guardian*, 21 May 1987.
115 Letter delivered to Prime Minister Andreas Papandreou on 14 May 1987, in SU/8613/C/3.
116 Moscow world service in English, 28 June 1987, in SU/8610/A3/5.
117 See R. B. Remnek, 'Soviet military interests in Africa', *Orbis*, 28: 1 (Spring 1984).
118 K. Brutents, Deputy Head of the CPSU Central Committee International Department on Soviet television, 28 February 1987, in SU/8506/C/4.
119 Tass in Russian and English for abroad, 24 March 1987, in SU/8525/A4/1.
120 Statement by Indian Foreign Minister, Sarwan Sing, on 9 August 1971, cited in *Times of India*, 10 August 1971, and Jain, ed., *Soviet–South Asian Relations 1947–1978*, vol. 1, p. 118; speech by A. N. Kosygin on 28 September 1971, in *Pravda*, 29 September 1971.
121 For the full text see *New Times* (Moscow), 33 (1971), 4–5. For English translations of the texts of all Soviet friendship and cooperation treaties signed with Third World states referred to in this study, apart from the 1984 treaty with North Yemen, see Z. Imam, *Towards a Model Relationship. A Study of Soviet Treaties with India and other Third World Countries* (New Delhi: ABC Publishing House, 1983). This contains an interesting breakdown of the provisions of all these treaties. See also Z. Imam, 'Soviet treaties with Third World countries', *Soviet Studies*, 35: 1 (January 1983), 53–70.
122 See Haselkorn, 'The Soviet collective security system'.
123 See A. Kapur, 'Indo-Soviet treaty and the emerging Asian balance', *Asian Survey*, 12: 6 (June 1972), 465–6.
124 Ayub Khan's account of his discussions with Soviet leaders during his visit to Moscow in April 1965, cited in Jain, ed., *Soviet–South Asian Relations 1947–1978*, vol. 2, pp. 37–8.
125 See H. Malik, 'Soviet intervention in Afghanistan and its impact on Pakistan's foreign policy', in H. Malik, ed., *Soviet–American Relations with Pakistan, Iran and Afghanistan* (London: Macmillan, 1987), pp. 153–4; for the discussions on the no-war pact see pp. 149–50.
126 B. G. Khabirov, 'O mezhdunarodno-pravovykh aspektakh neprisoedineniya', *Sovetskoe gosudarstvo i pravo*, 12 (1973), 115.
127 Information from an Indian diplomat involved in negotiating the Indo-Soviet treaty interviewed in New Delhi in December 1984.
128 Yodfat, *The Soviet Union and the Arabian Peninsula*, p. 19.
129 For the text of the Treaty of Friendship and Cooperation between the USSR and the United Arab Republic see *Pravda*, 28 May 1971; for the text of the Treaty of Friendship and Cooperation between the USSR and the Republic of Iraq see *Pravda*, 10 April 1972; for the text of the Treaty of Friendship and Cooperation between the USSR and the Somalian Democratic Republic see *Pravda*, 12 July 1974.
130 See K. Dawisha, *Soviet Foreign Policy Towards Egypt* (London: Macmillan, 1979), pp. 61–2; A. Sella, *Soviet Political and Military Conduct in the Middle East* (London: Macmillan, 1981), p. 39. The Soviet leadership presented its general image of the treaty in a letter to Sadat before its negotiation; see M. Heikal, *Sphinx and Commissar: The Rise and Fall of Soviet Influence in the Middle East* (London: Collins, 1978), pp. 227–8.
131 R. A. Tuzmukhamedov, ed., *Dvizhenie neprisoedineniya v dokumentakh i materialakh* (Moscow: Nauka, 1975), p. 46.
132 Radio Moscow in Arabic, 30 August 1973, in SU/4389/A1/7.
133 For Sadat's decision to abrogate the treaty see Heikal, *Sphinx and Commissar*, pp. 269–70.
134 Cited in Dawisha, *Soviet Foreign Policy Towards Egypt*, p. 77.

135 *Diplomatiya razvivayushchikhsya gosudarstv* (Moscow: Mezhdunarodnye otnosheniya, 1976), pp. 58–9.
136 Tuzmukhumedov, ed., *Dvizhenie neprisoedineniya*, p. 90; R. A. Tuzmukhamedov, ed., *Dvizhenie neprisoedineniya v dokumentakh i materialakh* (Moscow: Nauka, 1979), pp. 22–3.
137 Yodfat, *The Soviet Union and the Arabian Peninsula*, p. 65.
138 Soviet–Indian Joint Declaration, 11 June 1976, in Jain, ed., *Soviet–South Asian Relations*, vol. 1, p. 463.
139 Tuzmukhamedov, ed., *Dvizhenie neprisoedineniya* (1979), p. 23; R. A. Tuzmukhamedov, 'Neprisoedinenie: nekotorye voprosy mezhdunarodnogo prava', *Sovetskõe gosudarstvo i pravo*, 6 (1981), p. 115.
140 B. D. Porter, *The USSR in Third World Conflicts: Soviet Arms and Diplomacy in Local Wars, 1945–1980* (Cambridge University Press, 1984), p. 194.
141 Buszynski, *Soviet Foreign Policy and Southeast Asia*, p. 169; D. Zagoria, ed., *Soviet Policy in East Asia* (New Haven and London: Yale University Press, 1982), p. 158.
142 Editorial in *People's Daily*, 10 November 1978, attacked by Radio Moscow in Standard Chinese, 14 November 1978, in su/5971/A3/1.
143 Buszynski, *Soviet Foreign Policy and Southeast Asia*, p. 171.
144 Radio Moscow in Vietnamese, 31 October 1979, in su/6263/A3/2.
145 Text of message on 2 November 1979, Moscow home service, 2 November 1979, in su/6263/A3/1.
146 See *Beijing Review*, 25, 22 June 1979, 20; 34, 24 August 1979, 19.
147 Speech on 5 September 1979, cited in *New Times* (Moscow), 38 (1979), 29.
148 *Pravda*, 6 December 1978. Bradsher is mistaken, therefore, in overstating the military commitment established by this article, see H. S. Bradsher, *Afghanistan and the Soviet Union* (Durham, NC: Duke Press Policy Studies, 1983), p. 97.
149 Text of report of Taraki's statement on Moscow TV; Tass in Russian for abroad, 6 December 1978, in su//5989/A3/1.
150 Ratification of the treaty examined during meeting of Presidium of 10th Supreme Soviet on 20 April 1979, reported in *Pravda*, 21 April 1979.
151 L. B. Teplinskiy, *SSSR i Afganistan 1919–1981* (Moscow: Nauka, 1982), pp. 233–4.
152 Agreement announced after visit by S. M. Dost, DRA Minister of Foreign Affairs, to USSR 13–14 March 1980, in *Pravda*, 15 March 1980.
153 In Article 10. For the text of the treaty see *Izvestiya*, 26 October 1979.
154 Radio Moscow in Arabic, 26 October 1979, in su/6257/C4 and 5.
155 Yodfat, *The Soviet Union and the Arabian Peninsula*, p. 110; for an analysis of this treaty see pp. 109–10.
156 Katz, *Russia and Arabia. Soviet Foreign Policy Toward the Arabian Peninsula*, p. 87. For details on such military ties see Yodfat, *The Soviet Union*, pp. 111–12.
157 Interview on 26 September 1980; cited in K. Dawisha, 'Soviet decision-making in the Middle East: the 1973 October War and the 1980 Gulf War', *International Affairs* (London), 57: 1 (Winter 1980/1), 59.
158 Text of treaty in *Pravda*, 9 October 1980.
159 For such an assumption see Dawisha, 'Soviet decision-making in the Middle East', p. 59.
160 See P. Ramet, 'The Soviet–Syrian relationship', *Problems of Communism*, 35: 5 (September–October 1986), 40–1.
161 *Pravda*, 17 December 1985.
162 Katz, *Russia and Arabia*, pp. 26, 47.
163 Text of treaty in *Pravda*, 11 October 1984.
164 Speech on 9 October 1984, cited in *Pravda*, 10 October 1984.
165 Colonel G. Malinovskiy, 'Natsional'no-osvoboditel'noye dvizhenie na sovremennom etape', *Kommunist Vooruzhennykh Sil*, 24 (1979), 33; cited in M. Katz, *The Third World in Soviet Military Thought* (London: Croom Helm, 1982), p. 108.
166 See *Diplomatiya razvivayushchikhsya gosudarstv*, p. 58; Ye. Yu. Bogush, *Kurs KPSS na sotrudnichestvo SSSR s razvivayushchimisya stranami* (Moscow: Mysl', 1984), p. 12.
167 Imam, *Towards a Model Relationship*, pp. 94–5.
168 Article in *Pravda*, 8 August 1981.

169 See, for example, speech by N. S. Reddy, President of India, at dinner in honour of L. I. Brezhnev's visit to New Delhi, 8 December 1980, cited in *Pravda*, 8 December 1980.

170 The treaty was signed on 15 January 1966; for the provisions see *Pravda*, 16 January 1966.

171 Cited in S. T. Hunter, 'The Soviet Union and the Islamic Republic of Iran', in Malik, ed., *Soviet–American Relations with Pakistan, Iran and Afghanistan*, p. 257.

172 See Yodfat, *The Soviet Union and the Arabian Peninsula*, p. 109.

173 Speech by Brezhnev on 3 November 1978, Moscow home service and Tass in English, 3 November 1978, in su/5961/A3/5; speech by Le Duan, 3 November 1978, in su/5961/A3/6.

174 Joint communiqué of visit to Moscow by Vietnamese delegation 1–9 November 1978; VNA in English, 9 November 1978, in su/5966/A3/1 and 2.

175 See *Pravda*, 14 December 1978; Tuzmukhamedov, ed., *Dvizhenie neprisoedineniya* (1979), p. 24.

176 Buszynski, *Soviet Foreign Policy and Southeast Asia*, p. 170.

177 Speech on 5 September 1979, cited in *New Times* (Moscow), 38 (1979), 29–30.

178 Agreement signed in Moscow 31 October 1983, in Hanoi 4 November 1983; published in *Pravda*, 5 November 1983. See Rosenberger, 'The Soviet–Vietnamese alliance and Kampuchea', pp. 229–30.

179 For example, Mikhail Kapitsa on Soviet television, 19 February 1987, in su/8504/A3/8.

180 Speech on 5 December 1978, in *Pravda*, 6 December 1978.

181 Tass in Russian for abroad, 6 December 1978, in su/5989/A3/1.

182 *Pravda*, 21 April 1979.

183 Teplinskiy, *SSSR i Afganistan*, p. 225.

184 *Pravda*, 21 April 1979.

CONCLUSION

1 V. M. Molotov, *The International Situation and Soviet Foreign Policy* (New York: 1955), p. 33; cited in G. Ginsburgs, 'Neutrality and neutralism and the tactics of Soviet diplomacy', *The American Slavic and East European Review*, 19 (1960), 555.

2 Letter of 6 October 1981 from Kirkpatrick to permanent representatives of sixty-four non-aligned countries and letter of 16 October 1983 from Reagan to Prime Minister Indira Gandhi, in R. Jackson, *The Non-Aligned, the United Nations and the Superpowers* (New York: Praeger, 1983), pp. 300, 297–8.

3 Yu. Alimov, 'Dvizhenie neprisoedinenie n vazhnom rubezhe', *Kommunist*, 7 (1983), 103–4.

4 K. Brutents, 'Dvizhenie neprisoedineniya v sovremennom mire', *Mirovaya ekonomika i mezhdunarodnye otnosheniya*, 5 (1984), 38.

5 *The Non-Aligned Movement: Aims, Principles, Practice. Supplement to New Times* (Moscow), 1986, p. 11.

6 *New Times* (Moscow), 37 (1986), 7.

7 *Izvestiya*, 16 August 1986.

8 *Izvestiya*, 9 September 1986.

9 Message of greetings from Gorbachev to Mugabe, Tass in English, 31 August 1986, in su/8353/A1/1.

10 Response by Gorbachev upon receipt of appeal of the Harare Conference, in Moscow home service (and Tass in English), 8 October 1986, in su/8386/A1/5.

11 Speech to the Indian Parliament, 27 November 1986, in *Stability and Security – A Common Concern. Visit of the General Secretary of the CPSU Central Committee Mikhail Gorbachev to India November 25–28, 1986* (Moscow: Novosti, 1986), p. 27.

12 V. Oleandrov and A. Kozyrev, 'International dialogue on building a secure world. Results of the 41st session of the UN General Assembly', *International Affairs* (Moscow), 4 (1987), 13.

13 Joint Soviet–Syrian statement, Tass in Russian for abroad. 26 April 1987, in su/8553/
A4/3; meeting between Gorbachev and Assad, Moscow home service, 24 April 1987,
in su/8552/A4/1.
14 *Ibid.*
15 *Pravda*, 17 September 1987.
16 The Communist Party Programme and Party Statutes, Final Version. In *Current Digest
of the Soviet Press*, Special Supplement, December 1986, p. 22.

Select bibliography

BOOKS AND COLLECTIONS OF DOCUMENTS

Addresses Delivered at Sixth Conference of Heads of State or Government of Non-Aligned Countries (Havana: Editorial de Ciencias Sociales, 1980)

Alim-Khan. *The Non-Aligned Movement: Achievements, Problems, Prospects* (Moscow: Novosti, 1985)

Allard, Sven. *Russia and the Austrian State Treaty: A Case Study of Soviet Policy in Europe* (University Park and London: Pennsylvania State University Press, 1970)

Allison, Roy. *Finland's Relations with the Soviet Union, 1944–84* (London: Macmillan, 1985)

Artem'ev, P. A. *Podlinnye i mnimye druz'ya dvizheniya neprisoedineniya* (Moscow: Nauka, 1982)

Baratashvili, D. V. *Novye gosudarstva Azii i Afriki i mezhdunarodnoe pravo* (Moscow: Nauka, 1968)

Berg, Eugène. *Non Álignement et nouvel ordre mondial* (Paris: Presses Universitaires de France)

Bhargava, G. S. *South Asian Security After Afghanistan* (Lexington, Mass.: Lexington Books, 1983)

Bhushan, Shashi, ed. *Twenty Years of Bandung and Problems of Peace and Security in Asia* (New Delhi: Allied Publishers, 1975)

Bogush, Ye. Yu. *Kurs KPSS na sotrudnichestvo SSSR s razvivayushchimisya stranami* (Moscow: Mysl', 1984)

Bondarevsky, G. L. and Sofinsky, V. N. *Politika neprisoedineniya: istoriya i sovremennost'* (Moscow: Znanie, 1976)

Non-Alignment: Its Friends and Adversaries in World Politics (Moscow: Social Sciences Today Editorial Board, USSR Academy of Sciences, 1978)

Bowman, Larry W. and Clark, Ian, eds. *The Indian Ocean in Global Politics* (Boulder, Colorado: Westview, 1981)

Bradsher, Henry S. *Afghanistan and the Soviet Union* (Durham, NC: Duke Press Policy Studies, 1983)

Braun, D. *The Indian Ocean, Region of Conflict or 'Peace Zone'?* (London: Hurst, 1983)

Brezhnev, Leonid. *On Relations Between Socialist and Developing Countries* (Moscow: Progress, 1984)

Broinowski, Alison, ed. *Understanding ASEAN* (London: Macmillan, 1982)

Brutents, K. N. *Osvobodivshiesya strany v 70-gody* (Moscow: Politizdat, 1979)

Brzezinski, Zbigniew. *Power and Principle. Memoirs of the National Security Adviser 1977–81* (London: Weidenfeld and Nicolson, 1983)

Buszynski, Leszek. *Soviet Foreign Policy and Southeast Asia* (London: Croom Helm, 1986)

Chand, Attar. *Nonaligned Solidarity and National Security* (New Delhi: UDH Publishers, 1983)

Chirkin, V. and Yudin, Yu. *A Socialist-Oriented State* (Moscow: Progress, 1983)

Clissold, S., ed. *Yugoslavia and the Soviet Union 1939–1973 – A Documentary Survey* (Oxford University Press, 1975)

Colombo Summit. Documents and Selected Speeches of the Fifth Conference of Heads of State or Government of Non-Aligned Countries (New Delhi: People's Publishing House, 1976)

Conference of Foreign Ministers of Non-Aligned Countries (New Delhi), 9–13 Feb. 1981. (Proceedings) (New Delhi: Ministry of External Affairs, 1981)

Conference of Heads of State or Government of Non-Aligned Countries, IVth, Algiers. Speeches (1973)

The Conference of Heads of State or Government of Non-Aligned Countries, Belgrade, Sept. 1–6, 1961 (Belgrade: 1961)

Cuba's Presence in the Movement of Non-Aligned Countries (Havana: Political Publishers, 1983)

Dawisha, Karen. *Soviet Foreign Policy Towards Egypt* (London: Macmillan, 1979)

Diplomaticheskiy slovar, vol. 2, Gromyko, A. A., Golunskiy, S. A. and Khvostov, V. M., eds. in chief (Moscow: 1961)

Diplomaticheskiy slovar, vol. 2, Gromkyo, A. A., Zemskov, I. N. and Khvostov, V. M., eds. in chief (Moscow: 1971)

Diplimaticheskiy slovar, vol. 1, Gromyko, A. A., Kovalev, A. G., Sevost'yanov, P. P. and Tikhvinskiy, S. L., eds. in chief (Moscow: Nauka, 1984)

Diplomaticheskiy slovar, vol. 2, Gromyko, A. A., Kovalev, A. G., Sevost'yanov, P. P. and Tikhvinskiy, S. L., eds. in chief (Moscow: Nauka, 1985)

Diplomatiya razvivayushchikhsya gosudarstv (Moscow: Mezhdunarodnye otnosheniya, 1976)

Dismukes, B. and McConnell, J. M., eds. *Soviet Naval Diplomacy* (New York: Pergamon, 1979)

Donaldson, Robert H. *The Soviet Union in the Third World: Successes and Failures* (Boulder, Colorado: Westview, 1981)

Dvizhenie neprisoedineniya (Moscow: Nauka, 1985)

Dvizhenie neprisoedineniya v dokumentakh i materialakh (Moscow: Nauka, 1983)

Dzasokhov, A. S. *Dvizhenie solidarnosti narodov Azii i Afriki* (Moscow: Nauka, 1977)

Efremov, A. Ye. *Sovetsko-avstriyskie otnosheniya posle vtoroy mirovoy voyny* (Moscow: Gospolitizdat, 1958)

Etinger, Ya. Ya., ed. *Vneshnyaya politika razvivayushchikhsya stran. Obshchie problemy i metodologiya issledovaniya* (Moscow: Mezhdunarodnye otnosheniya, 1983)

Dvizhenie neprisoedineniya v sovremennom mire (Moscow: Mezhdunarodnye otnosheniya, 1985)

Etinger, Ya. Ya. and Melikyan, O. *Neytralizm i mir: Neytralistskaya politika stran Azii i Afriki* (Moscow: Mysl', 1964)

Fiedler, H. *Der Begriff der Neutralität in der sowjetischen völkerrechtlichen Theorie und praktischen Politik* (Cologne: 1959)

Final Documents. Seventh Conference of Heads of State or Government of Non-Aligned Countries (New Delhi: March 1983)

Fedotova, E. M. *SShA i neprisoedinivshiesya strany* (Moscow: Nauka, 1975)

Fritsche, Klaus. *Blockfreiheit aus sowjetischer Sicht* (Cologne: Weltforum Verlag, 1986)

Gafurov, B. G. *Neutralism and the National Liberation Movement* (Moscow: Novosti, 1966)

Gal, Choidogiin, ed. *Socialist Community and Non-Alignment* (New Delhi: Allied Publishers, 1979)

Ganyushkin, B. V. *Sovremenny neytralitet (Politika neytraliteta i postoyanny neytralitet v usloviyakh bor'by za mir)* (Moscow: Inst. mezhdunarod. otnosheniy, 1958)

Neytralitet i neprisoedinenie (Moscow: Mezhdunarodyne otnosheniya, 1965)

George, Alexander L. *Managing U.S.–Soviet Rivalry: Problems of Crisis Prevention* (Boulder, Colorado: Westview, 1983)

Ginsburgs, George. 'Neutralism à la Russe', in Ginsburgs, G. and Rubinstein, A. Z., *Soviet Foreign Policy Towards Western Europe* (New York: Praeger, 1978)

Girenko, Yu. S. *Sovetsko-yugoslavskie otnosheniya* (Moscow: Mezhdunarodnye otnosheniya, 1983)

Grinevich, E. A. and Gvozdarev, B. I. *Kuba v mirovoy politike* (Moscow: Mezhdunarodnye otnosheniya, 1984)

Halliday, Fred. *Threat from the East? Soviet Policy from Afghanistan and Iran to the Horn of Africa* (Penguin Books, 1981)

Harkavy, Robert E. *Great Power Competition for Overseas Bases: The Geopolitics of Access Diplomacy* (New York: Pergamon, 1982)

Haselkorn, A. *The Evolution of Soviet Security Strategy 1965–1975* (New York: Crane Russak and Co. Inc., 1978)

Heikal, Mohammed. *Sphinx and Commissar. The Rise and Fall of Soviet Influence in the Middle East* (London: Collins, 1978)

Horn, Robert C. *Soviet–Indian Relations: Issues and Influence* (New York: Praeger, 1982)

Hough, J. F. *The Struggle for the Third World: Soviet Debates and American Options* (Washington: Brookings, 1986)

Hyman, Anthony. *Afghanistan Under Soviet Domination, 1964–81* (London: Macmillan, 1982)

Imam, Zafar. *Towards a Model Relationship. A Study of Soviet Treaties with India and other Third World Countries* (New Delhi: ABC Publishing House, 1983)

Jackson, Richard L. *The Non-Aligned, the United Nations and the Superpowers* (New York: Praeger, 1983)

Jain, R. K., ed. *Soviet–South Asian Relations 1947–1978*, vols. 1 and 2 (Oxford: Martin Robertson, 1979)

Select bibliography

Select bibliography

Select bibliography

Select bibliography

Jankowitsch, Odette and Sauvant, Karl P., eds. *The Third World Without Superpowers: The Collected Documents of the Nonaligned Countries* (Dobbs Ferry, NY: Oceana, 1978), 4 vols.

Jansen, G. H. *Afro-Asia and Non-Alignment* (London: Faber and Faber, 1966)

Jukes, Geoffrey. *The Soviet Union in Asia* (Sydney and London: Angus and Robertson, 1973)

Kapitsa, L. M. *Razvivayushchiesya strany i novy mezhdunarodny ekonomicheskiy poryadok* (Moscow: Znanie, 1981)

Katsman, V. Ya. *Vneshnyaya politika stran sotsialisticheskoy orientatsii Afriki* (Moscow: Nauka, 1985)

Katz, Mark N. *The Third World in Soviet Military Thought* (London: Croom Helm, 1982)

  Russia and Arabia. Soviet Foreign Policy Toward the Arabian Peninsula (Baltimore and London: Johns Hopkins University Press, 1986)

Khabirov, B. *Mezhdunarodno-pravovoy status i vneshnie funkstii neprisoedinivshikhsya gosudarstv*, candidate thesis in juridical science (Moscow: 1972)

Khan, Rasheeduddin, ed. *Perspectives on Non-Alignment* (New Delhi: Kalamkar Prakashan (P) Ltd., 1981)

Khrushchev Remembers II: The Last Testament, trans. and ed. S. Talbott (London: Penguin, 1977)

Khryashcheva, N. M. *Novy mezhdunarodny ekonomicheskiy poryadok i strany Azii* (Moscow: Nauka, 1984)

Klimenko, B. M. *Demilitarizatsiya i neytralizatsiya v mezhdunarodnom prave* (Moscow: 1963)

Kotlyarov, V. S. *Dvizhenie neprisoedineniya – aktivnaya politicheskaya sila sovremennosti* (Moscow: Znanie, 1983)

Kovalenko, I. I. *Bor'ba sovetskogo soyuza za mir i bezopasnost' v Azii* (Moscow: Nauka, 1976)

  Soviet Policy for Asian Peace and Security (Moscow: Progress, 1979)

Kurs mezhdunarodnogo prava, tom 3, Osnovnye instituty i otrasli sovremennogo mezhdunarodnogo prava, Kozhevnikov, F. I., chief ed., (Moscow: 1967)

Kozhakhmetov, Kenesbay. *Dvizhenie solidarnosti narodov Azii i Afriki v bor'be s kolonializmom i imperializmom (1955–1960)* (Alma Ata: Kazakhstan, 1983)

Krutskikh, A. V. *Politika SShA v Indiyskom okeane* (Moscow: Nauka, 1984)

Krylov, S. B. and Durdenevsky, V. N., eds. *Mezhdunarodno-pravovye formy mirnogo sosushchestvovaniya gosudarstv i natsiy* (Moscow: Inst. mezhdunarod. otnosheniy, 1957)

La Roumanie et les pays nonalignés (Relations de solidarité et de large coop amicale) (Bucharest: Agerpress, 1976), vol. 1

Lazarev, M. I. *Imperialisticheskie voennye bazy na chuzhikh territoriyakh i mezhdunarodnoe pravo* (Moscow: Inst. mezhdunarod. otnosheniy, 1963)

Löwenthal, Richard. *Model or Ally? The Communist Powers and the Developing Countries* (Oxford and New York: Oxford University Press, 1977)

Lyon, Peter. *Neutralism* (Leicester University Press, 1963)

MacFarlane, Neil S. *Superpower Rivalry and Third World Radicalism* (London: Croom Helm, 1985)

McMillen, Donald H., ed. *Asian Perspectives on International Security* (London: Macmillan, 1984)

Malik, Hafeez, ed. *Soviet–American Relations with Pakistan, Iran and Afghanistan* (London: Macmillan, 1987)

Martin, L. W. *Neutralism and Non-Alignment. The New States in World Affairs* (New York: Praeger, 1962)

Mates, L. *Non-Alignment: Theory and Current Policy* (Belgrade: The Institute of International Politics and Economics and Dobbs Ferry, NY: Oceana Publications Inc., 1972)

Matyunin, E. N. *Dvizhenie neprisoedineniya na sovremennom etape* (Leningrad: Znanie, 1981)

Melikyan, O. N. *Neytralizm gosudarstv Afriki* (Moscow: Nauka, 1966)

Mekhr, M. A. *Politika neytraliteta i neprisoedineniya afganistana,* candidate thesis in historical science (Moscow: 1970)

Menon, Rajan. *Soviet Power and the Third World* (New Haven and London: Yale University Press, 1986)

Misra, K. P., ed. *Non-Alignment: Frontiers and Dynamics* (New Delhi: Vikas, 1982)

Mitchell, R. Judson. *Ideology of a Superpower: Contemporary Soviet Doctrine on International Relations* (Stanford: Hoover Press, 1982)

Modzhoryan, L. A. *Politika podlinnogo neytraliteta – vazhny faktor bor'by narodov za mir i nezavisimost'* (Moscow: Znanie, 1956)

    Politika neytraliteta (Moscow: Znanie, 1962)

Mortimer, R. *The Third World Coalition in International Politics* (New York: Praeger, 1980)

Movement of Non-Aligned Countries September 1979–January 1983. Vol. I Chairmanship. Various Documents (Havana: 1983)

    Vol. II Ministerial Conferences and Plenary Sessions, Coordinating Bureau Meetings and Other Activities (Havana: 1983)

    Vol. IV Ministerial Conferences and Plenary Sessions, Coordinating Bureau Meetings and Other Activities (Havana: 1983)

New International Economic Order (Moscow: Social Sciences Today Editorial Board, USSR Academy of Sciences, 1984)

Non-Alignment: A Bibliography, Tandon, J. C., Batra, S., Muley, R., compilers (New Delhi: Lancers, 1983)

Nord, Lars. *Nonalignment and Socialism: Yugoslav Foreign Policy in Theory and Practice* (Stockholm: Raben and Sjögren, 1974)

Obminsky, E. *Cooperation on an Equitable Basis: Problems of Restructuring International Economic Relations* (Moscow: Novosti, 1978)

Papp, Daniel S. *Soviet Perceptions of the Developing World in the 1980s: The ideological basis* (Lexington, Mass.: Lexington Books, 1986)

Pashuk, V. V. *25 geroicheskikh let: (respublika kuba v bor'be za mir i mezhdunar. sotrudnichestvo)* (Kiev: Politizdat ukrainy, 1983)

Petrov, A. I., ed. *Vneshnyaya politika stran Azii* (Moscow: Mezhdunarodnye otnosheniya, 1983)

Poklad, B. I. *Real'nosti sovremennogo mira i politika konfrontatsii* (Moscow: Mezhdunarodnye otnosheniya, 1985)

Porter, Bruce D. *The USSR in Third World Conflicts: Soviet Arms and Diplomacy in Local Wars, 1945–1980* (Cambridge University Press, 1984)

Portnyagin, A. D. *Strategiya SShA v zone Indiyskogo okeana* (Moscow: Mezhduna-rodnye otnosheniya, 1985)

Postoyanny neytralitet (na sravitel'nom opyte Mal'ty), thesis submitted in Moscow University (Moscow: 1985)

Prasad, Bimal. *Indo-Soviet Relations 1947–1972: A Documentary Study* (New Delhi: Allied, 1973)

Prusakov, Yu. M. *Neytralitet v sovremennom mezhdunarodnom prave* (Moscow: Znanie, 1972)

Rakhim, Abdul. *Dogovorno-pravovoe regulirovanie sovetsko-afganskikh otnosheniy*, candidate thesis in juridical science for University of Kiev (Kiev: 1978)

Rao, T. V. Subba. *Non-Alignment in International Law and Politics* (New Delhi: Deep and Deep Publications, 1981)

Razvivayushchiesya strany v mirovoy politike (Moscow: Nauka, 1970)

Reshetar, J. S. Jr. *The Soviet Union and the Neutralist World* (Philadelphia, PA: The Annals of the American Academy of Political and Social Science, 1965)

The Road to Communism. Documents of the 22nd Congress of the Communist Party of the Soviet Union (Moscow: Foreign Languages Publishing House, 1961)

The Role of the Neutrals and the Non-Aligned in the Detente Process (Vienna: Peace and the Sciences 2, 1980)

Rubinstein, A. Z. *Yugoslavia and the Nonaligned World* (Princeton University Press, 1970)

Saxena, Munish N. *Non-Aligned Movement in the Eighties* (Moscow: Novosti, 1982)

Shevchenko, Arkady N. *Breaking with Moscow* (Moscow: Jonathan Cape, 1985)

Second Conference of Heads of State or Government of Non-Aligned Countries. Speeches (Cairo: 1964)

Selezneva, Ye. I. *Politika neprisoedineniya molodykh suverennykh gosudarstv Azii i Afriki* (Moscow: Mezhdunarodnye otnosheniya, 1966)

Sella, Amnon. *Soviet Political and Military Conduct in the Middle East* (London: Macmillan, 1981)

Sen Gupta, Bhabani. *Soviet–Asian Relations in the 1970s and Beyond: An Interperceptional Study* (New York: Praeger, 1976)

Afghanistan. Politics, Economics and Society (London: Frances Pinter, 1986)

Simoniya, N. A. *Dvizhenie neprisoedineniya – vazhny faktor mezhdunarodnoy politiki* (Moscow: Znanie, 1978)

Simoniya, N. A. *Non-Alignment: Its Friends and Foes* (Moscow: Novosti, 1979)

Singham, A. W. and Hune, S. *Non-Alignment in an Age of Alignments* (London: Zed Books, 1986)

Singham, A. W. and van Dinh, trans. and eds. *From Bandung to Colombo: Conferences of the Non-Aligned Countries 1955–75* (New York: Third Press Review books, 1976)

Sovetsko-afganskie otnosheniya 1919–1969 gg. Dokumenty i materialy (Moscow: Politizdat, 1971)

Soviet Military Power 1986, fifth edn (Washington: US Government Printing Office, 1986)

Soviet Military Power 1987, sixth edn (Washington: US Government Printing Office, 1987)

Stability and Security – A Common Concern. Visit of General Secretary of the CPSU Central Committee Mikhail Gorbachev to India (Moscow: Novosti, 1986)

Starushenko, G. B. *Neytralizm segodnya i zavtra* (Moscow: Znanie, 1966)

Stein, Arthur. *India and the Soviet Union: The Nehru Era* (Chicago and London: University of Chicago Press, 1969)

SShA i razvivayushchiesya strany 70-e gody, Kremenyuk, V. A., Lukin, V. P., Rudnev, V. S., ed. board (Moscow: Nauka, 1981)

SSSR–Avstriya, 1938–1979 gg.: Dokumenty i materialy (Moscow: Politizdat, 1980)

Sulitskaya, T. I. *Strany ASEAN i mexhdunarodnye otnosheniya v Yugo-Vostochnoy Azii* (Moscow: Nauka, 1982)

Taber, Michael, ed. *Fidel Castro Speeches: Cuba's Internationalist Foreign Policy 1975–80* (New York: Pathfinder Press, 1981)

Teplinskiy, L. B. *Afganistan – nash yuzhny sosed* (Moscow: Znanie, 1978)

SSSR i Afganistan 1919–1981 (Moscow: Nauka, 1982)

Tito and Non-Alignment. President Tito's Addresses at Conferences of Non-Aligned Countries (Belgrade: Socialist Thought and Practice, 1979)

Tiunov, O. *Neytralitet v mezhdunarodnom prave* (Perm State University, 1968)

Tuzmukhamedov, B. R. *Zony mira* (Moscow: Mezhdunarodnye otnosheniya, 1986)

Tuzmukhamedov, R. A. *Neprisoedinenie i razryadka mezhdunarodnoy napryazhennosti* (Moscow: Mezhdunarodnye otnosheniya, 1976)

Soviet Union and Non-Aligned Nations (New Delhi: Allied, 1976)

Razvivayushchiesya strany v mirovoy politike (Moscow: Mezhdunarodnye otnosheniya, 1977)

ed. *Dvizhenie neprisoedineniya v dokumentakh i materialakh* (Moscow: Nauka, 1975)

ed. *Dvizhenie neprisoedineniya v dokumentakh i materialakh* (Moscow: Nauka, 1979)

Two Decades of Non-Alignment: Documents of the Gatherings of Non-Aligned Countries, 1961–1982 (New Delhi: Ministry of External Affairs, 1983)

Valkenier, Elizabeth K. *The Soviet Union and the Third World: An Economic Bind* (New York: Praeger, 1983)

Vigor, P. H. *The Soviet View of War, Peace and Neutrality* (London: Routledge and Kegan Paul, 1975)

Vladimirov, V. Kh. and Kostin, V. G. *Kuba. 20 let novoy vneshney politiki (1959–1979 gg.)* (Moscow: Mezhdunarodnye otnosheniya, 1980)

Whelan, J. G. and Dixon, M. J. *The Soviet Union in the Third World: Threat to World Peace?* (Washington, New York, London etc.: Pergamon, 1986)

Willetts, Peter. *The Non-Aligned Movement: The Origins of a Third World Alliance* (London: Frances Pinter, 1978)

The Non-Aligned in Havana (London: Frances Pinter, 1981)

Wilson, D. *The Neutralization of South-East Asia* (New York: Praeger, 1975)

Yodfat, Aryeh Y. *The Soviet Union and the Arabian Peninsula* (London: Croom Helm, 1983)

The Soviet Union and Revolutionary Iran (London: Croom Helm, 1984)

Yahuda, Michael B. *China's Role in World Affairs* (London: Croom Helm, 1978)

Zagoria, Donald S. *Soviet Policy in East Asia* (New Haven and London: Yale University Press, 1982)

Select bibliography

ARTICLES

Alimov, Yu. 'Dvizhenie neprisoedineniya – vliyatel'naya sila mezhdunarodnykh otnosheniy', *Mirovaya ekonomika i mezhdunarodnye otnosheniya*, 11 (1976)
'Vazhny faktor mirovoy politiki (K itogam Deliyskoy konferentsii neprisoedinivshikhsya stran)', *Mirovaya ekonomika i mezhdunarodnye otnosheniya*, 6 (1983)
'Dvizhenie neprisoedineniya na vazhnom rubezhe', *Kommunist*, 7 (1983)
'Svyaz' vremen i sobytiy (k 30-i godovshchie Bandungskoy konferentsii)', *Mirovaya ekonomika i mezhdunarodnye otnosheniya*, 6 (1985)
'Dvizehnie neprisoedineniya: ot vneshnepolitichesko-kontseptsii – k mezhdunarodnomu obedineniyu', *Voprosy istorii*, 4 (1986)
Artem'ev, P. 'Neprisoedinenie – vazhny faktor mirovoy politiki', *Mirovaya ekonomika i mezhdunarodnye otnosheniya*, 3 (1981)
Artem'ev, P. and Klimov, A. 'Dvizhenie neprisoedineniya v mirovoy politike', *Mirovaya ekonomika i mezhdunarodnye otnosheniya*, 8 (1979)
Baratashvili, D. I. 'Pozitivny neytralitet v sovremennom mezhdunarodnom prave', *Sovetskoe gosudarstvo i pravo*, 6 (1963)
Bindschedler-Robert, D. 'Völkerrecht und Neutralität in sowjetischer Sicht', *Österreichische Zeitschrift für Aussenpolitik*, 5 (1965)
Blishchenko, I. P. 'Ponyatie i sushchnost' vneshnikh funktsiy neytralistskogo gosudarstva', *Pravovedenie*, 4 (1965)
Brutents, K. 'Dvizhenie neprisoedineniya v sovremennom mire', *Mirovaya ekonomika i mezhdunarodnye otnosheniya*, 5 (1984)
Chicherov, A. I. 'Non-alignment in contemporary world: some approaches and evaluations', *Review of International Affairs*, 37: 858 (1986)
Chirkin, V. Ye. 'Sotsialisticheskaya orientatsiya razvivayushchikhsya stran: edinstvo i protivorechivost' politicheskoy sistemy', *Voprosy filosofii*, 7 (1984)
Cviic, K. F. 'The Non-Aligned in Havana', *The World Today*, September (1979)
Dasgupta, K. K. 'Nonalignment: the NIEO and the socialist world', *The Nonaligned World*, 2: 2 (April–June 1984)
Durdenevskiy, V. N. 'Neytralitet v sisteme kollektivnoy bezopasnosti', *Sovetskoe gosudarstvo i pravo*, 8 (1957)
Durdenevskiy, V. and Osnitskaya, 'Neytralitet i atomnoe oruzhie' *Sovetskoe gosudarstvo i pravo*, 2 (1960)
Duncan, W. R. 'Castro and Gorbachev: politics of accommodation', *Problems of Communism*, 35: 2 (March–April 1986)
Efremov, A. Ye. 'Bandungskaya konferentsiya i rost solidarnosti stran Azii i Afriki v bor'be protiv kolonializma', *Problemy vostokovedeniya*, 2 (1960)
El'yanov, A. Ya. 'Bor'ba za novy mezhdunarodny ekonomicheskiy poryadok', *Narody Azii i Afriki*, 2 (1985)
Etinger, Ya. Ya. 'Dvizhenie neprisoedineniya: aktual'nye problemy', *Narody Azii i Afriki*, 6 (1981)
'Vazhny faktor mira i mezhdunarodnoy bezopasnosti', *Mirovaya ekonomika i mezhdunarodnye otnosheniya*, 3 (1983)

Fritsche, Klaus. 'The Nonaligned Movement in Soviet perspective', *The Nonaligned World*, 2: 3 (July–September 1984)
'Soviet views on non-alignment', *Review of International Affairs*, 37: 864 (1986)
Galina, A. 'Problema neytraliteta v sovremennom mezhdunarodnom prave', *Sovetskiy ezhegodnik mezhdunarodnogo prava* (1958)
Georgiev, N. and Klimov, I. 'Problems and prospects of the Non-Alignment Movement', *Far Eastern Affairs*, 2 (1977)
Ghebhardt, Alexander O. 'The Soviet system of collective security in Asia', *Asian Survey*, 13: 12 (December 1973)
Ginsburgs, George. 'Neutrality and neutralism and the tactics of Soviet diplomacy', *The American Slavic and East European Review*, 19 (1960)
Goncharov, L. 'Afrika v bor'be za novy mezhdunarodny ekonomicheskiy poryadok', *Mirovaya ekonomika i mezhdunarodnye otnosheniya*, 6 (1982)
Goncharova, T. V. 'K ideyno-politicheskim voprosam dvizheniya neprisoedineniya', *Latinskaya Amerika*, 6 (1982)
Harrison, Selig. 'Dateline Afghanistan: exit through Finland?', *Foreign Policy*, 41 (Winter 1980–1)
'A breakthrough in Afghanistan?', *Foreign Policy*, (Summer 1983)
Haselkorn, A. 'The Soviet collective security system', *Orbis*, 14: 1 (Spring, 1975), 250–1.
Hensel, Howard M. 'Asian collective security: the Soviet view', *Orbis*, 19 (Winter 1976)
Horn, R. C. 'Changing Soviet policies and Sino-Soviet competition in Southeast Asia', *Orbis*, 17: 2 (Summer 1973)
Imam, Zafar. 'Soviet view of non-alignment', *International Studies* (New Delhi), 20: 1–2 (January–June 1981)
'Soviet treaties with Third World countries', *Soviet Studies*, 35: 1 (1983)
Jackson, R. L. 'The United States and the Non-Aligned Movement', *Review of International Affairs*, 37: 860 (1986)
Joshi, Nirmala. 'The Soviet Union and the non-aligned countries: natural allies?', *Problems of Non-Alignment*, 1: 1 (March–May 1983)
Kapur, Ashok. 'Indo-Soviet treaty and the emerging Asian balance', *Asian Survey*, 12 (June 1972)
Kaushik, Devendra. 'Soviet perspectives on the Third World: ideological retreat or refinement?', *The Nonaligned World*, 1: 1 (January–March 1983)
Khabirov, B. G. 'O mezhdunarodno-pravovykh aspectakh neprisoedineniya', *Sovetskoe gosudarstva i pravo*, 12 (1973)
Khlestov, O. N. 'Zhenevskie soglasheniya po Laosu – vazhny shag v formirovanii sovremennogo ponyatiya neytraliteta', *Sovetskoe gosudarstvo i pravo*, 5 (1963)
Kim, G. F. and Ul'yanovskiy, R. A. 'Vtoraya godovshchina Bandungskoy konferentsii stran Azii i Afriki', *Sovetskoe vostokovedenie*, 2 (1957)
Kobo, Kh. 'Forum neprisoedinivshikhsya stran', *Latinskaya Amerika*, 1 (1980)
Kotlyarov, V. S. 'Neprisoedinivshiesya strany i gegemonizm Pekina', *Problemy dal'nogo Vostoka*, 4 (1973)
'The Nonaligned Movement: an important factor in world politics', *Asia and Africa Today*, 6 (1981)

'Dvizhenie neprisoedineniya – nekotorye itogi i perspektivy', *Narody Azii i Afriki*, 5 (1983)

Kovalenko, I. 'Bandung: Past and Present', *Far Eastern Affairs*, 3 (1980)

Kovalenko, I. and Tuzmukhamedov, R. 'Neprisoedinenie i sotsializm v mirovoy politike', *Kommunist*, 17 (1976)

Kremnyev, M. 'The Non-Aligned countries and world politics', *World Marxist Review*, 4 (1963)

Krutikov, K. 'Forum in Delhi', *Far Eastern Affairs*, 4 (1983)

Larrabee, F. S. 'The Soviet Union and the Non-Aligned', *The World Today*, 32: 12 (December 1976)

LeoGrande, W. M. 'Evolution of the Non-Aligned Movement', *Problems of Communism*, 22 (January–February 1980)

Levchenko, L. A. 'Avangardnaya rol' Kuby', *Latinskaya Amerika*, 4 (1979)

Light, Margot. 'Neutralism and nonalignment: the dialectics of Soviet theory', *Millenium: Journal of International Studies*, 14: 1 (Spring 1985)

Low-Beer, F. 'The concept of neutralism', *The American Political Science Review*, 58: 2 (1964)

Luard, Evan. 'Superpowers and regional conflicts', *Foreign Affairs*, 64: 5 (Summer 1986)

Lyon, P. 'Neutrality and the emergence of the concept of neutralism', *Review of Politics*, 22 (April 1960)

MacFarlane, S. N. 'The Soviet conception of regional security', *World Politics*, 38: 3 (April 1985)

Mehta, Jagat S. 'A neutral solution', *Foreign Policy*, 47 (Summer 1982)

Melikyan, O. and Etinger, Ya. 'Vneshnyaya politika mirolyubivykh stran Azii i Afriki i ee burzhuaznye kritiki', *Narody Azii i Afriki*, 6 (1961)

Melkov, G. M. 'Neytralitet v voyne', *Sovetskiy ezhegodnik mezhdunarodnogo prava* (1978)

Mendras, M. 'Le tiers-monde dans la doctrine soviétique des relations inter-nationales', *Relations Internationales*, 45 (Spring 1986)

Nasenko, Yu. P. 'Indiya: evolutsiya politiki neprisoedineniya', *Narody Azii i Afriki*, 6 (1968)

Nikolaev, V. N. 'Ot Belgrada k Gavane', *Latinskaya Amerika*, 4 (1979)

Nesterov, S. M. 'Dvizhenie neprisoedineniya – vazhny faktor mezhdunarodnykh otnosheniy', *Narody Azii i Afriki*, 6 (1977)

Neuhold, Hanspeter. 'Permanent neutrality and non-alignment: similarities and differences', *India Quarterly*, 35: 3 (July–September 1979)

Pastukhov, N. 'Neprisoedinivshiesya gosudarstva i bor'ba za mir', *Kommunist*, 9 (1964)

Pavlov, A. 'Dvizhenie neprisoedineniya i Pekin', *Aziya i Afriki segodnya*

Pavlovskiy, V. V. 'Kollektivnaya bezopasnost' – deystvenny faktor politiki v Azii', *Narody Azii i Afriki*, 1 (1975)

Polyakov, N. 'Put' k bezopasnosti v Indiyskom okeane i Persidskom zalive', *Mirovaya ekonomika i mezhdunarodnye otnosheniya*, 1 (1981)

Primakov, E. M. 'The new states and the opposing socio-political systems', *The Nonaligned World*, 1: 3 (July–September 1983)

Primakov, Ye. 'Osvobidivshiesya strany v mezhdunarodnykh otnosheniyakh', *Mirovaya ekonomika i mezhdunarodnye otnosheniya*, 5 (1982)

Ramet, P. 'The Soviet–Syrian relationship', Problems of Communism, 35: 5 (September–October 1986)
Remnek, R. B. 'Soviet military interests in Africa', Orbis, 28: 1 (Spring 1984)
Reznikova, O. B. 'Sotsintern i dvizhenie neprisoedineniya', Narody Azii i Afriki, 3 (1984)
Reznikova, O. B. and Etinger, Ya. 'Neprisoedinivshiesya strany i bor'ba za ustranenie yadernoy opasnosti, uprochenie mira', Mirovaya ekonomika i mezhdunarodnye otnosheniya, 2 (1986)
Rosenberger, Leif. 'The Soviet–Vietnamese alliance and Kampuchea', Survey, 27 (Autumn–Winter 1983)
Ryakin, Yu. and Stepanov, V. 'The Nonaligned Movement and Peking's intrigues', Far Eastern Affairs, 1 (1980)
Savel'ev, I. D. 'Protivniki politicheskogo uregulirovaniya polozheniya vokrug Afganistana', Narody Azii i Afriki, 2 (1984)
Selezneva, Ye. I. 'K kharakteristike vneshney politiki neytralistskikh gosudarstv Azii i Afriki', Narody Azii i Afriki, 4 (1963)
Sergeev, V. 'Neprisoedinenie i problema razoruzheniya', Aziya i Afrika segodnya, 1 (1983)
Sethi, J. D. 'Indo-Soviet treaty and nonalignment', India Quarterly, 27: 4 (October–December 1971)
Simoniya, N. 'Dvizhenie neprisoedineniya nabiraet silu', Aziya i Afrika segodnya
Stepanov, V. 'Peking and the Nonaligned Movement', Far Eastern Affairs, 3 (1982)
Tuzmukhamedov, R. A. 'Neprisoedinenie: "latinoamerikanskiy etap"?', Latinskaya Amerika, 1 (1972)
'Vliyatel'ny faktor mirovoy politiki', Kommunist 14 (1979)
'Neprisoedinenie: nekotorye voprosy mezhdunarodnogo prava', Sovetskoe gosudarstvo i pravo, 6 (1981)
Ul'yanovsky, R. A. 'Amerikanskaya politika "pomoshchi" i neytralizm Indii', Narody Azii i Afriki, 3 (1963)
Vaidik, V. P. 'Afghan non-alignment: changing faces', International Studies (New Delhi), 20: 1–2 (January–June 1981)
Valkenier, E. K. 'Revolutionary change in the Third World', World Politics, 38: 3 (April 1986)
Vivekandan, B. 'The Indian Ocean as a zone of peace: problems and prospects', Asian Survey, 21: 12 (December 1981)
Vlad, C. and Calina, N. 'The Non-Aligned Movement, the international system and Romanian foreign policy', The Nonaligned World, 2: 2 (April–June 1984)
Zagoria, Donald S. 'Into the breach: new Soviet alliances in the Third World', Foreign Affairs, 57: 4 (Spring 1979)
Zamostny, Thomas J. 'Moscow and the Third World: recent trends in Soviet thinking', Soviet Studies, 36: 2 (April 1984)
Zorina, I. N. 'Strany Latinskoy Ameriki na deliyskom forume neprisoedin vshikhsya gosudarstv', Latinskaya Amerika, 8 (1983)

Select bibliography

PRIMARY JOURNALS AND NEWSPAPERS

Soviet

Aziya i Afrika segodnya
Far Eastern Affairs
International Affairs (Moscow)
Izvestiya
Kommunist
Latinskaya Amerika
Literaturnaya gazeta
Mirovaya ekonomika i mezhdunarodnye otnosheniya
Narody Azii i Afriki
New Times
Pravda
Problemy dal'nogo vostoka
Sovetskiy ezhegodnik mezhdunarodnogo prava
Sovetskoe gosudarstvo i pravo
Sovetskoe vostokovedenie
Soviet Review (New Delhi, Embassy of USSR)
Voprosy istorii
World Marxist Review

Others

Far Eastern Economic Review
The Guardian
The Muslim
Peking Review, Beijing Review
Review of International Affairs (Belgrade)
The Times

Index

Index

Kovalenko, Ivan, 138–40
Kuala Lumpur, 133, 137
Kudryavtsev, V., 99, 110
Kuwait, 152–5, 157, 191

Laos
  Geneva Conference on (1962), 13, 25–6
  Geneva Declaration on the Neutrality of,
    26, 131
  and Indo-China federation, 195–6
  and neutralisation of Southeast Asia,
    135–7, 140
  neutralisation of, neutrality of, 13,
    25–6, 130–2, 136, 246
  and nuclear-free zone in Southeast Asia,
    145
  as socialist state in Non-Aligned
    Movement, 46, 53
Latin America, 39, 49, 56–7, 70, 76–7,
  90, 97–8, 109, 192–3
Lazarev, M. I., 200–1
League of Arab States, 35
Lesotho, 46
Liberia, 46
Libya, 53, 89, 154, 159–60, 171, 203–4,
  249
Lima Non-Aligned Conference, *see*
  conferences of non-aligned states
Luxembourg, 8, 127, 163

Madrid, Fifteenth Congress of the Socialist
  International (1980), 57
Madrid Review Conference, 19
Malaysia, 39, 132–7, 140, 144–5, 187
Mali, 45
Malik, A., 133
Malmierca, I. Peoli, 91, 193
Malta, 13–14, 88, 158–9, 204–5
Managua Non-Aligned Conference, *see*
  conferences of the non-aligned states
Mangal, Habib, 167
Mediterranean, 88–9, 147, 157–61, 245
Mendelevich, L. I., 86
Mehta, Jagat, S., 169–71
Mexico, 54, 74, 103
Micunovic, 60
Middle East, 73, 82, 90, 94, 148–9, 151,
  157, 171–2, 183, 190–1, 202
military denial, strategy of, 1, 3, 6–7, 27,
  181, 157, 195, 243, 245–7, 252
Molotov, Vyacheslav, M., 129, 198
Mongolia, Soviet–Mongolian Treaty of
  Friendship, Cooperation and Mutual
  Aid (1966), 217, 235–6
Morocco, 39, 46, 97
Mozambique, 46, 53, 76, 226–7, 237,
  240

MPLA, 71
Mugabe, Robert, 102, 107
mujahidin, 169, 175, 177–9

Nagy, Imre, 17–18, 60
Najibullah (Najib), Mohammed, 175, 178–9
Namibia, 74, 77, 90
Nasser, Gamal, A., 4, 40, 72
NATO, *see* North Atlantic Treaty
  Organisation
Nehru, Jawaharlal, 4, 72, 79, 80–1, 184
Nepal, 97
Netherlands, 8
neutral and non-aligned group (N and N),
  14, 19–20, 101, 104
neutralism
  concept of, 3–6, 21–8, 32–3
  and Europe, 3–4, 243
  Soviet view of, 3, 21–8, 32–3, 242
neutrality, atomic, 15–16
  and collective security, 8, 16, 243
  and Hungary, 17–18
  and international law, *see* international
    law
  and military relations, 11–12, 14–19,
    25–7, 243
  and neutralism, 13, 21–6
  permanent, 7–8, 10, 12–13
  positive, 13, 21–2, 25, 27–8, 42, 165
  socialist, 7, 11
  and Warsaw Pact, 9, 17–18, 20, 243–4
  wartime, 6, 8, 10–11, 13–14, 25
  in West Europe, 6, 8–10, 14–20, 243
neutralisation
  concept of, 6, 126–31, 137, 243, 246
  and demilitarisation, 127–30, 252
  and international law, *see* international
    law
  Soviet Union and, 126–79, 137, 246–7,
    252
  of Afghanistan, 126, 161–79, 247
  of Austria, 9, 17, 129
  of Belgium, 127
  of Berlin, 129–30
  of Cambodia, 13, 130–2
  of Germany, 9, 17, 129–30
  of Kampuchea, 126, 142–3, 146–7, 247
  of Laos, 13, 25–6, 130–2, 246
  of Luxembourg, 127
  of Mediterranean Sea, 147, 158–61
  of Nicaragua, 126
  of Persian Gulf, 147–61
  of Southeast Asia, 132–47
  of Switzerland, 127
New International Economic Order (NIEO)
  and Non-Aligned Movement, 59,
    113–24

294

Index